W9-CCJ-412

THE

LIFE AND TIMES

OF

JOHN HUSS

AMS PRESS
NEW YORK

THE LIFE AND TIMES OF JOHN HUSS;

OR, THE

Bohemian Reformation

OF

THE FIFTEENTH CENTURY.

BY

E. H. GILLETT.

IN TWO VOLUMES.

VOL. II.

BOSTON:
GOULD AND LINCOLN,
59 WASHINGTON STREET.
NEW YORK: SHELDON AND COMPANY.
CINCINNATI: GEORGE S. BLANCHARD.
1863.

Library of Congress Cataloging in Publication Data

Gillett, Ezra Hall, 1823-1875.
    The life and times of John Huss.

    Reprint of the 1863 ed. published by Gould and
Lincoln, Boston.
        1. Hus, Jan, 1369-1415. 2. Reformation—Czecho-
slovakia—Bohemia—Biography. 3. Bohemia—Church history.
I. Title.
BX4917.G5 1978   284'.3 [B]   77-85271
ISBN 0-404-16150-2

First AMS edition published in 1978.

International Standard Book Number:
Complete Set: 0-404-16150-2
    Volume II: 0-404-16152-9

Reprinted from the edition of 1863, Boston. [Trim size and
text area of the original has been maintained in this
edition.]

MANUFACTURED
IN THE UNITED STATES OF AMERICA

284.3
G47
v.2

CONTENTS.

CHAPTER I.

HUSS IN PRISON. HIS REFUSAL TO RECANT. FAREWELL
LETTERS. JUNE 8, 1415–JULY 1, 1415.

CHAPTER II.

FINAL AUDIENCE AND EXECUTION OF HUSS. JULY 1, 1415–
JULY 6, 1415.

57949

(iii)

CHAPTER III.

JACOBEL, GERSON, AND VOLADAMIR. MAY, 1415–AUGUST, 1415.

CHAPTER IV.

THE COUNCIL AND THE BOHEMIANS.—JEROME RECANTS.
AUG. 1, 1415–SEPT. 23, 1415.

CHAPTER V.

VIOLENCE OF THE TIMES. LETTERS OF THE BOHEMIANS.
ZISCA. SEPT. 23, 1415–DEC. 19, 1415.

CHAPTER VI.

NEW CHARGES AGAINST JEROME. CONFERENCE WITH BENEDICT. VINCENT FERRARA. DEC. 19, 1415–FEB. 16, 1416.

CHAPTER VII.

JEROME BEFORE THE COUNCIL. FEB. 16, 1416–MAY 26, 1416.

CHAPTER VIII.

SENTENCE AND EXECUTION OF JEROME. MAY 26, 1416–MAY 30, 1416.

CHAPTER IX.

INEFFICIENCY AND TUMULTS OF THE COUNCIL. ILL-SUCCESS AND RETURN OF THE EMPEROR. MAY 31, 1416–JAN. 27, 1417.

CHAPTER X.

BENEDICT DEPOSED. PROGRESS OF REFORM. MARTIN V. ELECTED. JAN. 27, 1417–NOV. 21, 1418.

CHAPTER XI.

MEASURES OF THE POPE AND COUNCIL AGAINST THE BOHE-MIANS. NOV. 22, 1417–APRIL 15, 1418.

CHAPTER XII.

FUTILE ISSUE OF THE COUNCIL. ITS DISSOLUTION. JAN. 1, 1418–APRIL 28, 1418.

CHAPTER XIII

VIOLENCE OF PARTIES IN BOHEMIA. SIGISMUND'S ARMY BEFORE PRAGUE. APRIL 15, 1418–JAN. 9, 1420.

CHAPTER XIV.

DEFEAT AND RETREAT OF THE EMPEROR. JAN. 9, 1420–JULY 28, 1420.

CHAPTER XV.

TABORITES AND CALIXTINES. JULY 28, 1420–AUGUST 5, 1420.

CHAPTER XVI.

THE CAMPAIGNS OF ZISCA. AUG. 5, 1420–OCT. 11, 1424.

CHAPTER XVII.

THE LAST CRUSADE. DEFEAT OF THE IMPERIALISTS. OCT. 11, 1424–JAN., 1432.

CHAPTER XVIII.

THE COUNCIL OF BASLE. CALIXTINE ASCENDENCY. 1432–1467

CHAPTER XIX.

THE TABORITES AND MORAVIANS. 1460–1517.

CHAPTER XX.

REFORMATION IN GERMANY. THE BRETHREN. 1517–1602.

CHAPTER XXI

PROTESTANTISM IN BOHEMIA, DOWN TO THE CLOSE OF THE THIRTY YEARS' WAR. 1602–1650.

THE

LIFE AND TIMES OF JOHN HUSS.

———————

CHAPTER I.

HUSS IN PRISON. HIS REFUSAL TO RECANT. FAREWELL LETTERS.

DEPRESSING CIRCUMSTANCES OF HUSS. — DENIED AN ADVOCATE. — HIS LETTERS AND
CONVERSATION IN PAST YEARS BROUGHT FORWARD.— WANT OF BOOKS.— HOPE-
LESSNESS OF HIS CASE. — PRISON REFLECTIONS. — ZABARELLA'S FORM OF RECANTA-
TION PRESENTED TO HIM. — REPLY OF HUSS. — GRATITUDE FOR KINDNESS. —
PERSUASIONS OF HIS FRIENDS. — ARGUMENT OF A MEMBER OF THE COUNCIL TO
OVERCOME HIS SCRUPLES. — THE CRIME OF HUSS IN REFUSING SUBMISSION TO
THE COUNCIL. — HIS UNSHAKEN PURPOSE. — VISIT OF PALETZ. — ARGUMENT OF
ONE OF THE DOCTORS. — EXPLANATORY LETTER OF HUSS. — HIS ESTIMATE OF
THE COUNCIL. — THE TREATMENT OF HIS BOOKS. — THE COUNCIL CONDEMNS IT-
SELF. — LETTER TO HIS COUNTRYMEN AT PRAGUE. — TIME OF HUSS' EXECUTION
DEFERRED. — GENERAL EXPECTATION THAT HE WOULD RECANT. — PROPOSED DE-
CREE IN SUCH A CASE. — REASONS OF THE EXPECTATION. — HOPES EXCITED IN
HUSS BY THE DELAY. — LETTER ON THE PROLONGED SPACE GIVEN TO PREPARE
FOR DEATH. — NO SURPRISE TO BE FELT AT TRIBULATION. — REJOICING THAT
HIS BOOKS HAD BEEN READ BY HIS ENEMIES. — THE EMPEROR ANXIOUS TO HAVE
HIM RECANT. — HIS FIRMNESS. — HIS OPINION OF THE EMPEROR. — FAREWELL
LETTERS. — ASKS AN AUDIENCE. — ASKS A CONFESSOR. — PALETZ DENIED HIM.—
VISIT OF PALETZ. — DREAMS OF HUSS. — SCRIPTURAL CONSOLATION. — CHLUM.—
DUBA. — CHRISTIANN. — SECOND FAREWELL TO FRIENDS AT PRAGUE. — GREET-
INGS. — POSTSCRIPT. — DEBTS. — ASKS CHLUM TO STAY TO THE LAST. — LETTER
TO MARTIN. — ADDRESSES ALL CLASSES. — MALICE OF CAUSIS. — HUSS IN PRISON.

JUNE 8, 1415–JULY 1, 1415.

WHAT must have been the feelings of Huss as the
guard escorted him back to his cell! For six months
he had been kept a close prisoner. His health had
given way under the hardships to which he had been

subjected. Once his life had been in such danger
that the council were like to lose their victim, and
from policy rather than compassion he was removed
to a more airy and comfortable cell, and the pope's
physician had been sent to attend him. With the
interval of a slight recovery, he was again attacked
with a new access of his severe distemper. " I have
been," so he writes, " a second time dreadfully tormented with an affection of my bladder, which I
never had before, and with severe vomiting and fever; my keepers feared I should die, and they have
led me out of my prison."[1] This was probably for
a few moments to enjoy the fresh air. His keepers
seem to have been moved to compassion by his sufferings,[2] and some of them appear to have shown
him no little kindness.[3] After four months' imprisonment at Constance, Huss was removed to Gottlieben. Here his situation was changed much for the
worse. His prison was the tower.[4] In the day-time
he was chained, yet so as to be able to move about.
At night, on his bed, he was chained by his hand to
a post. His subsequent treatment was still more
harsh. His keepers were changed after the flight of

---

[1] Epis. xxxviii.

[2] Huss' jailers were kind and noble-
hearted men. They became very
strongly attached to their prisoner,
and at their request Huss wrote several brief treatises on prominent duties
and doctrines of Christianity. The repeated conversations between them
satisfied the jailers that the doctrines
of Huss were those of scripture, and it
was the sympathy and affection which
they were led to feel for him, that drew
them to the scene of his execution.

[3] Epis. lii.

[4] At Gottlieben, the narrow cell is
still pointed out in the castle—at present the property of the Count of Ber-
oldingen, of Stuttgard—in which Huss
was confined. A late visitor at the
Castle writes,—" High up under the
roof, at the top of a long stair-case,
and shaded by thick pines, is a garret
in which one cannot stand upright.
This is the prison of the martyrs John
Huss and Jerome of Prague." Becker,
84, 85.

the pope—and not for the better. His friends were not allowed to see him. New attacks of his disease,—violent head-aches, hemorrhage, colic,—followed in consequence of this close and cruel confinement. For more than two months his sufferings were extreme. It was not till the beginning of the month of June that he was removed from his prison at Gottlieben, and conveyed to Constance. Without the uninterrupted quiet of even a single day, his trial proceeded. He found himself compelled to meet it in infirm health, and in a most weak and exhausted condition. He had demanded of the judicial committee an advocate to manage his cause for him, but this, which he was at first encouraged to expect, was finally refused him, on the ground that no such privilege could be granted to a heretic.[1] He was thus presumed guilty even before he was tried. Gerson did not hesitate afterwards to ascribe the condemnation of Huss to the injustice of this proceeding. " Had he been allowed an advocate, the council would never have been able to convict him of heresy." Huss was undoubtedly disappointed at the refusal of a request so just and reasonable. Yet he calmly submitted to the wrong. " Well, then," said he, " let the Lord Jesus be my advocate, who also will soon be my judge."

He was thus forced of necessity to depend upon himself alone for his defence. In chains, and in the endurance of the most severe sufferings, he was obliged to draw up his answers to the charges presented. And here he found, to his grief and indignation, that the most unfair advantages had been

[1] Epis. xlix.

taken of him. Passages from intercepted letters, in
part distorted, and conversations with theologians
once his friends, but who had now deserted him, in
which he had used familiar expressions in confidence,
were recalled and employed to his prejudice.[1] His
letters to his friends at Prague, by a system of es-
pionage as well as through their indiscretion, had
fallen into the hands of his enemies, and been used
against him. Paletz sometimes visited him in prison,
and sought to overwhelm him by harsh language.
"Sad greeting"[2] Huss calls it, as well he might. He
speaks of Paletz generally as his fiercest enemy, who
did him the most injury. Still his Christian spirit,
overcoming every revengeful thought, led him to
pray, " May God Almighty forgive him." " Yet," says
he, " never in my whole life did I receive from any
man harsher words of comfort than from Paletz." In
such circumstances as these Huss had to look around
him for the means of making his defence. But he
found himself totally in want of books. At first he
had not even a Bible, and was obliged to ask his
friends to procure him one.[3] He says, indeed, that
he had brought with him the Sentences of Lombard
and a Bible, but he could not have taken them with
him into his prison. Could the cruelty of his enemies have deprived him even of these? It must
have been so.

All these things were enough to have driven any
ordinary man to despair. To be denied an advocate—to have his few books withheld from him—to
have numerous and skilful enemies taking every pos-

---

[1] **Epis. xliii. xlviii.**   [2] " Salutatione horribilissima." Epis. xlvi.   [3] Epis. lii. liii.

sible advantage of his helplessness, in framing charges
of which he was long kept in ignorance—to know
that the learning, talent, and sympathies of the
whole council, spurred on by the bitterest malice,
were arrayed against him,—was enough to discourage
the efforts and palsy the energies of any man whose
help was not in a more than mortal arm. Enfeebled
by disease, worn out with suffering and want of sleep,
he had been called to appear before the council and
enter upon his defence. On every side he saw hostile
faces and prejudiced judges. His conscientious scruples were met by derision, and his arguments were
answered by ridicule. He was frequently interrupted or cut short in his replies. New articles were
presented, which he had never seen or heard of until
the moment when they were produced. His request
for a further and fuller hearing was met by threats
of the consequences should he persist in his demand
of what had been promised. A form of retraction
had been presented him, which he could not conscientiously adopt. His request to be instructed in
what respects he had erred, that he might intelli-
gently disavow his errors, was set aside. He saw
before him, instead of an impartial jury, a band of
men, through malice or prejudice, conspiring to effect
his ruin. Well might he look around him as he left
the council, disheartened and despondent. We can
but follow him as he is led back to his prison, with
the sympathies ever due to the innocent and the
wronged. How slowly and sadly must the hours of
a sleepless night have dragged along, bringing new
burdens and anxieties, instead of repose to his ex-

hausted frame! Now his mind reverts to the scenes
of the previous day,—and the tumultuous assembly,
like a stormy sea of angry faces, is present before
him. He recalls the years that are past, and stands
again in his Bethlehem chapel, in the presence of
those who had been awakened to a new life by his
thrilling words. Forgetting the tragedy of which
he is to be the victim, he is only anxious that the
cause for which he has labored may still live on,
nurtured to a more vigorous growth by the ashes of
his funeral pile. The light of another day at last
steals in upon the prisoner, restless on his bed, and
brought back to self-consciousness by the clanking
of his chain. He recalls, as his exhausted energies
will permit him, the points on which he alternately
hopes and despairs to be permitted to address the
council. How fondly he lingers over the possibility
that some at least in that assembly who shall hear
his words, shall carry them away in memory, and
thus in after days be enabled to repeat to others the
lessons of his dying testimony. Fully convinced he
is, that the truth he has preached shall still live.
The God of truth will not suffer it finally to perish.
A century or even centuries may pass over it, buried
beneath martyr's dust, but the time of its resurrection and triumph will come at last.

At his last appearance before the council, Huss
had vainly been urged to accept the terms they had
presented. But he could not conscientiously recant
doctrines that he had never held, nor could he disavow those of the error of which he was not convinced. A milder form of abjuration had been

promised him by Zabarella, the Cardinal of Florence.
This, it was intimated, he might safely subscribe. To
this course he was advised and urged by some of his
friends, more anxious for his life than he was himself.
This form was brought to Huss in his prison by the
Cardinal of Ostia, the president of the council. It
had been drawn up by their order, and the tenor of
it was as follows:

"I, John Huss, etc., in addition to the protestations made by me, which I hereby renew, do protest,
moreover, that although many things are imputed to
me which I never entertained the thought of, I submit myself with humility to the merciful orders and
correction of the sacred council, touching all things
that have been objected or imputed to me, or drawn
from my books, or, in fine, proved by the deposition
of witnesses—in order to abjure, revoke, and retract
them, and to undergo the merciful penance imposed
by the Council, and generally to do all that its good-
ness shall judge necessary for my salvation, recommending myself to its pity with entire submission."[1]
In this formula of recantation there was manifest a
greater leniency than was exhibited by the Bohemian enemies of Huss. Cardinal Zabarella, by whom
it was probably drawn up, was evidently more inclined to moderation and mercy than many other
members of the council.[2]   And although no one
dared openly to advocate his cause, we have every
reason to believe that among the few in the council

---

[1] Van der Hardt, iv. 329.

[2] Becker says, I know not on what
authority, that Zabarella held that
if one of the greatest scandals of the
church was to be done away, the celibacy of the clergy must be given up
—p. 105.

who were kindly disposed to him, or at least sought to save his life, there were some of no little influence. The presiding cardinal, John de Viviers of Ostia, treated him with humanity and kindness. There were strong inducements, not only in the hope of saving his life, but in the entreaties and persuasions of his friends, to lead Huss to adopt the form of recantation that had been drawn up. But it was here, and in these very circumstances, that his character shone forth most brightly. He had no ambition to found a sect, or attain notoriety by putting forth new and strange dogmas. His constant appeal—and this was his real crime in the eyes of the council that had judged the pope, and allowed no other being, human or divine, to share its tribunal—was to the word of God. Nobly did he exhibit, and heroically did he adhere to that principle which was the stronghold, a century later, of the great German reformer.

Huss could not accept the form of recantation drawn up for him, grateful as he expressed himself for the kindness by which it had been modified, if not dictated. He felt that to adopt it would be a compromise of principle. Calmly and clearly he stated his reasons for rejecting it: "My father," said he, in reply to the cardinal, "may the Almighty Father, most wise and holy, count you worthy the reward of eternal glory, through Jesus Christ. Most reverend father, I am truly grateful for your kind and fatherly favor. But I dare not submit, according to the tenor of this proposition made by me to the council. For in such a case I must needs condemn many truths, an act which (as I have heard from their own lips) they call scandalous. Besides, through such an abjuration I must perjure myself by the confession that I have held errors. By these things should I give scandal to the people of God, who heard from me in my preaching that with which this would be inconsistent. If therefore Eleazar, under the Old Testament, of whom we read in Maccabees, would not falsely confess that he had eaten meat by the law forbidden, lest he should sin against God, and leave an evil example to those that should come after him,—how shall I, a priest of the New Testament, although unworthy, for fear of a punishment which will soon be passed, consent, by a grievous sin, to transgress the law of God,—first, by departing from the truth; secondly, by committing perjury? In truth, it is better for me to die, than, by flying from a momentary pain, fall into the hands of God, and perhaps have fire and everlasting contempt for my portion. And, inasmuch as I have appealed to Jesus Christ, the most powerful and righteous Judge, committing his own cause into his hands, I do therefore abide by his most holy decree and sentence, knowing that he will judge each man, not according to false testimony, nor according to fallible councils, but according to truth and individual desert."

Such an answer, from one whose words meant what they expressed, was worthy of, and could have proceeded only from a spirit lifted above the world, and made heroic by faith in God. Many, no doubt, of the friends of Huss regretted the decision which he

had made. Under the pressure of the immediate
danger of his life, they would at least have counselled
him to temporize. One of these,[1] a member of the
council, whose kindness Huss had before experienced,
sought to overcome by gentle persuasions the scruples which he felt in regard to recanting. "As to
your first objection," said he, " let not this, my most
loving and beloved brother, have weight with you,
that you thus condemn the truth. For it is not we,
but they, who condemn it—they who now are your
and my superiors. Consider the saying, ' Lean not
to thine own understanding.' There are many
learned and conscientious men in the council. ' My
son, hear the law of thy mother.' This much to
your first objection.

" As to the second, in regard to perjury: This perjury, *if it be* perjury, would recoil not upon you, but
upon those who require it. Your views on these
subjects are not heresies unless you persist obstinately
in maintaining them.[2] Augustine, Origen, the Master of Sentences, and others have fallen into error, but
they cheerfully forsook it. I have many times believed myself to be acquainted with matters in which
I was ill-informed. When set right, I joyfully returned to correct views.

"I write, moreover, briefly, for I write to a man
of understanding. You will not recede from the
truth, but will approximate to the truth. You will
not perjure yourself, but will better yourself. You
will not give scandal, but you will edify. Eleazar

---

[1] Some imagine this friend to have
been John Cardinal, a Polish doctor ;
others, less probably, that it was Cardinal de Viviers himself.

[2] Epis. xxxi.

was a noble Jew. Judas, with his seven sons and
the eight martyrs, was nobler. St. Paul was let
down from the wall secretly in a basket, that he
might work out better things. May Jesus Christ, the
judge of your appeal, grant you apostles,[1] and these
are they. Conflicts yet await you for the faith of
Christ."

By others, also, Huss was urgently pressed to recant. Again and again, both in private and public,
he was beset by the importunities of those who felt
for him a strong attachment, or who, highly respect-
ing his character and talents, wished to snatch him
from the flames. The council, moreover, with all
the eagerness of some of its members for the severest
measures, could not be altogether blind to the wiser
policy of forcing Huss to acknowledge publicly the
supremacy and infallibility of their judgment. The
question, in fact, was reduced to this : The council, or
private judgment—which must yield? The council
would allow no rival. They had deposed a pope,
and the acknowledgment of their supremacy was
with them a vital point. Huss could not blindly
submit to place them in the seat of Christ—to en-
throne them above the word of God. This was his
crime. In the eyes of the council it was an aggravated one, and it ensured his doom.

The prisoner remained steadfast in his purpose.
His conscience forbade him to sacrifice the truth. To

---

[1] These words, " Jesus Christ grant
you apostles," etc., are quite obscure
in their meaning. It is plain that
they have some reference to the appeal of Huss. Letters dismissory
from the jurisdiction of the court
were sometimes obtained in cases of
appeal from the judge who had condemned. These were called " apostles." If these were not obtained
within a certain time, the appeal was
null and void.—*L'Enfant*, i. 343.

all the solicitations of friendship, to all the authoritative advice of members of the council, to public and private persuasions, he remained equally unmov̦ed. "I would sooner," said he, "have a millstone bound about my neck, and be cast into the sea, than give occasion of scandal to my neighbor; and, having preached to others constancy and endurance, I will set them an example, looking for help to the grace of God."[1] There was never in the prisoner a moment's wavering. Among others that visited him was Paletz, his former friend. He evidently had not counted on the constancy of Huss. Resolved to humble him as a rival, he could scarce have sought his life. All the persuasions of Paletz were employed to shake the prisoner's firmness. "Put yourself," said Huss, "in my place. What would you do if you were thoroughly assured that you had never held the errors which they wish you to retract?" "I confess," said Paletz, "it is hard," and for once the tears filled his eyes.[2] The persecutor paid his victim the tribute of sympathy, wrung out by respect for truthful constancy, and perhaps the memory of former friendship. It is not impossible that remorse for his conduct, which was leading to a strangely fatal result, had something to do with his tears.

In one of his letters[3] Huss gives the substance of the argument of one of the doctors who was urging him to a blind submission to the council. "Even though the council," said he, "should tell you that you have but one eye, and you have two, you would be bound to assent to their statement." "And I,"

<hr />

[1] Ep. xxxiii.   [2] Ib. xxx.   [3] Ib. xxxiii.

replied Huss, " while God spares my reason, would
never allow such a thing, though the whole world
were agreed upon it, because I could not say it without wounding my conscience." No wonder the doctor was confused by the reply. The illustration he
had selected was too ridiculous for ridicule. It only
set the conscientiousness of Huss, as well as the absurdity of the demands made upon him, in a too obvious light.

Nothing now remained for Huss but to prepare
himself and his friends for the fatal result which his
own constancy rendered inevitable. Carefully and
clearly does he lay down the principles upon which
his conduct was based. He does not trifle with his
fate. His words are calm and serious, as were befitting his circumstances. " Often," says he, " have
the demands of the council upon me been urged.
But, inasmuch as they imply that I recant, abjure,
and submit to penance, in matters of truth which I
must give up—requiring me to abjure, and perjure
myself by confessing errors falsely imputed to me—
demanding that I should give offence to many of
God's people to whom I have preached,—for which I
should deserve that a mill-stone should be tied about
my neck, and I be cast into the midst of the sea—
and because, if I should submit, in order to escape a
temporary trouble and penalty, I should plunge myself into far greater, unless I should repent,—for
these reasons I cannot yield. And for my consolation, I think of the seven martyrs of the Maccabees,
who chose rather to be cut in pieces than disobey
God by eating flesh. I think, moreover, of Eleazar,

who would not even say that he had eaten flesh contrary to the law, lest he should set an evil example to those that should come after him, choosing rather to endure martyrdom. Wherefore, having these before my eyes, as well as many holy men and women of the New Testament who gave themselves up to martyrdom because they would not consent to sin; and, moreover, having preached so many years on the duty of constancy and endurance, I cannot but say of a course by which I must utter many falsehoods, and commit perjury, giving offence to many of God's children—far be it, far be it from me! For my Master, Christ, shall be hereafter my reward, while even now he gives me the aid of his presence." [1]

Such were the reasons which Huss repeatedly and on different occasions urged in defence of his course. They were neither fanciful nor fanatical, but such as would be appreciated by his friends and followers at Prague. To these he wrote from time to time as occasion offered, and his letters were publicly read in the Bethlehem chapel, where his voice had once been so often heard. "My dear brethren, (so he writes back to Bohemia,) I have thought that it might be well to admonish you how my books written in the Bohemian language have been condemned in the council of Constance—though itself full of pride, avarice, ambition, and almost every vice—as being heretical. They have hardly been seen or read, or, if read, not understood. . . . If ye had been present here at Constance, ye would have seen this council,

[1] Epis. xx.

called holy, and therefore claimed to be infallible, as though it could not err, to be shameful and scandalous; for the very citizens of this country say, as I have heard, that this city will not recover in thirty years from the sins and scandals of this council." He bids his friends not to be frightened at the decision against his books. " They have attempted to frighten me from the truth of Christ, but the strength of God in me they have been unable to overcome. . . . They would not venture to discuss with me, though I professed my willingness to be instructed, on the authority of the Sacred Scriptures. . . . Not by these, but by terrors and threats have they tried to overcome me. But the God of mercy, to whose word I bow, is with me, and still will be, as I am confident, and in his grace will keep me even until death."

In another letter Huss reminds his friends of the treatment of the books of Jeremiah—full as harsh as that which his own had experienced, and yet they were not suppressed. In later times the sacred writings were burned, as well as the works of several of the fathers, but they could not be suppressed. He bids them not to neglect his books, or give them to his enemies to be burned. As to themselves, they need not be terrified. The forces of Antichrist would perhaps leave them at peace. The council of Constance would scarcely come to Prague, and some of his followers, he believed, would sooner die than give up his books.

Even in the danger in which Huss found himself of his life, he did not fear to give free expression to the severe judgment he had formed of his judges. He speaks of their having condemned their head, while many of themselves were guilty of the same crimes. " Would to God," says he, " that in this council it had been said by divine authority, Let him that is without sin among you first pass sentence. Undoubtedly they would have gone forth, one after the other. Why, then, have they heretofore bowed to him, kissed his feet, called him Most Holy, when they have known and seen that he was a heretic, a murderer, a reprobate wretch, as they have publicly charged him with being? Yea, why did the cardinals speak of him as holy, when they knew that he murdered his predecessor? Why did they allow him, while he was yet pope, to drive such a traffic as he did in holy things? They are his counsellors for the very purpose of giving him the best advice, and if they failed to do it are they not equally guilty? . . . I think we may plainly see Antichrist revealed in the pope, and others present at the council."

Such were the views which Huss had held at Prague—now confirmed by his experience at Constance—and in the conviction of the truth of which he was willing to die. In full anticipation of the final result, he wrote, on the tenth of June, a letter to his friends in Prague, in which he gives them for the last time—as he feared—his counsel and encouragement. In this parting address, that might be almost dated from the martyr's stake, he speaks with an apostolic earnestness and unction. He forgets no class, neither rich nor poor, male nor female, but adapts his words to the circumstances of each.[1]

"I, Master John Huss, in the hope that I am God's servant, wish, on behalf of all the faithful of Bohemia who love God, that they may live and die in the grace of God, and at last be saved. Amen. Ye princes, high and low, I pray for and admonish you, that ye obey God, reverence his word, and live according to it. I beseech you to abide in the truth of God, which I have preached and written to you from his word and from the holy prophets. I beseech you, if any one among you has heard from me, by public speech or otherwise, or has read in my books, anything contrary to the truths of God, that you reject it, although I am not conscious of having written or taught any such error.

"I beseech, moreover, if any one has observed any levity in my speech or conduct, that he copy not my example, but intercede with God in my behalf that such levity may be forgiven me. I beseech you to love and hold in high esteem those priests who discharge well the duties of their office, especially those who labor in the word of God. But beware of the wicked, especially those Godless pastors that go about, as the Master says, in sheep's clothing, but inwardly they are ravening wolves. Ye nobles, I beseech you, deal fairly with your subjects, and maintain just government. Ye burghers, I beseech you that ye each live in his estate in such a manner as to keep a clear conscience. Ye artisans, labor faithfully, and earn your bread in the fear of God.

[1] Epis. xii.

Ye servants, serve your masters in truth. Ye school-masters, instruct the youth to purity of life, and teach them with diligence and fidelity. First of all, that they fear God, and keep him before their eyes. Then, that they study with all diligence, not for gain or the honor of the world, but for God's glory, the good of men, and their own salvation. Students in the university, and all other pupils, I pray you be obedient to your masters in all that is honorable and praiseworthy, following their good example, and dili-gently studying, that by your means God's glory may be promoted, and yourselves with others advance in all that is good.

"Finally, I pray you all gratefully to regard the excellent lords Wenzel de Duba, John de Chlum, Henry Plumlow, William Zagetz, and other nobles from Bohemia, Moravia, and Poland, and treat them with studious respect. For many a time have they set themselves against the whole council, and man-fully defended the truth, exerting themselves to the utmost to save my life, expecially Duba and Chlum, to whom you may give full credit in the entire ac-count which they will render you of what has taken place. For they have been often by, when I have answered before the council, and they know who those Bohemians are who have treated me with severity and harshness, and how the whole council cried out against me when I merely answered the questions which they asked.

" I beseech you, moreover, to pray to God for the emperor, and for your king and queen, that the God of mercy may be with and among you forever.

"This letter have I written to you in prison and in chains, and this morning I have heard of the decision of the council that I must be burned. But I have full confidence in God that he will not forsake me, nor permit me to deny his truth, or with perjury confess as mine the errors falsely imputed to me by lying witnesses. But how gently God my Master deals with me, and supports me through surprising conflicts, ye shall learn when, amid the joys of the life to come, we shall, through the grace of Christ, behold one another again.

"Of my dear friend, Master Jerome, I hear nothing, except that he is kept close in prison, where, like me, he awaits death for the faith which he has manifested in Bohemia. But our bitterest enemies, the Bohemians who have ill-treated us, go from bad to worse. I beseech you, pray God in their behalf. But this one thing I do especially beseech of you, that ye cherish the Bethlehem church, and faithfully attend to it as long as God shall give you grace, that God's word be preached therein; for of such a church is the devil the sworn enemy, and he raises up against it the priests and their tools, for he sees that by its means his kingdom is in danger of being broken up. But I hope in God that he will sustain the church in his good pleasure, and cause his word to be imparted there through others more largely than it has been by my poor efforts.

"I beseech you, love one another—swerve not from the truth. Meditate upon it—how the righteous may not be crushed. Given on Monday night before the day of St. Vitus, by a faithful messenger."

Such was the calm and manly tone of this letter of Huss, written under the impression that it would be his last! It manifests throughout a noble and Christian spirit. There is no railing at his enemies. There is no wild fanatic enthusiasm. There is no despondency. In a more than human strength he prepared himself to meet his fate.

But events of which Huss was not aware led to a postponing of the time of his execution. While the council had resolved that if he should refuse to recant he should be burned, and this fact had been communicated to him to awe and frighten him into submission, they had also secretly resolved, in the confident expectation that he would consent to the form of recantation, that, after having given this consent, he should for the remainder of his life be doomed to close imprisonment. The tenor of this proposed decree, giving hope of the issue which the council most desired, shows that among its members there were those who entertained no doubt of being able to persuade Huss to recant, and save his life. This proposed decree is worthy of being given entire, as it shows what the tender mercies of the council would have been even in case Huss had submitted. It is as follows :[1]—

" But, inasmuch as from some manifest signs it is conjectured that the said John Huss experiences contrition for his former sins, and, influenced by sound advice, is desirous of returning to the truth of the church of God, with a pure heart, and with faith unfeigned,—therefore this holy council cheerfully allows

[1] Van der Hardt, iv. 432.

him to present himself voluntarily, for the purpose
of abjuring and revoking all heretical pravity and
error, specially the errors of John Wickliffe, receiving him, upon confessing of his own accord, with the
prodigal son, the sins he has committed, and manifesting penitence, and absolving him, humbly seeking
absolution from the sentence of excommunication
which rests upon him. But, inasmuch as from the
doctrines of the said John Huss, unsound, inconsistent with the faith, and full of error, innumerable
scandals and seditions have sprung up in the church
of God, and among the people, and through him
grievous sins have been committed against God and
the holy church in the matter of perverse doctrine,
and contempt for the keys and censures of the church,
to the imminent danger of the Catholic faith,—therefore this present most holy council decrees and declares that the said John Huss, as a man scandalous,
seditious, pernicious to the holy church of God, shall
be deposed and degraded from the sacerdotal rank,
or whatever rank in the church he may hold; committing, nevertheless, to the most reverend fathers in
Christ, the archbishop of Milan, the bishops of Feltri,
Asti, Alexandria, Bakora,[1] to execute in a becoming
manner, as the order of the law requires, the degradation of John Huss in the presence of this most
holy council; and the council pronounces and decrees
that John Huss, as a man dangerous to the Christian
faith, for the aforesaid reasons, shall be immured and
imprisoned, and ought to be immured and imprisoned, and thus perpetually to remain, and shall be

---

[1] Bachorensi (Bangor ?)

proceeded against in other respects according to canonical sanctions." [1]

This sentence was to have been read in case Huss should consent to abjure, when his degradation from the priesthood was immediately to follow. The impression, thus shared by the council, that Huss would yet be induced to recant, was due in part undoubtedly to the hopes of the prisoner's friends, rather than to any words or actions of his own. From first to last, the idea of escaping by a feigned retraction seems never to have entered his mind. On the morning of the tenth of June, such an announcement of the action of the council was made to him—with the intention, no doubt, to induce him to recant—as led him to believe that he was to be executed the following day. Under this impression he wrote his farewell letter to the Bohemians. But the next day came, and the next, and the execution of the sentence was still deferred. It is not surprising that in the mind of the prisoner there should have sprung up a faint hope that he might yet be delivered from the power of his enemies. In his letters, which he still continued to write to his friends in Prague during this interval, we see traces enough of this latent and feeble hope to show us that Huss did not regard death with the indifference of a stoic, or prolonged life with the repugnance of a misanthrope. He felt, in the sense in which Paul did, that it was Christ for him to live, but if truth demanded a victim, he was ready to be offered up. In the doubtful hope that he might yet be by some means rescued, he writes: "Our Saviour

[1] See Mansi. Van der Hardt, iv. 432. L'Enfant, 234.

recalled Lazarus to life after he had lain in the grave four days, and had upon him the smell of corruption. He preserved Jonah three days in the belly of the fish, and sent him back to preach again; he called forth Daniel from the den of lions, to record the prophecies; kept the three young men in the furnace from the power of the flames, and liberated Susannah when already condemned to death. Therefore, easily might he deliver me too, poor mortal!—if it served to promote *His own* glory, the progress of believers, and my own best good—for this time, from prison and from death. For *His* hand is not shortened, who by his angel led Peter, while the chains of his hands fell off, from the dungeon, when already condemned to die at Jerusalem. But ever let the will of the Lord be done, which I desire may be fulfilled in me, to his glory and to my own purification from sin."

Huss did not fail to write again to his friends at Prague as soon as the opportunity was afforded. " God be with you," he says, " my most beloved in the Lord. I had strong reasons to believe that my previous letter to you would be my last, so near then was the prospect of the goal of death. But now, when I learn that I am spared, my joy is that I may write to you yet once again, and testify my gratitude. As it concerns my death, God knows why I and my dear brother, Master Jerome, are not executed. He, as I hope, will die innocent and blameless, and he gives evidence that he will suffer and die more courageously than I, poor sinner! But God has kept us so long in prison, that we may think so much the

more humbly on our past sins, and so much more
deeply repent of them; and he has given us time and
space for the severe conflict which blots out great
sins, and that our conversation may be so much the
more abundant. Yea! he has given us time enough,
in order that we might so much the more fully reflect
upon the shameful ignominy and cruel death of our
loved King, the Lord Christ, and be so much the
more patient to suffer. Thus may you learn that
eternal joys are not to be reached through the joys
of this world, but the saints, through much tribulation
and anguish, have pressed into the kingdom. For some
of them were hewn asunder; some were spit upon;
some sodden; some flayed alive, or buried alive,
stoned, crucified, crushed between mill-stones, and
dragged hither and thither until they died. Some
were drowned, burned, hung, torn in pieces, and, before they died, shamefully and cruelly treated in
prison. But who could undertake to recount all the
forms of pain and martyrdom which were endured
under the Old Testament, and have been repeated
since, to the shame and disgrace of those who inflicted them—the ecclesiastics! Why should any
one then be surprised that now, with all their base
deeds and the injuries they inflict, they remain unpunished? Indeed, I rejoice that they have been
forced to read my books, in which their baseness is
plainly set forth; and I know that they have read
them far more diligently than they read the holy
gospel, only that they may discover something with
which they may be able to find fault."

The anxiety of the council, and especially of the em-

peror, to induce Huss to retract, led them to continue
efforts of exhortation and persuasion. The emperor
at least could not contemplate the prospect of the
execution of Huss without apprehension as to the
results that might follow. It would undoubtedly
exasperate the whole Bohemian nation, and their
execration would fall, not without reason, upon his
own head. The cry of an indignant people, and perhaps the secret reproaches of his own conscience,
arose before him and made him hesitate. He had
gone too far with the council already to attempt to
shield Huss from the sentence of death, unless some
retraction on his part could be secured. The attempt
to do it would only exasperate the council and lead
it to counteract his schemes, or perhaps regard him
as implicated in heresy. The abjuration of Huss
alone could relieve the emperor from his perplexity;
and to obtain it he spared neither prayers, persuasion, nor threats. From first to last, all these efforts
were vain. "I have refused to abjure,"—so Huss
writes to the University of Prague,—" at least till the
articles I hold are proved to be erroneous on the
authority of Sacred Scripture." [1] He disavowed any
wish to cling to anything incorrect which could be
found in his writings. "I exhort you," he says, "to
hold in detestation whatever you shall find to be
false in my articles." [2]

The efforts of the emperor to induce Huss to abjure, only filled the prisoner with a sad and melancholy pity for his oppressor. He would not have
exchanged places with him for the world. "Place

[1] Epis. xviii.   [2] Epis. xi.

not your confidence in princes of the earth,"[1] wrote
he to his Bohemian friends. Sorely had he been deceived in his estimate of the character of Sigismund.
He now acknowledged the more correct apprehensions of his friends. "Truly did they say that Sigismund would himself deliver me up to my adversaries;
he has done more,—he has condemned me before
them."[2]

Thus by his firmness Huss forced the emperor to
incur the disgrace of his own conduct, and, had he
sought revenge for the violation of the imperial faith,
he had it in denying him the power to rescue him
from the funeral pile.

The most sanguine friends of Huss must by this
time have become fully convinced that his doom was
sealed. The firmness of his purpose was proof
against all persuasions. His mind was fully made up
to meet the result which appeared inevitable. His
main anxiety now was to secure such an audience
before the council as had been promised him by the
emperor.[3]

It only remained for him to take a final leave of
his earthly friends and interests. In letters of touching pathos he utters his farewell to those to whom
he was bound by a mutual attachment. He wrote
to Hawlik,[4] his successor in Bethlehem chapel, urging
him not to oppose the doctrine of the cup. He exhorted Christiann of Prachatitz to diligence in pas-
toral duty, and requested him to greet, in his name,
Jacobel and the friends of truth.[5] He admonished
the members of the university to mutual love and

---

[1] Epis. xxxv.   [2] Ib.   [3] Ib. xxxv.   [4] Ib. xvi.   [5] Ib. xvii.

sobriety of conduct, stating to them also the reasons which forbade him to recant, while he prayed for his enemies that God would forgive them. He begged them to stand by Bethlehem chapel, and to appoint Gallus as his successor. To their love and confidence he recommended his faithful friend, Peter the Notary.[1] To his benefactors[2] he returns his hearty thanks, admonishing them to stand fast in their fidelity, and expressing his confidence that God would repay them for what they had done in his behalf. He expresses his apprehension that a severe persecution of the true servants of God in Bohemia would follow his death, unless God should make use of the civil power to prevent it.[3]

To his friends generally, whom he does not venture to name lest the unavoidable omission of some should give offence, he extends his salutations, declaring it his unshaken purpose not to recant, yet protesting his desire to be instructed that he might disavow any article which could be shown to be false. He expresses his sense of obligation to the king and queen, the barons and nobles of Bohemia and Moravia, and especially to the Bohemians in Constance, for their friendly offices, and their efforts to secure his liberation.[4] From his own experience, he admonishes his friends not to put their trust in an arm of flesh.[5] To Chlum (June 29) he addresses cheering words of the future glory with Christ, of those who suffer for him now.[6] Of his different friends, including Martin, Peter the Notary, Duba, the family of Liderius, and others, he takes leave, in tender and

---

[1] Epis. xviii.   [2] Ib. xxiv.   [3] Ib. xix.   [4] Ib. xx.   [5] Ib. xxi.   [6] Ib. xx. xxii.

affecting words.   He urges that care should be taken
of his letters, and that they should be carried back
to Bohemia, lest his friends should be implicated or
brought into danger by means of them[1].   The lines
which he received from time to time from his friends,
he immediately destroyed.[2]

In the letter in which he narrates his sad interview
with Paletz, he expresses his joyful assurance of the
heavenly glory that shall crown his martyrdom, and
his confidence in the strength which Christ alone can
impart, praying for "a fearless spirit, a true faith, a
firm hope, and perfect charity."[3]   He does not forget
his nephews, (sons of his brother,) but directs that
they should be placed in some secular calling, since
he feared that if they were educated for the priesthood, they would not discharge its duties as they
ought.[4]   He dissuades his friends generally from
coming to him at Constance, for fear of the consequences; and the sight of Christiann, who had come
in the vain hope of serving him, completely un-
manned him, and melted him to tears.   All the provision which he could make for the payment of his
debts at Prague, was made, and in case it proved insufficient, he begged his creditors to forgive him for
the sake of their common Master, Christ.

Disburdened of other cares, Huss was now anxious
only for a final hearing before the council.   He begged that the emperor might be present, and that he
might himself have a place assigned him near the
imperial presence.   He requested also that the noble
knights, Chlum, Duba, and Latzembock, would take

---

[1] Epis. xxvii.   [2] Ib. xxxiv.   [3] Ib. xxx.   [4] Ib. xxviii.

good care to be present, to witness to his words, and
prevent any false reports in regard to his statements
from going abroad.[1]

In the prospect of the doom before him, Huss
sought a confessor. Whom would he select? Scarcely
could he wish for such a one as the council would
appoint. He could value but lightly the absolution
conferred by hands stained with simony and corruption. His conscience was void of offence, and at
peace with God, and no superstitious reverence for
the priesthood induced him to believe that his salvation was dependent on sacerdotal absolution. It
was undoubtedly more with the desire of a full and
free conference with his former friend, than from
any other motive, that he sought the privilege of
having a confessor granted him, and asked that
Paletz might be appointed.[2]

Nothing could more fully testify the humility and
the forgiving spirit of Huss than this request. He
felt that he had been wronged by those Bohemians
who, before the council, had pursued him with unrelenting hostility. Among these Paletz had held the
foremost rank, and he it was whom Huss, with a
magnanimity unsurpassed, selected to hear his dying
confession. Of him he had most to complain, and
to him he had the most to forgive. "Alas!" said
he, "the wounds which we receive from those persons
in whom our soul has placed its hope, are the most
cruel; for to the sufferings of the body are joined
the pangs of betrayed friendship. In my case it is
from Paletz that my most profound affliction pro-

---

[1] Epis. xlix.   [2] Ib. xxxi.

ceeds." Again he says, " Paletz is my greatest adversary; it is to him that I wish to confess myself." This request of Huss was refused him, and in his place the bishops sent a monk, whom he speaks well of, and who, after having given him absolution, recommended to him to submit, but without absolutely commanding it.[1]

Paletz, moreover, who had previously been applied to, had refused. He recoiled from the painful task which the humility and magnanimity of Huss had imposed. He was, however, vanquished by the nobleness and generosity of the prisoner's conduct, and he determined to visit him in his cell.

When Huss saw him enter, he addressed him not in the language of reproach or passion, but in a mild and melancholy tone. " Paletz," said he, " I uttered some expressions before the council that were calculated to offend you. Pardon me." This was undoubtedly the confession which he most desired to make. And now he had made it, and Paletz was his confessor. His persecutor was deeply affected, and entreated Huss to abjure, undoubtedly with the deepest sincerity; for he never seems to have apprehended that his prosecution would cost him the life of one that was once his friend, and whom he could never have ceased really to respect. " I conjure you," said he, " do not look to the shame of retracting, but only to the good that must result from it." " Is not the opprobrium," replied Huss, " of the condemnation and the punishment greater in the eyes of the world than that of the abjuration? How, then," asked

[1] Epis. xxxi.

Huss, as if in gentle reproach for the imputation of such a motive—" How, then, can you suppose that it is a false shame which prevents me?" It was on this occasion, probably, that Huss asked the question before referred to, of Paletz, what he would do if the case were his own, and he were required to retract errors that he never held. With tears Paletz confessed that the case would be hard indeed. "Is it possible," rejoined Huss, "that you, who are now in this state before me, could have said in full council, when pointing to me, 'that man does not believe in God?'" Paletz denied having said it. "You said so, however," repeated Huss; " and, in addition, you declared that since the birth of Jesus Christ there never was seen a more dangerous heretic. Ah! Paletz, Paletz, why have you wrought me so much evil?" Paletz replied by again exhorting him to submit, and then withdrew, weeping bitterly.[1]

It is no wonder that, in the excited state of the prisoner's mind, and in the solitude of his cell, his dreams should have partaken of the character of his waking thoughts, or that they should have assumed a prophetic aspect. He believed that in this manner he had received intimations of future events. "Know," he writes to his friends, "that I have had great conflicts in my dreams. I dreamed beforehand of the flight of the pope, and after relating it, Chlum said to me in my dream, 'The pope will also return.' Then I dreamt of the imprisonment of Jerome, though not literally according to the fact. All the different prisons to which I have been conveyed have been

represented to me beforehand in my dreams. There
have also appeared to me serpents, with heads
also on their tails, but they have never been able to
bite me. I do not write this because I believe myself a prophet, or wish to exalt myself, but to let you
know that I have had great temptations, both of
body and soul, and the greatest fear lest I might
transgress the commandment of our Lord Jesus
Christ." [1]

What must have been the strength of the consolation by which Huss was sustained amid all the gloomy
scenes and trials of his tedious and cruel imprisonment, and especially with no prospect of relief except
by death! In the noble letter which he wrote on
the eve before the festival of St. John the Baptist,
he displays the grounds of his comfort, peace, and
confidence. "Much consoles me," he says,[2] "that
word of our Saviour, 'Blessed be ye when men shall
hate you. Rejoice ye in that day, and leap for joy,
for, behold, great is your reward in heaven.' A good
consolation; nay, the best consolation; difficult, however, if not to understand, yet perfectly to fulfil, to
rejoice amid those sufferings. This rule James observes, who says, 'My beloved brethren, count it all
joy when you fall into divers temptations; knowing
this, that the trying of your faith, if it is good, work-
eth patience.' Assuredly it is a hard thing to rejoice
without perturbation, and in all these manifold temptations to find nothing but pure joy. Easy it is to
say this, and to expound it, but hard to fulfil it in
very deed. For even the most steadfast and patient

[1] Epis. xxiii.   [2] Epis. xxx.

warrior, who knew that he should rise on the third day; who, by his death, conquered his enemies, and redeemed his chosen from perdition, was, after the last supper, troubled in spirit, and said, 'My soul is troubled even unto death;' as also the gospel relates, 'that he began to tremble, and was troubled;' nay, in his conflict he had to be supported by an angel, and he sweat, as it were, great drops of blood falling down to the ground; but he who was in such trouble said to his disciples, 'Let not your heart be troubled, and fear not the cruelty of those that rage against you, because ye shall ever have me with you to enable you to overcome the cruelty of your tormentors. Hence his soldiers, looking to him as their king and leader, endured great conflicts, went through fire and water, and were delivered. And they received from the Lord the crown of which James speaks, i. 12. That crown will God bestow on me and you, as I confidently hope, ye zealous combatants for the truth, with all who truly and perseveringly love our Lord Jesus Christ, who suffered for us, leaving behind an example that we should follow in his steps. It was necessary that he should suffer, as he tells us himself; and we must suffer, that so the members may suffer with the head; for so he says, 'whoever would follow me, let him take up his cross and follow me.' O most faithful Christ, draw us weak ones after thee, for we cannot follow thee if thou dost not draw us. Give us a strong mind, that it may be prepared and ready. And if the flesh is weak, succor us beforehand by thy grace, and accompany us, for without thee we can do nothing; and least of all, can we face a cruel death. Give us a ready and willing spirit, an undaunted heart, the right faith, a firm hope, and perfect love, that patiently and with joy we may for thy sake give up our life." Such was the letter of Huss—worthy of the noblest of the martyrs. Only in its subscription does it show any trace of the errors or peculiarities of the Romish church. It closes thus : "written in chains, on the vigils of St. John, who because he rebuked wickedness was beheaded in prison : may he pray for us to the Lord Jesus Christ."

Huss had written what he supposed was his farewell letter to his countrymen. During the season of his reprieve—if such it may be called—he writes to various friends. Some of these have already been referred to. But one of the last was addressed to Chlum, who seemed to him dearer than a brother. Many a time had his cheering words, or the warm grasp of his hand, or his genial sympathy, brought comfort to the lonely and neglected prisoner. Huss now expresses to this noble knight his joy at hearing that he meant to renounce the vanities and toilsome services of the world, and, retiring to his estates, devote himself wholly to the service of the Lord Jesus Christ, whose service was perfect freedom. In like manner, he expresses his joy at learning that the knight Duba had resolved to retire from the world and marry. "It is even time for him," he writes, "to take a new course, for he has already made journeys enough through this kingdom and that, jousting in tournaments, wearing out his body, squandering his money, and doing injury to

his soul. It only remains for him therefore to renounce all these things, and, remaining quietly at
home with his wife, serve God, with his own domestics around him. Far better will it be, thus to serve
God, without cares, without participation in the sins
of the world, in good peace, and with a tranquil
heart, than to be distracted with cares in the service
of others, and that, too, at the imminent risk of his
own salvation."[1] To his friend Christiann, the rector
of the university, he writes : " My friend and special
benefactor, stand fast in the truth of Christ, and embrace the cause of the faithful. Fear not, because
the Lord will shortly bestow his protection and increase the number of his faithful. Be gentle to the
poor, as thou ever hast been. Chastity I hope thou
hast preserved ; covetousness thou hast avoided, and
continue to avoid it ; and for thy own sake, do not
hold several benefices at once ; ever retain *thy own*
church, that the faithful may resort for help to thee
as an affectionate father." Jacobel, moreover, with
" all the friends of the truth," are saluted. The letter is subscribed—" written in prison, awaiting my
execution at the stake."[2] Last of all, Huss wrote
his second farewell letter to his friends at Prague.
He besought them that for his sake who would be
already dead as to the body, they would do all that
lay in their power to prevent the knight of Chlum
from coming into any danger. " I entreat you," he
writes, " that you will live by the word of God ; that
you obey God and his commandments, as I have
taught you. Express to the king my thanks for all

[1] Epis. xxiii.　　　　　　[2] Epis. xviii.

the kindnesses he has shown me. Greet in my name your families and your friends, each and all of whom I cannot enumerate. I pray to God for you: do you pray for me ? To him shall we all come, since he gives us help."

This letter of Huss, so full of Christian kindliness of feeling, was written probably on the fourth day of July, in the immediate expectation of his martyrdom. In the addition which he made to it on the following day, was a sort of postscript to inform them of his approaching execution. "Already I am confident I shall suffer for the sake of the word of God." He begged his friends, for God's sake, not to allow any cruelty whatever to be practised against the servants and the saints of God. He makes the bequest of his fur cloak with a small sum of money, to the friendly notary, Peter ; to others, small legacies, or some of his books : it was nearly, if not quite all that he had to give. Instead of being rich, as was charged in prison, he had to request his friends to discharge for him a few small debts, that his creditors might not suffer.

One of the last requests that Huss had to make of his friends was addressed to the faithful Chlum. He wished this brave man whom he loved so tenderly, to remain with him to the last. "O thou, the kindest and most faithful friend," said he, " may God grant thee a fitting recompense! I conjure thee to grant me still this—not to depart until thou hast seen everything consummated. Would to God that I could be at once led to the stake before thy face, rather than be torn away in prison, as I am by perfidious manœuvres! I still have hope—I still have confidence—that Almighty God will previously snatch me from their hands to himself, through the merits of his saints. Salute all our friends for me; and let them pray to the Lord that I may await my death with humility and without murmuring."

It was in this spirit that Huss prepared himself for the final scene. Many were the letters written and messages sent, which spoke in the calm and touching eloquence of a martyr, to the persons to whom they were addressed.[1] His first and last anxiety was, that they should be faithful to the truth—not of his own teachings, for they might be in some respects erroneous—but of the word of God. To some who might be called to follow him to the stake, he addressed such exhortations as were enforced by his own example. "Fear not to die," said he to priest Martin, one of his disciples, "if thou desirest to live with Christ, for he has himself said, 'Fear not them that kill the body, but cannot kill the soul.'" And yet Huss gave his friend this rare counsel, as remarkable for prudence as modesty: "Should they seek after thee on account of thy adhesion to my doctrines, make them this reply: I believe that my master was a good Christian; but, in regard to his writings and instructions, I have neither read all, nor comprehended all."[2]

In his adieus, Huss showed no respect of persons.

---

[1] The letters of Huss are not chronologically arranged, and it is sometimes, therefore, difficult to determine their date. In most cases, however, it may be ascertained from internal evidence.

[2] Epis. xxviii.

He remembered the poor as well as the rich. He speaks of the cordwainers in the same breath with the doctors and the magistrates. Several of the families of his church in Prague are mentioned in one of his letters as specially to be saluted. His words to them "recommend them to be zealous for the love of Christ, to advance in humility with wisdom, and not to indulge in comments of their own making, but to recur to those of the saints."

Among the enemies of Huss none had shown a more inveterate and unrelenting malice than Causis. Unlike Paletz, his heart was moved neither to sympathy and compassion, nor to remorse. Several times the hardened wretch had gone to the prison where Huss was confined, and exclaimed, exulting in the savage cruelty of his nature over his destined victim, "By the grace of God, we shall soon burn this heretic, whose condemnation has cost me much money." [1] But even this failed to excite in Huss any revengful feelings. "I leave him to God, and pray for this man most affectionately," was the language in which he spoke of the virulent persecutor.

A noble object does Huss thus present for our study and admiration. Sometimes depressed by the fears and weakness of the flesh, but never declining the crown of martyrdom—loving his own life in the hope of future usefulness, but far more anxious for the truth he had preached—surrounded by the extreme of human terrors, yet still exclaiming, "The Lord is my light and my salvation; whom shall I fear? the Lord is the strength of my life; of whom shall I

[1] Epis. xxx.

be afraid ?"   Kindly does he remember his friends
while he forgives his enemies.   His last hours and his
last earthly counsels are given to the cause he loved,
and to his friends—some perhaps soon to follow
him in the thorny path of suffering for the cause of
truth.

CHAPTER II.

FINAL AUDIENCE AND EXECUTION OF HUSS.

JULY 1, 1415—JULY 6, 1415.

Up almost to the last moment, urgent persuasions were addressed to Huss to induce him to recant. In meeting his objections, a casuistry was adopted worthy the acuteness of the Jesuit doctors, Sanchez and and Escobar. Many, whom Huss calls pedagogues, and a few of the fathers, almost overwhelmed him with their importunities. Among others, an Englishman attempted to influence him by the example of those who, in England, had abjured the opinions of Wickliffe. "By my conscience," said he, "if I were in your case I would abjure." Causis, however, pursued a different policy. He, in all probability, had no wish to have Huss escape the flames. By his means the prisoner's situation had been rendered more harsh and grievous. None of his friends were permitted to see him ; the wives of his jailers, who were disposed to show him kindness, were henceforth denied the privilege. Sigismund, to whom he might have applied, and probably with success, for relief, had left Constance. Under the pretence of recreation, he had withdrawn to a village some miles distant, attended by numbers of his court. We can readily believe, without the hints of the annalist, that other than his avowed reasons had their influence. Among these, his own conduct suggests that he might not have wished to be too near the victim he had himself betrayed. From the twenty-third to the twenty-eighth of June, he remained at Ueberlingen, returning in season to hear the public refusal of Huss to retract.

An assembly was held on the first of July in the Franciscan monastery, and Huss was brought before it and publicly urged to abjure. He now presented a paper, drawn up by his own hand, in which he once more stated the grounds of his refusal. " I, John Huss, in hope, a priest of Jesus Christ, fearing to sin against God and fearing to commit perjury, am not willing to abjure all and each of the articles which have been produced against me on false testimony. For, God being my witness, I have not preached, asserted, nor defended them as they have said that I have preached, defended, or asserted. Moreover, in regard to the extracted articles, if any of them implies anything false, I disavow and detest it. But through fear of sinning against the truth, and speaking against the views of holy men, I am unwilling to abjure any of them. And if it were possible for my voice now to reach the whole world —as every falsehood and every sin which I have committed will be brought to light in the day of judgment—I would most cheerfully recall everything false or erroneous which I ever spoke or thought of speaking, and I would do it before the world. These things I say and write freely, and of my own accord."

In this language we recognize, not the obstinate and bigoted partisan—not the terrified and yielding supplicant—but the sincere lover of truth, and the conscientious confessor. But such a position as Huss had taken did not pay that homage to the infallibility of the council which was considered essential. He was sent back to his prison. For four days the council were engaged in discussing other subjects. Gerson brought up the propositions of John Petit. Business in regard to the abdication of Pope Gregory was discussed.

On the fifth of July came a deputation from the

emperor, once more to inquire if Huss would not recant. The deputation consisted of the cardinals of
Cambray and Florence, the patriarch of Antioch,
six bishops, and a doctor of laws. They were accompanied by the two brave knights, Chlum and
Duba.[1] They asked Huss whether he had determined to abjure the articles which he acknowledged
as his, and which had been proved by witnesses;
whether he was willing to asseverate that those
which he did not acknowledge, but had been
proved by witnesses, were not held by him, but that
he chose rather to think with the church. He answered, that he still would abide by the decision
which he had given in writing to the council, when
he last appeared before them, on the first day of
July. Upon this he was plied with new arguments
aud persuasions. It was represented to him that he
ought not to cling to his own opinion, but rather
yield to the opinion of the whole church, and bow
to the authority of the many learned men who composed the council. But all their arguments were
vain. The purpose of Huss still remained unshaken
in the near prospect of death. It was a trying moment to his friends who had accompanied the deputation. What counsel should they give?

Knowing well the attachment to Huss of his noble
friend, and the strong influence which his words
would have upon his mind, the emperor had besought
Chlum,[2] along with his associate Duba, to accompany
the deputation. He thought it probable that Huss
might be induced to listen to their united representa-

---

[1] Fleury, xxvi. 86.   [2] Mon. Hus., ii. 345.

tions; but for once he was mistaken. Had they attempted to persuade Huss to recant, they would probably have failed. But they did not. Chlum was the first to address him. " Dear master," said he, " I am not a learned man, and I deem myself unable to aid you by my counsels ; you must therefore yourself decide on the course which you are to adopt, and determine whether you are guilty or not of those crimes of which the council accuses you. If you are convinced of your error, have no hesitation — be not ashamed to yield. But if, in your conscience, you feel yourself to be innocent, beware, by calumniating yourself, of committing perjury in the sight of God, and of leaving the path of duty through any apprehension of death." [1]

Such language—so different from the unqualified exhortations to recant which were addressed to him by the council, and of the sincerity and affection of which he could not doubt—almost overpowered the prisoner, and he replied with a flood of tears. " Indeed," said he, " as I have done before, so now I call the Almighty God to witness, that if I were aware of having taught or written anything contrary to the law or orthodox doctrine of the church, I would retract it with the utmost readiness; and even at the present time, I desire exceedingly to be better instructed in sacred learning. If therefore any one will teach me a better doctrine than I have inculcated myself, let him do it. I am ready to hear him ; and, abandoning my own, I will fervently embrace the other, and confess that I have erred." [2]

Mon. Hus., i. 25. See also ii. 345. [2] Ib. L'Enfant, 267. Van der Hardt, iv. 386.

"Do you, then," asked one of the bishops, "believe yourself to be wiser than the whole council?" "I conjure you," replied Huss, "in the name of Almighty God, to give me as my instructor in the divine word the least person in the council, and I will sub-scribe to what he says, and in such a manner as that the council will be satisfied."

"See," said the bishops, "how obstinately he per-severes in his errors!" It was enough. The depu-tation plainly perceived that further attempts to per-suade Huss blindly to abjure, and pay the homage of sacrificing his conscience and reason to their idol—the council's infallibility—would be utterly futile. Huss, who had been led forth from his prison to meet the deputation—little disposed, even for a single hour, to share its comforts—was ordered back under the care of his jailers, and the deputation re-turned to report to the emperor.[1]

Nothing now remained but the promised audience and the final sentence. It was on the following day, July 6, that Huss appeared for the last time before the council, now in its fifteenth general session. There was a full attendance. The Cardinal de Viv-iers presided. The emperor himself was present, seated upon his throne, surrounded by the princes and the insignia of the empire. An immense crowd had assembled from all quarters, interested to behold the scene, or to receive the earliest intelligence of what was to transpire. The celebration of mass had already commenced when Huss arrived, but he was kept outside the door till the religious services, in-

---

[1] Van der Hardt, iv. 386–7. L'Enfant, 270. Mon. Hus., ii. 345.

cluding the litanies, were over, under the pretence
that the holy mysteries would be profaned by the
presence of so great a heretic.

At length Huss was brought in. A high platform
had been erected in the midst of the assembly, and
on it was placed a box containing the sacred vestments of the priesthood, with which Huss was to be
robed previous to his degradation. He was required
to take his stand in front of the platform, on a foot-
stool, by which he was so raised as to be visible to
the whole council. Here he fell upon his knees, and
remained for some time engaged in prayer in a low
tone.

Meanwhile the Bishop of Lodi ascended the pulpit from which the decrees of the council were
usually announced. He had been selected to deliver
the sermon which was to whet the appetite of the
council for the blood of a heretic. His text was
taken from Rom. vi. 6—" That the body of sin
might be destroyed." His object was, to expose the
evils of heresy, and justify the measures necessary
to its extirpation. He began his sermon by a quo-
tation from Aristotle, following it up by a citation
from Jerome, in order to enforce his persecuting
and bigoted doctrine. After venting his indignation upon Arius and Sabellius, the speaker proceeds to discriminate the most dangerous kinds of
sins. Among these he places schism in the first
rank. To this he traces the aggravated iniquities
and corruptions of the times—the discords and conflicts which desolated the nations—the vices and
simony which deformed the church. " How many

heresies," he exclaims, "have made their appearance! How many heretics remain unpunished! How many churches have been broken in and plundered! How many cities oppressed! How many religious rites fallen into neglect! How many discords among the clergy! How many slaughters among Christian people! Look, I pray you, at the church of God, the spouse of Christ, the mother of the faithful, how she is daily given up to contempt! Who now venerates the keys of the church? Who fears her censures? Who defends her privileges? nay, rather, who does not offend against them? who does not invade them? Who is there that does not dare to lay violent hands upon the patrimony of Jesus Christ? The property of the clergy, bought by sacred blood, and of the poor, as well as the food of pilgrims, is plundered and wasted." In the prevalent disorders the speaker seems to see *the abomination of desolation* brought into the sacred temple. Tyranny is destroying the bodies, and schism the souls of men. Those guilty of the first, may sin in ignorance; the last are without excuse. As the result, the speaker sees before him the church, like a boat upon the waves, endangered by pirates or thrown upon the rocks. Heresies have sprung up on all sides, and discord has entered among the flock of Peter and the fold of Christ. Many had toiled in vain to suppress these,—kings, princes, and prelates: "Wherefore," exclaims the bishop, turning to the emperor, "most Christian king, this glorious triumph has awaited thee, this unfading crown is due to thee, and a victory ever to be celebrated is thine, in order that by thee the

wounded church may be bound up, the inveterate
schism removed, simony restrained, and heretics rooted
out.   Do you not see how great will be this lasting fame, how celebrated this glory?   What could
be more just, what more holy, what more fitting,
what, in fine, more acceptable to God, than to extirpate this nefarious schism, restore the church to its
former liberty, put an end to simony, and destroy and
condemn errors and heresies from among the flock
of believers?   Surely nothing could be better, holier,
more desirable for the world, or acceptable to God.

"To execute this, so pious and holy a work, thou
hast been elected by God,—deputed in heaven, before chosen on earth.   Heavenly principalities made
thee emperor before the suffrage of the imperial
electors was cast.   And especially was this, in order
that thou mightest destroy and condemn, by imperial
ordinance, the heresies and errors which we have
here before us, in our hands, already condemned.
To the performance of so holy a work, God has conferred upon thee the wisdom of divine truth, the
power of royal majesty, and the justice of right
equity.   As the Most High has said, Jer. i., 'Lo, I
have put my words into thy mouth by imparting
wisdom, and I have placed thee over the nations and
kingdoms by conferring power, that thou mightest
root up and destroy by executing justice.'   So mayest
thou destroy heresy and error; and especially this
obstinate heretic, by whose malign influence many regions have been infected with the pest of heresy, and
by reason of whom many things have gone to ruin.

"This sacred labor, O glorious prince, is left to

thee. On thee is it the more incumbent, to whom
has been given the supremacy of justice. And as
the result, from the mouth of babes and sucklings
shall thy praises be long celebrated, as the destroyer
of its enemies and the avenger of the Catholic faith.
The which, that it may prosperously and happily become thy lot, may he who is blessed for ever more,
Jesus Christ, grant. Amen." [1]

Such was the discourse, delivered in full council,
and upon the Sabbath—the session was held on that
day—by which the minds of men were to be brought
into a frame devout enough to give over an innocent
man to the flames. It seems as if the black deed
would not have been perfect in its horror, without
this dark feature of Sabbath profanation.

Immediately after the sermon, the decree was
read, by which the council enjoined silence. Its
language betrays the self-sufficient and arrogant tone
of authority which the council had assumed. " The
holy council of Constance, lawfully assembled by
the influence of the Holy Spirit, decrees and orders
every one, with whatever dignity he may be invested,
whether imperial, royal, or episcopal, to abstain, during the present session, from all language, murmur,
and noise which may disturb this assembly, convoked
with the inspiration of God; and this under pain of
incurring excommunication, and imprisonment of two
months, and of being declared an abettor of heresy."
The procurator of the council then demanded a
vigorous prosecution of the process which they had
in hand, insisting that there should be no pause or

---

[1] Van der Hardt, tom. iii., gives the discourse in full.

cessation in the proceedings till Huss was finally condemned and sentence pronounced.

The council now directed that sixty articles of Wickliffe, extracted from the two hundred and sixty which had been brought before them by the English deputation, should be read. After sentence against these was pronounced, the council proceeded to the works of Huss. Thirty articles were presented, some of which had not before been publicly read, but most of which were in substance those upon which he had been interrogated in the presence of the council. Some with which he had first been charged were found to be but duplicates of others, or implied in them, and were consequently left out, reducing them to the number mentioned above.[1] A statement was then made of the character and scope of the several articles, together with the testimony by which they were severally supported. Instead, however, of giving the names of the witnesses, only their office or ecclesiastical rank was stated. This was the course that had been pursued on the trial of John XXIII. In that case there could have been little or no objection to it, for the pope, when summoned to confront the witnesses against him, had declined the privilege, and had confessed to the justice of his sentence by a voluntary submission. But in the case of Huss, this course was one of manifest injustice. He was not permitted to confront his witnesses. In few instances could he even know who they were. His enemies were permitted to testify, without scrutiny or question, whatever they pleased.

[1] Van der Hardt, iv. 408.

In these circumstances, it was but natural that
Huss should seek to meet each article, as it was read,
by a final statement.[1] This he wished and attempted
to do, but the privilege was denied. As the first
article was read, "that there is one Catholic church,
which is composed of the body of believers predes-
tined to salvation." Huss added in a distinct and
and clear voice, "Indeed, I have no doubt that there
is one holy Catholic church, which is the congregation of all the elect, not only in this world, but in
the world of spirits, embracing those who belong to
the invisible body of Jesus Christ, of whom he is
the head." To the succeeding articles Huss also attempted to reply, but was interrupted by the Bishop
of Cambray, who ordered him to be silent, and when
he answered, to reply to all at once. "But," said
Huss, "you forbid me to answer to each, while it is
out of my power to remember the whole list of accusations." As another article was read, Huss again
attempted to reply. Upon this, the Cardinal of Florence arose and exclaimed, "You deafen us,"—a
strange complaint after the previous scenes of uproar
and confusion of which the council had had experience. The ushers of the council were ordered to
seize him and force him to be silent. So gross a
wrong Huss could have borne for himself, but he
was unwilling that the immense crowd assembled
upon the occasion should receive the articles of the
council as a reliable statement of his real views.
With a loud voice, and with his hands lifted to
heaven, he exclaimed, "In the name of Almighty

[1] L'Enfant, 271.

God, I beseech you, deign to afford me an equitable
hearing, that I may clear myself at least before those
who surround me, and remove from their minds the
suspicion of errors. Grant me this favor, and then
do with me what you will."

Here he was again interrupted and required to be
silent.[1] Finding that he was not to be permitted the
privilege of speaking and vindicating himself from
such a multitude of accusations, he kneeled down,
and raising his hands and eyes to heaven, commended
his cause in prayer to God, the most righteous judge.

At length the old accusation which had before
been abandoned, was brought forward. It was
charged that Huss had written and taught, that in
the consecration of the eucharist the material and
substantial bread (the matter and substance of bread)
remained. To this was added the article "that a
priest in mortal sin cannot baptize," etc., with other
articles of a similar tenor, or that had before been
fully answered. When Huss wished to reply to
these, the Cardinal of Florence again enjoined silence. But again Huss urgently entreated that he
might be heard kindly, at least on account of those
around him, whom he would not have misled by the
imagination that he defended such errors as were
now adduced. "For," said he, "I utterly deny that
I ever believed or taught that after the consecration
in the sacrament of the altar, the material bread remains. Moreover, I assert that baptism and consecration, and the administration of other sacred rites,
performed by a priest guilty of mortal sin, is infamous

[1] Mon. Hus., 346.

and hateful in the sight of God. Whenever he is
full of impurity, he is least of all a worthy minister
of sacred and divine offices." To other accusations
upon the list he replied briefly in much the same
manner as he had done before in writing, either
briefly refuting some, or candidly confessing others.

Huss was now accused of giving out that he was
the fourth person—now added—of the Holy Trinity.[1] This was established by the testimony of a
single doctor, whose name was not mentioned. " Give
me the name," said Huss, " of that doctor who testifies thus against me." But the bishop who read the
accusation refused this request. He merely replied,
" There is no need of it." Huss, mastering his indignation, solemnly ˙declared, " God forbid that such an
imagination as that I should call myself a fourth
person of the Trinity should have been thought of
by me, nor, by the love of Christ, has it ever entered
my mind." He then repeated the article from the
Athanasian creed upon the Trinity, declaring in it
his firm and abiding belief. At length the words of
his appeal to God, as supreme Judge, were read, and
this solemn appeal was pronounced an impious error.
To the council Huss had no reply to make in his defence. Mastering his emotions, he looked up to
heaven, and said, in a tone that should have thrilled
the assembly, " Most blessed Jesus, behold how this
council holds as error, and reprobates thine own deed
and the law which thou didst prescribe, when thou
thyself, overwhelmed by enemies, didst commend thy
cause to thy Father, God, the most holy Judge, leav-

[1] Mon. Hus., ii. 346.

ing us an example in our woe and weakness, that, with prayer for aid, we should suppliantly flee in our wrongs to the most righteous Judge." Here he paused a moment, and then added, " But I—I say confidently, that the surest and safest of all appeals is to the Master, Christ. For he it is whom no one can sway from the right by any bribes, nor deceive by false testimony, nor snare in any sophistry,—since to each he gives back his own reward."

He was next charged with having treated the papal excommunication with contempt,[1] still unwarrantably continuing in the exercise of his office, even to the celebration of mass. " I did not," said Huss, " despise the excommunication, but publicly in my sermons I appealed to him who is the Judge. And thus it was that I continued to discharge the sacred offices. Meanwhile, I thrice sent to the chief pontiff those who should act as my procurators, to give satisfaction in my behalf. For, for good and satisfactory reasons I could not appear in my own behalf, as has been stated. Yet I was never able to obtain a hearing. My representatives, moreover, were cruelly treated. Some were imprisoned, some were insultingly rejected, or subjected to torturing hardships. The records will readily certify you of this, in which my case, and the injustice done, are written out. For this reason I came hither freely to this council, relying upon the public faith of the emperor, who is here present, assuring me that I should be safe from all violence, so that I might attest my innocence, and give a reason of my faith to all who compose it."

[1] Mon Hus., ii. 346.

As Huss spoke of the public faith—the safe-conduct which he had received—he fixed his eyes
steadily upon the emperor. A deep blush at once
mounted to the imperial brow.[1] Sigismund felt the
shame and meanness of which he had been guilty,
and his own previous declarations before the council
deprived him of any chance to vindicate his integrity
or honor. This circumstance was not soon forgotten
in Germany. To it, perhaps, the safety of Luther
and the success of the German reformation a century
later were in part due. When Charles V., at the
celebrated diet of Worms, was pressed to consent to
the seizure of Luther in contempt of his safe-conduct, his Spanish honor revolted at the proposal.
"No!" said he, "I should not like to blush like
Sigismund."

At length, when the several articles of accusation
had been read, one of the judges of the court arose,
and made a statement of the manner in which Huss
had been repeatedly asked whether he would maintain or disavow them. In his prison at Gottlieben
he had promised to submit himself to the decision
of the council. He had afterward repeated this
before the commission sent to him upon his removal
to Constance. A third time he had made a similar
declaration, and had given it in writing under his
own hand. This, as already presented, was then read,
and it was added, that on the day preceding, (July 5,)
Huss had been once more asked by the prelates dep-
utized to visit him by the council, whether he would
abjure the articles which he acknowledged to be his,

[1] Mon. Hus., ii. 346. L'Enfant, 272.

promising no longer to hold them, and no more to
teach those which he did not acknowledge; but he
chose still to abide by his previous declaration, unmoved from his purpose by all the means of persuasion which could be employed.

The Bishop of Concordia, Italian by birth, whose
bald head and advanced years gave him a venerable
aspect, had been selected to read the two sentences
of the council, one condemning the books of Huss to
be burned, and the other requiring his degradation
from the priesthood, in order that he might be given
over to the secular arm. Upon the requisition of Henry
de Piro, the prosecutor of the council, these sentences
were then read. The first, against the books of
Huss, was as follows: [1] "This most holy general council of Constance, representing the Catholic church,
etc., etc.:—Because, as the truth itself testifies, an
evil tree brings forth evil fruit, hence it is that John
Wickliffe, a man of damnable memory, by his destructive doctrine,—not like those holy fathers of old,
who in Jesus Christ, through the gospel, begot believing children,—but against the saving faith of Christ,
like a root of poison,—has begotten sons of perdition, whom he has left behind him as successors
in the inheritance of his perverse doctrine, against
whom this holy council of Constance is compelled to
rise up as against bastard and illegitimate sons, and
cut off their errors as noxious tares from the garden
of the Lord, by watchful care, and the knife of ecclesiastical authority, lest, like a canker, they spread
abroad to others' destruction; and since, moreover,

[1] See Mansi. Also, Mon. Hus., ii. 346. Van der Hardt, iv. 429–432.

in the sacred general council lately held at Rome, it
was decreed that the doctrine of John Wickliffe, of
damnable memory, ought to be condemned, and his
books which contain this said doctrine should be
burned as heretical, and this decree was carried into
effect,—therefore should this said decree be approved
by the authority of this present sacred council. And
yet, nevertheless, a certain John Huss, in this sacred
council, here present in person, a disciple, not of
Christ, but rather of the heresiarch John Wickliffe,
after and against this condemnation and decree aforesaid, with venturous audacity, has dogmatized, asserted, and preached many of his errors and heresies,
which have been long condemned by the most reverend fathers in Christ, their lordships the archbishops, the bishops of different kingdoms, and masters
of theology in many universities,—especially in his
resisting, along with his confederates in the schools,
and in his sermons in public, the scholastic condemnation of the articles themselves of Wickliffe several
times pronounced in the University of Prague ; and in
favor of his doctrine he has declared, in the presence
of a multitude of the clergy and the people, that
John Wickliffe was a Catholic man, and an evangelical doctor.   He has, moreover, published certain
articles hereinafter written, and many others deserving of condemnation, asserting them to be Catholic,
which articles are contained, as is notorious, in the
books of this very John Huss.   Wherefore, full and
sufficient information being had in the premises, as
well as careful deliberation on the part of the most
reverend fathers, their lordships the cardinals of the

holy Roman church, the patriarchs, the archbishops, the bishops, and other prelates, and doctors of scripture and of laws—composing a large assembly—this most holy council of Constance declares and decrees, that the articles hereinafter written, which have been found on collation, by many masters of the sacred page, to be contained in his books and treatises written by his own hand, and which, moreover, this same John Huss, in the presence of the fathers and prelates of this sacred council, has confessed to be contained in his books and treatises, are not Catholic, nor to be taught as such; but some of them are erroneous, some scandalous, others offensive to pious ears, many of them rash and seditious, and some notoriously heretical, and long since by the holy fathers and general councils reprobated and condemned; and to preach, teach, or in any way approve them, is prohibited. But since the hereinafter written articles are expressly contained in his books or treatises, viz., in the book which he has entitled "*De Ecclesia*," and in his other works, therefore, the aforesaid books, and their doctrine, and each of his other treatises and works, edited by him in Latin, or in the vulgar Bohemian, or by him or others, one or more, translated into some foreign idiom, this most holy council reprobates and condemns; and doth decree and appoint that they shall be burned, solemnly and publicly, in the presence of the clergy and people, in the city of Constance, and elsewhere, adding, moreover, for the reason aforesaid, that his whole doctrine is and ought to be suspected as to faith, and should be avoided by all the faithful of Christ. And that this pernicious doctrine may be rooted out from the midst of the church, this holy synod orders, that, by the ordinaries of different localities, treatises and works of this nature, by means of ecclesiastical censure, and even, if need be, under penalty of favoring heresy, shall be carefully sought out, and, when found, shall be committed publicly to the flames. And if any one be found to violate or despise this sentence and decree, this same holy synod ordains that such persons shall be proceeded against, as suspected of heresy, by the ordinaries of different localities, and the inquisitors of heretical pravity."[1]

As this sentence was read, Huss replied, " Who are ye, that ye can justly condemn my writings? For I always desired that they should be corrected by a better application and understanding of Christian truth, and this is still my wish. And yet, hitherto ye have not presented any solid arguments against them, nor have ye convicted of error a single word of my writings. Why, then, have ye been impelled to destroy my books, whether rendered in the Bohemian, or other language—those, moreover, which doubtless ye have never seen? And if ye were to see them, your ignorance of the Bohemian language would prevent your understanding them." But after complaining of other injustice in the accusation, he knelt down, and with his eyes to heaven uttered fervent prayer.

The sentence against Huss himself was then read. " The things done and to be done in the cause of inquisition of, and concerning the heresy of, John Huss

[1] Mansi.

being considered, and a faithful and full report of
the commission deputed to act in this case having
been had, as well as of other masters in theology
and doctors of law, in, of, and concerning the acts
and words of witnesses worthy of credit, and in
great number—which testimony has been openly and
publicly read to John Huss himself before the fathers and prelates of this sacred council, by which
testimony it is made most clearly manifest that this
same John Huss has taught many things evil, scandalous, seditious, and dangerously heretical, and has
preached the same through a long course of years;
this most holy council of Constance—the name of
Christ being invoked—having only God before their
eyes, doth by this definitive sentence, in these writings, pronounce, decree, and declare, that the said
John Huss was and is a true and manifest heretic,
and that he has taught errors and heresies long
time condemned by the church of God, and many
things, moreover, scandalous, offensive to pious ears,
rash, and seditious; and that he has publicly preached
them, to the grievous offence of the divine majesty,
the scandal of the Catholic church, and the prejudice
of the Catholic faith; that he has, moreover, treated
with contempt ecclesiastical censures and the keys
of the church, persisting obstinately in this spirit for
many years, sandalizing Christian believers by his
extreme stubbornness, while neglecting ecclesiastical
rules; that he has interposed his appeal to the Lord
Jesus Christ as supreme Judge, in which appeal he
has laid down many positions, false and unjust, scandalous in regard to the Apostolic See itself, contemn-

ing ecclesiastical censures and the keys :—wherefore, for the aforesaid reasons, as well as many others, this holy synod pronounces John Huss to have been heretical, and concludes that he ought to be judged and condemned as a heretic, and by these presents doth condemn him, reproving his appeal as unjust, scandalous, and derisive of ecclesiastical jurisdiction, and himself as having seduced Christian people from the faith, especially in the kingdom of Bohemia, by his preaching and by his writings, and as having been not a true preacher of the gospel of Christ according to the exposition of the holy doctors, but rather a misleader of the people.

"But because, by those things which it has seen and heard, this holy synod knows this same John Huss to be pertinacious, incorrigible, and, moreover, of such a disposition as not to desire to return to the bosom of holy mother church, nor abjure the heresies and errors which he has publicly defended and preached,— therefore this holy synod of Constance declares and decrees that the same John Huss be deposed and degraded from the order of the priesthood, or other dignity with which he is invested, giving in charge to the ever reverend fathers in Christ, the archbishop of Milan, the bishops of Feltri, Asti, Alexandria, Bangor, and Lavaur, the due execution, in the presence of this most holy synod, of the said degradation, as the canonical rule of order requires."

As the charges of the sentence were read, Huss interposed brief comments. It was in vain that they forbade him to speak. His indignant sense of the wrong done him would not permit him to be silent. When

the accusation of obstinacy was read, he promptly
denied it. "This," said he, "I do utterly deny. I
have ever desired and I still desire to be better instructed from scripture; and I solemnly declare that
such is my zeal for the truth, that if by a single word
I might confound the errors of all heretics, there is
no danger that I would not face in order to do it."
Who could doubt the sincerity and conscientiousness
of the speaker?

When the reading of the sentence was concluded,
Huss again fell upon his knees, and in earnest and
distinct tones prayed for his enemies. "O Lord
God, through thy mercy I pray thee deign to pardon
all my enemies, for thou knowest that I have been
unjustly accused by them, overcome by false witnesses,
oppressed by fictitious accusations, and unrighteously
condemned. For thy mercy's sake, therefore, remit
their sins." The scene, in its circumstances, had a
deep and solemn significance that might have reminded the judges of the prayer once offered on the
cross of Calvary. But the history of persecution
was to carry out the parallel of the tragedy in a still
more striking manner. Scorn and derision were
traced in the features of the members of the council,
and were uttered in their sneers. They saw in Huss
a victim, of whom they felt they might safely make
an example.

The ceremony of degradation—the first step in the
execution of the sentence—was now commenced.[1]
By the direction of the bishops he was clothed in
priestly robes, and, as if he had been about to cele-

---

[1] Mon Hus., i. 28, and ii. 346.

brate mass, the chalice was placed in his hand. As they put the white robe upon him, Huss could not forbear to say—"My Master, Jesus Christ, when he was sent away by Herod to Pilate, was clothed in a white robe."

At length, being clad, the prelates admonished him to retract while he yet might, and abjure the errors with which he stood charged. But he replied aloud, as he stood upon the platform to which he had been raised—turning as he spoke toward the people, with tears in his eyes and his voice trembling with emotion—"Behold, these bishops persuade and exhort me to retract. But I fear to do it, lest hereafter I be charged with falsehood before God, in case I should confess myself to be guilty of errors of which I was never conscious, which I have never taught, and thus sin against my conscience and divine truth at once. Never have I asserted those articles, but they are unjustly imputed to me on false testimony,—while I have written and taught the exact opposite. Above all, I fear lest the minds of so great a multitude as that to which I have preached so long, as well as of others who are faithful ministers of the divine word, should, through the offence thus given, be torn away from truth." [1]

[1] The language, as given by another historian, though to the same purport, is more spirited. "How could I," asked Huss, "after such a hypocritical abjuration, lift my face to heaven? With what eye could I support the looks of that crowd of men whom I have instructed, should it come to pass, through my fault, that those same things which are now regarded by them as certainties, should become matters of doubt; if, by my example, I caused confusion and trouble in so many souls, so many consciences, which I have filled with the pure doctrine of Christ's gospel, and which I have strengthened against the snares of the devil? No! no! it shall never be said, I preferred my life to their salvation."—*Bonnechose*

Such language, while it might have moved some to pity and respect, only provoked the bishops. "See," said they—and the murmur went round the assembly—"how perverse he is in his wickedness, and how tenacious of his heresy!"

The bishops now directed Huss to descend from the platform. They then began to strip him of the sacerdotal habit in which he had been clothed. They took from him first the chalice, accompanying the act with the words—"O thou accursed Judas, who, breaking away from the counsels of peace, hast consulted with the Jews! Behold! we take from thee this chalice, in which the blood of Jesus Christ for the redemption of the world is offered." Unmoved by the united curse and outrage, Huss exclaimed, in a clear, loud voice, to be heard by all, "But I have all hope and confidence fixed in my God and Saviour, that he will never take from me the cup of salvation; and I abide firm in my belief that, aided by his grace, I shall this day drink thereof in his kingdom."

The bishops proceeded to strip him of the remaining symbols of the priestly office, accompanying the removal of each with a correspondent curse. "All these insults," said Huss, "I can endure, undisturbed and calm, for the name and truth of Jesus Christ."

When this work of removing the sacerdotal habits was accomplished, it still remained to efface the marks of the tonsure, and thus take away the last symbol of the priestly office. Here a singular and ludicrous controversy arose.[1] In order to crop the hair, some were for using a razor, and some insisted

---

[1] Mon. Hus., ii., 347.

that the shears were the proper instrument. Some
would be satisfied if the tonsure were but disfigured;
others would have the hair entirely removed.

The scene was one that Huss, even in his circumstances, felt to be ridiculous. " Ah ! " said he, turning
to the emperor where he sat upon his throne, edified
doubtless by the pious heresy of some on the question under discussion—" Ah ! these bishops cannot
easily agree among themselves, even in regard to the
method by which to insult me."

At last the shears-party was triumphant. His
hair was cut in four directions, so as to leave bare
the form of a cross. This was then washed, as if to
remove the oil of his anointing by which he was
consecrated to the priesthood. It was then declared
that " This holy council of Constance doth now remove John Huss from the order of the priesthood
and the offices of honor which he has discharged,
thus declaring that the church of God disowns this
man, and gives him up, no longer shielded by her
protection, to the secular arm." As they were about
to place upon his head the paper crown which he
was to wear to the place of execution, and which in
derision was covered with pictured fiends, they said,
" We devote thy soul to the devils of hell." " But
I," said Huss, lifting his eyes to heaven and reverently folding his hands—" I commend it to my most
merciful Master, Jesus Christ." The crown was now
set upon his head. It was a sort of pyramidal mitre,
rising to a considerable height. On each of its three
sides the frightful figure of a demon was painted,
while on each was written, so as to be visible to all

and from every direction, the crime for which he was condemned—*Heresiarch.* Huss looked at it and calmly said, " My Lord Jesus Christ, though innocent, deigned to bear to an infamous death, for wretched me, a far rougher and weightier crown of thorns."[1]

The ceremony of the degradation of Huss was now complete. He was disowned by the church, and no longer as a priest was subject to its exclusive jurisdiction. Given over to the secular arm, it belonged to the emperor—such was the orthodox theory of persecution—to do with the prisoner as Pilate with Jesus—what the priests could not—execute capital sentence. Sigismund committed Huss to the charge of Louis, the Elector Palatine, directing him to go and see that he was delivered into the hands of the proper officers. Huss was given over by the elector to the mayor of Constance, and by the latter was placed in the hands of those to whom it belonged to see the sentence executed. They were commanded to burn him, with his clothes, and all indiscriminately that belonged to him, even to his knife and to his purse, from which they were not to take so much as a single penny.

He was led to the place of execution, walking between two officers of the Elector Palatine, and without being chained; two of the police of the city preceded and two followed him. The princes, with an escort of eight hundred armed men, and followed by an immense multitude, drawn by curiosity, interest, or anxiety, accompanied them to the place of execution.

[1] Mon. Hus. ii. 347 ; also i. 28.

The procession, instead of taking the direct route thither, moved first in a nearly opposite direction, in order to pass upon the way the episcopal palace, in front of which a pile of the prisoner's writings had been heaped up for the flames. The fire was kindled and the books burned as the procession passed. They had been first condemned, and were first to be consumed. But to Huss the scene appeared simply ridiculous, as indeed it was. Nor did it need a prophet's sagacity to discern that the course pursued was like to defeat its own object. It was altogether out of the power of the council to obtain and thus destroy all the writings of the reformer. They were too widely scattered and too deeply cherished, and this act of impotent vengeance would only make them the more prized—would attach to them a new importance, and excite a more eager curiosity for their perusal. The scene, even in the solemn circumstances in which Huss was placed, did not fail to draw from him a smile at the senile malice which it displayed.

As the procession passed on, they reached a bridge at which it was necessary to pause. It was not considered safe for the whole multitude to pass over it at once. The armed escort first proceeded, one by one, and then the crowd of citizens followed. Huss improved the occasion to say a few words to the throngs that pressed around to catch a sight of him. He told them, in the German language, that it was not for any heresy that he had been condemned, but through the injustice of his enemies; that they had not been able to convict him of any error, al-

though he had challenged them to do it so often and
so urgently. As he approached the place where he
was to be burned, which was a meadow adjoining
the garden on the north side of the city, outside the
Gottlieben gate, the procession paused, that everything might be made ready for the execution. Here
Huss kneeled down, and lifting his eyes toward
heaven, prayed—using the language of some of the
penitential psalms, especially the thirty-first and
fiftieth.[1] Repeatedly he used the petitions, "Lord
Jesus, have mercy on me," and "O God, into thy
hands I commit my spirit." The crowd around him
were surprised at such an exhibition of devotion in
one whom they had been taught to regard as a
heretic. "What this man may have done before,"
said they, "we know not, but now, certainly, we
hear him speak and pray in a godly and devout
manner."[2]

Huss was then asked by some who stood by—
probably in the hope that the fear of death might
lead him to recant—if he would have a confessor.
A priest near by on horseback, clothed in a green
gown drawn together with a sash of red silk, heard
the question asked, and, more anxious for the execution than for a recantation which might even yet
snatch the victim from the flames, declared that a
confessor ought not to be allowed him because he
was a heretic. Huss, however, replied that he would
be glad to have one. Ulric Reichenthal—one of the
historians of the council—as he himself relates, called for a priest then present to come and receive the

---

[1] More probably the fifty-first.   [2] Mon. Hus., ii. 347.

prisoner's confession. The name of this priest was
Ulric Schorand, a man of repute for learning and
integrity, and highly esteemed by the council. He
asked Huss whether he was willing to renounce the
errors for which he had been condemned to the
punishment which he now saw awaiting him. If so,
he was ready to confess him ; but if not, he must be
aware that a heretic, according to the canon law,
could neither administer or receive the sacraments.
Huss having heard the conditions on which he might
be confessed, declined to accept them. He replied,
that he did not deem it necessary for him to confess,
inasmuch as he did not feel himself to be guilty of
any mortal sin. He desired, however, the privilege
of improving the occasion to address the people in
the German language. But the brutal elector, true
to the instincts of his cruel nature and in perfect consistency with his previous course, instead of allowing
permission, gave orders that he should immediately
be committed to the flames. Huss at once lifted up
his voice in prayer. " O Lord Jesus, I would endure
with humility, for thy gospel, this cruel death ; and I
beseech thee, pardon all my enemies." Such were
some of the expressions of his prayer. While he
was thus engaged in his devotions, with his eyes
toward heaven, the paper mitre, which had been
placed upon his head in the council, fell off. As
Huss turned to behold it, a smile played over his
features. Perhaps he saw in the frail thing an em-
blem of that impotent malice which in vain attempted to affix calumny to his name. The soldiers, however, more inclined to sympathize with their harsh

leader, replaced the mitre upon his head, and, referring to the images painted upon it, declared he ought
to be burned with the devils he had served.

Having asked and obtained permission to speak to
his keepers, Huss thanked them for the kind treatment which he had received at their hands.[1] " Ye
have shown yourselves," said he, " not merely my
keepers, but brethren most beloved. And be assured
that I rest with firm faith upon my Saviour, in whose
name I am content calmly to endure this sort of
death, that I this day may go to reign with him."
These words were spoken in German. We have
other testimony, also, to show that even among his
jailers, Huss must already have seen the fruits of
his fidelity. He now wished, with his dying breath,
to seal the impression that had been made by his
life.

He was now stripped of his garments and bound
fast to a large stake, through which holes had been
bored to secure the cords. Of these there were six
or seven, which had been wet in order longer to resist the heat of the flames. One was bound about
his ankles, one below and another above the knees,
while others were distributed over the upper part
of his body as far as the armpits. His hands had
previously been bound behind his back, and he was
now made fast in this position. The stake was driven
downward and made to stand erect in the earth, so as
to support the victim while the flames consumed him.
By some accident it had happened that Huss, as
bound to the stake, stood facing the east.[1] This was

---

[1] Mon. Hus., ii. 347.　　[2] Ib 348.

observed by some of the bystanders, and the order was given that he should be turned so as to face the west. As a heretic, he might not die with his eyes directed toward the Holy Land. The order was immediately obeyed. The neck of the prisoner was now bound to the stake by a black and sooty iron chain, which had been used by a poor man, its former owner, for suspending his kettle over the fire. Huss bent his head somewhat so as to obtain a sight of it, but instead of turning pale with affright, he beheld it with a cheerful smile. "The Lord Jesus Christ," said he, " my beloved Redeemer and Saviour, was, for my sake, bound with a harsher and more cruel chain. Why, therefore, should wretched I blush, for his most holy name, to be bound with this sooty one ? "

Two piles of fagots were placed about the feet of Huss, which had been stripped of their covering. Bundles of straw were placed erect around the stake, reaching as far upward as the neck of the victim. Every thing was now ready for the kindling of the flames. Before the torch was applied, however, one more effort was made to induce Huss to recant. It was the wish of the emperor even yet, undoubtedly, to save if possible his honor with the prisoner's life ; and it was probably by his direction— given beforehand, for he did not choose to witness the scene—that the marshal of the empire with the elector approached the funeral pile, and exhorted Huss yet to save his life by retracting and abjuring his doctrines. It was the last opportunity. Would Huss now hesitate ? In a loud, clear voice, he replied, with a firmness which the immediate prospect of death could not shake, "I call God to witness, that I have never taught nor written those things which on false testimony they impute to me; but my declarations, teachings, writings, in fine, all my works, have been intended and shaped toward the object of rescuing dying men from the tyranny of sin. Wherefore I will this day gladly seal that truth which I have taught, written, and proclaimed—established by the divine law, and by holy teachers—by the pledge of my death."[1]

On hearing this final decision of Huss—unshaken in his purpose to the last—the marshal and the elector left him. The executioners kindled the flames. Amid the smoke and blaze, Huss could be heard engaged in prayer. "O Christ, thou Son of the living God, have mercy on me." The prayer was repeated, and again he was heard uttering the words of the creed, when the wind, rising with the flames, kindled the pile to a fiercer heat, and he was suffocated by the smoke that prevented his saying more. Still was he observed for one or two minutes obviously engaged in devotion. He bowed his head, and his lips were seen to move as if in utterance of prayer. At last all was silent. The charred carcass was motionless, and the spirit had fled.[2]

As the fagots burned away, they left the body visible, still hanging to the stake by the iron chain. The executioners with poles pushed the fragments of the burning brands back around the stake, and heaped up new fuel about the half-consumed skele-

[1] Mon. Hus., ii. 348.   [2] Ib.

ton. They struck at the bones and limbs, to break
them in pieces, that they might the sooner be consumed. His head rolled down. It was beaten into
pieces with a club and thrown back into the flames.
His heart, found among his intestines, was pierced
by a sharp stick of wood, and roasted at a fire apart
until it was reduced to ashes. One of the executioners was seen still having in his possession some
of the garments of Huss. The elector, on observing
it, commanded that these and all that belonged to
Huss should be cast together into the flames, promising the executioner compensation for the loss. "The
Bohemians," said he, "would keep and cherish such
a thing as a sacred relic." When every thing had
been consumed, the ashes, and every fragment or
memorial of the scene of martyrdom, were shov-
elled up and carted away, to be emptied into the
Rhine.

Thus perished, upon his forty-second birthday, in
the full vigor of his powers, and in the strength and
promise of manhood, one of those men whom the
world has been constrained to acknowledge well
worthy of the martyr's crown. Even his enemies
could not but eulogize his noble bearing, and respect
his manly and heroic spirit. "They went," said
Æneas Sylvius, who afterward filled the papal chair,
and who knew all the circumstances of the execution of Huss and Jerome—"They went to their punishment as to a feast. Not a word escaped them
which gave indication of the least weakness. In the
midst of the flames they sang hymns uninterruptedly
to their last breath. No philosopher ever suffered

death with such constancy as they endured the flames."[1]

The question here rises—What were the real causes which led to the condemnation of Huss? He himself would never allow, even to the last, that he had departed from the orthodox standards of the church —the scriptures and the fathers. In fact, with the exception of his late approval of the views of Jacobel in regard to the communion of the cup, there was scarce a doctrine which he held, upon which he could not have found many members of the council to agree with him. When questioned upon transubstantiation and the Trinity, he replied by a full and frank confession of the Catholic formula. In regard to confession, he did not reject it, though like many of his contemporaries whose orthodoxy passed unsuspected, he did not attach to it that supreme and superstitious importance which belonged to it in the eyes of many. On other points of belief,—as intercession of the saints, the adoration of images, works, purgatory, and tradition, his replies before the council show that his views differed but slightly from those of the French theologians, and the more intelligent and liberal members of the Roman Catholic church. As to the doctrine of the absence of the spiritual character in bad priests—a doctrine so long obscure in his mind, and which at first he seems to have adopted from Wickliffe—he finishes by giving it an orthodox explanation, declaring that in the ministry of an unworthy priest, God works worthily and effectually by unworthy hands. Even with re-

[1] Æneas Sylv., xxxvi.

gard to indulgences, he declares himself indisposed to withhold any prerogative which God may have given to the Roman pontiff, but merely denies that they were of any value when given for unworthy purposes. Many of the propositions attributed to him by the council he publicly disavowed, and others he explained in such a manner that they could not properly be regarded as heretical. Huss attacked, not so much the doctrines of the Romish church, as their abuse, and in this respect might have found sufficient precedent for his justification, had he sought it, among the writings of members of the council.

Nor can we ascribe the condemnation of Huss to the severe language which he used in regard to the corruption and degeneracy of the church. No language to be found in his writings can exceed, if even equal, in severity, that which was employed upon this subject by Gerson, Clemengis, and D'Ailly. Many a sermon was preached before the council, in which plain and terrible expositions of the prevalent depravity were presented, startling enough to fill the mind of every hearer with astonishment and horror. No one ever attempted to deny the truth of what Huss asserted on this subject. The Cardinal of Cambray merely complained that it was said inopportunely.

One prominent feature of the criminality of Huss may perhaps be found in some lines written in an old manuscript copy of his works. " As long as John Huss merely declaimed against the vices of the seculars, every one said that he was inspired by the Spirit of God ; but as soon as he proceeded against ecclesiastics, he became an object of odium, for he then really laid his finger upon the sore."

Huss traced, like Wickliffe, a large part of the excesses of the clergy to the riches which, by the violation of ecclesiastical order, they had been enabled to accumulate. He saw them becoming lords and princes, entangled in worldly business, and inspired by worldly ambitions. He believed that it was the right and duty of the secular power to secure the proper employment of the property of the church, and when it had been perverted from its uses, it might be taken away altogether. This doctrine was a heinous one in the eyes of the clergy. It gave a mortal blow to their worldly rank and temporal authority. Undoubtedly its avowal made Huss many enemies, and these of a most unrelenting and vindictive character.

Various parties in the council stood arrayed against Huss upon distinct grounds. The theologians of the University of Paris saw in him an adherent of the philosophy of the Realists, and the *odium philosophicum*, full as much as the *odium theologicum*, brought them as Nominalists into bitter conflict with him. The English deputation, indifferent, or perhaps hostile to the philosophical views of the Parisians, taking but little delight in the verbal quibbles with which the dialectic skill of the Cardinal of Cambray sought to entrap Huss into self-contradiction, regarded him yet as a disciple of Wickliffe, and when they heard him defending his memory, resolved to give him up

as another victim to their hatred of their own countryman.

The deputation of the German nation, moreover, had
come to Constance, many of them bitterly envenomed
by prejudice against Huss. They regarded him—
some of them, at least—almost in the light of a personal enemy. They charged him with being the
principal agent in the measures which led to the virtual expulsion of the German nation from the University of Prague. Among those who are mentioned as
especially eager to secure his conviction and condemnation, we find many who in all probability had
studied in that university, and carried back with
them from Bohemia the inveterate hostility and
prejudice which had there been excited.[1] The most
pertinacious antagonist of Huss—according to the
historian, the only one who could vanquish him in
argument—was John Zachariæ, professor of theology, who represented the University of Erfurth in
the council of Constance, and who is spoken of as a
man of extensive learning and consummate ability.
To him the same historian ascribes the prevailing
influence which secured the sentence of Huss. However this may be, there can be no doubt that the
German nation in the council, to which Huss should
have looked for defenders, was envenomed against him
by the reports that had gone forth from the University of Prague.

To bring the various interests, antipathies, and
prejudices of the several parties to bear against the
prisoner, there were only needed the skill and malice

---

[1] Van der Hardt, iv. 395.

of men like Paletz and Causis. Paletz, a former companion and associate, soon a rival in influence, at
length in a moment of terror yielding up his better
convictions to secure his own safety, and virtually
sold over to the enemies of the man whom he now
pursued, not so much for the purpose of taking his
life, as for the privilege of triumph over a prostrate
foe ;—Michael de Causis, a villain from the start, and
schooled by all the practised arts of fraud to do the
meanest things which the tool of other men's malice
needs to do, while he gratifies his own :—these were
the leaders in a plot of which bribery was an ac-
kowledged element, and which combined and wove
into its web of intrigue the basest passions, and the
most unhallowed and even conflicting interests.

And yet it is probable that all those arts by which
they poisoned the minds of the council, and all the
false testimony which they heaped together in order
to convict Huss, would have proved vain, but for
that which was in reality, after all, the chief crime
that rested upon his head. He would not admit the
infallibility of the council. He had too much good
sense, not to say piety, to allow the word of any
man, or any body of men, to silence or overthrow
the clear authority of the word of God. He had
appealed from the pope to Christ, the supreme
Judge, in vain, if any council was to sit in judgment
on Christ himself, wrest his words from their true
meaning, or replace them by human decisions from
any source. He demanded, and again and again did
he repeat the demand, that he should be set right
and instructed by the authority of the Sacred Scrip-

tures. To these alone, and not to the *dicta* of any body of men, was he willing to submit. Here was the root of the difficulty. Huss was a Protestant before the name was known. He protested against superseding the plain word of Christ by any inventions or decisions of fallible men. This constituted his crime. To this position he remained steadfast to the last. Sigismund, like a second Nebuchadnezzar, required that Huss should bow down and worship the great image of synodical infallibility which he had set up in place of the pope. The council itself repeated the demand. Obedience and submission were the only terms on which his life would be spared. These conditions Huss rejected with disdain; and his doom was sealed. He went to the stake with a clear conscience, forcing the very flames which his enemies had kindled, to emblazon before the world in fiery letters his reverence for the word of God. Had his life been spared, we can readily believe that new light would have dawned upon him, and that Luther would have been preceded in his career by a man who combined some of the noblest qualities of the martyr spirit with a firmness and decision fully equal to his own.

The character of Huss is one that the most virulent calumny has scarce dared to touch. The purity of his life, the simplicity of his manners, his love of truth, his deep conscientiousness, his aversion to all assumption or display, his strong sympathy for the poor and ignorant, his chivalrous readiness to obey each prompting of duty, though it might carry him to the prison or the stake, are plainly legible in the

whole story of his life. He has no false pride that
forbids him to retract an error, or reject a truth. He
only asks to be convinced, and he is willing to confess his mistake. We can see at times the impetuous-
ness of his nature breaking out under the indignant
sense of wrong or injustice. He utters his feelings
in sharp and even burning words. Fearing not the
face of man, he dares avow his doctrines before the
world; and, if the occasion demands, can lash the
vices of men in power with unsparing invective and
reproof. And yet, so thoroughly is he master of himself, so perfectly has he schooled his passions to self-
control, that rarely a word escapes his lips, or a step
is taken, which he needs to recall. In all the
prominent men of his age we look in vain for that
combination of qualities by which he was eminently
fitted for the task committed to his hands. He
showed throughout his trial a presence of mind, and
a power and quickness of apprehension, which are
perfectly surprising, when we consider the hardships
of his severe and protracted imprisonment—for the
most part deprived of books—and the tumultuous
scenes in the council, which at times made it more
like a mob than a body of men assembled to deliberate and judge. In other reformers we can in
almost every instance detect some weakness or excess that led them into blunders, and which we sadly
regret. Luther might have been too defiant, Melanchthon too compliant. Jerome, the associate of
Huss, was impetuous, perhaps to an extreme; but
Huss himself pursued a course in which his decision
and moderation, his conscientiousness and docility, his

loyalty to truth, and his respect for the rights and judgment of others, are happily blended. We could scarcely wish him to have been other than he was. Even without the crown of martyrdom, we should have been constrained to pronounce him brave and true,—the possessor of a manly, noble nature.

I have not thought it necessary to sum up at length the character of Huss; for its leading features are quite distinctly brought out in the course of the narrative. Frank, genial, and confiding, he scorned all disguise of his views or feelings. His motives are transparent and avowed, and he is never ashamed to confess them. The man stands forth before us, delineated in his own words and deeds.

That he valued and desired the love of all good men is obvious; but he seems never to have been carried away by the mere love of applause. Severely, and perhaps at times morbidly, conscientious, his moral character is above the reach of calumny. The malice of his enemies could not detect in it a flaw or stain. In his familiar letters, he censures himself for faults which most would have scarcely esteemed foibles. He reproaches himself for playing chess, and for an attention to dress which was unbecoming. But his gentleness and charity, his purity and integrity, are above question. They were eloquently attested, as we shall see hereafter, by the document in which the university vindicated his memory from the charges of the council.

In his controversies he never descends to personal abuse. He expresses, in strong language, his disapproval of the course of some of his party in the use of reproachful epithets. Yet it is evident that he lacked neither the occasion or ability, had he been so disposed, to cover his opponents with ridicule, and convert his success into a personal triumph. But this his loyalty to truth as well as the kindliness of his nature forbade.

His social affections were warm and tender. His letters in exile and from prison unfold his heart to us. We have, indeed, in Huss a man whose faculties were admirably balanced,—true and devoted as a friend, powerful yet courteous as an antagonist, eloquent in the pulpit, faithful as a witness to the truth before the council, a hero in the prison, and a martyr at the stake.

CHAPTER III.

JACOBEL, GERSON, AND VOLADAMIR.

May, 1415—August, 1415.

During the period which intervened between the first appearance of Huss before the council and his final sentence, there were other subjects of discussion, of grave importance, which claimed the attention of the members of that body. The Bishop of Litomischel, as we have already seen, entered his complaint against the innovation introduced by Jacobel at Prague. The matter had been given in charge to the theologians of the council, who were directed to examine and report. The result of their labors was a small treatise, in reproof of the innovation.[1] This treatise was submitted to the council, and furnished

---

[1] Van der Hardt, tom. iii., pt. xvii., p. 586.

the grounds upon which their subsequent decree (June 15th, 1415) was based. It pronounces the authority and long practice of the church a sufficient warrant for the withholding of the cup, and declares heretical any who should maintain the contrary opinion; and such persons, as heretical, are to be proceeded against, wherever they may be found, by the diocesans, their vicars, or the inquisitors of heretical pravity, even to the infliction upon them of severe penalties.[1]

The conclusions of the doctors and the penal decree of the council were not calculated to set the question at rest. As to the first, by their admissions they stultified themselves. As to the latter, Jacobel was not a man to be intimidated by its terrors. The doctors had admitted—as they could not well deny— that as the sacrament was instituted by Christ, and observed by the early church, the communion of the cup had been allowed. Their argument for withholding it from the laity was based upon the practice and authority of the church. A custom long observed, had, they remarked, the force of law, and the church had the right to make or adopt such changes in the sacraments as she deemed fitting. On these grounds, which would allow age to sanctify error, and permit the institutions of Christ to be mutilated or abrogated by human caprice, they justified the practice of the church in the withholding of the cup.

But the plea in its favor, drawn from custom and precedent, was by no means a strong one. Scarce two centuries had passed since the cup had been first

---

[1] Van der Hardt, iv. 332.   Fleury, xxvi· 103.

withheld. In England the practice seems first to
have prevailed, and yet, from the writings of Anselm
we infer that he knew nothing of it. The celebrated
Thomas Aquinas is the first of any eminence who
taught that the communion of both kinds was unnecessary, inasmuch as the body and blood of our Lord
are found in each. Bonaventura goes further, and
advises the withholding of the cup from the laity.
These two men, whose names supplied the place of
authority with the Dominicans and Franciscans respectively, first gave an impulse to the innovation.
The mendicant monks, swarming all over Europe,
carried the practice with them. By degrees the communion of the cup fell into disuse. In order that
laymen might communicate in both kinds, a dispensation was at length required by the popes. This
gainful prerogative, once secured, was not likely to
be given up. It was a new jewel in the tiara of
papal prerogative.[1] The first ecclesiastical statute dis-
coverable on the subject, dates from the year 1261.
It was enacted at a general chapter of the Cistercian
order, and is grounded on the pretence that evils
arise from making the communion of the cup general. In the middle of the fourteenth century, yet
less than fifty years before the birth of Huss, the
denial of the cup to the laity had become common.
But in Bohemia, on the confines of the Greek church,
the innovation made slower progress. Matthias, who
died at Prague in 1389, and who is said to have
maintained the same doctrine on the subject with
Jacobel, must have seen and conversed with those

[1] Spittler's History of the Cup.

to whom the cup had been allowed. Many of the
citizens of Prague, who had as yet scarce passed
middle life, must have remembered how Charles IV.,
and Blanca his wife, at their coronation in 1347, had
been allowed to partake of the communion in both
kinds. In Bohemia, therefore, at least, the arguments of the council, futile and inane as they were
in themselves, would lose all their force. So far as
the inhabitants of that kingdom were concerned, the
communion of the cup had in its favor the practice
of twelve centuries. One, or even two hundred
years of innovation was a poor offset—even on the
grounds upon which the council argued—against a
precedent of such long and continuous standing. But
Jacobel did not rest the weight of his arguments
even upon this ground. He had already learned,
like Huss, to go back to the original records of Christianity itself; and to the authority of these—sustained
as it was by the unanimous voice of the Christian
fathers—he was willing to leave the question. His
controversy with Broda already referred to, shows
that he had informed himself in regard to the whole
subject, with care and diligence. He could scarcely
have been taken by surprise at the announcement of
the conclusions and the decree of the council. These
were published on the fifteenth of June, and must
have been known at Prague before the death of
Huss.

But at nearly the same time the report of the
views which Huss entertained upon the subject must
have been received. His words would carry especial
weight with them, as the dying testimony of one

whom tens of thousands revered and loved. In his case, it was to be presumed, there was no blinding motive of self-interest to lead him to a wrong conclusion. In the circumstances of the case his authority would, with the mass of the citizens of Prague, more than counterbalance that of the council. The latter had exposed itself to contempt, not only by its treatment of Huss, which excited the deepest indignation, but by its notorious intrigues and corruptions, unblushingly proclaimed by members of its own body. Huss, on the other hand, had been almost canonized in the affections of his countrymen, by the injustice which the council had inflicted upon him. Contrary to their design, they had crowned their victim with a dignity and power with which their own could not compete. The preacher was to be elevated into the confessor, the hero into the martyr. Powerful as the words of Huss might be from his pulpit in Bethlehem chapel, they were more eloquent as traced by his manacled hand in the cell of his Gottlieben prison. The decree of the council stood little chance of securing favor or recognition when the views of Huss were once known.

Jacobel was encouraged and strengthened by the approval of his countryman at Constance. His own convictions had been deliberately formed, and, confident of the rectitude of his course, he did not quail before the storm. But although the decree of the council doomed him as a heretic to inquisitorial vengeance, it failed to frighten him from the stand which he had made. He took it up, along with the conclusions on which it had been based, and hurled it back in the face of the council, riddled through and through by the arrows of scripture logic.[1]   He brought the array of the Christian fathers in unbroken phalanx against an innovation of less than three hundred years' standing at the utmost.   Nor did he fail to improve so fair an occasion of speaking some plain truths upon kindred topics.

The argument of Jacobel displays throughout an uncompromising love of truth, a thorough detestation of all hypocrisy and injustice, a devoted fidelity to the authority of scripture, as well as a most vigorous intellect and a glowing eloquence.   As he takes up the conclusions of the doctors, adopting the first, and exposing the more fully thereby the fallacy and absurdity of the last, and then proceeds to attack the decree of the council, which, in its cruel severity, bore its condemnation on its face, all his powers and feelings are aroused, and his argument grows fierce and terrible as it clothes itself in the mantle of injured and insulted truth.   His irony, contempt, sarcasm, and grave reproof, not unmingled with a sadder tone that breathes a dirge-like music over the bleeding wounds of persecuted truth, carry us along on the tide of argument, and we feel that resistance is vain.   The man's words come from the deepest fountains of feeling and conviction.   His heart is a volcano, pouring forth a lava tide of fiery logic that scathes and burns all it touches.   He does not fight as one that beateth the air.   He feels that he is dealing with real antagonists.

Each paragraph is sharp and pointed as a dagger.

[1] The entire discussion on both sides is to be found in Van der Hardt, tom. iii.

Every sentence stings. " If we are Christ's priests," he says, " I know not whom we should follow rather than Christ himself." " If Christ is the foundation—as we have heard from their own mouth in regard to this doctrine—not only the doctors of the council of Constance, but the gates of hell shall not prevail against it." " Whoever loves the truth, let him dismiss these doctors, even though there were a legion of them, and hear him who is the Truth— Christ, that great Prophet, the well-beloved of the Father." " Into such senselessness do they fall, who, when anything obscure prevents them from discerning the truth, have recourse, not to the words of the prophets, the writings of the apostles, or the authority of the gospel—and so become masters of error because they never were disciples of the truth."

Jacobel takes occasion to show how the disciples of Christ, who truly followed in his steps, have been persecuted and charged with heresy. Abel was killed, Joseph sold as a slave, Isaiah sawn in sunder, Christ, the Lamb slain from the foundation of the world, crucified. Paul, after the manner that men called heresy, worshipped the God of his fathers. " Such men the council takes on false testimony, convicts and condemns them of heresy, and then delivers them over to the secular arm to be punished. O Jesus Christ, the author of this truth ! do they not, as far as in them is, make thee an heresiarch ? They give up thee and thy holy primitive church to the secular arm, and still wish to be called guiltless of murder, and charitable ! As of old the Pharisees and the priests, so holy that they would not enter the prætorium, or the house of a Gentile, gave up the Innocent One to be crucified, while they said 'It is not lawful for us to put any one to death,' so now is their example copied by those, who first defame, then cite to trial, excommunicate and hastily arrest, and degrade, cursing body and soul as far as in them lies, and handing their victims over to the secular court. And as the Jews then said, 'If thou lettest this man go, thou art not Cæsar's friend,' so now these men say—'Powerful master, this man is under your jurisdiction; the church has no more to do with him, and so he must be restrained by the civil power.' . . . O King of kings and Lord of lords, tribulations are on every side, thou Eternal Father! For if, according to thine own command, I am to hear thy well-beloved Son, and listen to the gospel, as that well-beloved Son himself gave commandment, and so live after the example of the primitive church, I shall be excommunicated, accounted a heretic, condemned, burned, or in some other way put to death by this Roman church, which savors not the nature or practice of the primitive one. But if I do not obey the gospel, eternal death and everlasting fire will be my portion when our Lord Jesus Christ shall be revealed from heaven with his angels, to take vengeance upon those that know not God and obey not the gospel of our Lord Jesus Christ. What choice then shall I make? But I know that if I should please men, I should be no more the servant of Jesus Christ. . . . . Fear not those, therefore, who can only kill the body. Not a hair of your head shall perish without our Father; in patience possess ye your souls.

"Since, then, all power is given to Christ, in heaven and on earth, who would dare to bring him into subjection to his own rules, shaping His gospel law according to his own caprice—who, but the son of perdition, who is exalted above all that is called God?"

Jacobel does not spare the persecuting doctrines of the council embodied in their decree. "Ye know not what spirit ye are of. Christ came, not to destroy men's lives, but to save them. Mahomet taught his followers to persecute and kill; Christ did not. . . . By their fruits ye shall know them,—yea, those who invoke the secular arm against such as practice gospel truth. . . . Antichrist, as Thomas says, forces, by threats and torture, those whom he cannot otherwise subdue." Jacobel seems to see fulfilled before his eyes the prophecies in regard to the last days. He quotes the language employed in previous centuries by those whom the church still honored, and shows how severely it bore against those who chose to obey, and force others to obey, men rather than God. Their final doom he holds up as a fearful warning.

The whole treatise is written in a bold, manly, and uncompromising spirit. It was the gauntlet of defiance thrown down at the feet of the council. From first to last, it breathes not a note of fear or submission. While perfectly decorous in language, it tears away the last thread of apology with which the council would veil its tyranny and iniquity. The occasion upon which it was written lent it a new force. The whole Bohemian nation were indignant at the outrage offered to their countryman. Jacobel's

words gave expression to the convictions of thousands.
They sank deep into the hearts of the people, and
animated them to a noble resistance of ecclesiastical
tyranny.[1]

The council, meanwhile, did not neglect the subject of the schism of the church. By deposition they
had disposed of John XXIII., but Gregory and Benedict still maintained their rival claims to the pontificate. The former, however, worn out with years and
care, was unequal to the task of long defying the authority of the council. At the opportune moment
he had intimated his willingness, on certain conditions,
to resign his office, and thus remove another obstacle
to the union of the church. Negotiations upon the
subject had been commenced, and the matter was so
far matured that in the fourteenth session, two days
before the death of Huss, the act of abdication was
solemnly executed. Charles Malatesta, Lord of
Rimini, was authorized by Gregory to act as pleni-
potentiary in his behalf. The two conditions of abdication which his master insisted upon were, that
the council should consent to be convoked anew by
him so that he might regard it as legitimate, and
that a cardinal of his obedience should preside over
the council. The first of these conditions was admitted without much difficulty, the council readily per-
ceiving that although its previous sessions would thus

---

[1] The various treatises of Jacobel
and his antagonists are given by Van
der Hardt, in his third volume. Jacobel left none of their arguments
unanswered. His familiarity with
scripture and the fathers, and his
remarkable logic and eloquence, rendered him a most formidable opponent. The closing treatise of the
series is remarkable as controverting
the doctrine of Wickliffe on transubstantiation—presenting those views
which the Calixtines, of whom Jacobel was the leader, subsequently held.

bear the imputation of being unauthorized, even Gregory himself would admit the justice of the process by which his rival, John XXIII., had been deposed. The other condition the council refused to grant, but compromised the matter by directing the emperor to preside while the abdication of Gregory took place.[1]

The council forbade any steps to be taken for a new election without its permission.[2] There might have been reason for apprehension lest the united cardinals, weary of the council's delay, might assume their prerogative, and give the church a new head from among their own number. The usages, rights, and privileges, allowed in previous elections, were therefore suspended. The council reserved to itself the authority of regulating the time, place, and form of this election.

It was, moreover, decreed that the council should not be dissolved until such an election had taken place, and the emperor was invoked to maintain and defend its rights. To this request Sigismund acceded. He published an edict, threatening severe penalties against any who should conspire, or attempt anything to the prejudice of the liberty of the assembly.

Upon his abdication Gregory was allowed by the grateful council to retain the dignity of cardinal, and to hold the highest rank in the college of which he was a member. His six cardinals were confirmed in their offices, and the two obediences were united.

The council terminated its fourteenth session by the reading of a decree[3] summoning Benedict XIII.,

---

[1] Fleury xxvi. 112, 118.   [2] L'Enfant, 265.   [3] Fleury, xxvi. 121.

the last recusant pope, to keep his promise, and abdicate the pontificate within ten days, under pain of
being proceeded against as schismatic, incorrigible,
devoid of faith, and perjured.   In case of contumacy,
the emperor was authorized to act in the matter according to his discretion.

Another subject, which in the minds of some of
the members of the council was of scarcely less importance than the unity of the church, had already
been brought to the notice of the council.   This was
the affair of John Petit.[1]   We have heretofore noticed the part which he took on the questions that
arose out of the murder of the Duke of Orleans by
the Duke of Burgundy.   The last—bold, perfidious,
and desperate in his daring—had awed the court of
France by the terror and power of his name.   He
boldly avowed the wicked deed by which he removed
an odious rival, and demanded and received from the
weak king of France, the brother of the murdered
man, the pardon of his crime.   But no sooner did he
return to his hereditary states than the scale turned
against him.   His deed ceased to be regarded in the
light of a patriotic act, and his enemies represented
it as being—what it really was—a heinous, inexcus-
able, and deliberate murder.   The Duke of Burgundy needed the aid of logical casuistry to justify what
he had done in the eyes of those who did not fear
the glitter of his sword.   He found it in the person
of John Petit, a member of the university, who,
grateful for the patronage of the duke, by whom he
had been educated and supported, offered his bene-

---

[1] Monstrelet.   Gers. op. v. 391.   Van der Hardt, iv. 345.

factor the aid of an unscrupulous conscience, a strong
intellect, and the ability of a thorough master of
scholastic arts.

This Franciscan friar was just the man for the occasion. A blind and violent logician, scrupling not to
reason against reason, and justify murder by scripture
and all the principles that should condemn it, he
entered upon his task. Prompt where all others
hesitated, taking by storm what others would
patiently besiege, almost raving in his furious advocacy or invective, yet always master of himself, and
calculating with cool reason the effect of his very
paradox, he was the person to carry along with him,
by the logical energy of his nature, the mass of
minds whose weakness or timidity demanded a leader.
He preached before the university a discourse as remarkable almost for its scholastic logic as for its
daring doctrine. In this curious but masterly production he hews his way to his conclusion with a
direct and straightforward energy,—leaving each
granite step by which he mounts, visible and defiant
to every eye.[1] His enemies must have admired the
art and boldness of the man they denounced, and
few there were who could safely venture to encounter such a disputant.

But the thing must be done, and upon Gerson, as
the ablest man in France, the task was devolved.
Nor did he shrink from it. Although, like Petit, he
was a debtor to the charities of the house of Burgundy, his mind and heart were both arrayed on the
side of justice. He hated the logic that defended

[1] Monstrelet, i. 61–81.

the crime, as he detested and boldly denounced the
deed itself.   With a chivalrous devotion to his cause,
Gerson threw himself into the midst of the discussion.   For a long time he struggled in vain.   The
Duke of Burgundy carried the university with him,
and triumphed temporarily in the person of Petit.
But his violence made him odious.   The relations of
parties were in a state of constant change.   At last,
in 1412, Gerson secured from the university the condemnation of seven articles from Petit's writings, in
which he had maintained that a subject may justly
put a tyrant to death on his own responsibility, and
even deserves to be recompensed therefor.   The king
of France, in consequence of these proceedings, directed the Bishop of Paris and the Inquisitor of the
Faith to join to themselves such a number of the
doctors of the university as they should see fit, and
give judgment upon the disputed propositions ! Thus
originated the celebrated assembly called the Council
of the Faith.   By this body thirty-seven propositions,[1]
drawn from the writings of Petit, who had meanwhile deceased, were condemned to be publicly
burned.   The sentence was duly executed, and was
inscribed, by the king's order, in the register of each
parliament of the kingdom.

The Duke of Burgundy felt that this blow was
aimed at him.   In stamping the argument of his
apologist with infamy, the council had left him without an apology for his crime, and he stood charged
before the world with the murder of his relative.
He appealed to the Apostolic See.   John XXIII. was

---

[1] L'Enfant (242) gives only the seven first condemned.

not indisposed to listen favorably to the cause of a powerful ruler, who hated his rival, Benedict XIII., with a venomous malice equal to his own. Three cardinals, appointed to examine into the affair, reported in favor of the Duke of Burgundy. They quashed the sentence of the Bishop of Paris. The question was thus brought to the notice of the world, and the issue joined in the face of Christendom. It remained for each party to present his cause at the council of Constance, and strive to secure its judgment in his favor.

The Duke of Burgundy had now, however, the manifest advantage. He merely needed to have the council reject the appeal of the opposite party. Silence—a passing over of the whole subject—was all that he demanded. Each party nerved itself for the struggle, and each was strongly supported in the council. Among the representatives of the Duke of Burgundy were Peter Cauchon, who afterward sat in judgment on the celebrated Joan of Arc, and Martin Porree, bishop of Arras, who had purchased his mitre by the advocacy of the doctrines of Petit. Among the bishops and doctors of the other party, representing Charles VI., the king of France, stood forth illustrious above all others John Gerson, a host in himself. Scarcely had he reached Constance before he took measures to bring the question that had agitated France before the council. He wished to have it committed to those members who were known as the commission of the faith, and the reformatory college. It was the business of this body to examine into all causes concerning faith, doctrine, and reformation. They were, after investigation, to pronounce judgment, subject to the definitive sentence of the council. To this step Martin Porree, as well as the other representatives of the Duke of Burgundy, objected. They sought to keep the cause of their patron entirely disconnected with questions that concerned the faith. "It was nothing more," they said, "than a simple question of morality, and religion had no connection with it." But the council on this point did not at first agree with them.

Foiled here, the Bishop of Arras, who showed himself an adroit tactitian and an able advocate, studied the composition of the commission to whom the question was to be submitted. He found upon it, perhaps in part secured the appointment to it, of the three cardinals of John XXIII., who had already reported in favor of the Duke of Burgundy. But along with these, also, was found D'Ailly, cardinal of Cambray, whose views upon the question of Petit's doctrines varied little, if any, from those of Gerson himself. From such a man, bold, able, and influential, a leading mind among any with whom he might come in contact, the Bishop of Arras had everything to fear. He resolved, if possible, that he should not be suffered to sit and act as judge.[1] He entered before the council a solemn protest against his serving on the commission, at least in the cause at issue between the Duke of Burgundy and the king of France.[2]

By this time Gerson must have begun to grow

---

[1] Van der Hardt, iv. 337.

[2] The Bishop of Arras proposed to bring charges of heresy against D'Ailly. Had he carried out his purpose, he might have made as good a case against him, perhaps, as the cardinal had against Huss.—*L'Enfant*, 325.

somewhat anxious as to the result. He found himself circumvented by management and intrigue.
Although he had secured one object—to have the
doctrines of Petit regarded as matters pertaining to
the jurisdiction of the commission on faith—yet the
commission itself was so composed that his confidence
must have been not a little shaken in the result at
which they would arrive.

Other events occurred that might well have increased the despondency of Gerson. The weak and
vacillating monarch of France withdrew from him
the authority previously granted, to act in his name
in bringing the affair of Petit before the council.[1]
Gerson could hence act in his own name only, as a
private member of the body. The Duke of Burgundy had agreed to adopt the same policy with the
French monarch, and direct the Bishop of Arras and
his colleague to proceed no longer on the authority
of his name. But he did not keep his promise. It
was not to have been expected that he would do so
against his own interest. Guilty already of perfidy
and murder, this violation of his word was but another grain thrown into the scale of his enormous
crimes.

Gerson had therefore to act in his own name against
the avowed representatives of one of the most powerful princes of his time. Nor was the duke himself
idle. Deeply anxious to secure from the council the
silence that would be for him virtually a verdict of
acquittal, he had approached near the confines of the
city where the council was assembled.[2] This con-

---

[1] L'Enfant, 248.   [2] Michelet, ii. 79.

fidence of security made his power more terrible.
His pretence was, he wished to hear by night the
belling of the stags. But with his tent pitched in
the great forest of Argilly, we can see the proof of
the eager and anxious feelings with which he watched the proceedings of the council. The earliest intelligence was conveyed to him. We seem to see
the princely criminal walking amid the twilight
glooms of the deep woods, visited by the spectres of
ancient crime, and hourly haunted by memories that
drove him almost to desperation, in his efforts to cir-
cumvent the great chancellor. Nor did he labor in
vain. The terror of his name was felt. The power
of his intrigues and the skill of his agents were producing their impression. His lavished gold was an
argument which Gerson could not refute.

Meanwhile new obstacles rose into view with more
threatening front. England and France were on the
brink of a war, in a few months to be made forever
memorable, to the dishonor of France, by the terrible
battle of Agincourt. On the sixteenth of April, 1415,
Henry of England had announced to parliament his
intention of making a descent upon France. On the
twenty-ninth, he ordered all his barons to hold
themselves in readiness.[1] The English church shared
in the feeling of the English nation, which demanded
war. Henry's claim to the crown of France found men
to justify it who wore the robes of the ecclesiastical
order. The Archbishop of Canterbury was directed
to summon his vassals. In such circumstances it was
obvious that the two enemies of France, the English

---

[1] Rapin's England, i. 511.

monarch and the Duke of Burgundy, would be inclined to yield each other a mutual support. The last derived a new accession of strength from the virtual alliance of the former.

Intelligence of these things would reach Constance while the commission on the faith was holding its sessions, and discussing this very question. Its influence could not fail to be felt, not only on the English members of the body, but upon others inclined to the prudent measure of not offending a powerful ruler. Still, with all these things against him, Gerson did not despair. Undoubtedly he had hoped to humble the powerful duke. He had meant that in his person the council should manifest its power to rebuke sin even in high places, and make the criminal tremble. But in this hope he was doomed to disappointment. The council refused to implicate, in the matter brought before them, the powerful Duke of Burgundy, or any of his partisans. It did not even venture to pronounce the name of his apologist, John Petit. In the most general terms it condemned the principal proposition of the apology as erroneous in faith and subversive of civil order.[1] This proposition was expressed in such a way, that the condemnation could scarcely have found an opponent. It was as follows: "That any tyrant may lawfully and ought meritoriously to be put to death, by any subject or vassal, whether by ambush, lure, or treachery, notwithstanding any oath or treaty, and without waiting for the sentence or authority of any judge." Such a principle one would

---

[1] L'Enfant, 275.

Lincoln Christian College

scarce suppose admitted even of debate. In later years it became, however, a dangerous weapon in the very city where it was first forged by the bold scholastic skill of Petit. Its import has become forever memorable in connection with the dagger of Ravaillac, and the murder of the heroic Henry IV. Its condemnation was secured in the council in great measure by the urgency of the emperor, who denounced it in no measured terms. This condemnation, general as it was, cost Gerson the most strenuous efforts.

D'Ailly, who in this matter had been rejected as a judge, appeared by his side. These two men exhausted the stores of their eloquence in describing the necessary results of such a dangerous principle.[1] They took up the several arguments urged by the advocates of the Duke of Burgundy, for leaving the matter at least in doubt, and not regarding it as a question of the faith, and demolished them one after another with a merciless logic. D'Ailly did not hesitate to declare that the doctrine of Petit merited condemnation infinitely more than the proposition of Wickliffe, which asserts that if princes fall into error, their subjects may reprehend and correct them.

The condemnation of Petit's doctrine was pronounced while Huss was on his way to the scene of his martyrdom.[2] To Gerson, the moment must have one of the deepest anxiety. The council had just sent Huss to the stake, and now, in a condemnation so general as to leave the real offenders unmolested,

---

[1] See vol. v. of Gerson's works.   [2] Fleury, xxvi. 129.

denounced a principle which would overthrow all
the foundations of social and civil order. Something
had been obtained, but far from what he had hoped.
Was it all that he could expect? Gloomy thoughts
must have filled his mind, as he reverted from the
victim who had just been sentenced to the flames, to
the character of those judges who had been tampered
with by the agents and the bribes of the Duke of
Burgundy. We may well believe that at such a
moment bitter words may have escaped his lips;
that in the soreness of disappointment, he gave utterance to statements which his convictions declared
true, but which others might account rash. Did he
begin to doubt whether after all it might not have
been that in the case of Huss the council had committed a judicial murder? Did the image of the
holy man, on bended knee before the assembled
council, appealing to the sentence of the great Judge,
haunt him with the presentiment that he too must
answer at another bar to the charge of injured, of
murdered innocence? We cannot tell. We only
know that he boldly avowed that if Huss had been
properly defended, he would never have been sentenced to the stake. We know that his deliberate
opinion of the council, years afterward, was such that
he could speak of it with a severity equal to that of
Huss' prison letters, and declare, "I would rather
have Jews and pagans for judges in matters of faith,
than the deputies of the council."

It is but a little while after Huss has been burned
as a heretic, that Gerson himself, one of his judges,
is arraigned on charges, some of which were not

altogether dissimilar.[1] His enemies were resolved to
break down his influence in the council, and no effort
was spared to make him odious.[2] It is true he triumphed in the conflict. His position, standing, and
acknowledged abilities, carried him safe through
the ordeal; but had his circumstances been only like
those of Huss, who could have foreseen the result?

Another affair in which Gerson took a deep interest was that of the complaint of the king of Poland
against the Teutonic knights.[3] This order had arisen
during the crusades, at the siege of Acre. Some
German merchants from Bremen and Lubeck had
witnessed the sufferings of the Christian army, and,
under the promptings of humanity and charity, had
formed themselves into an organization to afford relief. They applied to the pope for the charter of an
order, whose rule was to be similar in many respects
to that of the Templars. The original object of the
association was to defend the Christian religion
against infidels, and to take care of the sick in the
Holy Land. Driven out from Palestine, the order
was first removed to Venice, and afterward was
called in by the Poles to aid them against their infidel neighbors, the Prussians. They accepted the
invitation, and with the arguments of sword and
battle, at last succeeded, in the space of fifty-three
years, in accomplishing the task.

---

[1] One of the articles for which Gerson was charged with heresy, was his
declaration "that if John Huss, whom
the council condemned and pronounced a heretic, had had an advocate, he would never have been convicted." Another was his language,
noted above,—" Malo in causis fidei,
Judæos vel Gentiles judices habere,
quam deputatos concilii."—*Fleury,*
xxvi. 161.

[2] Ger. op. v. 439.

[3] L'Enfant, 160, 268, *et seq.* Van
der Hardt, iv. 546.

Meanwhile the order increased in strength and numbers, and enlarged its territories in such a manner as to become a formidable power. At the commencement of the fifteenth century they had reached the highest point of their prosperity. Grown insolent with success, and utterly regardless of the object of their institution, they were ready at the first opportunity to arm against the king of Poland. If we are to believe the statements of the latter, presented in a letter to the Emperor Robert, in which he implores his aid, they dealt out an indiscriminate and impartial vengeance alike to Christian and infidel. Mutual recriminations were followed by frequent and bloody battles. The knights extended their ravages beyond the regions to which they could fairly lay claim, attacking the allies of Poland, already Christianized, without sparing the territory of those whom they should have regarded as their benefactors, the Polish nation itself. The knights were defeated in numerous battles, but soon contrived to recover from the loss. They complained that the king of Poland was become indifferent to the conversion of infidels, as was indeed the case if his zeal was to be measured by their violence and ambition. His humanity is attested by the tears he shed when battle was successively forced upon him. At last he had recourse to the council of Constance. His ambassadors were charged to bring the matter to its notice. It was committed for investigation to Cardinal Zabarella, assisted by two deputies from each of the nations composing the council. It was on the eleventh of May that the commission was appointed.

The question brought before them was, "Is it right, under the pretext of propagating religion, to invade foreign territory and wage war upon it?" It was a question in regard to which humanity and justice demanded to be heard. The old doctrine of the church had been, not merely in theory, but in practice, that as all the kingdoms of the world belonged to Christ, an infidel king had no right to reign, and might justly be deposed. The bloody record of the Albigenses had attested the faithful application of this principle, when Simon de Montfort had signalized his infamy by the slaughter of thousands, and turned the fertile fields of Southern France into an uninhabited desert. The career of the Teutonic knights could be justified on the strength of this principle alone. Strictly considered, it was the principle of the religious bigot everywhere. It built up the inquisition, and invented its tortures. It triumphed in the crusades, and was vindicated in the execution of Huss. But men of that day did not see it in the whole extent of its application. Gerson could allow Huss to be sent to the flames, but was nobly inconsistent with himself when the same principle was to be applied on a more extended scale. His sympathies were strongly enlisted on the side of the Polish king, and his ambassador, Paul Voladimir.

The latter, on the day previous to the burning of Huss, (July 5,) presented to the German nation, by them to be considered and communicated to the other nations, a treatise, entitled "A Demonstration," in which he undertook to prove against the Teutonic knights, "that Christians are not permitted to employ

violent means for the conversion of infidels, nor under
this pretext to plunder them of their goods." After
stating the excesses and ferocious cruelties of the order
which—invoked by Poland as a shield—had become
a lash, and giving a brief history of the peaceful
progress of Christianity among those who were now
molested by them, he proceeds to show, in fifty-two
consecutive propositions,[1] that such conduct, and the
doctrine by which it is sustained, are equally opposed
to natural equity and the law of God. Some of his
positions would scarcely be allowed at the present
day, but others are characterized by sound sense and
true humanity. Infidels, he maintains, if not of the
fold of the church, are yet of the fold of Christ;
as he said, "I have other sheep not of this fold."
From this he infers that Christ's successor should
protect them and defend them in their right, while
they live as good citizens, instead of maltreating
them, or suffering them to be maltreated. Even he,
though he may send preachers among them whom
he may sustain, must not constrain them by force to
embrace the gospel. They must be left to the freedom of their own will, inasmuch as conversion is
God's work, and faith is not to be forced by blows.
He condemns the cruelty which had been too common in Europe in the treatment of the Jews and
other unbelievers, contending that Christian princes
ought not to plunder them, or expel them from their
lands. He enforces the teachings of natural reason
in regard to the rights of individuals, by the command of the proverb not to trespass on a neighbor's

---

[1] Van der Hardt, iii. 10, *et seq.*

landmarks. Infidels possess their authority as rulers from God, and by no guilt of their own. Voladamir, while he inconsistently excepts heretics from the privileges allowed to infidels, declares that they are not to be dealt harshly with, untried and uncondemned. He maintains that even letters of the Roman pontiff, conferring privileges upon any man or order, are to be interpreted in accordance with law and the rights of individuals—a doctrine that would have spared the world the sight of many a horror, now to be charged to the claims of papal infallibility. He condemns the principle of doing evil that good may come. We are not to injure our neighbor, and thus transgress the commandment in order to convert him. The decision of the council of Toledo is referred to, as condemning the use of violent and hard methods, and recommending only the arts of persuasion and gentle means. Voladimir goes even beyond the spirit, not of his own, but, we may even say, of the present age, in maintaining that the individual soldier must be convinced of the justice of the cause in which he is engaged. If a subject, and the matter is in doubt, it may be possible that his sovereign's command may be paramount. But no fear of temporal losses should induce him to take part in a war which he knows to be unjustly waged. In these views, the Polish ambassador unconsciously passes the limit of that servile rule which proscribes the right of private judgment. He is unconsciously arguing against the infallible authority, whether of pope or council. It shows, moreover, the liberal spirit by which he was animated, that he dares to throw off the bigoted scruples of the age, and assert that a Christian prince might, in case of danger, justly seek the alliance of an infidel. He closes his treatise by picturing the horrid results that would follow the adoption of the principle of his adversaries. If all unbelievers were *ipso facto* disqualified from ruling; if they might be assaulted with force of arms to bring them to the adoption of the Christian faith, the door is opened to all manner of violence. The command, " Thou shalt not kill," stands in the way, and forbids all these forms of cruelty and injustice.[1]

Erroneous as some of the positions of Voladimir were, the humane and sensible character of others shows the ability and Christian feeling of the man. As rector of the University of Cracow, and representative of the king of Poland, he honored the office and position which he occupied in the council. In many respects he and Gerson found themselves drawn together by strong sympathies. And as if the more to unite them in feeling, they had much the same experience of the character of the council. It was for a long time in vain that Voladimir sought to obtain from the council some judgment in favor of his proposition. But he too had *his Duke of Burgundy*. The Teutonic order was powerful, and not lightly to be offended. Sigismund, earnest as he was for peace, was unwilling to do anything which should tend to alienate their sympathies from the great cause he had at heart,—the union of Christendom against the Turk. And might not some of the principles of Voladimir's demonstration rise up to

---

[1] Van der Hardt, iii. p. 2.

protest even against his cherished project? In vain did Gerson lend all the weight of his influence to enforce the representations of his Polish brother. Weightier motives than those of simple justice, he must once more have felt, in the bitterness of his soul, controlled the action of the council.

But Voladimir had not only his Duke of Burgundy in the Teutonic order, but the order itself had its John Petit in the person of a Dominican monk, John Von Falkenberg.[1] The latter became, at the instance of the order, their apologist against the king and kingdom of Poland, and he showed himself not unworthy in some respects of his Parisian prototype. The apology itself, as a whole, has perished, but fragments of it have been preserved, enough to show the venomous spirit that pervades it. It is directed to all kings, princes, prelates, and to Christendom generally, and the author promises eternal life to all that will league together to exterminate the Poles and Jagellon their king. He was accused of maintaining that the king was an idol, and his subjects idolaters; that both should be hated, as they deserved to be; that they were heretics and shameless dogs, turning back to their vomit by falling into heathenism; that to kill the Poles and their king is more meritorious than to slay pagans; that secular princes who shall do it at the risk of earthly dignity will merit eternal glory, while those who tolerate them or aid them will be damned; and that all Poland, with Jagellon its king, is to be accounted criminal as committed to schism and heresy.

[1] L'Enfant, 578–9.

This treatise, which the emperor met with in Paris a few months after the subject had been brought before the council, was subsequently condemned to be burned, as erroneous in faith and morals, seditious, cruel, scandalous, injurious, impious, offensive to pious ears, and heretical. But no sentence was passed upon it in public session. The order exerted their influence with Martin V., just then elected pope, (1418,) and he dared not offend so powerful a body. In vain did the French and Polish deputations, who felt that their cause was one and the same, urge the matter.

Neither Falkenberg's book, nor Petit's apology, odious as they both were, could be brought to share the fate to which the works of Huss had been doomed. Falkenberg himself was imprisoned, but to leave the matter there seemed to Gerson a mockery of all justice. His deliberate view of the matter, as he saw it in retrospect, is expressed in his works.[1]

The course of the council, so he remarks, "gives the Bohemians just occasion to accuse it of a most criminal partiality, in treating with indifference a matter so vital to Christian morals and civil society, while other heresies less fatal are dealt with so harshly. It opens the gate to robbery, perjury, massacre, and assassination. It takes from bishops the power of repressing heretics, or correcting those who err within their diocese; for if they see that the council had no such authority, they will not dare to undertake its exercise. Secular princes will find themselves under the necessity of using temporal

---

[1] Ger. Op. tom. v. 1014.

weapons against such as teach pestilent doctrine in
their states. Thus the authority of the council is
made cheap; its deeds are null and void; it becomes
a laughing-stock for infidels, schismatics, especially
for Peter de Luna (Benedict XIII.) and his adherents,
who will not fail to exult at the result of a measure
so exciting in expectations, so futile in its issue."

It is more than possible that motives of a more
personal and worldly nature than Gerson was aware
of, found a place in his heart. His zeal was quick-
ened, perhaps, by a sense of what he considered in-
dignities offered to himself. He had boldly stemmed
the tide of popular opinion, when the power of the
Duke of Burgundy was at its height in Paris. His
name had been mingled with the curses of the populace. His house had been sacked, and his life endangered by a lawless mob.[1] He doubtless felt himself to have been a persecuted man. Nor had his
treatment in the council been such as he might deem
justly due to his position and his ability. He found,
to his sorrow and disappointment, that human nature
was much the same at Constance and at the French
capital. The scenes of the council were such, that to
take a part in them must at times have wounded his
own self-respect. They were anything but models
of decorum and order. Shouting, stamping, recrimination, and almost every form of confusion, were not
infrequent. In Von Falkenberg he found another
John Petit, and the cause each defended was much
the same. Nay, the former had even volunteered,
incited, doubtless, by the bribes of the Duke of Bur-

[1] Sketch of Gerson's Life in Van der Hardt.

gundy, and to secure his alliance, to become the avowed champion of Petit. In this character he assaulted D'Ailly and Gerson in no measured terms. His pamphlets teem with insults, full of abuse and contemptuous insolence. He speaks of Gerson as so unversed in logic that he should be sent to school to learn its rules. Not the glory of the University of Paris, but the disgrace of its ignorance, is manifest in the stupidity of its chancellor. No wonder, he says, if such a man as he, unacquainted with the rudiments of logic, occupied that post, the Bishop of Paris, with the doctors of his council of faith, should have blundered into the error of condemning the propositions of Petit.

It is not strange that Gerson's zeal was inflamed by some sense of the personal outrage to which he was subjected. The consciousness of his own integrity perhaps needed this new spur to rouse him to the most strenuous effort. And that effort was put forth. The great man, with his noble heart and gigantic intellect, toiled on, hoping against hope, and trusting with the fondness of affection to the action of a council that was forever humbling his idolatrous respect for it by showing itself but a prostrate Dagon. Efforts that would have crushed others in weeks, were by him continued without intermission for years. It was with feelings that none can envy, that he at last withdrew from a scene that, at once, had witnessed his glory and humiliation. The dreams of early years were dashed to the earth. His enemy, the Duke of Burgundy, was triumphant. The council, which he had at first idolized, dared not touch

the powerful criminal. The University of Paris was
no longer his home. The murderer of the Duke
of Orleans ruled there still; and the broken-hearted
exile found the only repose—the only real peace he
was again to enjoy on earth—in the humble monastery of a distant city. There, at Lyons, we see that
intellect, which found not its peer in the assembled
representatives of the Christian world, engaged in
the instruction of little children, and teaching them—
in a humility which had been taught by adversity—
as they should pass the spot where his ashes would
soon rest, to "pray for poor John Gerson!"

CHAPTER IV.

THE COUNCIL AND THE BOHEMIANS.—JEROME RECANTS.

AUG. 1, 1415—SEPT. 23, 1415.

THE execution of Huss, as the intelligence of it went abroad, was variously received. To some it afforded occasion for exultation; in the minds of others it excited only grief and indignation. The enemies of the reformer gained nothing by it. The council had only aggravated its own infamy by the cruel deed. Sigismund had forever alienated from himself the sympathies of the Bohemians, by the complacency with which he had tolerated the violation of his safe-conduct. The instigators of the prosecution had covered their own memory with an odium which would follow them to their graves.

There were some, undoubtedly, who exulted in
the fate of a man charged with heresy,—one whose
name had been so long coupled with that of Wickliffe, or who had been recognized by them only as
a dangerous innovator. But there were not wanting those, even at Constance, who regarded the proceedings of the council, in the case of Huss, with indignation and abhorrence. The doctrines for which
he was willing to die assumed a new importance. The
persecuting bigotry of the council, in their method
of dealing with him,—the outrage committed, in his
imprisonment, trial, and execution, upon all the forms
of justice,—combined, with the notorious corruption
of the council itself, to tear from the eyes of men
the veil of its false assumptions. Any public manifestations of the feelings which had thus been excited
would have been hazardous in the extreme, and yet
their expression could not be entirely suppressed. It
would have been difficult to conceive anything more
bitterly severe than the method which was taken to
set forth the contempt which the council had invited
upon itself. On the day after the execution of Huss,
the following writing was found affixed to the doors
of all the churches in the city. "The Holy Ghost,
to the believers in Constance, greeting:—Pay attention to your own business. As to us, being occupied
elsewhere, we cannot remain any longer in the midst
of you. Adieu." [1]

None would dare to avow the authorship, and few
perhaps would approve the spirit of this pasquinade.
Yet many were dissatisfied and disgusted with the

[1] L'Enfant. Van der Hardt.

proceedings of the council. It was not many months after the death of Huss, that an Augustinian monk, of Mayence, preached before it a sermon, the severe rebukes of which were terrible truths or atrocious libels. "It is related," said he, "of Socrates, that he once laughed at seeing great robbers drag little ones to the gibbet; more reason would he have to laugh if he were here now at this council of Constance, where we see great rogues, that is, Simonists, suspend little ones." [1] In truth, one only needs to note the measures of the council in connection with the sermons preached before it, to be convinced that, so far as morality and religion were concerned, the whole business of the assembly was a pompous farce. But for the blood and crime accumulated upon the hands of the actors, the council would have seemed but a theatre, on which, before the eyes of Europe and to the scandal Christendom, was played out, in the name of religion, a grand "comedy of errors." Scarce a sermon was preached, for months after the execution of Huss, which was not its virtual condemnation. The most frightful pictures of the prevalent immorality and corruption of the clergy were successively presented to view, and presented by men who were eye-witnesses of what they described, and looked the council in the face while they exhibited the memorials of its disgrace. A Carmelite doctor from Montpelier preached, a few weeks after the martyrdom of Huss, a discourse on the necessity of a reformation of the church. He demanded that most prompt and effectual measures should be

[1] L'Enfant.

adopted by the council to correct the prevalent
abuses,—" the insatiable avarice, the indomitable ambition, the gross ignorance, the shameful indolence,
and execrable impurity of the ecclesiastics.[1] Still,
a few weeks later, another preacher before the council expatiates on the same theme. After depicting
the wretched condition of the church, he traces it to
its causes,—" in the avarice and cupidity of the ecclesiastics, their haughtiness and pride." " Who," he
asks, " are those that most oppose reform ? Secular
princes ? No ! far from it. They are the ecclesiastics, who tear the robe of Christ in pieces, and
whom we may compare to famished wolves, who
come into the fold in sheep's clothing, and who, under the habits of religion, conceal hearts impious
and heinous with enormity."[2]

Still later (October 25) the Bishop of Lodi, who
had urged the council to severity against Huss at
the session in which his sentence was pronounced,
preached a funeral sermon on the death of Landolph
Maramour, Cardinal de Bari. He says not a word
of the dead, but takes for his subject of discourse
the vices of the ecclesiastics, and the necessity of
reform. The council might well blush at such reproof, if any sense of shame was left it. " Instead of
being," says the bishop, " an example to the people,
it is they, (the people,) perhaps, that will need to
teach us how to live. Do we not see in the laity
more gravity, decorum, exemplariness in morals and
conduct, more respect and devotion in church, than
in the ecclesiastics themselves ? Are we to be sur-

---

[1] L'Enfant.   [2] Ib., 330.

prised that secular princes despoil, persecute, and
scorn us, making of us a public mockery ?   This is a
just judgment of God, who will not allow this persecution to cease until we remove its cause by a change
in our lives." He represents the clergy as so plunged
into excess of luxury and brutal indulgence, that, in
his opinion, Diogenes, seeking a man among them,
would only find beasts and swine.[1]

As if the subject was too large to be exhausted,
we find an English preacher, the following week,
proceeding in the same strain in a sermon before the
council. With his English aversion to the mendi-
cants, he empties out upon them the vials of his
wrath, and then proceeds to administer his rebuke
to the bishops and doctors, who neglect scripture,
theology, and morals, for the contentious and lucra-
tive study of the canon law. He depicts the ignorant and sensual ecclesiastics, who leave their
charges and churches, and go to the great cities to
live in wantonness and splendor. He applies to them,
on the part of the church, the language of scripture:
" ' My husband is not at home ; he has gone a long
journey: he has taken with him a bag of silver, and
will not return until the full moon '—that is," says
the preacher, "until autumn, when he shall find the
granaries and cellars full, and with his full purse may
return to buy many rich benefices." [2]

It would be tedious even to sketch the successive
discourses, which turned almost uniformly upon this
theme. Nothing could have justified them, nothing
could have secured them a hearing in the council,

---

[1] L'Enfant, 339.   [2] Ib. 340.

but the notorious and undeniable truth which they contained. The facts upon which they were based were too patent to be denied.

The deliberations of the council in its assemblies, moreover, were often characterized by a confusion approaching to mob violence. Repeatedly the attempt to read a statement or a protest would be clamored down. Crimination and recrimination were rife, and Gerson had reason for saying that he would sooner have Jews and pagans for his judges, than the deputies of the council. Thus all the language which Huss had used at Prague, in reference to the corruption of the church, was more than justified in the eyes of his countrymen. The council itself had exhibited the proof that the charges brought against it were true. It had refuted, beforehand, those who would have been its apologists. It had deposed the pontiff by whom Huss had been excommunicated. The mutual recriminations of its members had exceeded in severity the calmer and more moderate statements of Huss.

It was inevitable that, as the intelligence of the execution of their countryman reached the citizens of Prague, it should at once be coupled in their minds with the confessed character of a large portion of his judges. The known purity of Huss, the notorious corruption of the council—the constant appeal of one to the authority of scripture, the tyrannic demand of the other for a blind submission in which perjury was implied—presented contrasts too obvious to allow hesitation as to which party should receive their sympathies. The whole city was in commotion.

Grief, indignation, and resentment pervaded the community. The exasperated multitude flocked, as by one common impulse, to the Bethlehem chapel. It was the place hallowed to them now by every memory of him whose words still seemed to echo along its walls. All classes alike felt the enthusiastic impulse to demand revenge. The dictates of prudence could scarce restrain them from an instantaneous rising. The torch of the executioner at Constance had set the nation on fire.

The ashes of Huss had been carefully gathered up and thrown into the Rhine. The council had rightly suspected that his disciples might seize upon them, if the occasion was offered, to bear them off as treasured relics. But the ingenuity of their malice went further. As a last insult to the memory of the martyr, a dead mule was buried on the spot where he was burned. "It was," says a Protestant author, "that the stench proceeding from the body might lead the people to imagine that it came from the heretic."

But all this was of no avail. The earth itself, about the funeral pile,—in place of the martyr's ashes,—was taken up, and carried into Bohemia.[1] Huss was honored as the apostle and the martyr of the nation. The cruelty and faithlessness of the council were denounced in no measured terms. Nor was it merely a blind and misjudging crowd that paid this homage. The barons and nobles of the kingdom met together, and, with hand on sword, swore to avenge what they regarded at once as an

---

[1] Æneas Sylvius' His. Boh., cxxxvi.

outrage upon innocence, and a national insult. The University of Prague sympathized strongly in the popular feeling. The presence at Constance of those members of it who were hostile to Huss, relieved it of the opposition which might, perhaps, have sought to silence its voice, or stay or modify its decision. Prague was no place for them now. Their participation in the measures that led to the fatal deed, would have concentrated upon them the national vengeance. The doctors of the university indignantly appealed, and with a unanimity that awed all dissent,—even if there was any,—to the whole of Europe, against the sentence of the council, and the reproaches that had been directed against themselves. " In the midst of our innumerable and poignant subjects of grief," said they, " we consider it an imperious necessity to defend the insulted reputation of our university, hitherto always esteemed so pure, against the attacks of blasphemers. To all the other motives which induce us to adopt this course, is added the remembrance of the honor and the virtue of that man who is now lost to us forever. . . . We desire to do this, that the great renown of one of our own children, John of Hussinitz, surnamed Huss, should not fade away, but shine forth more and more in the eyes of the universe. . . . We desire the more ardently that our words may be heard by all believers, because the presence of so great a man among us has produced so much good, before God and before man. . . . For his life glided on before our eyes, from his very infancy, and was so holy and pure, that no man could show him to be guilty of a single fault.　O man, truly pious, truly humble! thou who wast conspicuous with the lustre of such great virtue—who wast accustomed to despise riches, and to succor the poor, even to experiencing want thyself—whose place was by the bedside of the unfortunate—who invitedst, by thy tears, the most hardened hearts to repentance, and soothedst rebellious spirits by the inexhaustible mildness of the word! thine it was to root out from every heart, and particularly from that of a clergy, rich, covetous, and haughty, their manifold vices, by applying to them the ancient remedy of the scriptures, which appeared as new doctrines in thy mouth;—thou, in fine, following in the footsteps of the apostles, restoredst the morals of the primitive church, in the clergy and the people! . . . Ah! beyond a doubt, nature had loaded this man with all her gifts, and the divine grace was so abundantly shed around him, that not only was he virtuous, but it may even be permitted to assert, that he was virtue itself! But why employ words when acts speak?　A frightful death, inflicted by his enemies, and supported with such wonderful patience, proves that he placed his trust on a heavenly foundation. . . . It is, in fact, a divine thing—it is the effect of a courage inspired by God alone, to endure so many outrages, so many tortures, and so much infamy for the divine truth, to receive all these insults, with a visage calm and serene, to shine forth by the greatest piety, in the face of tyrants, and thus to terminate an irreproachable life by the most bitter death." [1]

Mon. Hus., i. 82.

Language like this from the university of which Huss had once been rector, and whose members could claim with him an intimate acquaintanceship of years, is significant. Its testimony to his ability, purity, and worth is above impeachment.

The council seem to have imagined that, with the terrible example of Huss before him, his friend and associate, Jerome, could be more easily brought to retract. It was on the nineteenth of July,[1] nearly two weeks after the execution of Huss, and two months after his own examination at the time of his capture, that he was again—after having been visited in his prison by the commission—brought before the council. These two months had been to him a period of suffering and hardship. The severity of his imprisonment had affected his health, and he fell dangerously ill.[2] To his bodily sufferings was added, also, a more oppressive mental anxiety. The fate of Huss must have been felt as a terrible blow. We have scant record of the prison examination, or of his appearance before the council.[3] A manuscript history states, that among the questions put him were those on the real presence, and on the Realist doctrine of universals. On these points his views agreed with those of Huss. After this public examination, Jerome was left to the sadness of his prison meditations. The council hoped that the execution of Huss would have a salutary and mollifying influence upon the mind of his disciple. They had, moreover, other matters of importance upon their hands, and could well afford their prisoner

[1] Fleury, xxvi. 145.   [2] L'Enfant, 184.   [3] Ib. 302.

leisure for reflection. One victim at least sufficed for the present; and the issue of their policy in the case of Huss—it was soon to be found—was not such as to invite them to repeat the experiment. The argument of fire had inflamed rather than terrified those to whom it had been addressed. Jacobel persisted in his reform, which the council had pronounced an heretical innovation. The minds of the Bohemians were in no mood to relish further the logic of the stake, and the emperor also was now about to set out upon his expedition to Spain to confer with Peter de Luna, (Benedict XIII.,) and the king of Aragon, by whom he was supported, so that the council might well feel it necessary to proceed with extreme caution.

With all the weight and authority of his influence, Sigismund had urged the condemnation of the propositions of John Petit, and had even gone so far as to say that he would not set out upon his journey until that condemnation was pronounced. Perhaps he felt that his own life was in danger from the Duke of Austria. One of the ostensible reasons of his leaving Constance during the few days preceding the final hearing of Huss, was his dissatisfaction with the council in the slackness with which they prosecuted the subject. He was reported to have said that he would not return to the city until steps had been taken toward the result which he desired. The council therefore saw fit to condemn a proposition represented as that of Petit, and in doing so—by this temporary and unwilling compromise of hostile parties—made the emperor its dupe. Sigismund seems

to have regarded the measure, as Gerson wished to
have it considered,—the necessary initiative to further
process against the defenders and promoters of Petit's
views; and, contenting himself as well as he could
with the progress already made, commenced preparations for his journey.

The proposed conference was to have taken place
before the emperor actually set out, but he wrote
for, and obtained, the privilege of a month's delay.
Great anxiety was felt by the council in regard to
the result of his enterprise.   Another pope could not
well be elected while Benedict XIII., with the adherence of Spain and Scotland, stood in the way.   It
was especially important that the king of Aragon
should be withdrawn from his allegiance ; and the
presence and influence of the emperor, it was hoped,
would most effectually promote this desired result.
The greater portion of Spain—Aragon, Castile, and
Navarre—the counties of Foix and Armagnac, and
the kingdom of Scotland, still acknowledged the
jurisdiction of Benedict.   Everything that could
possibly be done to withdraw these from his allegiance must be attempted.   It was—so it seemed—the
only course to be adopted.   And yet by some it was
fondly hoped that Benedict would consent to a voluntary abdication.   They little understood the spirit
of the man.   In his feeble and attenuated frame
glowed a spirit that aspired to rival a Gregory VII.
or an Innocent III.   It was no Gregory XII. with
whom the council had now to deal.   Benedict saw
himself the sole claimant of the tiara.   He evidently
hoped, to the last, that such he might be suffered to

remain. His old secretary, Clemengis, had written [1]
—of his own accord, according his statement,—yet
perhaps not without some urgency of Benedict—to
the council, remonstrating with them against their
decision that neither of the contestants for the tiara
should be a candidate for their election. What
might his influence be with his old friends, Gerson
and D'Ailly? To what terms might not the council
be brought by the untiring perseverance of Benedict?
The last was at least resolved that his dignity should
not be lost without a struggle. We shall see with
what result he defied the council and the emperor.

In the sixteenth session, Sigismund announced, in
a formal manner, his intended departure.[2] The
council named to accompany him, and to assist him
with their counsels, fourteen deputies, of whom four
were bishops, and ten doctors, selected from the
several nations. The cardinals bore it ill that none
of their number were appointed. But the council
was too suspicious and distrustful of them, to accept
their nominations. The deputies were authorized to
act as plenipotentiaries with the emperor for the
transaction of everything that should be found
necessary to secure the abdication of Benedict.

The seventeenth session (July 15) was devoted
to measures preparatory to the emperor's journey.
After mass and sermon, Sigismund, laying off his imperial robes and crown, knelt with bared head before
the altar, to receive the benediction of the council.
With a cardinal upon either side of him, he awaited
the close of prayers adapted to the occasion, when

---

[1] See the letter in the works of Clemengis.   [2] L'Enfant, 299.

the presiding officer gave him the benediction, while the words were chanted—" Lord, preserve the king." [1]

Among the decrees then read was one which the Jesuit, Maimbourg, does not regard as infallible. He considers it an arrogant assumption over the temporal power of kings and princes. But the council did not deem it unnecessary; and rumors of previous attempts on the emperor's life, and his own sensitiveness to Petit's doctrine, effectually preserved him from any remonstrance.[2] The decree was to the effect that " The sacred council threatens with excommunication, and with the deprivation *ipso facto* of their dignities, whether secular or ecclesiastical, whomsoever—whether king or prince, bishop or cardinal—who shall in any manner impede the journey of the emperor or his suite." [3] These certainly, on the part of the council, were lofty pretensions. Had their object been other than the emperor's security, they would scarcely have passed unquestioned. Sigismund's anxiety for his own life led him to pawn the prerogative of exclusive secular dominion for the hope of security found in the council's decree.

To add new importance to the emperor's mission, a solemn mass and procession was decreed, every Sabbath during his absence, for the fortunate issue of his journey. A hundred days' indulgence was granted to all who should assist at these devotions, as well as to the officiating priests. A forty days' indulgence was extended to such as should substitute an *Ave Maria*, or *Pater Noster*, instead.[4]

The emperor hastened to the place of meeting.

---

[1] Fleury, xxvi. 142.
[2] Ib. 144.
[3] L'Enfant, 300.
[4] Fleury, xxvi. 144.

This had been changed from Nice, the city first designated, to Narbonne, as nearer to Perpignan, the
residence of Benedict. But neither the king of Aragon nor Benedict was there. The first was dangerously ill, the last hesitated and delayed to come.
At last he appeared, as if for armed conference,
with soldiers and armed cavalry. But his real
strength was in his own resolute and unbending will.
The fire of ambition glowed like a volcano in the old
man's heart, and he met the emperor in no cringing
or fawning manner. He was resolved to fall—if fall
he must—a pope to the last. He had kept the first
appointment of the conference for June, and when
the emperor did not appear, had the insolent assurance to accuse him of contumacy, and issued a proclamation publishing the fact that he had not kept
his appointment.[1] When Sigismund reached Perpignan, Benedict was absent at Valentia. To the emperor's notification and request to meet him, he replied by demanding a safe-conduct which should be
granted to him as supreme pontiff. The emperor
escaped the dilemma which would force him to a fatal
acknowledgment, by replying that on the territory
of a foreign ruler it was not for him to grant a safe-
conduct. Nor did he hesitate to say that he altogether ignored the claims of Benedict. He might
come as cardinal, but could not be received or recognized as pope. Benedict scorned the offer as an insult.
He replied by demanding, as the conditions of his
renunciation of the papacy, the assembling of a council in the immediate neighborhood of his jurisdiction,

[1] L'Enfant, 329.

in which his claims should be confirmed; after which, he should remain perpetual legate *a latere*, with full temporal and spiritual power throughout his whole obedience—saving only the name of pope, which should be given up. The emperor refused the conditions, and summoned Benedict to appear at Perpignan. He came at last, but not to surrender his claims.[1] The emperor was soon to find that he dealt with a wily foe.

The council made but slow progress during Sigismund's absence. Some of its members were well content that this should be the case. Many showed a strong disposition to leave the city, either willing that the council should be broken up, or dissatisfied with the little progress made, and disgusted with its proceedings. Surely they might imagine that the Holy Ghost had taken his departure, if indeed he had ever been present. Never did any city present a more vivid picture of Vanity Fair than Constance had presented, up to the time of the emperor's departure. It was Europe in miniature. It was the compendium of its splendor and its vice. It was the focus of ecclesiastical and princely intrigue. Each nation, each ruler, had diplomatists there to look after their interests. A very small fraction of the council had any concern to secure more than an individual and personal advantage. The knights and nobles had their sports and tourneys. Cardinals, bishops, and doctors tilted with the weapons of logic and sophistry, and, if more deeply in earnest, played a more hazardous game.

[1] L'Enfant, 354.

Acts of violence in the streets and neighborhoods of the city were not infrequent. It was difficult to control the immense multitude, made up of all classes and characters, and impelled by so many diverse and conflicting interests, with which the city was filled. Pillage and assassination were of frequent occurrence, not only without, but even within the walls.[1] The princes did not hesitate to use their authority to the prejudice of the liberty of the council. Many were forced, by fear, to vote against their conscientious convictions. The council was under the necessity of passing a decree for the protection of its members, in coming to and going from it, in which they threatened with severest penalties all persons—emperor, pope, kings, princes, ecclesiastics, seculars—who should make any attempt on the life, person, or property of any connected with the body. The disposition to leave the city had become so manifest, and threatened such dangerous consequences, that, in the session held previous to the emperor's departure for Spain, the council appointed a commission to look after the absentees, and, under threat of the severest penalties, bring them back or keep them at their posts. Some, doubtless, were led to believe that the emperor's departure would be the signal for a general dispersion. In fact, but little was expected of, and little accomplished by, the council in his absence. The time was mostly spent in fruitless and angry discussions.

Gerson preached a sermon before the council, at or about the time of the emperor's departure,[2] in which he endeavored to bring the action already taken by

---

[1] L'Enfant, 299.   [2] Ib. 303.   Fleury, xxvi. 145.   Ger. op. ii. 273.

the council to bear upon the case of John Petit. Assuming "that a general council holds its authority immediately from Jesus Christ, and that every man, even the pope, is bound to obey such a council in all matters of faith, extirpation of schism, and reformation of the church, in head and members," he proceeds to lay down the rules of procedure by which it should be guided. He maintains that, the authority of the council being supreme, it should shrink from the examination of no error, by whomsoever held or defended. "The general council may, and should judge, in cases of heresy, all classes of persons, however high in position, without fear, favor, or acceptance of person." "It must condemn all erroneous or heretical propositions, even though it finds itself thereby necessitated to proceed against such as assert them." Gerson then lays down other rules, certainly not above criticism,—as that many propositions with their authors may be condemned, although, by the rules of grammar or logic, or by some gloss, they admit of being understood in a good sense; that propositions may and ought to be condemned, which cannot be disproved by scripture, without calling in the exposition of the doctors and the usage of the church. These positions were indeed implied in the action of the council, with respect to Wickliffe, Huss, and Jacobel, and it would have been difficult for any one to deny it. Gerson adroitly makes use of this fact, to take away every excuse for not proceeding further, even to the condemnation of Petit's propositions, and to process against the Duke of Burgundy himself. But the

emperor had left the council. The weakness of the
king of France was despised, and, notwithstanding
the frequent letters of the emperor enjoining action
in the condemnation of Petit's propositions, little
progress could be made. The Duke of Burgundy
and his partisans were too powerful to be summarily
dealt with.

It was a few days after Gerson's sermon, when the
council at last found leisure to give the Bohemians
a tardy notice of what they had done with Huss.[1]
Twenty days had already elapsed since his execution.
The popular feeling in Prague was in a state of intense excitement, and the letter of the council was
only calculated to increase it. It was but attempting
to quench the flame by covering it with new fuel,
and it blazed the more fiercely. The letter is addressed to the bishop, the chapter, the suffragans, and
the whole of the clergy of Prague. It begins with
a protestation, on the part of the council, of the evils
that had sprung up from schism and heresy, to the
grievous affliction of the church, and of the profound
grief and anxiety with which the council were constrained to regard them. It sets forth their estimate
of the perverse doctrines of Wickliffe, to whom it
concedes the first rank among pestiferous heretics,
and states the sentence which had been passed in the
condemnation of his doctrines, the burning of his
books, and the exhumation of his bones. It then
proceeds to show how his heresy had spread, infect-
ing the minds of Huss, Jerome, and others, to the
manifest injury of the church, and the destruction of

[2] Mon. Hus., i. 81.

the Catholic faith. Impelled by the earnest desire of restoring peace and delivering Bohemia from the desperate men who filled it with their pestilent doctrines, the council had yielded to the urgency of persons of the Bohemian nation, and carefully deliberated on the course to be pursued. The matter was not one of small moment. The evil was like to spread, not only among the ignorant, but the learned. The council, therefore, had proceeded to the examination of Huss and his writings, and employed all the means in their power to induce him to recant his false doctrines. The letter then states briefly the measures that had been taken, his examination, his public audience, the testimony against him, and the *charity* with which he had been treated. But all efforts had proved vain. The benevolence of the council, which sought not the death of the sinner, but rather that he should turn and live, was utterly defeated. Huss was convicted of the most manifest and intolerable heresy, and, after being condemned and degraded, had been given over to the secular arm.

The letter then urges upon the Bohemian clergy the most strenuous efforts to perfect the work thus begun. It gives Wenzel, the king, credit for a deep anxiety to witness and aid such a desirable work. It praises the Bishop of Leitomischel for his diligence in defence of the honor of the king and kingdom, and the defence of the Catholic faith. It then beseeches them, " by the bowels of Jesus Christ, to silence all those pestiferous men who teach or preach the doctrine of Wickliffe and his zealot Huss, so that this most dangerous corruption may be extirpated from the very extremities of the kingdom." If any should offer opposition to this good work, they were hereby denounced beforehand, and threatened with process, according to canonical sanctions, so that their correction should serve as an example to others. The admonitions and directions of the letter were enforced by the terrors of the greater excommunication, the deprivation of benefices, and degradation from the priesthood.[1]

But all these threats were of no avail. An indignant and outraged people treated them with contempt. Jacobel still preached without molestation. The offended nobles and princes of Bohemia were strengthened in their regard for the memory of Huss, and in their confidence of the soundness of his doctrines, by the measures of the council, rendering itself continually more and more odious. Even the king, steeped as he was in the brutality of a sensual nature, showed some signs of resentment at the affront which had been offered him in the violation of the liberty, and in the execution, without his assent, of one of his own subjects. Daring thoughts and bold designs grew up in the minds of many during the few weeks that followed the death of Huss.[2] He was gone from among them—and was no more present to repress and restrain the popular tumult by his saintly presence and calm counsels. The multitude were impelled by motives of a more worldly and personal character than he would have allowed.

The importance attached to the communion in

[1] Mansi. Council of Constance, xxvii. 781.   [2] Æneas Sylvius, ch. 36. Cochleius.

both kinds—an outward visible symbol calculated to appeal to fanatic feeling—swelled the tide of indignation and vengeance. This, undoubtedly, Huss would have sought to restrain. He would never have allowed a mere rite to engross to itself the place of a fundamental truth, however much he might admit or even urge its propriety. The princes, knights, and nobles of the kingdom were many of them rude, bold men, who little appreciated orthodoxy of doctrine, but who did not lack the sensibility to wrong and outrage which urged them to resentment. They met at once, and drew up a letter of protest and remonstrance addressed to the council. We shall have occasion to notice it more fully hereafter.

The attention of the council was now directed, in a somewhat different spirit than heretofore, to the case of Jerome. No efforts or persuasions were spared to induce him to recant.[1] He had already been twice examined, first at the time of his arrest, (May 24th, 1415,) and again briefly on the nineteenth of July, when he had been brought before the council assembled in the church of St. Paul. For nearly two months more he was left in prison. His third examination took place on the eleventh of September. Meanwhile, however, the most strenuous exertions had been put forth to induce him so far to submit that the council might be spared the necessity of inflicting capital sentence. We can well believe that in his circumstances they would be not without effect. He had for four months been pining in chains. The greatest harshness and severity had

[1] De Vrie, apud Van der Hardt, i. 170.

been shown in his treatment. He had been pros-
trated by sickness in his noisome dungeon, and his
legs were already afflicted with incurable ulcers.
Sufferings so protracted may have well depressed
his spirit and exhausted his energy. In these circumstances, he was taken out of prison and brought
before the council. Under terror of being burned,
he was called upon to abjure his errors and subscribe
to the justice of the execution of Huss.

Had one been asked beforehand in regard to the
two men, Huss and Jerome, which was most like to
meet the ordeal unmoved, his answer probably would
have been—Jerome. Nature seems to have endowed
him with an eminently fearless spirit, a resolute
energy, a noble generosity of soul, and a chivalrous
oblivion of self, which his religious views had nurtured rather than repressed. He seemed born to be a
hero. Had it been his destiny to have led armies to
the field, he would have been found sharing every
danger, nor shrinking from the hardships of the
meanest soldier. In days like those of English ship-
money, he would have been seen breasting the
storm, the foremost man of all to expose himself for
others—a Hampden or a Cromwell, to bid tyranny
concentrate its bolts upon his head. But there was
wanting in Jerome what was found in Huss—that
truly Christian self-distrust, which would lead him in
prayerful humility to throw himself into the arms of
Omnipotence. Jerome was self-reliant. Under the
impulse of conscious strength, he rushed too reck-
lessly to the hazardous encounter. By sore trial he
had to learn the lesson that taught him to be a bet-

ter man, and a nobler because a Christian hero.
The hardships of his imprisonment had unnerved
him—had made the bold man fear and quail. The
terrors of a cruel death awed him to a base submission. Human weakness prevailed. The promises
and threatenings of the council shook his purpose.
He signed a paper by which he declared his submission to the council, and approved the condemnation
of the errors of Wickliffe and of Huss.

Yet it was at no slight sacrifice of feeling that this
compliance was wrung from him. He gave as an
excuse for his course, that he was not aware that the
errors imputed to Huss had been truly held by him.
We can scarcely admit the sincerity of such a defence.
If any one should have known what Huss taught,
Jerome was the man. He must have heard him and
read his books. As his intimate friend and associate,
he must have frequently conferred with him, and
may almost have been said to have read his heart.
But a prison was an irksome place; and death at the
stake was no pleasing prospect, and in a weak hour
the strong man fell.[1] And yet there lingered so
much of conscience and self-respect, that Jerome was
forced to add conditions or explanations of his submission, that could have been in nowise acceptable to
the council. While he subscribed to the condemnation of the articles of Wickliffe and Huss, he added
that he was not to be considered as thereby doing
any prejudice to the holy truths which these men
had taught and preached. Explaining himself after-

[1] Many facts in regard to Jerome's
treatment are brought out upon his
trial. Others are to be found in the
two narratives contained in the last
volume of Huss' *Monumenta.*

ward upon the subject, he said, of Huss particularly, that he still repeated that he did not mean to do anything tending to the prejudice of his person, and his excellent morals, any more than to the many truths which he had heard from his mouth. He confessed that he had been his intimate friend, and that he was disposed to defend him toward and against all, for the gentleness of his conversation and the holy truths which he had heard him explain to the people, but that now, on being better informed by reading his works themselves, he was unwilling to befriend his errors, though he had loved his person. *Esto quod sint amici et Plato et Socrates, sed magis amica veritas mihi est et esse debet.* Let Plato and Socrates be my friends, yet I love and ought to love truth more. Such was his attempt at justification, by which he essayed—and perhaps for the time successfully—to deceive himself. He added still other remarks. He declared, that in condemning the errors of Huss he did not thereby intend to make a recantation, because, although he had often heard and read the condemned articles, he never had held them to be articles of faith, and had never preferred his own judgment to the authority of the church.

The terms of this submission were too vague and ambiguous to satisfy the council. It was not the unequivocal condemnation of Huss which they demanded. They saw the necessity of using further influence to secure a more unqualified submission. The time between this present and the following session was employed to secure this object.[1]

---

[1] L'Enfant, 333.

The nineteenth general session was to have been held on the twentieth of September, but was deferred until the twenty-third of the month—doubtless in order to bring Jerome to better terms. The greater part of it was taken up with the effort to induce him to retract unconditionally. The articles of Wickliffe and of Huss were again read, that he might publicly anathematize them. The Cardinal of Cambray announced the form of retraction drawn up by Jerome in his own hand-writing, conceived in the following terms.[1]

"I, Jerome of Prague, master of arts, acknowledging the true Catholic church and Apostolic faith, do anathematize every heresy, especially that in regard to which I have hitherto been defamed, and which in past times was taught and held by John Wickliffe and John Huss, in their works, books, or sermons to the clergy and the people, on which account they were condemned with their dogmas and errors, as heretical, by this the said council of Constance, and their doctrine aforesaid was especially condemned in sentence passed by this sacred council, upon certain express articles. I assent, moreover, to the holy Roman church, to the Apostolic See, and to this sacred council, and with heart and mouth profess, in and in respect to all matters, specially the keys, sacraments, orders, offices, and censures of the church, indulgences, relics of the saints, ecclesiastical liberty, rites, and whatever pertains to the Christian religion,—as the Roman church itself, the Apostolic See, and this sacred council profess: and specially

---

[1] L'Enfant, 334. Fleury, xxvi. 171.

that of the aforesaid articles many are notoriously
heretical, and long since reprobated by the holy fathers, some are blasphemous, others erroneous, others
scandalous, some offensive to pious ears, and some
of them rash and seditious. As such, the aforesaid
articles were by this sacred council recently condemned, and Catholics were forbidden, each and all,
under threat of anathema, venturing to preach, teach,
or hold the said articles, or any of them.

" Moreover, I, the aforesaid Jerome, inasmuch as in
some scholastic exercises, in order to enforce my views
on the tenet of *Universalia a parte rei*, and to show
that many qualities of the same species might be specified by one essence, described, in order to present an
illustration obvious to the senses, a triangular figure
which I called the shield of faith ; therefore, to prevent any erroneous or scandalous understanding,
which some might perhaps receive therefrom, I say,
assert, and declare, that I did not draw the said figure,
or name it the shield of faith, with any such intention
of exalting the doctrine *De Universalibus* over its opposite, as if it was in such a sense the shield of faith,
that, without it, faith or catholic truth could not be
protected or defended, since I would by no means
stubbornly adhere to it. But the reason of my calling that figure by such a name was, because, in the
figure of the triangle describing the three different
persons (supposita) of the divine essence, the Father,
Son, and Holy Spirit, I regarded this article of the
Trinity as the principal shield of faith, and the foundation of Catholic truth.

" Besides, that it may be plain to all what were

the reasons for which I was reputed an adherent and
an approver of the said John Huss, I make it known
by these presents, that when on many occasions I
heard him in his sermons and scholastic lectures, I
believed him to be a good man, and not in any way
proceeding contrary to the traditions of holy mother
church, and the holy doctors. Yea, even when of
late certain articles laid down by him, and condemned
by this sacred council, were shown to me, I did not
believe them to be his, at least in that form. And
when, from certain eminent doctors and masters in
the sacred page, I had heard it affirmed that they
were his, I asked fuller information, and that the
books might be shown me in which the said articles
were reported to be contained. These being presented
to me in his own hand-writing, which I know as well
as I do my own, I found that the said articles were
written, each and all, in that very form in which they
had been condemned. Whence I have apprehended,
and do now apprehend, that he and his doctrine,
with those that follow it, were not undeservedly condemned by this sacred council as heretical and insane.
And all these things aforesaid, I say sincerely and
absolutely, as now having been fully and sufficiently
informed of the aforesaid sentences pronounced by
this holy council against the doctrines of the said
Wickliffe and Huss, and against their persons, to
which sentences, I, as a devoted Catholic, in all and
regarding all, consent and adhere.

" Also, I, the same aforesaid Jerome, who on another occasion voluntarily, freely, and of my own
accord explaining and declaring my views before the

most reverend fathers, etc., in this same place, made
a threefold distinction, which as I afterward perceived
by some was understood as if I meant to say that
there was faith in the church triumphant, while nevertheless I believe that with them, there is beatific
vision excluding doubtful knowledge,—I do now say,
assert, and declare, that it was never my intent to say
that there was faith there *as faith*, but a knowledge
which, implying all that faith could apprehend, exceeds it.   And in general, whatever I there or before
said, I refer and submit with all humility to the decision of this holy council of Constance.

"I moreover swear, both by the holy Trinity and
by these most holy Gospels, that I will abide undoubt-
ingly in the truth of the Catholic church; and I do
pronounce all those that shall contravene this faith,
with their dogmas, worthy of eternal anathema.
And if I myself shall ever presume (far be it from
me) to think or preach anything to the contrary, I
will subject myself to the severity of the canons, and
shall be found exposed to eternal punishment.   This
copy of my confession and profession, before this holy
general council, I freely and voluntarily present, and
the same and each of these have I subscribed with
my own hand."[1]

Such was the form of recantation which Jerome
had been induced to subscribe.   When his purpose
to present it had been announced by the Cardinal
of Cambray, Jerome came forward to read it before
the council, prefacing it with a few remarks.   Addressing himself to each and all the members of the

[1] Mansi Concilia, xxvii. 791, 793.   Van der Hardt. iv. 499, 506.

council, whom he embraced in one "glorious assembly," he proceeded: "Since from the history of the Holy Bible it is evident, indeed and truly, that in the temple of God all may not present offerings of equal value, but each according to his ability, as some gold, some silver, some precious stones, etc., if I, with the meanest of the people, shall present in this temple of God, acceptably to God and to you, but skins of goat's hair, I shall account that I have done enough; since the poor woman in the temple, giving from her poverty, according to the words of our Saviour, is said to have bestowed more than kings, who furnished cedar, onyx-stones, gold, and silver for the structure of the temple. Nor is this to be wondered at, since it is not things presented, but the spirit of the one that bestows them, that is to be taken into account. But by the temple of the Lord, I mean this present most holy general council. Nor as I imagine without reason, since the apostle Paul, writing to a particular church, says, *The temple of the Lord is holy, which temple ye are.* As to you, therefore, most eminent men, and those who resemble you, like the men of the days of Solomon, here present in this sacred temple of God, long time have you presented and offered the gold of shining wisdom; and you that are less eminent, the silver of divine eloquence; and others still of a lower order, by your various virtues and efforts, the scarlet, purple, and hyacinth, for the larger vessels of the temple, for restoring the curtains and roof of the militant hierarchy. I, after you, so many, so great, so distinguished men, who in comparison with you am but nothing, having my head bowed down by almost every kind of faultiness—what shall I offer? Lest, however, placed in this holy temple in the presence of God and of you, I may appear entirely destitute, I may offer at least the skins of my beast-like deeds, and the goat's hair of my unworthy conduct, with a free heart, beseeching you each and all with deep earnestness that I may not be wholly despised or condemned in this, nor be driven forth and ejected with obloquy from this temple of God, which ye are. For even these offerings of mine may be of service, in their own way and time, in the temple of God. Thus to show, with your approbation, that not only clusters of grapes, but leaves also, may contribute to render the vineyard of the Lord of Hosts not only spacious, but specious, I have prefaced this much, like one who goes through steep and hidden ways, forewarning of their nature. After this entrance upon them, follows this my offering, which I present voluntarily for the honor of God and of the holy faith."

Jerome then read the paper which he had drawn up, and which seemed to meet the demands of the council. They had forced him by the terror of the flames to an act of hypocrisy, and of treason to his own convictions. How far at the time the sophistry of his own fears led him to believe his course to be justifiable, it is difficult to say. None could condemn it more heartily than he afterward did himself. For the present his declaration satisfied the council. He was led back to prison and treated less harshly.

CHAPTER V.

VIOLENCE OF THE TIMES. LETTERS OF THE BOHEMIANS.
ZISCA.

New Commission on Heresy. — Annates. — Ravages of the Turks. — Conference of Benedict XIII. and Sigismund. — Canonization. — Commission Appointed.— Gerson's Treatise. — Violence and Anarchy of the Times. — Narrative of Bernard Witt. — Frederic of Austria and the Bishop of Trent. — Measures of the Council Against the Former. — Caroline Constitution. — Nason's Complaint. — Letter from Bohemia. — Mission of the Bishop of Leitomischel. — Reply of the Bohemian States. — Vindication of the Bohemians Presented to the Council. — The Principles Avowed by the Latter on Keeping Faith with Heretics. — They Fail to Convince the Bohemians. — Measures Adopted at Prague. — Zisca. — Permission Granted Him by Wenzel.

Sept. 23, 1415 — Dec. 19, 1415.

In the same session in which Jerome abjured, a decree was read, which intimated the purpose of the council to follow up the task which it had begun, of extirpating heresy. The Patriarch of Constantinople and the Bishop of Senlis were appointed a commission to examine such as adhered to Huss, and inquire into their doctrines, as spread throughout Bohemia and Moravia. Other heresies, that might call for notice, were also to be referred to them. They were to hear, decide, and judge them, with all things thereto appertaining. No state, grade, rank, order, or condition was allowed exemption from their jurisdiction. They were empowered to cite before them, in person, all who were subject to suspicion, and to

(146)

proceed in their case to a definitive sentence.[1] This
commission was appointed over another to which the
general subject of heresies had been committed. It
was doubtless the intention of the council, by its
appointment, not only to expedite business, but to
place the matter in safe hands.

Many matters of local as well as general interest
occupied, from time to time, the attention of the
council. The subject of the papal abuse of *annates*
had been strongly urged, especially by the German
and some of the French nation, but the question what
means should be provided for the support of the
Roman court, if annates were dispensed with, furnished a problem for which a satisfactory solution
was difficult. After long, tedious, and often angry
discussions, the subject was for the time deferred.

The absence of Sigismund in Spain had furnished
an occasion for the Turks to renew their inroads upon the provinces bordering on his kingdom of Hungary.[2] Relieved of all apprehension by his distance
from the scene, they extended their invasions so far
that the council itself was not altogether free from
anxiety upon its own account. Startling reports
reached Constance of the terrible ravages by fire and
sword which had been already committed. Sigismund's territories were singled out for vengeance.
His purpose to unite Christendom in a grand crusade
against the Turk was no secret. The council felt
that in his absence it became them to repay the generosity of his service by exerting themselves in his

[1] Van der Hardt, iv. 562, 573.   [2] Niem, apud Van der Hardt, ii.
Fleury, xxvi. 176.   416.

behalf. They wrote to the king of Poland, urging
him to interfere to restore peace. They sent one of
the bishops present at the council to engage the
nobles of Hungary to remain faithful to their master.
The influence of the king of Poland was at once exerted, and the negotiations for peace were like to be
successful, when the violence of the Hungarians, in
arresting the Polish ambassador as a spy, excited the
resentment of the Turks, and hostilities were resumed.
The Hungarian army was defeated, and many of its
nobility were slain.

Meanwhile the council, anxious that the negotiations with Benedict XIII. should be brought to
a favorable conclusion, despatched the Archbishop
Wallenrod of Riga to aid the emperor with his
counsel. His influence with Sigismund was well
known. His energy and decision were not checked
by any conscientious scruples, or enfeebled by any
feelings of sympathy or humanity. The treatment
of Huss, who had been committed to his charge,
could attest the harsh, unscrupulous spirit of the
man. The council feared lest the attention of the
emperor, whose plans looked toward the securing of
such a peace among the nations as to favor his project of a crusade, might be somewhat withdrawn
from the matter of the union of the church, or be
misled by the artifice of Benedict. But they had
no good reason to distrust his perseverance or fidelity
in the task in which he was engaged. He had already
gained over the king of Aragon, who resolved to
withdraw obedience from Benedict if he would not
abdicate his office. The latter too gave such signs

of readiness to consider the proposals of the emperor, in his first conference with him, that some were
deceived with the hope that he would accept the
terms offered.[1] He received the emperor with all
respect, in a castle which bore his own name. In a
conference of two or three hours, he seemed to give
such evidence of good intentions, that the report of it
at the council was welcomed with joy. He wept freely
during the interview, but his tears had the virtue of
the crocodile's. The hypocrisy that belonged to the
part he played called for tears, and they were shed
as a matter of business. It was not long before
their true value was discerned.

It was at about this time that the subject of
the canonization of new saints by the church was
brought, in a special manner, before the council. The
king of Sweden had written to John XXIII. soon
after his arrival at Constance, urging him to grant
the canonization of three of his subjects who had
sustained a high reputation for sanctity.[2] But John
XXIII., however facile he might have shown himself in complying with the request, was too much
absorbed in the conduct of his own affairs to pay
much attention to others, and St. Bridget alone secured his favorable regard. He was soon placed in
such circumstances that any further action on his
part would have been strongly opposed, or at least
sharply controverted. The ambassadors of the Swedish king, therefore, laid their letter before the council. A commission was appointed, to which the

---

[1] L'Enfant, 354–358. Van der Hardt, iv. 1240, *et seq.*   [2] Van der Hardt,
iv. 490.

subject was referred. They were to examine into the claims of the pretended saints, the life they had led, and the miracles they had performed, and to consider generally whether it were not better to diminish the number of saints than to increase it. The members of the commission were selected from the cardinals, bishops, and doctors. Beside the cardinals of Cambray and Cologne, and the bishop of Lodi, Gerson was placed upon it. The subject which they were now to consider was one that for a long time had claimed the serious consideration of thoughtful minds. Wickliffe had denounced in the most severe terms that worship of the saints, which was derogatory to the honor of Christ as the one and only mediator. There are those, he says, that deem it right that all other intercessors should be discarded. The frequency of canonization he imputes to cupidity and ignorance of the true faith. It was obvious that the possession of a saint's bones often ensured, to the body that held it, a large income. It was but a just inference that the frequent appeals to the court of Rome for canonization were connected with the profits that were to be the result. But, said Wickliffe, some would choose a king's fool to intercede for them with his master; and these saints are but the buffoons—fools of the court of heaven. Moreover, in the multiplication of saints through the cupidity of men, there was great danger that mistakes would be made, and it might even come to pass that men would adore and serve the devil canonized as a saint.

But such views as these were not shared by Wick-

liffe alone. Henry de Hassia, or Langstein, as he was
also called, a member of the University of Paris,
and afterward a teacher at Vienna, had written on
the subject in a manner that secured the approbation
of Gerson who had for a time known him—and perhaps been his pupil. Clemengis too, the Cicero of
the university, and friend of Gerson, while exhaust-
ing the store of his wonderful eloquence in depicting the vices of the church, did not suffer the evils
of frequent canonizations to escape his notice. He
pronounces the advent of a new saint in the calen-
dar a tremendous curse.[1]

Gerson entered upon the subject with an earnestness which showed that he had not been an inattentive observer of the evils connected with it. In regard to the pretended saint and vision, he lays down
the rule of investigation grounded on the principle,
" By their fruits ye shall know them." The formula
was: " Ask who, what, why, to whom, how, and
whence." [2] Under these several heads, he enters into
a close and searching investigation of the claims put
forth in behalf of pretended saints and their visions.
These last might present a thousand truths; but if
they contained a single falsehood, that would be fatal
to them. If they came from the Spirit of God, and
were intended for men, they would be intelligible,
instead of obscure, as they often were. They would
declare some truth which was consonant with scripture, but not rendered unnecessary previously by
Bible revelation. They would be concise, lest their

---

[1] Clemeng. Op. 104.   [2] Tu, quis, quid, quare, cui, qualiter, unde, require,
Ger. Op. i. 39.

prolixity should at length make them more burdensome than the law of the Old Testament. Gerson,
moreover, represents visions as sometimes springing
from injury or weakness of the brain. A person's
temperament might superinduce a tendency to visions, with which nothing but a mere human spirit
had any concern.

Gerson expresses, in connection with the examples
he cites, his conviction that the claims of pretended
saints were to be closely scrutinized, and that *prima
facie* there was strong reason for rejecting them.
"The demon once presented himself," so Gerson relates, "transfigured as Christ, to one of the holy
fathers. 'I am Christ,' said he, 'personally visiting
thee, because thou art worthy.' But the holy father
at once shut his eyes, covering them with both hands,
and cried out, 'I have no wish to see Christ here, it
is enough to see him in glory.' Upon this the demon immediately vanished." Another of the fathers
had a similar vision, but he kept his humility, and
and was kept by it. "But see," said the holy man,
"to whom you have been sent; for surely I am not
such a one as is worthy to behold Christ here."
Another person was unwilling to enter the church,
saying, that it was enough for him that with his
bodily eyes he had seen Christ; but by harsh discipline of chains, and fasting from flesh and wine, his
swollen fanaticism was reduced, and he was cured.

Gerson declares that it was impossible to say what
deception had grown out of this prevalent curiosity
to know future and hidden things, or see and perform miracles. It had turned many away from the

true religion. Superstition had spread abroad in Christendom, like the demand for signs and wonders of old in Judæa, till men put more faith in the uncanonized, and in writings that were not even authentic, than they did in holy men and in the gospel.[1] Few were able to judge the claims put forth by those whom the people would regard as saints. Many were, consequently, deceived.

Gerson's sound sense placed him on this question by the side of Wickliffe and of Clemengis; more mild in tone, he was, in reality, scarcely less severe than they. Clemengis undoubtedly would have said, if the question in its present shape had been brought before him, that it might be worth while to make the council itself holy, before multiplying saints of a character almost as questionable as their own. In his deference for general councils and their decisions, he stands on the same ground with Huss himself. "It seems to me," he says, "rash to say that a general council cannot err or be deceived." In this case, however, partly through Gerson's influence, they took the right course. They declined to increase the number of the saints.

Among matters of less importance which now claimed attention, were those that respected the liberty of ecclesiastics, the privilege of prelates of the council to receive the fruit of their benefices, while absent at Constance, and rules for the better observance of the constitutions of the mendicant orders. These last had been for a long time the light infantry of the papal army. They had gone all over Chris-

[1] Ger. Op., i. 41.

tendom, at first welcomed for their poverty, their
moral superiority to the ordinary clergy, and the
earnestness of their preaching. But with their reputation they increased in wealth and power, till at
last, in their corruption, they were very generally
regarded as the nuisance of the church. The University of Paris had complained of their rapacity,
vice, and violence, and Gerson was their bitter
opponent. He had attacked them in his writings,
almost with Wickliffe's severity. But they could
not be suppressed, and it only remained for the council to make a feeble and ineffectual attempt to reform
the order.

The attention of the council was moreover directed
to acts of violence which had been committed against
its members. Europe generally, as well as France,
was torn by feuds and dissentions. The bishops and
counts were at continual strife. Bernard Witt, a
Benedictine monk, gives us, in his history of Westphalia, a picture of the anarchy which prevailed a
few years previous, and which even still defied the
power of the emperor to restrain it. "Here," he
says, "you might hear the clashing of battle; there,
the shrieks of fugitives, and the complaints of the
oppressed. Now, dwellings are torn down or burned;
and again, villages ravaged, and the crops trampled
to the earth. These things and others of a like
character—the acts of insolent power, abusing the
defenceless—are frequent."[1] Nor could the church,
or rather the papacy, be regarded as guiltless in the
premises. Many of these evils sprang directly from

[1] Ber. Wit., p. 464.

the extortion or the perfidy of the pontiffs. Sometimes rival claimants for a benefice deluged in blood
the diocese for which they contended. The history
of the archbishops of Cologne for successive centuries might furnish a parallel to the enormities that
rendered the history of the last days of the empire,
founded by Constantine, illustrious in crime and carnage.   Sometimes dissentions arose between the
clergy and the people. This was the case at Worms
in 1406.[1] For three years the clergy were expelled
from the city. Although the Emperor Robert was
on their side, they succeeded at last only by force
of spiritual arms, against which the steel of their
enemies was no sufficient defence. Henry of Lunen-
berg, only two years previous, had been taken captive by Count Bernard, who released him on his oath
to pay as his ransom 100,000 florins. But he had
only to go to Rome to receive absolution from his
oath by the abuse of papal authority.

We have already seen the turbulent character of
the Duke of Burgundy. France without an energetic
king was torn by factions. The nobility were themselves sovereign in their own territories, and were
continually at variance. There was no common
authority to command respect. Nor within the
bounds of the German empire was the state of things
much better. On every side there were turbulence
and lawless license. Frederic, Duke of Austria,
though reconciled formally with the emperor, was
still busy with his plots and schemes. With restless
impatience he endured the restraint of a forced sub-

[1] Ber. Wit., p. 484.

mission. At last he proceeded to the overt act of arresting the Bishop of Trent, and seizing upon the city as his own domain. The matter was brought by complaint before the council. They issued their monitory against the duke, commanding him to restore, within twenty days, what he had taken away, with damages for the evil done. They authorized the bishop to invoke against him, in case of refusal, the secular arm. The penalty of disobedience was most severe. The council—assuming a right which they had exercised in the decree concerning the emperor's absence,—authority over secular princes— threatened his disobedience with a deprivation of all the feoffs and privileges which he held from the church or the empire, stripping him of all authority, power, and title to reign, and his posterity after him to the second generation. The subjects of Frederic were to be released from their oaths of allegiance. He, with his accomplices who were to share his fate, was to be summoned before the council, and the ecclesiastics who should favor him, were to be excommunicated.

The council probably would have scarcely dared to assume such an attitude toward any other prince than Frederic of Austria. The emperor hated him still, notwithstanding their formal reconciliation, and gave some credit to the report of attempts made by the duke to take his life. The council were confident of being sustained by Sigismund in their course. Frederic was not the powerful Duke of Burgundy— a criminal whom they dared not touch. Despoiled of a large part of his possessions, and deprived of the

favor of the emperor, he was just the object over
which they might safely presume to domineer. Violent and reckless as he may have been, his conduct
in this instance demanded more judicial formality,
more investigation in regard to its justice or injustice,
than was allowed by this summary sentence.

The facts of the case were these. George of Lichtenstein had been appointed Bishop of Trent, to the
great dissatisfaction of its inhabitants. They had, as
their leader, a nobleman by the name of Rodolph,
who aspired to occupy the post of the unacceptable
official. This could only be secured by acts that
bordered at least on violence, and tended to the
expulsion of the bishop. But the latter found a
friend and ally in Henry of Rottenberg, who marched
upon Trent with his army and took summary vengeance upon the inhabitants. He seized and kept
possession of the city, having first ravaged it with
fire and sword, and put Rodolph to death. Frederic
of Austria observed with anger and indignation this
harsh and violent proceeding. It is not to be presumed that he was much moved by such a method of
installing a bishop in his diocese, for on another occasion, if his own interests had demanded it, he would
probably have been willing to have adopted it himself without a scruple.

But Trent was a friendly city bordering on his
own domain. Undoubtedly, as he looked around
upon his lost jewels—the territories that had been
taken from him for his adherence to John XXIII.—
he felt an anxious desire for their recovery. But
whatever motives may have influenced him, he

marched to Trent, drove out the obnoxious bishop, and took the citizens under his protection. All this seems to have taken place after the emperor had set out for Spain. In the twentieth session of the council, (Nov. 6,) the decree against the duke, already referred to, was read. His advocate, John Eling, protested against the decree as a nullity. For months after this, the matter made little if any progress. Frederic appeared at Constance.[1] But he found little hope of justice in the action of the council. He seized the occasion that offered, to escape secretly from the city back to his own dominions, which had been plundered in his absence. He left behind him a public placard, in which he complained of the injustice of the council, " who," he said, " had shut the mouth of his advocate." This was the thirtieth of March, 1416, after the matter had been depending for more than six months. The council, however, were indignant, not only at Frederic's escape, but at his placard, which they considered libellous. They wrote to the emperor against him, and found Sigismund only too ready to put the turbulent duke under the ban of the empire. Frederic, moreover, found a dangerous rival in his brother Ernest, who had in his absence seized upon large portions of his estates. Yet notwithstanding all the influences and terrors that were arrayed against him, the duke maintained his ground. He defied alike the emperor and the council. He still kept the Bishop of Trent in durance, and deprived of his diocese. The effort

[1] Some difficulties appear in the statement of the matter, only to be met by supposing the assault on Trent to have taken place before Frederic's first arrest.

to induce his subjects to renounce his allegiance was
but partially successful, and the threatening decree of
the council fell at his feet as a mere *brutum fulmen.*

The duke was, however, in the course he pursued,
but a fair specimen of the petty princes and nobles
of Europe. To restrain their violence, the council
revived the memorable *Carolina Constitutio,*[1] by
Charles IV., on the subject of the liberty of ecclesiastics. It affixed the several penalties to the crime
of trespassing on the rights, person, or privileges of
the clergy. They who transgressed it were to be
accounted infamous, deprived of their honors, and no
more to be admitted to the privileges or councils of
their order. All this was aggravated by the terrors
of the imperial ban, and the canonical as well as divine judgments which were denounced upon the of-
fender. Undoubtedly severe restraints and penalties
were necessary to repress the prevalent violence; but
when the clergy and prelates were often the chief
offenders, their immunity only the more provoked
indignant reprisals. The justice of the council should
have taught them not to launch the terrors of the
Caroline Constitution and their own anathema, till
their project of reform had become so far effectual
that the clergy could be regarded as deserving of such
protection.

The work of reform, however, made but slow
progress. At a congregation held on the nineteenth
of December, John Nason, president at that time of
the German nation in the council, gave utterance to
his complaints on this subject. " The council," said

Van der Hardt, iv. 523.

he, "has been assembled for three principal objects,
—to put an end to the schism, to condemn heresies,
and to reform the church in its head and members.
John Huss has been already most justly condemned,
and John XXIII. has been deposed. But those same
crimes are still every day committed which were
the ground of his deposition, and especially the crime
of simony. The German nation has hitherto redoubled its urgency for the condemnation of this and
every other abuse, as well as for the exemplary punishment of those that are guilty. But, to the shame
of the council, the most criminal indulgence and dissimulation have been practised."

After this complaint and protestation, he besought
the members to proceed without delay in the matter.
Nor did he fail to call attention to a subject in which
his own personal feelings were enlisted—the case of
Jerome. He seemed dissatisfied with what had
already been done, and put no faith in the recantation which Jerome had made.[1] In this respect he
was probably a fair representative of the feeling of
the German nation. They were earnestly bent upon
a reform of the church. They had complained repeatedly of the abuses which they wished to have
corrected. In the discussion of the papal claim of
annates they had been especially interested, but
their defeat in regard to these matters was only a
premonition of what they were still to expect. In
regard to Jerome, their complaint was more successful. If there were those in the council who preferred
to save him, and avoid again provoking the Bohe-

---

[1] Van der Hardt, iv. 556.

mians, many of them were still more cautious of offending the German nation. It was less hazardous to give up an unfriended and powerless individual, whose cause, without a Duke of Burgundy or a Teutonic order to represent it, might be trampled upon, *perhaps* with impunity.

And yet they might well have hesitated, on mere principles of worldly prudence, to deal harshly with Jerome; for this same day another letter from Bohemia was laid before them.[1] The bearer of it was a friend of Jerome, and yet he boldly ventured to present it to the council, although its contents could not but have been exceedingly offensive. It bore the seals of four hundred and fifty-two persons of the Bohemian nation. Some of these were barons and nobles, and most of them persons of distinction. The language was plain, direct, and earnest. They blamed the council for the condemnation and punishment of Huss. They declared Huss to have been a holy and just man, whose equal for integrity and sanctity could not be found. The council had sinned and wrought evil in what they had done, and on this account the Bohemians declare that they will neither adhere to it, nor yield it obedience. This was indeed a bold step to take, but the council had provoked it. The popular feeling in Bohemia resented the injustice offered to their countryman, and it was felt that it would be treason to his memory, to honor his murderers.[2]

---

[1] The principal letters from Bohemia and Moravia, addressed to the council in a tone of bold remonstrance, are to be found in Mon. Hus. 58–63. The first two are from the Bohemian barons. The third is from Bohemia and Moravia. The fifth is from fifty-four Moravian nobles.

[2] Van der Hardt, ii. 425.

The state of feeling in Bohemia is still more clearly seen in another letter which at about the same time must have been laid before the council. The barons and magnates of the kingdom met to reply to the letter which the council had written them, informing them of the execution of Huss, and vindicating their own proceedings. The letter had been despatched to Bohemia by the hands of the Bishop of Leitomischel. He was charged, moreover, with the task of endeavoring to extirpate the heresy of Huss from the kingdom. But he found that the work exceeded his powers. Although noble by birth and rank, and a man of great ability and iron will, rank, ability, eloquence, and energy were of no avail. He found few disposed even to listen to him. On all sides he was met with coldness or hostility. Scarcely did he dare to show himself in public. He professed fear of person as well as of property. Certainly his presence, as a member of the council, and charged to extirpate the heresy of Huss, was peculiarly obnoxious to the nation at large.

The first meeting of the magnates to reply to the letter of which he was the bearer, was held at Sternberg. A second meeting was held at Prague on the second of September, when the assembly united in a detailed statement of their grievances and complaints. Their letter was addressed "To the most reverend, the fathers, lords, lord cardinals, patriarchs, primates, archbishops, bishops, ambassadors, doctors and masters, and the whole council of Constance," and was signed by nearly sixty of the Bohemian and Moravian magnates, embracing the most important officers

and nobility of the land.[1]   "Inasmuch," say they,
"as each one, by natural and divine law, is commanded to do to others as he would have them do to
himself, and is forbidden to do to another what he
would not have done to himself, according to the
words of our Saviour, 'All things whatsoever ye
would that men should do unto you, do ye even so
to them, for this is the law and the prophets,'—yea, he
who was a chosen vessel, cries out, 'Love is the ful-
filling of the law, and the whole law is fulfilled in
one word, Thou shall love thy neighbor as thyself;'
we, therefore, walking as near as we may to the
aforesaid divine rule and direction, as God is our
witness, express our affection as neighbors to him
who was our dearest neighbor, the reverend master,
John Huss, of blessed memory, bachelor of sacred
theology, and preacher of the gospel, whom lately
you—we know not by what spirit led—have condemned,—neither confessing his crime, nor lawfully
convicted, as was becoming, and no manifest errors
or heresies being brought against him, but at the
accusation, instigation, and information, unfair, false,
and urgent, of those who were *his* capital enemies
and traitors, as well as those of our kingdom and of
the march of Moravia,—as an obstinate heretic, and
have put him, thus condemned, to a cruel and most
shameful death, to the perpetual infamy and disgrace
of our most Christian kingdom of Bohemia, and the
most renowned march of Moravia, as well as of us all.
As we before transmitted in writing to Constance,
to the most serene prince and lord, Sigismund, king

[1] Mon. Hus., i. 78.

of the Romans and of Hungary, heir of our king and master, which writing was read and published in your congregations, and—which we would be glad to disbelieve—thrown, to our contempt and dishonor, to the flames: so also now we have thought that our letters patent, by these presents, should be addressed to you in behalf of the said Master John Huss; publicly, by heart and mouth, professing and protesting that Master John Huss was certainly a man excellent, just, and Catholic, for many years spoken of as praiseworthy, in life, conduct, and reputation, in our kingdom. The gospel law, and the books of the prophets, both of the Old and New Testaments, according to the exposition of the holy doctors, and those approved by the church, did he teach and preach in a Catholic manner to us and our subjects; and many of the same things has he left to us in writing, uniformly detesting all errors and heresies, and faithfully admonishing all believers of Christ to detest the same; exhorting to peace and charity, as far as possible by words, writings, and works, so that we never heard, or could learn by diligent inquiry, that the aforesaid Master John Huss taught any heresy or error in his sermons, or preached or asserted the same; neither in any way, by word or deed, did he scandalize us or our subjects; but ever in Christ, living in piety and gentleness, did he exhort all to keep the gospel law, and the institutions of the holy fathers, for the edification of holy mother church, and the salvation of our neighbors; and this he did in word and deed with the utmost diligence. Yet all these premised—perpetrated to our confusion and that of our kingdom of Moravia—did not suffice for you; but that honorable master, Jerome of Prague, a man indisputably a flowing fountain of eloquence, master of the seven liberal arts, as well as an illustrious philosopher, him, not seen, heard, confessed, or convicted, but at the malicious information of those that were traitors to him and us, you have mercilessly arrested and thrown in prison, and perhaps even now you have put him, as you did Master John Huss, to a most cruel death.

" Besides, it has come, we regret to say, to our hearing, and from your letters we plainly gather, that certain slanderers, odious to God and men, and enemies and traitors of our kingdom and Moravia, before you and the council, have calumniated us most gravely and basely, asserting, though falsely and treacherously, that in the aforesaid regions diverse errors have sprung up, grievously and extensively affecting our hearts, and the hearts of many faithful inhabitants, so that unless the rule of correction is soon applied, the aforesaid regions, with their Christian believers, will be subjected to irrevocable loss and ruin of souls.   Such atrocious and prejudicial wrongs as these, which, notwithstanding our many demerits bring them upon us and our kingdom, etc., are yet falsely and lyingly imputed,—how can we endure them?   Since, by the grace of God, while almost all other kingdoms of the world are often vacillating, cherishing schism and antipopes, our most Christian realm of Bohemia, and the most reputable march of Moravia, have, from the very time when they received the Catholic faith of our Lord Jesus Christ, adhered most firmly and unceasingly, without rebuke, to the holy Roman church.   At what exceeding charge and effort, and with how sacred regard and reverence, holy mother church and her pastors have been regarded by the princes and their followers, is manifest, beyond dispute, to the whole world.   And you yourselves, if you are willing to confess the truth, can testify to all these things.   But in order that, according to the apostolic doctrine, we may provide that which is good, not only in the sight of God, but of men; and lest, through a negligence of the most untarnished reputation of the aforesaid kingdom, etc., we be found guilty of cruelty toward those who are our neighbors; therefore, having in Christ Jesus our Lord a firm hope, a sincere conscience and purpose, and a sure orthodox faith, we, by the tenor of these presents, to you and to all the faithful in Christ, make known, and maintain, professing it publicly with heart and mouth, that whatsoever man, of whatever state, eminence, dignity, condition, grade, or religion he be, shall say or assert, that in the aforesaid kingdom of Bohemia, etc., errors and heresies have sprung up, and infected us and other Christian subjects of the aforesaid realm, every and each such individual, the person only of our most serene prince, our Lord Sigismund, king of the Romans and of Hungary excepted, whom we believe and hope to be guiltless in the premises,—each such individual *directly lies in his teeth*, as a most wicked wretch and traitor toward the aforesaid kingdoms, and is our most perfidious, and our only most injurious heretic, the child of all malice and iniquity, as well as of the devil, who is a liar, and the father of the same. Nevertheless, leaving these aforesaid wrongs to the Lord and his vengeance, which will abundantly mete retribution to the proud, we shall prosecute them further before the apostle to be elected, whom God will place as only and unquestioned pastor of his holy church ; to whom, God willing, we, as faithful children, in all things lawful and honest, and consonant to reason and the divine law, exhibiting due reverence and obedience, shall seek and demand in regard to each and all the matters aforesaid, according to the law of our Lord Jesus Christ, and the institutions of the holy fathers, that fitting remedy be devised for the satisfaction of us and the aforesaid kingdom, etc. These things aforesaid notwithstanding, we will defend and protect the law of our Lord Jesus Christ, and his devoted, humble, and constant preachers, even to the shedding of blood, all fear, and human statutes enacted to the contrary, being cast beneath our feet.—Given at Prague, Sept. 2, A. D. 1415, in full council of magnates, barons, lords, and nobles of the realm of Bohemia and the march of Moravia, with the affix of our seals."[1]

The council could not mistake the tone of this letter. It was bold, manly, and even defiant. It breathed a deep and indignant sense of wrong. It expressed the only too unanimous convictions of the nation. The violation of the imperial safe-conduct was an act, the infamy and outrage of which were palpable to the most rude and unlettered. The common people and barons alike were already arraign-

[1] Mon. Hus., i. 78, 79.

ing and condemning it in no measured terms. And now the letter of the Bohemians, with the report of what was taking place at Prague, forced the council so far to pay homage to the sentiments of public morality as to make at least an attempt to vindicate the breach of public faith with which they themselves and the emperor stood charged. The council first discusses the validity of safe-conducts, given to heretics by secular princes.[1] "The present synod declares that every safe-conduct granted by the emperor, by the kings and other secular princes, to heretics, or persons accused of heresy in the hope of bringing them back from their errors, must in no way serve to the prejudice of the Catholic faith or ecclesiastical jurisdiction, nor prevent these persons from being examined, judged, and punished according as justice shall require, in case these heretics shall refuse to revoke their errors; and this to be, although they shall have come to the place of judgment merely and only on the faith of the safe-conduct. And he who shall have promised them safety shall not in this case be under obligation to keep his promise, by whatever pledge he may be engaged, since he has done all that depended on him." This general principle, that faith is not to be kept with heretics, and which outraged the public sentiment even of that age, finds its specific application in the case which it was designed to cover—that of Huss. The decree stands recorded on the same page with the letter of the Bohemians, and was evidently intended to meet objections from that source.[2] "The most holy

[1] L'Enfant, 385.   [2] Van der Hardt, iv. 521–522.

council, etc.   Inasmuch as some persons, ill-disposed or ill-informed, or perhaps assuming to be wiser than they should be, slander not only his royal majesty, but even the sacred council, as is reported, by their cursed tongues, in public and in private, saying or suggesting that the safe-conduct given by our most invincible prince and Lord Sigismund, king of the Romans and of Hungary, to the late John Huss, heresiarch of damnable memory, was unduly violated against justice and honor, while nevertheless the said John Huss, perversely assaulting the orthodox faith, has forfeited all safe-conduct and privilege, so that no faith or promise is, by natural, divine, or human law, to be kept with him, to the prejudice of the Catholic faith; therefore this said holy council declares, by the tenor of these presents, that the said most invincible prince, in respect to the late John Huss aforesaid, had done, according to the obligations of justice, what was permitted, and what became his royal majesty, commanding and requiring all and each of the faithful of Christ, of whatsoever dignity, grade, eminence, condition, state, or sex they may be, that none shall hereafter detract from, or speak against, the holy council, or his royal majesty, in regard to what was done in the case of the late John Huss aforesaid.   And he who shall violate this command, is to be punished as a favorer of heretical pravity, and guilty, beyond pardon, of the crime *Læsæ Majestatis.*" [1]

It was indeed fitting, that deeds which would not bear the light, should be cloaked with apologies.

[1] Mansi.

Few criminals like to have their conduct canvassed, unless they furnish the commentary by the light of which it is to be judged. The council at least found that their policy did not bear discussion well, and therefore employed all their art and skill to draw up a plausible defence. But their apology was only an endorsement of their crime. No slander of their enemies could be so damaging as their libel upon themselves, when, to excuse the infamy of a single act, they adopted the broad principle that faith was not to be kept with heretics. And yet this was the only resource left them. It was the only semblance of a moral rule which could be invented, on which to base and defend their extraordinary course. But the Bohemians were not duped by its sophistry. It required some deeper casuistry to satisfy them, or suppress their instincts and convictions of what was right and just. They never forgot the outrage on public faith of which their enemies had been guilty.

And yet up to this point they had no intention of breaking with the Romish church. With their letter to the council, they sent deputies who were to speak publicly in defence of their course. Anxious for the spread and success of the gospel as they had heard it from the lips of Huss, they resolved that all the churches throughout the kingdom should be provided with faithful pastors, who should preach the word of God without molestation; that if a priest was accused of any error, he should be cited before his bishop, in order, if he should be convinced of having taught any doctrine contrary to the word of God, that he might be punished and expelled; that if a bishop should chance to condemn and punish secretly, of his own individual impulse and through hatred of the gospel, any priest not convicted of error, no such bishop should be any more allowed to cite a priest before him, but the matter should be referred to the judgment of the university, to be examined according to holy scripture; that priests of their dependence should be required to allow the excommunications of their bishops, and obey them when they were legitimate, but, on the contrary, resist them when they were unjust or precipitate, and launched through hatred of the word of God, or any other cause which could not be lawfully known. And they declare that they are fully purposed to obey from the heart the lawful citations and excommunications of their bishops. The assembly then expresses its earnest prayer that it will please God speedily to bestow upon the church a good pope, in order that they may bring before him their lawful complaints; and they declare that they will obey him in all which he shall command conformable to the word of God.[1]

Nothing more strikingly manifests the influence of the doctrines of Huss, or their prevalence throughout Bohemia, than the respect which is here, and throughout all their proceedings, testified by the assembly for the authority of the scriptures. They did not as yet perceive the fatal inconsistency between the claims of the council or the church, and the position which they had themselves assumed. They were simple enough to believe that if they were faithful to the spirit and precepts of the gospel,

[1] Mon. Hus. i. 77, 78.

they were faithful subjects of the Romish church. The council, however, was more fully aware of the bearing and tendency of the principles avowed by the Bohemians. They saw that if scripture was allowed to be the test of truth and doctrine, the council itself was but of secondary authority. Its claims were invalid. Its sentence was of but small account. Nor were they stupid enough to disregard the significance of the popular commotion at Prague. There was no one there on whose fidelity they could rely. The archbishop himself was powerless, and it is possible that he already leaned to the doctrines of Jacobel, which he subsequently embraced. The king was unreliable and inefficient at the best, while all the fragments of manliness left in him were but so much tinder for kindling his resentment against the council.

Among the nobles of his court, moreover, the one who had perhaps the strongest influence over him was John de Trocznow, his chamberlain. This was the man who afterward became so famous under the name Ziska, or one-eyed, for the bold hero had lost an eye in battle. Ziska proved to be one of the greatest and most successful generals of his age. He was born of a poor but noble family in the village whose name he bore. The memory of a sister, so it is narrated, who had been seduced and violated by an ecclesiastic, had kindled and fed his resentment against the whole monkish and priestly order.[1] The treatment of Huss and Jerome had reawakened all his past indignation, and excited within him the

[1] L'Enfant, 331.

deep but temporarily smothered purpose to avenge
the outrage. He brooded gloomily over the national
insult. His features bore the marks of his abstrac-
tion,—engrossed in the one thought of avenging the
wrong which he, as an individual, suffered in common
with the nation. The king observed him, on one occasion, walking in the court of the royal palace, lost
in revery. He called him, and asked what was the
matter that occupied his thoughts so intensely.
"The grievous affront," said he, "which the punishment of John Huss has offered to the Bohemian
nation." "Neither you nor I," said Wenzel, "are in
circumstances to avenge this affront; but if you can
devise the means to do it, take courage, and avenge
your compatriots." These words confirmed Ziska in
his bold purpose.[1] He at once began to devise
measures to execute it. The permission of the king,
who was but a cipher, gave him yet an immense advantage, by the mere authority it conferred. It relieved him from all apprehension, for the present at
least, of any obstruction to his designs from the fickle
and dissolute monarch. The magnates and nobles of
the land would now venture to speak out, in the fearless tone they had used in their letter to the council.
The doctors at Constance could judge by that tone,
of the strength and unanimity of the national feeling.

[1] L'Enfant, 331.

CHAPTER VI.

NEW CHARGES AGAINST JEROME. CONFERENCE WITH BENE-
DICT. VINCENT FERRARA.

More Lenient Feeling Toward Jerome. — Nason's Taunt. — Resignation of the
Commission in Jerome's Case. — A New One Appointed. — Gerson on the
Method of Dealing With Heretics. — New Charges Against Jerome. — Re-
port from the Conference with Benedict. — His Terms. — The Emperor's
Disgust. — Spanish Propositions. — Cheering Intelligence. — Defection of
Vincent Ferrara from Benedict. — His Wonderful Career as a Preacher
— His Gifts, Eloquence, and Virtues. — The Emperor at Paris. — He En-
deavors to Secure a Peace Between France and England. — Petit's Case
in the Council. — Sermon of Theodoric of Munster. — Invective Against the
Clergy.

Dec. 19, 1415—Feb. 16, 1416.

In the council there were those who were decidedly in favor of treating Jerome with leniency.
They doubtless, and wisely, imagined that it was the
most prudent course to be satisfied with his retraction. More would thus be gained for the authority
of the council than by sending him to the flames.
There might, moreover, be danger in offering a new
provocation to the Bohemians. But the enemies of
Jerome were bent on burning him. They professed
to have no faith in the retraction he had offered, and
probably they were sincere. They knew that he had
been "convinced against his will," if convinced at all,
and they did not intend that he should thus escape.
They therefore busied themselves in raking together

(174)

new accusations. Causis and Paletz distinguished themselves by their zeal in the matter. They urged his enemies at Prague to draw up new accusations.[1] Charges that before had not been thought of, were now devised. His enemies insisted that he should be called to undergo a new trial. His judges, the cardinals of Cambray, Ursinis, Aquilea, and Florence, opposed the application. They represented—with prudence, if not some lingering of conscientious feeling—that such a course would be unjust, and that Jerome, having shown obedience to the council, must be set at liberty.

But this show of clemency only irritated the enemies of Jerome. Nason, the president of the German nation, whom we have seen urging the condemnation of the prisoner, is said to have replied to these representations with much asperity.[2] "We are much surprised, most reverend fathers," said he, "that you are willing to intercede for this wicked heretic, who has done us so much mischief in Bohemia, and who might yet do you the same. I am quite apprehensive that you have received presents from these heretics, or from the king of Bohemia."[3] Such language was extremely irritating. The cardinals regarded it as an insult. Unwilling to be driven by such invidious accusations or suspicions to further process against Jerome, they chose to throw up their office, and ask as a commission to be discharged. Their request was granted. The enemies of Jerome triumphed in securing the appointment of a new commission. At the head of it stood the Patriarch

[1] L'Enfant, 340.   [2] Ib., 341.   [3] Mon. Hus., ii. 352.

of Constantinople, who had shown the spirit of an
unrelenting persecutor, in urging forward the sentence and execution of Huss.   Gerson, moreover,
joined the assailants of Jerome.   On the twenty-
ninth of October he had produced a treatise on the
subject "Of Recanting and Protesting in Matters of
Faith."[1]   Jerome's name is not mentioned in it, but
it is evident that it was aimed at him.   Its whole
scope is to show, that though a man may recant, he
may do it in such a way, or it may be accompanied
with such evidences, as to leave him still under suspicion of heresy.   Gerson thus volunteered to become
the casuist of the enemies of Jerome.   He maintains
that there are men with whom ignorance is crime;
and among these he classes those whom he describes
in drawing the picture of Jerome himself—men possessed of natural vivacity of mind, a shrewd judgment, the faculty of discernment, remarkable learning, extensive acquaintance with scripture, or with
canon and civil law.   Moreover, the question is
asked, May not a man sin against his conscience by
recanting?   "The answer," says Gerson, "is plain.
He must lay aside his conscience in the case supposed,
of his obstinacy."   The treatise of Gerson is a fine
piece of casuistry.   He evidently disliked boldly to
arraign the case of Jerome; but he weaves his web
skilfully around it, and overlays it with suspicions.
The tendency of his argument would be to encourage
Jerome's assailants.   Gerson's dislike of the man
seems to have been even greater than that which he
felt toward Huss.   Undoubtedly he was conscien-

[1] Van der Hardt, iii. 40.

tious in considering him a dangerous heretic. He
was, perhaps, the only man in Europe who could
fairly be considered Gerson's rival in those very arts
in which he excelled.   As a disputant, he would have
hesitated on no occasion to challenge the great chancellor himself. The two men were, moreover, opposed
in their philosophical views, and Jerome had shown
himself an able champion of the Realists.   Could
Gerson's mind have been warped by these considerations? It is more than possible. The fervency of
his feelings sometimes blinded his judgment. The
noble bearing and matchless eloquence of Jerome
won him friends in the council, but Gerson was not
among them. The generosity of his heart was seared
by prejudice, and in cherishing that prejudice he
thought to do God service. But the most diligent
efforts were made, by persons even less disinterested
than Gerson, for Jerome's condemnation.   Intelligence of his retraction had reached Prague, and his
enemies there became apprehensive lest, after all, he
might escape. The monks especially, who had been
stung by his insults and contempt, were resolved to
spare no effort to secure the doom of their destined
victim.[1] New charges were drawn up against him
and forwarded to the council, where the sincerity of
his abjuration was already strongly suspected. The
bearers of the new list of accusations were Carmelite
friars from Prague. They demanded that Jerome
should again be put upon his trial, and required to
answer to the charges which they should present.[2]
In spite of the protest of Jerome against this new

---

[1] Mon. Hus., ii. 351, 352.   [2] L'Enfant, 340, 380.

injustice, and the objections of the commission who had hitherto conducted his case, the monks, aided by Paletz and Causis, and especially by Gerson, finally succeeded in carrying their point. In this they were materially aided by the sympathies of the new commission, composed of members more of their own stamp.

On the twenty-ninth of January, 1416, the ambassadors who had accompanied the emperor to Spain, returned to make their report to the council.[1] The king of Aragon had died; but Ferdinand, his successor, had manifested a disposition to comply with the views and sustain the policy of the emperor. He resolved to withdraw obedience from Benedict, unless he would abdicate the pontificate. But the old man was not to be moved by any such terrors. He still refused to recede from his terms.[2] He demanded the rejection of the council of Pisa, the dissolution of that of Constance, the convocation of another near his own obedience, his own confirmation as pope, and provision for his honorable maintenance on his resigning his dignity. He maintained, throughout all the conferences, that he was the true pope, and that though this might reasonably have been doubted before, it could be doubted no longer, since one of his rivals had resigned, and the other had been deposed. He maintained that it was not he who was guilty of keeping up the schism, but the council of Constance, since, in order to end it, it was only necessary to recognize his claims; that to proceed to a new election would be only to renew

[1] Van der Hart, iv. 583.   [2] De Vrie, apud. Van der Hardt. i. 203, 204.

the schism, since there would then be two popes; that
he was resolved to maintain his right to his last
breath, because he could not in conscience abandon
the vessel which God had committed to his care; that
as his age increased, he was the more bound to discharge his duty, and resist with all his might the
storm raised against him; moreover, if for peace'
sake another pope was needed, he alone could be
elected, for he was the only one of the cardinals that
had been promoted to that office before the schism
by Gregory XI., and that consequently he, as the
only one whose promotion was indisputable, was
eligible to the office, even on the principles of his
enemies themselves. It is said that for seven long
hours the old man continued his harangue, without
showing any fatigue either in his countenance or the
tones of his voice, although he had almost reached
his threescore years and ten.[1]

The emperor saw that any attempt to conquer the
resolution of Benedict was vain, while his conditions
were utterly inadmissible. His show of compliance
had been but part of the game which he was resolved to play out, and thus amuse the world with
hopes never to be realized. The emperor, with the
ambassadors of the council, withdrew in disgust.
He was about to return to Germany. But the king
of Aragon, with the ambassadors of Castile, Navarre,
and Scotland, as well as others of Benedict's obedience, who had now come to a better knowledge of
his character, sent to the emperor at Narbonne, begging him not to hasten his departure. They assured

[1] L'Enfant, 355.

him that Benedict should yet cede, or be abandoned by his whole obedience.

Negotiations were consequently resumed. The ambassadors of the emperor returned to Perpignan. The kings and princes exerted themselves to the utmost to overcome the old man's obstinacy. They were met at every point, however, by the artifice and subtlety of Benedict. All their persuasions and arguments were lost upon him. Their threat of withdrawing their obedience produced no effect. At last matters reached such a crisis of exasperation and excitement, that there was danger of violence. Benedict seized his moment, and withdrew secretly from the city. He did this, says Niem, in concert with Ferdinand, with whom he had a secret understanding. This, however, was but a public rumor. Benedict withdrew to Callioure on the sea coast. But even here he was followed by deputies, who urged him to cede and acknowledge the council of Constance, which he might do by sending his attorneys to Perpignan, or by coming there in person. In case of his refusal, he was to be threatened with harsher measures. But even here, Benedict, who saw himself virtually a prisoner—for the deputies had taken pains to seize his galleys and prevent his escape—replied haughtily that he should still abide by the declarations which he had made at Perpignan, whence he had withdrawn only that he was restricted of his liberty, and that he should not give any more explicit answer till he had reached the place for which he had set out. Even this was not enough to show his defiant spirit. He ridiculed the pretended care of Ferdinand for the

Catholic church. That was his own business, he
said, as legitimate pontiff. He moreover hurled his
fulminations against all,—cardinals, patriarchs, archbishops, bishops, kings, and emperors,—threatening
them with the spiritual and temporal power, if they
dared on this point to usurp any of his rights. Benedict's cardinals also were summoned to Perpignan.
At first they replied in the spirit of their master.
On the second summons—with the exception of the
cardinals connected with his own family—they all
forsook him for the conference at Perpignan.

Benedict's affairs were in a desperate condition.
But the heroic old man did not despond. A tame
submission he despised. He found means to escape
from Callioure, and fled to Peniscola, some two hundred miles from his enemies, upon the sea-coast. The
place was a strong one, and it was said to have belonged to the house of Luna.[1] Here Benedict could
at least more safely defy his enemies. But they followed him even to Peniscola. A third and last
deputation was sent him, requiring him to cede. But
like those that preceded it, it proved futile. Benedict replied,[2] that he could not recognize the council
of Constance, inasmuch as it was held in a city subject to the emperor, who managed everthing there
just he chose, as was exemplified in the case of John
XXIII., whose safe-conduct had been violated. He
maintained that the emperor persisted in continuing
the council in that city, only in order to elect a pope
devoted to his own interests, that he might do as he
pleased in Italy, and seize upon the possessions of

---

[1] L'Enfant, 356.   [2] Van der Hardt, ii. 515.

the church. He declared, moreover, that he could not accept a council composed of the cardinals of John XXIII. and Gregory XII., because this would be joining schismatics to his own Catholic subjects; and beside all, he did not deem that the place where the council was to be held should be left to the option of the emperor; that for these reasons he could not cede the pontificate without sinning against God and scandalizing the church, at least since his enemies were unwilling to accept the conditions on which he offered to cede. He added, also, that it did not belong to the council to choose a pope, but to the college of cardinals; that his reasons for withdrawal were not false, as had been pretended, and that the attempts that were made upon him every day were his sufficient justification. Moreover, he protested against all that should be done in regard to himself, on the ground of his being schismatic, as null and void. As to the reports that were circulated, that the king of Aragon was on the point of withdrawing from his obedience, and engaging others to unite themselves with him in aiding the emperor and council in proceeding against him, and deposing him from the pontificate, he besought them by the bowels of divine mercy not to afford occasion for such a scandal, which, so far from putting an end to the schism, would only cherish and extend it. He represented that the king of Aragon, especially, could not listen to such counsels without rebellion against himself, since of him he held his states, was his feudatory, and had given him the oath of fidelity. He added, that even though these protestations should not reach

the ears of those for whom they were intended, he
should not fail to proceed against them in all requi-
site ways, as he was authorized and even bound by
the interests of the church to do; and he referred
them, for a commentary upon his words, to one of his
bulls, given at Marseilles in 1407. Yet, to show that
he had ever at heart the union of the church, he declared that with this object he had already convoked a
council for the month of February next ensuing, and he
urgently besought the king of Aragon not to employ
menace, as he was said to have done, to prevent the
prelates from assembling. He said, finally, that having learned that his enemies had published that he
had advanced in his discourses or writings propositions contrary to the Catholic faith, he declared that
if such were the case—though he did not believe it
—he disavowed them, as having been always inviolably attached to the faith of the church, to whose
judgment he referred himself for all that might be
alleged against him.

Such obstinacy on the part of Benedict disgusted
many of those who, up to this time, had still adhered
to him, and they now determined to withdraw from
him their obedience. By them propositions were
sent to Narbonne, to the emperor and his council.[1]
These were, in substance: 1. That the three obediences assemble and compose a council without the
permission of Benedict, and without being under
the necessity of making any further requisition of
him. 2. That they proceed against the said Benedict, and do all that they shall judge to be fitting

[1] L'Enfant, 359.

for the union of the church. 3. That whatever process or anathema be designed against Benedict, it shall be sustained by all, or a greater part of, those who in the council were of the obedience of Benedict.

Upon this ensued a war of protests and manifestoes. The Archbishop of Tours took up the defence of the emperor and the council, in a document addressed to the Catholic church. He gave a brief history of the schism, the means employed to put an end to it, and the obstacles thrown in the way by the obstinacy and inconsistencies of Benedict. The archbishop closed by exhorting all Christendom to regard him as a common enemy. The ambassadors of the princes now entered into consultation with the emperor, and, in view of the obstinacy of Benedict, agreed, on the thirteenth of December, 1415, to twelve articles known as "The Capitulation of Narbonne."[1] These articles were skilfully framed. They allowed the council of Constance to be called merely an assembly, and not a council, until those of the obedience of Benedict were united with it. Both parties were to write letters of summons to form a council at Constance, while those already there were to speak of themselves as "the cardinals, patriarchs, archbishops, bishops, etc., assembled at Constance." In general nothing was to be done or allowed to the prejudice of those who had hitherto been of the obedience of Benedict. The proceedings of the council of Pisa were to be regarded as null, since in case of their validity the Spaniards would be con-

[1] Van der Hardt, ii., 542.

victed of having obeyed a deposed pope. All the decrees of Gregory against the obedience of Bene dict were to be quashed. The cardinals of Benedict were to be received *ad eundem* in the council. The members of his court were to be provided for. Those who had hitherto adhered to him should see to it, that in· case of his death no successor was elected in his place. Safe-conducts were to be procured by the emperor for Benedict or his officials, if they wished to attend the council to prosecute the business of his cession.

With these articles, the archbishop presented to the council two other documents. One of these was an edict of the king of Aragon, by which he renounced the obedience of Benedict, and enjoined his subjects to follow his example. The other was a letter, stating that the kings of Castile and Navarre, with the counts De Foix and Armagnac, had resolved to pursue the same course. The result was hailed with the greatest joy. Public thanksgivings were ordered for the favorable issue of the negotiations, so soon as they were known at the council. They were published by the sound of trumpet through the whole city of Constance. A public procession was announced, which took place the next day (January 30, 1416) with imposing pomp.

One of the greatest blows to the cause of Benedict was the defection of Vincent of Ferrara, by universal consent the most eloquent preacher of his age. He belonged to the Dominican order, and was at this time its most distinguished ornament. He had been Benedict's confessor, and master of the sacred palace. He was born at Valencia, A. D. 1350, and early distinguished himself for his extraordinary attainments. His days and nights were devoted with tireless assiduity to study. He read and re-read the fathers; but the Bible was his favorite book. In this we recognize the fountain from which he imbibed that zealous, humble, and devoted spirit, which he manifested in the midst of all the corruptions of his age. His eloquence and sanctity soon won for him the title of the Apostle of the West.[1] His labors were wonderful. He travelled over Europe, mastering the language of each people, and addressing them with unwonted earnestness in their own vernacular. The discernment of Benedict led him to attach to himself and his court the most able and talented men. He induced Clemengis to become his secretary, and Vincent his confessor. One was the most eloquent writer and the other the most eloquent preacher of the age. Both long cherished an affectionate regard for Benedict, even after the vices of his court had driven them from Avignon for purer air. In fact, the most valuable testimony to the merit of Benedict is found in the continued adherence of two such men,—both able, both incorruptible, both indignant protestants against the corruption of the church, and diligent students of the Sacred Scriptures. To Vincent, the common people ascribed the power of working miracles—a claim in

[1] A quite full account of the life, labors, and character of Vincent Ferrara is to be found in an article of the "Pres. Quarterly Review," for July, 1860. The materials for it were drawn mainly from the Letters of Clemengis, and "Historie des Hommes Illustres d l'Ordre de St. Dominic, tom. iv. Paris, 1746. With the fervor of a Baxter, Vincent combined the missionary zeal and activity of a Whitefield.

his behalf which in them was natural, in view of his amazing gifts, his wondrous eloquence, and the multiplied conversions of which he was the instrument,— but a claim which we have no evidence that he sanctioned himself.

The stories of his ability and success as a preacher border indeed on the miraculous, but are well attested. He was the itinerant apostle of Western Europe. Wherever he went his fame preceded him, and thronging thousands hung entranced upon his lips. "Men of every grade, order, and dignity," says Clemengis, "welcomed him as if he had been an angel of God." His knowledge of scripture, his lucid exposition and apposite adaptation of it, excited the admiration of this learned ex-rector of the University of Paris. The word of God, from his mouth, had such a burning, blazing power, that the coldest and most frozen hearts were melted into penitence.[1] The most obdurate were forced to cry out in the groans and anguish of conviction. His delivery, his gesture, the whole expression of his person, contributed to the effect. Sometimes he personated others, and made his sermons assume the form of dialogue. The farmer quitted his harvest field, the artisan forsook his worshop, to catch a sight or to hear the voice of the wonderful man. Nor did he speak only in the cities or villages. No church could have held the crowds that flocked to hear him. He took his stand in the broad plain, where thousands might be gathered to listen to his voice. They came from leagues around, and many of them

---

[1] Clemengis Lit. p. 315.

came not in vain. They saw and heard, only to be
convicted, converted, and reformed. They found in
Vincent a John in the wilderness, a man severely
simple and abstemious, whose life corresponded with
his words, and who practised what he preached.
" He did not belong," says Clemengis, " to the Phari-
see class, who occupy Moses' seat, who say and do
not." The gifts that were offered him he refused.
True to his vow of poverty, his fare was simple and
his raiment plain. He would not own a change of
raiment, and only accepted the offer of a new garment when the old was worn out. Thus he went
from province to province, and from kingdom to
kingdom, leaving behind him in the results of his
labor, and the reform effected, the seals of his ministry. One of the noblest testimonies to his true
worth and integrity is the fact, that all the public
applause that trumpeted his name over Europe left
him still the same humble, devoted, incorruptible
witness to the truth that he was when he first
tremblingly ventured, at repeated solicitations, to
ascend the pulpit. His ability and integrity are attested by the fact of his appointment as an arbitrator
in various matters, but especially in one that concerned the inheritance of the Castilian crown.[1]

The defection of such a man from the cause of
Benedict gave it a mortal blow in the popular esteem. The last evasions of the obstinate old man
had satisfied him that he was fully determined to
persist to the last in his schism, and Vincent was no
longer his dupe. He did all in his power to persuade

[1] Godeau, xxxvi. 313.

Benedict to yield, but the eloquence that had swayed nations was powerless to change the purpose of his former master. From a devoted adherent, Vincent became a zealous opponent. It was he who preached on the occasion of the publication of the edict for withdrawing obedience, which he himself read from the pulpit.

Vincent's course seems to have been conscientious throughout. In no instance do we discover him influenced by motives of selfish interest or personal advantage. His renunciation of the pope bears, therefore, those marks of sincere conviction which entitle it to our respect. We find the effort afterward made by Gerson to induce Vincent to come to Constance.[1] Undoubtedly he would have found in him a congenial spirit and a well-wisher, if not a colaborer in his projects of reform. But there is reason to believe that Vincent felt that Constance was no place for him, and that his powers would be wasted upon an assembly of whose real character he must by this time have been fully aware. Like Clemengis, he chose to keep space enough between himself and the council. Was he suspicious lest they should be inclined to question his orthodoxy? They might have done so with almost as much reason as in the case of Huss. His sympathy with the Flagellants at least might have raised suspicion of heresy.

The Bohemian reformer and the apostle of the west were brothers in spirit, and we can scarce doubt that had they truly known each other, they would

[1] L'Enfant, 487.

have bid and received a mutual good-speed in their noble work.

The emperor had accomplished all that was possible for him in Spain. The other princes, beside the king of Aragon, had given hopes of joining with him in renouncing Benedict's allegiance. But there was opposition in their states, and some wavered. The emperor directed his course to Paris. The great battle of Agincourt had been fought, but a few weeks previous, (Oct. 25, 1415,) and English valor had won the day. It was a terrible blow to France. The right hand of her power was cut off; her army and a large number of her nobles and knights were slain, or taken captive. The emperor sought to restore peace to the warring nations. The common foe of Christendom was thundering at the gates of the empire, and the story of Turkish invasion and cruelty was ever ringing in Sigismund's ear. He wished to unite the nations in a crusading warfare against the infidel. By his mediation he succeeded in procuring between England and France a truce of ten years.

But already the blow struck at Agincourt was producing its effect. The humiliation of the weak king of France was relatively the exaltation of the powerful Duke of Burgundy. Henry V. of England had only fought the duke's battles. The fruits of victory did not cross the English channel. The most obvious result was that the murderer of the Duke of Orleans was delivered from all danger on the side of France. It was all in vain that at this moment the French king wrote to the council to

urge the condemnation of Petit's propositions.[1] It
was in vain that the university reiterated its complaints.[2] It was in vain that the emperor himself
wrote once and again expressing his indignant abhorrence of principles that exposed his own life to
the stroke of the assassin.[3] The advocates of the
Duke of Burgundy became more bold and earnest
in their opposition. A majority of more than two-
thirds of the eighty-four doctors, who were directed
to give in their written opinions on the subject, were
against Gerson and France.[4] These last appealed to
the council in full session. The discussions were
violent and protracted. The difficulties in the way
of proceeding were continually aggravated. Day
after day the nations assembled to discuss the subject, but no advance was made. Nothing could be
concluded. The council declared expressly that no
condemnation of the propositions should prejudice
the person or honor of individuals.

The intelligence of the articles of "The Capitulation of Narbonne," meanwhile, (Feb. 4, 1415,)
reached Constance. The council assembled to hear
them read, and to swear to their solemn observance.
They did this, not as a council, but as an assembly
of cardinals, bishops, etc. Instead of the Cardinal
de Viviers, the president of the council, the Archbishop of Tours was the moderator of the assembly.
Sixteen cardinals, more than fifty bishops, more than
twenty abbots, and more than one hundred ambassadors and deputies took oath to observe the articles
of "the capitulation." Some, however, protested

[1] L'Enfant, 312.   [2] Ib., 368.   [3] Ib., 354.   [4] Ib., 373.

against portions of them, or against their being understood in a sense prejudicial to what they claimed as their right.[1]

It was while these matters and those of John Petit were occupying the public attention of the council, that Theodoric of Munster (Feb. 16, 1416) preached a sermon, in part with reference to Benedict XIII., but mainly bearing upon the vices of the clergy and the abuses of the church.[2] It serves to show the feelings and opinions of at least a respectable minority of the council, and how strongly some of them must have sympathized in a portion of the views of the man whom they had sent to the stake. He took for his text the words, "Go ye also into my vineyard," and improved the occasion, naturally, to condemn the indolence of the ecclesiastics, and the abuses and disorders in which it resulted. By the vineyard he understands, first, the Holy Scriptures, which the bishops and priests are to cultivate by study; and, in the second place, the church, which is confided to their care. The negligence, idleness, and vicious life of the clergy are severely rebuked, and their conduct in leaving their flocks to indulge in luxury is sharply arraigned. "Yet," says the preacher, "it would be something tolerable if, in their dislike to labor in the vineyard, they would at least serve as scarecrows, to drive away the birds; but since they merely spread around them the stench of their vices, they can only be regarded as carrion, to attract ravenous beasts to trample and ravage the vineyard of the Lord. Such prelates deserve to be

---

[1] L'Enfant, 365.   [2] Ib., 370.

deposed, not only as useless servants, but as nuisances that make others breathe their pestilent corruption. . . . . It is a great error to believe, as some do, that a pope should be deposed only for heresy, if by this we are not to understand sins public, scandalous, and maintained with shamelessness and obstinacy." In these words he refers to the grounds on which Benedict might be proceeded against. He then goes on to condemn other faults of the ecclesiastics: their neglecting the study of Holy Scripture, to apply themselves to canon law and the decretals, for purposes of gain. Not that he would have the latter absolutely neglected; but the principal study of prelates and pastors should be the word of God, in order to preach, inasmuch as this is the original authority by which all positive law—which, moreover, is necessarily faulty and subject to change—must be tried. Enforcing his position by examples, he remarks, in language little respectful to the papacy, "That the convocation of the council and the deposition of one of the rival pontiffs would have been impossible, if it had been required to follow the new canon law which gives to the popes alone the right of assembling councils, and which lays down the principle that the pope cannot be judged except for heresy alone." Again the preacher remarks, "Now we see positive laws,—that is, the canon law, the decretals, and constitutions of the popes,—exalted above the law of God and the commandments of Jesus Christ. This is the case even in this council, where the prelates fear more to disregard the authority of the Clementines, than that of the decalogue.

They take more pains to see that court rules are observed, than to prevent propositions being advanced opposed to faith and to gospel morals."

Such language was bold enough, and could scarcely have been acceptable to the majority of the council. But many of its positions had fully been illustrated in the proceedings that had taken place, especially in the case of Huss. The speaker's reference to the scriptures as above all the authority of what he called positive law, fully coincided with the position taken by Huss upon his trial. It seems difficult to explain how such language could have been used,—so much in the spirit of invective employed by the Bohemians, and so fully justifying what the council had branded as heresy. But it is evident that there were those at the council—and if united, forming a powerful minority—who were yet anxious and earnest on the subject of reform. It was impossible to silence them altogether, and it might have been a politic measure to allow them the satisfaction of having their views expressed. The statements which they presented were, moreover, so indisputably true, that the only answer they could receive was a silent acquiescence.

CHAPTER VII.

JEROME BEFORE THE COUNCIL.

CITATION OF THE BOHEMIANS. — THE DECREE. — DISPOSITION OF THE COUNCIL TO-
WARD JEROME. — HIS CONDITION AND STATE OF MIND IN PRISON. — REFUSES TO
RECOGNIZE HIS NEW JUDGES. — THE LIST OF CHARGES AGAINST HIM. — HIS RE-
PLIES. — ON WICKLIFFE. — ON CONTUMACY. — VARIOUS CHARGES. — PHILOSOPH-
ICAL SUBTLETIES. — TRANSUBSTANTIATION. — SONGS WRITTEN AND SUNG. — ALL
MAY PREACH. — UNJUST EXCOMMUNICATION INVALID. — INDULGENCES. — TREAT-
MENT OF THEM THAT SOLD THEM. — PAPAL BULLS. — PICTURES OF THE SAINTS. —
RELICS. — MARTYRS OF PRAGUE. — FAVOR TO THE GREEK CHURCH. — JEROME'S
RECANTATION HYPOCRITICAL. — HIS LETTER TO VIENNA. — DISHONEST PURPOSE IN
COMING TO CONSTANCE. — WILL NOT ACKNOWLEDGE HIS ERRORS. — REFUSES TO
FAST. — DEMAND THAT HE SHOULD ANSWER ON OATH. — EXTENDED PERIOD OF
JEROME'S LIFE COVERED BY THE CHARGES. — JEROME'S REPLIES. — ADMISSIONS,
EXPLANATIONS, AND DENIALS. — JEROME ALLOWED A GENERAL DEFENCE. — HIS
VIEWS AND FEELINGS. — HIS SPEECH. — REFERS TO ANCIENT MARTYRS. — UNI-
VERSITY OF PRAGUE. — EULOGY OF HUSS. — HIS COURSE. — JEROME'S VISIT TO
CONSTANCE. — HIS TREATMENT. — HIS RECANTATION DISAVOWED. — HIS VIEWS OF
WICKLIFFE. — HIS SUBSTANTIAL ORTHODOXY. — HIS FATE SEALED BY HIS AP-
PROVAL OF HUSS. — HEROISM OF JEROME. — POGGIO BRACCIOLINI. — HIS LETTER IN
PRAISE OF JEROME. — ABLE DEFENCE OF THE LATTER. — HIS MANLY BEARING. —
HIS RETORTS. — WONDERFUL POWERS. — HIS MEMORABLE ELOQUENCE.

FEB. 16, 1416 — MAY 26, 1416.

THE condition of things in Bohemia had now become such as to excite the well-founded alarm of the
council. Their proceedings were boldly arraigned,
and their authority contemned. The Bishop of Leitomischel, bearing their commission, found himself
unable to execute it. His person, and even his life,
were considered as endangered in the attempt. The

(195)

whole nation was in a ferment. At length, on the twentieth of February, 1416, the matter was brought before the council. It was decreed that the followers of Huss, in Bohemia and Moravia, should be cited to appear and answer such accusations as had been, or should be, brought against them.

The main ground of citation was the charge against the council, implied in the statement that Huss "had been unjustly executed, and in violation of all truth;" in the assertion that "he was a good and holy man, of excellent and innocent life and pure in faith;" and in ascribing his execution to "the envy of a luxurious and wanton clergy." The citation therefore extended to all those who had signed or affixed their seals to the letters addressed to the council. It comprehended the ablest and most learned men of Bohemia, as well as officers of the royal court.[1]

"We are confident that all Christendom is fully aware, as well by previous councils as by the present one, that Satan has, in these last times especially, excited heretics or ministers of damnation against the whole ecclesiastical edifice; that these attempts have been to overthrow the Catholic faith, and the laws and usages given by the holy fathers, and till the present time inviolably observed by Catholics; and among these men are John Wickliffe and John Huss, heresiarchs, as plainly appears from their works and writings. These persons unwarrantedly assume to be doctors, and wishing to pass among the people for new law-givers and rabbis, have plunged into ex-

[1] Van der Hardt, iv. 610.

travagant and damnable errors, in contempt of the
holy doctrine and the traditions of the fathers, in
such sort that the greater part of them are sectaries
of Satan, who, wishing to rise above all that is worshipped in heaven, have been plunged to the bottom
of hell, and cease not to draw men after them into
the pit of their damnation. These men, wishing to
raise themselves and their traditions above the hierarchy of the church militant, have associated many
with them, even of the priestly order, who, after the
manner of Theudas the Galilean, boasting to be new
law-givers, have seduced multitudes. And what is
more surprising is, that the number of the followers
of these heresiarchs goes on increasing continually, as
we know, alas! too well, by the report of many, and
by public rumor, especially in Bohemia and Moravia.
There are among them even persons of rank, who
are leagued together to maintain John Huss and his
errors, and who, adding sin to sin, nor content with
their malicious speeches and feigned devotion, write
out slanderous documents, confirmed by their seals,
in which they undertake the defence and eulogy of
John Huss, though he has been burned by the just
judgment of God and by our holy sentence. They
venture also to declare that they are resolved to
defend, even to the shedding of blood, these execrable heresies, and to maintain those who favor them.
And, as if to make themselves a spectacle to the
world by this monstrous error, they have been bold
enough to write us letters full of their venom and
poisoned lies. Touched, therefore, as a tender mother
by the ruin of so many unfortunate ones, whose eyes

have been fascinated by the devil, we have spared no pains to recover them from this diabolical obstinacy, and heal them of their frenzy, by writing to instruct them, sending them legates, and practising in regard to them a simulation, flattery, and patience that has, perhaps, been pushed too far. But, alas! all these remedies have only served to their injury. They refuse all obedience, they will not listen to the salutary instructions of the church, and instead of profiting by the counsels of peace and truth that have been given them, they rise up against the orthodox church, and strengthen themselves in iniquity. For these reasons we have resolved, by the aid of the Trinity, to oppose strenuously this damnable doctrine, and to proceed against these sectaries and followers of John Huss, through fear of incurring the indignation of the Most High by dissembling in regard to such great evils, after the example of the chief priest Eli, who, though in other respects a good man, drew down upon himself the divine vengeance for not having corrected the sins of his children, and sadly perished along with them. Therefore it is, that, wishing to proceed against them according to the *royal way*, after summary information; and having learned, on the testimony of people worthy of faith, that Czenko de Wesele, *alias* Wartemberg, supreme burgrave of Prague, Lasckow de Crauvartz, captain of the marquisate, and others who signed the letter of which we have spoken, are publicly charged and suspected in regard to the faith; and inasmuch as they may not safely be sought at their own dwellings, we cite them peremptorily,

by the present edict, which shall be publicly affixed
to the doors of all the churches of Constance."[1]

Leaving this citation to find its way to Bohemia,
let us return once more to the affairs of Jerome of
Prague. More than six months had passed away
since his recantation, and nearly a year since his first
arrest. The first term of his imprisonment had been
one of severe hardship. His treatment afterward
was more mild. There were those in the council
who were ready to set him free, or at least unwilling to subject him to a new trial. But over these,
the more moderate portion, embracing nearly if not
quite all those who had served on the commission in
his case, the opposing party prevailed. His enemies,
led or spurred on by personal hostility, welcomed the
announcement that new charges were to be presented
against him. Many of them, from the first, had been
suspicious of his sincerity in recanting. Doubtless
the conduct of Jerome must have tended to confirm
those suspicions. His was not a nature adroitly to
play the hypocrite. It was too frank, too impulsive,
too sensitive to self-disgrace, not sometimes to revolt
at the thought of his belying his own convictions.
During the last six months of his prison probation,
he had time to reflect. Memory could not but be
busy. Conscience must have sometimes reasserted
her sway; and, from his own confessions, we know
that the prisoner must have experienced an intense
wretchedness in reflecting upon his guilty weakness.
To the misery of a life prolonged on such conditions,
death was preferable. Jerome felt this. Remorse

[1] Van der Hardt and Mansi.

for the past was restoring him to himself, and when the hour of trial came again, as it now did, he was ready to meet it.

On the twenty-seventh day of April, (1416,) the council met, and the principal business before them was the case of Jerome. The processes for his trial had been issued more than two months previous[1] (Feb. 24). The Patriarch of Constantinople, and Nicholas Dinckelspuel, a theological doctor from Vienna, were directed, as a commission, to receive and examine testimony that should be adduced against him. These men visited Jerome, submitted to him the charges made, both the old and the new, and heard his answers. Their report was drawn up, and was now made to the council. It was read by John de Rocha, a theological doctor, a former friend and present defender of Petit, and in that matter one of Gerson's antagonists.[2] An old author of the "Life of Jerome" says, that he was reluctant to recognize this new commission that had been appointed for his second trial.[3] He certainly had the right to protest against its appointment over a previous commission, which had discharged its duty under the eyes and with the approval of the council. He refused at first to recognize the new commission, or reply to their questions. He demanded, as his right, a public audience.[4] Probably upon the assurance of this, he finally consented to defend himself in prison from the charges now presented.

The first head of accusation turned upon the con-

---

[1] Van der Hardt, iv. 607.   [3] Mon. Hus., ii. 352.
[2] L'Enfant, 380.   [4] L'Enfant, 380–383.

nection of Jerome with Wickliffe.[1] The answers of
the former to the several points, as they were read,
were also given. They were brief and direct. He
admitted that he had read the works of Wickliffe;
that he was aware of their having been condemned;
but to the charge of having taught the errors and
heresies contained in his books, he replied,—" For
myself, this much I have to say in answer, that it is
false that I taught errors and heresies out of his
books. But this I confess, that when I was a youth,
ardent in the cause of learning, I came to England,
and hearing of the reputation of Wickliffe, that he
was a shrewd and talented man, I transcribed, as I
could obtain copies, his Dialogue and Trialogue, and
carried them with me over to Prague."

The articles charged went over the most prominent acts of Jerome's life, bringing up as far as possible every instance in which he had shown a leaning
toward, or a disposition to defend, the views of Wickliffe. They maintained that he had been banished
from Bohemia for his violation of the edict in regard
to Wickliffe's books. He replied that he had not
been banished, but that when, through the letters
of the Archbishop of Prague, containing false statements, the king had been induced to deliver him up
to the archbishop, he had by the latter been gently
dealt with for some time, till the king sent one of
his barons, and ordered him to be released. Jerome
was charged, at the discussion in regard to Wickliffe
carried on in the university, with having maintained that Wickliffe was a Catholic, and that what

[1] Mon. Hus., ii. 352.

was contained in his books was most true. "I answer," said Jerome, "that I said that John Wickliffe had composed and written many good things in his books, but I did not say that all things contained in the said books were and are most true; for I had not seen them all. But this I do say, what good things Wickliffe wrote, let them be to his credit and not mine; and what he wrote ill, let him be blamed for, and not me."

He was then charged with having gone to Vienna, and there, on being arrested on the suspicion of heresy, having taken an oath to abide his trial and submit to his sentence, but instead of doing this had fled away by stealth. "I was violently arrested," replied Jerome; "but nothing was done judicially in regard to me, for I was of another diocese, and they had no jurisdiction; neither did I escape by stealth or through contumacy, but I did not choose to wait for their violent measures, as I was not obliged or bound to do."

Reminded that on the term for his appearance to be tried having expired, he had incurred by their sentence presumptive guilt of heresy, he answered, that after his departure they could have written in regard to him according to their caprice. The said processes, they continued, were published at Vienna, Cracow, Prague, and other places. "I am aware that they were published at Prague," said Jerome; "whether they were elsewhere or not, I do not know." He was then charged with contemning the keys of the church, in disregarding his sentence of excommunication for five years or more. He denied that he had contemned the authority of the church, adding that if he had ever been excommunicated, he had sought absolution. The Archbishop of Prague had prosecuted against him the process of Vienna, but without summoning him before him. As to his being incorrigible, he denied it. If he had been excommunicated, he even to this day was not aware of it; but whether lawfully excommunicate or not, he does not treat it with contempt, but asks to be absolved. Jerome was next accused of having slandered the pope, prelates, and lords; of having published these slanders abroad; of having, in the Bethlehem chapel while Huss was speaking, thrust his head out of the window and slandered the Archbishop Sbynco before the people; of having violently thrown the sacred relics, kept by a friar in the Carmelite monastery, to the ground; of having assailed the monastery with an armed crowd, and borne off a preacher who was speaking against Wickliffe, and kept him in durance for several days. Some of these charges Jerome denied. Other he explained. As to the last, he said, " I confess that in the case referred to, when I entered the monastery I found the monks contending with two citizens, whose servant they had thrown into prison. And when I spoke with them in a peaceable way, many of them, armed with swords, made a rush upon me. And although I had no means of defence at hand, I forcibly seized a sword from a certain layman who stood by, and protected myself as well as I was able. I then gave up two of the monks for trial, but one I kept with myself."

Other charges were added, some of them trivial,

and many of them referring to facts evidently distorted to his prejudice. He was then accused of
being a chief adherent of John Huss, approving of
him, in his doctrine and in his heresies, justifying him,
and seeking out defenders for him from Bohemia
and Moravia. To this he replied, that he loved John
Huss as a good man, and one who had diligently performed his duties, not drawn off by unchastity, and
of whom he had heard nothing heretical. Many
things, moreover, had been imputed to him, for which
he deserved no blame. As to his having been cited
to the court of Rome to abjure the heresy of adhering to Huss, Jerome denies that any citation had
reached him. As to his having excited seditions at
Prague by appearing in the streets at different times
with one and sometimes two hundred armed men in
company, he denied it, except as he had joined, with
a smaller number, the royal escort. Other articles
of accusation betrayed their origin in feelings of personal spite or malice. He was charged, moreover,
with having maintained, at different places, especially
at Paris, Cologne, and Heidelberg, certain propositions, more of a philosophical than theological nature.
Among them were the following :—" In God, or the
divine Essence, there is not only a trinity of person,
but a quaternity and quinternity of things (*rerum*),
such that each of these is not another and yet each
is God : in created things there may be a trinity in
a single essence, as memory, understanding, will, in
the essence of the human soul : the soul of man is a
perfect image of the trinity, with the single exception that it is created, and has but a finite perfection :

the memory, the intelligence, or will of an angel is
his essence, and yet not a person: God the Father
could not beget the Son by the absolute power of
deity: all things to come will take place by a con-
ditionated necessity: the substance of the bread is
not, by virtue of consecration, changed into the body
of Christ: John Wickliffe was not a heretic, but a
holy man: God cannot annihilate any thing." These
propositions Jerome was charged with having maintained.   Even as they stand, they fall far short of
that speculative wantonness of disputation which
only a few years before had prevailed at the University of Paris.   Jerome's reply to them was, that these
propositions, understood in the proper sense, were
true, though they were not presented in his style, yet,
in regard to some of them, what sounded as his language had been employed in order to express them.
[1] These charges and their answers having been read,
the council, by the instigation of his enemies, and at
the demand of its prosecuting officer, determined
that more should be added to the already extended
catalogue.   After some other business had been transacted, these also were read.   They were much more
extended than the first, and in fact substantially repeated them, though in a more ample manner, with
many additions.   They go back in their specifications
so as to cover a space of more than twelve years.
The mere recital of them, aggravated as they were
by the ingenious malice that drew them up, was well
calculated to prejudice the cause of the prisoner in
the minds of his judges.   Yet they are valuable—

[1] Van der Hardt, iv. 646.

even from the hostile source from which we derive them—as giving something of a picture, however distorted, of Jerome's life.

The first and main point charged in the new indictment, was the dissemination and defence of Wickliffe's doctrines. It stated the methods which Jerome had employed for this purpose: copying Wickliffe's books; recommending them to others; circulating them as he had opportunity, at Prague and elsewhere, declaring that those students who had not read them had but attained the mere bark of learning instead of discovering its roots; persuading them to reject their ordinary and approved text-books, to peruse those of Wickliffe; defending the reputation of the man, and showing himself so zealous a favorer and champion of him and his errors, that many persons, of both sexes, formerly Catholics, had been drawn away from the faith, and fallen into heretical pravity, becoming so blind and obstinate in their error, as to assert that their false opinions were gospel truths, and to boast that in all respects they followed the gospel and the doctrines of Christ. The indictment asserted, that after the various condemnations pronounced upon the writings of Wickliffe at Oxford, Rome, and Prague, Jerome, who could not be ignorant of the facts, had still persisted in maintaining Wickliffe's opinions, had defended them publicly, had disputed and offered to dispute in their favor, and had dared, in the lecture-room of Prague, and in the Bethlehem chapel, to speak of Wickliffe as a most holy man, a preacher of the gospel, and a teacher of the true faith. He had, moreover, pro-

ceeded to use violent means to silence opposition.
Here the indictment recapitulated charges already
mentioned. The opinions of Wickliffe on the eucharist, indulgences, etc., were then cited as endorsed by
him. For the space of ten years, at different times,
Jerome had maintained that in the sacrament of the
altar the material bread remained after consecration, and that in this sacrament the bread is not
transubstantiated into the body of Christ ; and this
he had induced many to believe, who still persevere
in their error. He had maintained, that in the sacrament of the altar Christ is not truly present, and the
argument used was this : Christ suffered on the cross ;
but the host never suffered, nor does suffer ; therefore,
Christ is not in the host, in the sacrament of the altar.
Again : Mice cannot eat Christ ; but mice can eat the
consecrated host ; therefore, the host in the sacrament
of the altar is not Christ. Again : The host in the
sacrament of the altar is not God,—for a priest cannot consecrate his Creator, that is, God ; but the
priest consecrates the host ; therefore, in the host of
the altar, the Creator, God, is not.

Jerome was accused of maintaining, that no one
could receive the heavenly crown who did not confess
with heart and mouth the doctrines of Wickliffe ; of
promising, after this life, the triumphs of glory to
those of all classes who should defend Wickliffe's
doctrines, and impugn the contrary ; of writing, and
procuring to be written, songs and doggerel verses,
ridiculing the mass, which were learned and sung by
the artisans, who said, that by these they also could
make the body of Christ, so that the priests were

subjected to seditions, wrongs, and insults. He moreover took the language of scripture, and versified it,
so that it might be sung, as it was in the streets,
leaving the impression, to the confusion of the ecclesiastics, that they (the singers) alone, and not the
church of Rome or any of the clergy, understood
the scriptures. After he had taught men these, he
had said and preached that the laity who had learned
them, and that too of both sexes, that is, men and
women of the Wickliffite sect, and holding Wickliffe's doctrine firmly and devotedly, might make the
body of Christ, baptize, hear confessions, or bestow
other sacraments of the church, provided they use
fit words, and adapted to the consecrating or sacramental act; and that the sacraments performed by
these are as efficacious and valid as if they were performed or bestowed by priests, according to the
church form. He had taught, moreover, in various
parts of Bohemia, but specially in the Bethlehem
chapel, the heresy held by John Huss—we may add,
by Clemengis, Gerson's intimate friend, also—that the
excommunication of the pope, or of any other bishop
or minister of the church, is not to be feared or regarded, unless it is evident that it has been preceded
by the divine excommunication; and he had taught,
moreover, that the excommunication of the defenders of Wickliffe's doctrine at Prague was to be accounted null, and to be disregarded, for God had
never bestowed on the pope, nor any other servant
of the church, any of his own attributes; and therefore, in spite of the interdict, the priests had been
compelled, in many places and cities of the diocese

of Prague, to celebrate and administer the divine
offices. Jerome, moreover, was accused of maintaining
that no authority for granting indulgences resides in
the pope or the bishops, and that no faith is to be
extended to letters, apostolic or episcopal, which contain indulgences.   Such indulgences were of no avail.
Those that preached them had been obstructed by
him in doing it, and been forced to desist. The indictment recounted the circumstances of the violent
opposition with which he had met them.   On one
occasion, John of Altamuta, and Benesius of Opta-
wich, had entered a manse belonging to a parish
church in a village of the diocese of Prague, intending to publish in the said church indulgences granted
by John XXIII.   Jerome heard of it, and gathering
a company of armed men around him, rushed into
the house in a state of excited passion, and with fury
in his looks.   He addressed the priests in harsh and
threatening language.   " Out with you, you deceivers, with your lies !   Your lord the pope is a false
heretic and a usurer.   He has no authority to grant
indulgences."   Jerome then threatened the priests,
drove them first into the church and then forth from
it, and followed them till he saw them outside the
walls of the village.   It was with difficulty, it was
said, that they escaped.   The indictment set forth,
moreover, that Jerome had said and asserted, in contempt of the keys and of the Apostolic See, that the
papal bulls were not to be credited, nor any faith put
in them, neither were the indulgences of the pope to
be believed in, inasmuch as they were null and void;
besides, it was out of the pope's power to give and

grant indulgences. When present himself at the preaching of them, he had hindered it; when absent, he had incited others to do it, and these men ran about through the city of Prague during sermon-time, entering the churches, disturbing those who preached indulgences, asserting that they were the deceivers and seducers of those among the people to whom they asserted that indulgences were of any avail. He had, moreover, taken the papal bulls, the letters apostolic containing the indulgences, and, putting them into a chariot with prostitutes, to whose breasts he bound them, had them drawn through the city. As the chariot moved on, it was surrounded with men crying aloud and shouting, "These are the letters of a heretic and a Russian, which we are taking to be burned." And in the street, near the centre of the city, he caused these bulls to be publicly burned.

Jerome, moreover, was accused of having held and taught, at Prague and elsewhere, that any educated or intelligent layman might, in any place, in a church or outside of it, without being licensed by pope, bishop, curate, or any one else, preach the word of God. He had, moreover, himself, though a layman and unshorn, preached, and thus practised what he preached, in different localities in Bohemia, as well as Moravia, on the ground that they who are called and sent of God seem to be sufficiently licensed. He had, moreover, said, asserted, and publicly preached, that pictures of Christ, of his crucifixion, of the Virgin and of canonized saints, are not to be painted, and that it is heretical to worship them. An image

of the crucifix he had insulted, and pelted with dung,
and procured others to treat it in the same way,
though many thronged to it in devotion.   The relics
of the saints he had declared were by no means to
be worshipped or adored.   He had said that the veil
and robe of the Virgin, in the cathedral church at
Prague, though reverently venerated by the faithful,
were of no more account, and to be held in no greater
reverence, than the skin of the ass on which Christ
rode.   Sacred relics he had torn from the altar, cast
to the earth, and trampled under foot.   He had
maintained, that those who died in defence of the
doctrine of Huss, which he claimed to be true and
Catholic, were true and glorious martyrs of Christ.
He had caused them to be borne in procession to the
grave, while the attendants chanted, "These are they
who gave up their bodies to punishment, according
to the will of God."   He had procured mass to be
said for them as martyrs, in the Bethlehem chapel,
and excited the multitude of that sect in such a way
that for several days scores of them went again and
again to the council-house of the city, saying that
those who had been beheaded were true martyrs,
and had died for the true faith of Christ, and that
they themselves were ready to undergo a like death
for the same faith.

The indictment then proceeds to specify other
articles classed by themselves, and evidently of less
weight or certainty, as that Jerome in Russia had,
on one occasion, openly forsaken the communion of
the Latin for that of the Greek church, publicly
offering insult to the former; that he had attempted

to seduce the Duke Withold, brother of the king of Poland, as well as others, to imitate his example; that when arraigned for his conduct before the Duke of Wilna, he had expressly declared that the aforesaid schismatics and Russians were good Christians. This he had done and repeated, in spite of the bishop's admonition to the contrary. At Pleskov again, Jerome had pursued the same course, giving his public approval to the infidelity, schism, and heresy of the said Russians.

The indictment then set forth that Jerome was not to be believed on oath, whether now or in time to come he should be sworn. His promises and abjurations were feigned, one way expressed by his mouth, but otherwise conceived in his heart. They had been made through hypocrisy, not with the purpose of abandoning his errors, but to afford him a chance to escape and scatter them abroad anew. A similar evasive course Jerome had pursued at Paris, where Gerson and others had endeavored to force him to recant, at Heidelberg, at Cracow, and again at Vienna, whence, notwithstanding his oath to submit to trial, he had secretly fled. It was stated, that after his flight from the latter place he wrote to the official of the church of Passau the following letter: "Venerable father, master, and lord! know that I am now at Wyetow, sound and well, in the company of many friends, and ready to serve ever you and yours. Hold me excused, if you please, from the promise extorted from me in respect to you, as you will do if you duly consider the nature of it. Not that we would prejudice justice, to which with due precaution we are ever ready to submit. But to stand among so many hundred enemies, alone, is what, if you love me, you would never advise. For my enemies have ploughed upon my back, and made long the furrows of their iniquity. But my soul has escaped like a bird from the snare of the fowler. The net has been broken, and we are at large. But I thank you, and ever shall thank you. Refer all my adversaries with their witnesses to me at Prague, and I will there take issue with them. Or, if it seem more fitting to them, let us each plead without witnesses in open court. But you must know that I was in your church in Laa, and there visited the master of the school and the notary of the city in memory of your kindness, and if I am ever able, I will serve you and yours. Farewell. Written at Wyetow. Yours ever, Jerome of Prague."

The same perfidy also, it was said, had been shown by Jerome in his coming to Constance, ostensibly to vindicate the purity of his orthodox faith, yet only with the intent to show himself off, and procure testimonials to strengthen his sect at Prague, in the belief that he had come off triumphant, and that the doctrine of Wickliffe was holy, just, and Catholic, and in no way to be reprobated. And yet he had secretly fled from Constance, and after having been brought back, and having, in his abjuration of the errors of Huss and Wickliffe, also promised that he would write to the king and the queen of Bohemia, the University of Prague, and others, that the condemnation of Wickliffe and Huss with their doctrines was canonical and just, he had yet, though

often admonished, refused to fulfil his promise aforesaid. Saying one thing while purposing another, he
had hitherto deferred writing; and even more than
this,—he had openly declared that he would not
write.

In the hope, moreover, that he had already satisfied
the council, and had taken measures to escape their
hands and custody, he had given himself up to an
elated, rebellious, and reprobate mind, refusing to
answer under oath to the articles charged against
him, and still refusing, in violation of his promise.
Instead of showing contrition, he maintains also that
he has ever been a good Christian, and free from all
stain of error or heresy. Neither will he submit to
be in any manner reproved. If this is attempted, or
he is charged with any guilt, he at once becomes
angry. He even asserts that injustice has been done
him in the imprisonment in which he is now held,
and demands damages therefor. He says expressly,
" I am an innocent man. Who will refund me damages ? " In his perverse obstinacy he still continues,
notwithstanding all his feigning in regard to his patient endurance of his imprisonment and his professions of apparent compunction, always intending to
defend the doctrine of Wickliffe, as argued by Huss.
This is plain, from his written statements, read in
this place of public session, where he said expressly,
among other things, " I call God to witness, that I
never have seen in his (Huss) conduct, or heard in
lectures and sermons by him, any thing exceptional.
Nay, I confess, that for his gentle and correct life,
and the sacred truths which he explained to the

people from the word of God, I was his intimate friend—for his person, and for truth's sake, a defender of his honor in whatever place I might find myself." From this, it is plain that he refused to write to the king and queen of Bohemia and the University of Prague. The same also may be inferred from many other things which evidence his extraordinary presumption, which was sufficient ground for his condemnation. Nor did the adversaries of Jerome forget to bring against him in the indictment the charge brought against Christ of old, that he did not practice fasting. They represented him as fond of good living, and more luxurious in his diet in prison than when at large.

They then ask that, as Jerome is a layman, and has ever borne himself as such, wearing a lay dress and a long beard, and notoriously bearing himself as a layman in public session, he may be forced, under pain of torture, to answer to each of the articles *credit* or *non credit*, to the end that he might no more, through hypocrisy, contrive to escape or secure relaxation from the severity of his imprisonment, so that, like hardened Pharaoh, he might afford comfort to his followers in their errors. If, however, after the matters aforesaid shall have been credibly proved against him, and he shall persevere in his contumacy, then, as an obstinate and incorrigible heretic, let him be given over to the secular court, according to the rules of the sacred canons.[1]

Such was in substance the long and tedious indictment against Jerome, which had been drawn up by

---

[1] The document is given in full by Van der Hardt, tom. iv.

the ingenious and unrelenting malice of his enemies. It occupies more than twenty folio pages of Van der Hardt's compilation. The reading of it must have been enough for a single session. It was in some respects most artfully framed. It went over a large part of Jerome's life,—followed him from Oxford to Paris, to Heidelberg, to Cracow, to Vienna, to Prague, and to Constance,—gathering up whatever could be found which could be so distorted or misrepresented as to excite prejudice against him. Many of the charges of the indictment were unquestionably true. Others, the prosecution would not be held responsible to prove. Undoubtedly they had been exaggerated, and in some instances must have been based merely on rumor. The statements in regard to his communing with the Greek church in Russia, Jerome pronounced false. Other charges he could undoubtedly have explained, in a manner to suffice for his perfect justification.

These charges were read on the twenty-seventh of April. On the ninth of May the judges of the commission made a report, by the mouth of the Patriarch of Constantinople, their president, in regard to the merits of the case and the forms of process to be adopted. This report was unanimously concurred in by the seven judges of the commission who were present. As Jerome was unchanged in his purpose of demanding a public audience, and refused to answer on oath before the commission which had been last appointed, a general congregation was assembled on the twenty-third of May, in order that he might be heard. He still refused to answer on oath in this assembly, unless they would first assure him full liberty of speech. This the council refused. The last portion of the indictment, containing the articles to which he had not answered, was now read, and Jerome replied to each, briefly, as the council required. This part of the indictment was drawn up in one hundred and one *items*, as the first part, already referred to, was in forty-five. As each article was read, the number of the witnesses by whom its truth was attested was also given. No names were mentioned, neither do we find the quality or office of the persons recorded, as in the case of the trial of John XXIII. There was the same or even greater mockery of the claims of justice than in the case of Huss.

To some of the articles read Jerome made no reply. Either he admitted their truth, or felt that the brief answer which he would be allowed to, make would fail to set forth the facts in their true light. As a general thing, the articles charging Jerome with violence were met by him with a prompt denial of their truth.[1] As to the matter of the songs which he was said to have taught and procured to be sung at Prague, in derision of the priesthood, as also with regard to the burning of the pope's bulls, he maintained that these charges were false. He admitted that he had studied the writings of Wickliffe, yet not without discriminating the good from the evil; that he had eulogized him as a philosopher and a learned man, not as a heretic; that he had placed his picture in his study just as he had the portraits of other em-

<hr>

[1] L'Enfant, 390, 391.

inent men, but had not placed a crown upon it as was charged. He claimed that he had not disputed in the Bohemian tongue on the sacrament of the altar; but admitted that he had spoken of John XXIII. as a usurer; that he had said that an unjust excommunication was of no validity; that there might be such a thing as indulgences, lawfully granted,—maintaining, however, that those which were bought and sold by the fiscal agents of the pope were mere extortion—they were not indulgences, but abuses of them; that, in regard to the privilege of every layman to preach the word of God, he had taken for his theme, on one occasion, the words, " As I do, so do ye also,"—and in this address he had introduced the remark that laymen and unordained clergy might preach.

Jerome had answered to scarcely more than half the articles, when the time of the sitting was consumed, and the assembly adjourned over two days, to the twenty-sixth of May.[1] On this occasion, he was still pressed to clear himself by oath in regard to the articles charged. But he refused to do it. Such a demand, he said, seemed to him to be strange and unwarranted, but he would continue his answers as he had begun. Many of the articles first read turned upon the subject of relics, and the violence which he had shown them. These he declared generally to be either false, or distortions of the truth. On many points we have no record of his answers. And yet, all the objectionable positions which he

It is said, (Mon. Hus. ii. 352,) that Jerome was not led forth to execution on the previous day, simply because the council was unable to go through with all the articles before the time of closing the session.

was said to have maintained at different universities, were read to him. To many of them, doubtless, no reply was made; on others, his answers, if we had them, would in all probability throw light enough to show that they had been misunderstood or misrepresented by his enemies. At the same time it must be observed that the scholastic arts of the universities claimed, even in this age, large liberty of discussion, abused, sometimes with impunity, to the defence of monstrous propositions, by the side of which the most extravagant of Jerome's appear tame and moderate.

The Patriarch of Constantinople, with the approval of his colleagues, then summed up the several charges against Jerome, taking notice also of his replies. He concluded that a fourfold conviction of heresy was proved against him. But, he said, that since Jerome had repeatedly besought a public audience to be allowed him, his request had been generally acceded to, so that he might now be heard in public audience and expose whatever vain obloquy rested upon him.[1]

He then turned to Jerome, and told him that if he had anything to say, he was at liberty to say it, since the present congregation had been called for his sake, and no other. If he wished to say, allege, or propose anything in defence of his innocence, he might do it; and, moreover, if he chose to revoke his error, the council, proceeding with gentleness and mercy, would receive him back to the bosom of holy mother church,—since there had been in the church many

---

[1] Van der Hardt, iv. 756.

heretics, who had recanted their errors, reformed
their lives, and received penance for the sins which
they had committed. But in case he should decline
to pursue this course, the council would then be
under the necessity of proceeding against him according to the forms of law.[1]

Jerome was prompt to improve the privilege he
had so long and so anxiously desired. The hours of
his tedious imprisonment had restored him to himself. Pale and worn as he was, he arose and boldly
faced the assembly. All could see at a glance that
he was master of himself, and, notwithstanding his
long imprisonment and suffering, of all his wonderful powers. The memory of his shameful and cowardly recantation had filled him with remorse, but a
remorse that stung him to the purpose of a noble
disavowal of what he now accounted his disgrace.
His whole appearance must have commanded respect. His bearing throughout betrayed neither
timidity nor weakness. In the portrait of him, which
has preserved his features for us, we read the restless
energy and the daring promptitude of the man.
Nature had stamped upon his face the chivalry of a
heroic nature. No common soul spoke out in those
large piercing eyes, and that bold high forehead, and
those lips that seemed instinct with the eloquence
they uttered. Men gazed upon him with admiration.
He felt himself that he stood before the world, and
was resolved, with death before him, to bear a noble
testimony to the justice of his cause.

Jerome prefaced his defence with a prayer that

[1] L'Enfant, 391.

God would deign to aid him, and inspire him to speak only such words as should be fitting and consistent with the well-being and safety of his soul. He then besought all those present, that they would pray God, the Blessed Virgin, and the whole heavenly host in his behalf, that they would so illuminate his mind and his understanding that he might speak nothing that could tend to the prejudice of his eternal welfare.

"I am aware," said he, "most learned men, that many excellent men have suffered things unworthy of their virtues, borne down by false witnesses, condemned by unjust judges." He proceeded to the statement of his own case, in which he wished to show that his own innocence had been subjected to a like hardship. "Although certain judges had been deputed by the council, to whose examination he had submitted, and who had found in him nothing on which to ground the charge of heresy, yet now, at the instance of his jealous enemies, new judges had been deputed in his case—those who now occupied the bench—an act which he had ever considered most abhorrent and repugnant to justice and his own rights. To the further examination of these judges he never had submitted himself, nor would he ever recognize them as his judges. He then passed in review many eminent and heroic men, who had been put to death, driven into banishment, or unjustly thrown into prison. "If I, myself," said Jerome, "should in like manner be condemned, I shall not be the first, nor do I believe that I shall be the last, to suffer. Still I have a firm hope in God my maker, that yet, when this life is past, they who condemn Jerome unjustly, shall see him take precedence of them, and summon them to judgment. And then shall they be bound to answer to God and to him, and give an account for the injustice with which he was treated at their hands." He then spoke of Socrates, unjustly condemned yet refusing the opportunity offered for his escape, unmoved alike by the fear of prison and death, although so terrible to mortal flesh. He then spoke of the captivity of Plato, the banishment of Anaxagoras, and the tortures of Zeno, as well as the unjust condemnation, the exile and shameful death of many distinguished heathen, referring to Boethius, Rutilius, Virgil, Seneca, and others. He then passed in review eminent men of the Hebrew nation—Moses, a deliverer and lawgiver of his people, yet by them wronged and slandered; Joseph, sold into bondage through the envy of his brethren; Isaiah, Daniel, and many of the prophets, reviled as impious or seditious, and wrongfully condemned. He referred to Susanna, sentenced on the false witness of two priests, though delivered by the wisdom of the prophet, and to the fate of many who, though most holy men, had perished by unrighteous judgment. He then came down to the New Testament record, spoke of John the Baptist—of Christ himself, condemned by false witnesses and false judges—of Stephen the protomartyr, who, in like manner, through false witnesses, was arraigned, imprisoned, and stoned. The apostles themselves were all condemned to death, not as good men, but as seditious, contemners of the gods, and doers of evil deeds. It was no wonder, therefore, if he, by his jealous and lying enemies, should be condemned to the fire. "Yet," said he, "it is an odious thing that a priest should be condemned by a priest: and yet this has been done. It is more odious to be condemned by a college of priests: yet this too has taken place. But the crowning point of iniquity is, when this is done by a council of priests: and yet we have seen even this come to pass." As Jerome uttered these words every eye was fixed upon him. His indignant eloquence thrilled and awed the assembly. Yet they did not venture to interrupt him. Jerome bearded the lion in his den. The wild beast quailed before the steady, searching gaze of conscious integrity and power.

After this eloquent and impressive introduction, Jerome proceeded to particulars. He said that no one had ever condemned him but his former friends, now alienated by hostility, and the Germans, who had gone forth from Prague. He gave a brief and concise statement of the origin of the university, its endowment by Charles IV., for the especial benefit of the Bohemian people—compelled to go abroad from a land rich in nature's wealth, to reap in a foreign land the harvests of learning. In this university, the old jealousy between the Germans and the Greeks, who were represented by the Bohemians, their descendants, was revived. "The Germans formed the majority, and engrossed to themselves the offices of honor and profit, to the prejudice of the Bohemians, who were stripped of all. If a Bohemian graduate had not other resources, he must, in order to live, leave the university and go out into the towns and villages and support himself by teaching school. The whole government of the university, moreover, was in the hands of the Germans. They disposed of its benefices. They kept its seal. They had charge of its keys. They had three voices out of four in its suffrages, instead of being counted as a single nation. They could do as they pleased. The Bohemians were of no account. The same was the case in the city government of Prague. Of the eighteen members of the council, sixteen were Germans and two Bohemians. The whole kingdom was governed by Germans, who held all the offices. The Bohemian laity were of no account. I perceived this, as did Master John Huss, whom I always held as a valiant, just, and holy man. We, therefore, in our anxiety to put a stop to these things, went to the present king of Bohemia to explain to him, in the presence of some of the nobility, how things were, and what ill effects might follow to the destruction of the Bohemian language."

Jerome then stated the measures he had employed —persuading Huss to add his influence with the people. At the mention of that name, all the tender memories of their former friendship were revived, and Jerome proceeded to speak of his former associate as a just, holy, upright, devout man, and one who had been found abiding inflexibly by the truth. With such aid as could be obtained, through Huss and the Bohemian nobles, Jerome stated that he secured a complete revolution in the relations of the two nations, so that the Bohemians occupied the place previously filled by the Germans. Such, he represented, were some of the grounds of hostility that had incited his persecution.

Subsequently to this, Huss had inveighed against the clergy and the ecclesiastical orders. He had pointed out how the priests indulged in pomp and show and luxurious living, spending in feasts and ostentation the money which belonged to the poor. He had spoken of the benefices as designed by God, that the poor might be fed, churches built up and maintained, and that they should not be perverted to vile and unworthy ends. Upon this—Jerome proceeded to say—the clergy rose up against Huss and himself. They persecuted Huss through envy, and sent Michael de Deutschbrod (Causis), not a Bohemian, but a German, to the court of Rome, to secure the citation of Huss before it.

The result of all this was, that John Huss was at last excommunicated by the judges deputed by that court. Yet Huss himself appealed from that excommunication, and still, by virtue of it, he was forbidden to preach. Things being in this state, Jerome stated that he had persuaded Huss that he ought to go to the council, at Constance, where he might fully set forth the real state of things, vindicate his innocence, and defend himself in reference to the penalties and pains unfairly imposed.

Jerome then stated the facts of Huss' going to Constance, his imprisonment, and the charges of heresy brought against him. He said that on learning these things, he himself fulfilled his promise made to Huss, and followed him to Constance. Thence, by the advice of men of power and influence, and from ap-

prehension of imprisonment, he had fled the distance
of a few miles to a village, where he remained for the
space of five days, writing meanwhile to the emperor
that great injustice was like to be done to Huss since
he had come provided with a safe-conduct, and even
a Jew or a Saracen ought to be free and unmolested
in coming, staying, stating and pleading his case, and
in departing, at his own pleasure, and according to
the tenor of the safe-conduct granted to Huss. Many
similar documents also he had sent to Constance,
which were affixed to the doors of the churches and
to the gates of the dwellings of the cardinals. Receiving no reply to these, he had departed from the
place where he had tarried, and set out on his return
toward Bohemia. On his way he was arrested, and
sent, by the council's direction, bound in chains to
Constance. Here, on his arrival, he had been cast
into prison.

All these circumstances Jerome dwelt upon, and
then described the treatment which he had received
at the hands of the council. He had been charged
with heresy. A commission was appointed to direct
the process against him. He had been over-per-
suaded, by certain great men, to refer himself to the
council, and submit to the conditions it should impose. It was their hope and expectation that he
would be kindly treated. In these circumstances,
afraid in his human weakness of the fire, the heat of
which was most cruel, and death by which was most
fearful, he had yielded to these persuasions, and
abjured, and had moreover written his abjuration to
Bohemia. He had also given his assent to the con-

demnation of the books of John Huss and their doctrine. But in this, said he, "I did not express my true belief." This much he confessed he had done in violation of his conscience, since the doctrine of John Huss, like his life, was holy and just, and in this conviction he would abide, and to it he would firmly adhere. And to confirm this impression, he had recalled the letter written to Prague, in which he had recanted the doctrine and the opinion which he had of Huss.

He said, moreover, of the books of Wickliffe and of his doctrine, 'that he never had met with the man whose writings were so excellent and profound.' This opinion he would adhere to, and he had done wrong in speaking otherwise. For as to what he had done in his recantation of his views of Huss and of his doctrine, he had not done it with the intention of desisting from them, but, through cowardice and fear, he had suffered the dread of the fire to extort it.

But whatever Huss or Wickliffe may have said erroneous in regard to the sacrament of the altar, and against the doctors of the church, he rejects, and, in this respect, does not follow or hold their opinion. His own views are those held by Gregory, Ambrose, Augustine, Jerome, and others, whose authority is admitted throughout the church. He also declared, that he considered the conduct and practice of the popes and cardinals, their disposal of benefices, their luxurious indulgence and style of dress, to be unwarranted, and indefensible on the grounds of truth and reason, as well as opposed to scripture and the order of the church. And on this point he

holds as Wickliffe and Huss hold, and he believes
that he is correct in so believing.

These scattered fragments of a speech, the impression of which must have been extraordinary, and the
spirit and ability of which filled even his enemies
with admiration, furnish us with a mere outline of
the plan and course of Jerome's argument. He seems
to have caught an inspiration in those prison hours,
when the thought of what others had endured before
him consoled his solitude, that lifted him as it were
above himself. On some points he is careful to state
his conformity to Catholic formularies, but on others
he avows his obnoxious opinions with a firm and uncompromising boldness. His doctrine on the subject
of the eucharist was not the one invented, in the
middle ages, for Berengar to tilt at, but the one held
by the early fathers. There was no real ground of
proceeding, however, against Jerome, except his endorsement of Huss and Wickliffe. The fact of his
approval of these men he did not attempt to conceal.
He frankly avowed it, and, as an act of simple justice
to the injured men, vindicated their memory. But
for this he might perhaps have yet been saved. He
had strong friends. His ability had found admirers;
men listened in astonishment and awe to his wonderful and impressive speech. But his enemies were
unrelenting, and his friends were disappointed. Instead of submitting to the council, he had impeached
its wisdom in the sentence of Huss. Instead of condemning the latter as a heretic, he had eulogized him
as a martyr. Thus his fate was sealed. None could
safely venture to be any longer his apologist. The

council appointed the following Sabbath, May 30th, as the time for pronouncing definitive sentence against Jerome.[1]

Thus passed from a transitory present into the permanent records of history, a scene that will be for ever memorable while truth is revered, or the martyr-spirit honored. Jerome was an orator. Nature had made him such. All the various learning of the age had helped to furnish his mind and discipline his powers. Gerson was perhaps the only man in Europe who could have been considered fairly his intellectual rival. But he was more than an orator —more than a learned man. It was the love of truth that made him eloquent, and it made him a martyr also. His false recantation had humbled him, but only to restore him to himself. He rose from his fall a wiser, a stronger, and a better man. He came from his prison, as if from the mount of transfiguration. There he had held communion with the mighty spirits of the past. There he had girded himself, in a more than human strength, for the mortal conflict. He remembered the example of Socrates, but he remembered also the example of Stephen; and his words and bearing remind us of both. Yet the philosopher is lost in the Christian martyr; and the man who does not gaze upon him with admiration, has lost, if he ever had, the power and sensibility to appreciate the noble and sublime in human action.

If any one was fitted to form a just estimate of the man and the occasion, it was one who witnessed it,

---

[1] Van der Hardt, 756–761.

and who has left us the record of the impression
which it made upon his own mind.　This man was
Poggio Bracciolini, who went to Constance as the
secretary of John XXIII.　He was a scholar.　His
taste had been formed on classic models.　John of
Ravenna taught him in the Latin tongue.　A knowledge of the Greek language, as well as of its orators,
poets, and philosophers, he had gained through the
celebrated Emanuel Chrysoloras, himself a native
Greek.　Above most of his Italian countrymen,
Poggio was an enthusiast in the cause of classical
learning.　To him we are indebted for the discovery
and preservation of the writings of Quintilian, Lucre-
tius, and others.　He travelled over Europe, and even
extended his journey to England, in search of the lost
treasures.　His merits continued him in office as papal secretary under seven popes.　He was a close
observer, careful and severe in his critical judgment,
and must be regarded a witness free from all suspicion of prejudice in Jerome's favor.[1]

Yet his account of the scene of Jerome's trial reminds us of Burke's eulogy of Sheridan's eloquence.
In spite of every bias against the prisoner, the papal
secretary was forced into an enthusiastic panegyric
of him.　Some portions of his letter to Leonard
Aretin, which have not already been incorporated
into the account of Jerome's speech, are of special
interest.　His descriptions are those of an eye-wit-
ness, and are truthful and vivid.　[2] " After having
spent some time at the baths, I wrote thence a let-

---

[1] Moreri. Dic. Histor.　　[2] Æneas Sylvius, p. 73.　Van der Hardt, i. 203.
Mon. Hus., ii. 358.

ter to our friend Nicholaus, which I think you must
have read. A few days subsequent, and shortly after
my return to Constance, the case of Jerome, charged
with heresy, was brought before the council. I determined to pass the matter in review before you, as
well for its own importance, as especially for the
eloquence and learning of the man. I confess that
I never saw one who approached so near, in pleading
his own cause—and that a capital one—to the eloquence of those ancient models which we regard
with such admiration. It was wonderful to see with
what language, what eloquence, what arguments,
what countenance, what oratory, and with what confidence he answered his prosecutors, and summed up
in his own defence. It is sad that so noble, so superior an intellect should have been led off to heretical
pursuits—if indeed the reports in regard to him are
true. But it is no business of mine to determine
this, for I but acquiesce in the sentence of those who
are accounted more wise. Do not expect from me a
documentary history of the case. That would be
tedious, and would require the labor of days. I will
only touch on some of the more prominent points,
by which you may understand the doctrine of the
man.

"After having produced many articles against him
to convict him of heresy, and corroborated them
by witnesses, they allowed him to answer to each
point urged against him. He was led into the midst
of the assembly, and required to reply to each charge
by itself. For a long time he refused to do so, declaring that he would plead his own cause before he

replied to the malice of his enemies. After he had
spoken and been heard in his own behalf, then he said
he would speak to the accusations and invidious
charges of his enemies. This condition the council
refused to grant. Jerome replied in an indignant
strain : ' What injustice ! you have kept me shut up
for three hundred and forty days, chained, in different prisons, in the midst of filth and stench, and in
want of every thing. You have given ear to my
enemies and slanderers, but will not listen to me for
a single hour. I do not wonder that when your ears
have been so long open to their persuasions, they
should have led you to believe that I was a heretic,
an enemy of the faith, and a persecutor of the clergy,
and that no chance of defending myself should be
allowed. You have by prejudice been led to account
me a criminal, before you could know that I was one.
But you are men—not gods, not immortal, but mortal men. You may err, be deceived, be misled. The
lights of the world, the wisest of the earth, are said
to be assembled here. It becomes you to see to it
that nothing be done rashly, unadvisedly, or contrary
to justice. I am a man, and my life is at stake. For
myself I do not speak. Sooner or later I must die.
But it seems an unworthy thing, that the wisdom of
so many men should proceed against me in violation
of equity, a course not so injurious for present results
as for future precedent.' [1]

" Much more did Jerome utter in the same noble
strain. But the noise and murmurs of the assembly
interrupted him in his speech. At length it was

[1] Mon. Hus., ii. 358.

decided that he should answer first to the charges against him, when full liberty of speech, as he demanded, should be allowed. The articles of accusation were read to him, one by one, with the testimony by which they were sustained, and he was then asked what objections he had to offer to them. It was wonderful with what ability he replied, and what arguments he urged in his own defence. He adduced nothing that was not worthy of a good man; and if his real belief was what he professed, not only could no cause of death be found in him, but not even the lightest ground of accusation. He declared that all that was urged against him was false, made up by the envy of his enemies. Among other things, when the article was read charging him with being a slanderer of the Apostolic See, an opponent of the Roman pontiff, an enemy of the cardinals, a persecutor of the prelates and the clergy, and an enemy of the Christian religion, he rose, and in tones of pathos, with lifted hands, exclaimed, 'Whither shall I now turn? Fathers, whose aid shall I implore? Whom shall I deprecate? Whom beseech? You? But these my persecutors have alienated your minds from me, in declaring that I am the enemy of all that are to judge me. For they imagined that, if the accusations which they have framed against me should seem light, you would condemn by your sentence one who is the common enemy and assailant of all, as they have falsely represented me to be. So that if you give ear to their words, I have no more hope of safety left.'[1] Often

---

[1] Mon. Hus., ii., 359.

his sarcasm was stinging.   Often, even in his sad and perilous situation, he forced the council to laughter as he exposed the absurdity of the charges against him, or met them with ridicule and sarcasm.

"When asked what he thought of the sacrament, he replied, 'First, bread in the consecration, and afterward the true body.' 'But,' said one, 'they say that you said, after consecration there remains bread.' 'Yes,' replied he, 'at the baker's.' A Franciscan monk inveighed against him: 'Silence, you hypocrite,' said Jerome. Another swore by his conscience. 'It is the safest way,' said Jerome, 'to carry out your deception.' One of his chief opponents he treated with derisive contempt. He spoke of him never except as 'dog' and 'ass.'"   Such was Jerome's defence on his second day of audience (May 23). Poggio characterizes it as able and pathetic. As he appeared at the next audience, (May 26,) the remaining accusations, with the testimony, were read, at somewhat tedious length. When the reading was ended, Jerome arose. "Since," said he, "you have listened so attentively to my enemies, it is befitting that you should give ear to me with equal readiness." Many clamored against it, but the opportunity at last was given him to proceed.[1]

Commencing with prayer to God for that spirit and that power of utterance which should tend to the advantage and salvation of his soul, he addressed the council in the language which we have already noted.[2] His exposition of his own life and pursuits, says Poggio, was admirable. It showed him great

[1] Mon. Hus., ii. 359.   [2] Pages 221–228.

and virtuous. The hearts of all were moved to pity.
As he discussed the differences of men in matters
of speculative opinion, he manifested a largeness of
mind and apprehension which was worthy to be
admired. " Of old, learned and holy men in matters
of faith had differed in opinion, yet not to the prejudice of faith itself, but to the discovery of truth.
Augustine and Jerome disagreed, nay opposed each
other on some points, yet neither was on this account
suspected of heresy."

Poggio pronounces Jerome to have been a man of
most remarkable ability.[1] " When interrupted, as
he often was in his speech, by clamors, or persons
carping at his language in a manner most provoking,
he left not one of them unscathed. All felt his vengeance, and were put either to shame or silence. If
murmurs arose, he paused and protested against the
disturbance. He would then resume his speech,
again and again interrupted, yet begging and beseeching them still to allow him liberty of speech,
whom they would never hear again. All the confusion did not break him down. He retained throughout his firmness and self-possession. How wonderful
was his memory, that never failed him, though for
three hundred and forty days thrust in the dungeon
of a dark and filthy prison ! Yet of this grievance,
which he indignantly complained, he said 'that as a
brave man it did not become him to moan about it
that he was treated with such indignity, but he was
surprised at the inhumanity which others had shown
him. In this dark prison he had no chance to read,

---

[1] Maximi ingenii fuit, Mon. Hus., ii. 359.

nor could he even see to do it.' I say nothing of his anxiety of mind by which he was harassed day after day, and which might well have destroyed his memory. Yet he adduced in his favor the authority of so many men of the highest wisdom and learning, so many doctors of the church whose words testified in his behalf, that you could not have expected more if the whole space of his imprisonment had been devoted in undisturbed leisure to the studies of wisdom. His voice was sweet, full, sonorous, impressive in its tones. His gesture was that of the orator, adapted, as occasion required, either to express indignation or to excite pity, which nevertheless he neither asked for, nor showed an anxiety to obtain. He stood before the assembly, so fearless and intrepid, not only scorning to live, but welcoming death, that you would have called him a second Cato. O man! worthy art thou to be forever remembered among men! I do not praise him in any respect in which he was opposed to the institutions of the church. I admire his learning, his extensive knowledge, his eloquence, and his skill in argument. I only fear that all nature's gifts have been bestowed to work his ruin."

CHAPTER VIII.

SENTENCE AND EXECUTION OF JEROME.

MAY 26, 1416 — MAY 30, 1416.

JEROME was borne back from the council to his dungeon, there to await his final sentence. The severity of his imprisonment, which had been somewhat relaxed, was now increased. He was more strictly fettered than before. His hands, his arms, and his feet were loaded with irons.

The members of the council were variously disposed toward him. Some were gratified, undoubtedly, that a stop was now to be put to his bold and agitating career. Others exulted over him as a fallen foe, and triumphed in his doom as the victim of their personal malice. Nearly all despaired of rescuing him. Those who had listened to his speech, and heard its candid and manly avowals, said to each other, " He has pronounced his sentence." Still there were many that could not thus abandon him. Numerous members of the council, embracing the most learned of the body, interested themselves in his behalf.[1] Poggio is said to have employed his influence to the same purpose. The Cardinal of Florence conversed with him, and endeavored to dissuade him from the resolution he had adopted. But all was in vain. Jerome saw no honorable way of escape from the fate to which he was doomed through his refusal to abjure. He was now at last resolved, living or dying, to remain true to his convictions. He scorned any more to dissemble, as he had done, and betrayed no longer any sign of weakness or hesitation. Death by fire was not so terrible as the disgrace and guilt of a feigned recantation,—the only one which it was possible for him to make.

If, in the earlier period of his imprisonment, Jerome showed himself tremulous and timid, as compared with Huss, these closing hours of his trial display his character in a nobler light. His prison experience was aggravated by some hardships from which Huss was spared. The latter had his friends, warm and true, who refused to desert him, and remained faithful to the end. In the enthusiasm of his gratitude, he writes of the generous countenance and sympathy afforded him by the Knight John de

---

[1] Poggio says that after his audience, (May 26th,) " Datum deine spacium pænitendi bidno. Multi ad illum accessere viri eruditissimi, ut ipsum a sua sententia dimoverent, inter quos Cardinalis Florentinus eum adiit, ut flecteret ad viam rectam."—*Mon. Hus.* ii. 360.

Chlum, and speaks of the consolation and strength which were thus ministered to him in his hours of weakness and despondency. The presence and counsel of those in whom he could confide lightened the load of his anxiety and anguish. They stood by him, and stood by him to the last. But when the deed was done,—when Huss was executed,—Constance was no longer the place for them. They departed, and Jerome was left alone. We hear no more of Chlum, Duba, or Peter the Notary. Jerome was kept a close prisoner; and, even had they remained, they would, probably, have been denied access to him in his prison-cell.

Who can enter into the anxieties and agony of the prisoner, wearing out his solitary hours in a close, foul, and gloomy cell, cheered by no friendly face or kindly word? And yet how noble, in such circumstances as these, was the self-recovery of Jerome! Uncounselled but by his conscience and his God, he rose from his fall, in the intrepidity and courage of a genuine martyr, blotting out, by an honest and hearty avowal of his error, the stain of what he thenceforth accounted his weakness and his disgrace.

The council met in its twenty-first session on Sunday, May 30th, 1416, to pronounce sentence upon the prisoner. There was no longer any doubt of the result—no chance, so far as any change in him was concerned, for averting his doom. A French writer,[1] quoting from Theobald's history of the Hussite war, gives a detailed account of the efforts employed to induce him to recant, some of which have been

[1] Bonnecnose, 122.

already referred to. "I will abjure," replied Jerome
to their urgent entreaties, "if you demonstrate to me
from the Holy Scriptures that my doctrine is false."

"Can you be to such an extent your own enemy?"
inquired the bishops.

"What!" replied he, "do you suppose that life is so
precious to me, that I fear to yield it for the truth,
or for Him who gave His for me? Are you not cardinals? are you not bishops? and can you be ignorant of what Christ has said: 'He that does not give
up all that he hath for my sake, is not worthy of me?'
. . . Behind me, tempters!".

The Cardinal of Forence presented himself. He
sent for Jerome, and said to him, "Jerome, you are
a learned man, whom God has loaded with the choicest of gifts; do not employ them to your own ruin,
but for the advantage of the church. The council
has compassion on you, and, on account of your rare
talents, would regret to behold you on your way to
execution. You may aspire to high honors, and be
a powerful succor to the church of Jesus Christ, if
you consent to be converted, like St. Peter or St.
Paul. The church is not to such a point cruel, as to
refuse a pardon if you become worthy of it. And
I promise you every kind of favor, when it shall be
found that neither obstinacy nor falsehood remains in
you. Reflect whilst it is yet time; spare your own
life, and open your heart to me."

Jerome replied, "The only favor that I demand—
and which I have always demanded—is to be convinced by the Holy Scriptures. This body, which
has suffered such frightful torments in my chains, will

also know how to support death, by fire, for Jesus Christ."

"Jerome," asked the cardinal, "do you suppose yourself to be wiser than all the council?"

"I am anxious to be instructed," rejoined Jerome, "and he who desires to be instructed, cannot be infatuated by ideas of his own wisdom."

"And in what manner do you desire to be instructed?"

"By the Holy Scriptures, which are our illuminating torch."

"What! is every thing to be judged by the Holy Scriptures? Who can perfectly comprehend them? And must not the fathers be at last appealed to, to interpret them?"

"What do I hear!" cried Jerome. "Shall the word of God be declared fallacious? And shall it not be listened to? Are the traditions of men more worthy of faith than the holy gospel of our Saviour? Paul did not exhort the priests to listen to old men and traditions, but said 'the Holy Scriptures will instruct you.' O Sacred Scriptures, inspired by the Holy Ghost! already men esteem you less than what they themselves forge every day! I have lived long enough. Great God! receive my life; thou canst restore it to me."

"Heretic!" said the cardinal, regarding him with anger, "I repent having so long pleaded with you. I see that you are urged on by the devil."

As the twenty-first session opened, the report of Jerome's firmness, as well as of his previous bearing in the prison conference, which had been noised abroad, drew multitudes together. His condemnation and execution made it to them, in anticipation, as it did to others afterward in retrospect, a memorable day. The emperor was still absent, but the Elector Pala tine occupied his place as protector of the council. By his orders the troops were called out and placed under arms. The Bishop of Riga then had Jerome led into the cathedral, once more to be cited to re-tract, and, in case of refusal, to hear his sentence.[1]

When he was formally called. upon to retract, according to some historians, previous to other pro-ceedings of the council in his case, he exclaimed, " Almighty God! and you who hear me, be wit-nesses! I swear that I believe all the articles of the Catholic faith, as the church believes and observes them; but I refuse to subscribe to the condemnation of those just and holy men whom you have unjustly condemned, because they have denounced the scan-dals of your life, and it is for this that I am about to perish." [2]

Jerome then repeated aloud the Nicene creed, and the confession of Athanasius, and spoke for a con-siderable time with as much ability as eloquence. All were lost in admiration at his knowledge and his admirable language. Several drew near him, and presented him with a new form of retraction, exhort-ing him to allow himself to be prevailed upon; but he refused to listen to any exhortation on that point.

The Bishop of Lodi then ascended the pulpit, and chose for his text [3] Mark xvi. 14. " Afterward he appeared unto the eleven, as they sat at meat, and

¹ Mon. Hus. ii. 353.   ² Ib.   ³ L'Enfant, 394.

upbraided them with their unbelief and hardness of heart." The sermon is curious in many respects. It betrays with a kiss—it stabs under the mask of charity. The logic of persecution whines and weeps, and recounts the evidence of its tenderness, as it strikes the victim. The introduction of the discourse is an attempt to show, that where milder measures fail more severe ones must be applied. "A hard knot cannot be split but by a heavy blow." "A virulent disease requires a more active remedy; a dangerous wound a more skilfully bound ligament. To bend the hard iron into shape, it must be subject to a hotter fire, and beat with a heavier hammer."

He then applied these principles to Jerome's case, and turning to the prisoner addressed himself directly to him: "I knew that thou wert stubborn, that thy neck was iron, and thy brow brass. But be assured that a hard heart shall have evil at last, and he that loves danger shall perish in it.

"Consider, also, that though my reproof sounds harshly to the outward ear, yet a charitable delight in mercy dwells within it. And, as by word and speech I ought not to spare you, so do I purpose, with good will and with gentle charity, to rebuke your faults. . . . Wherefore, think not that I wish to add afflictions to one already afflicted, or stir up the fire to a new heat by the sword. But that you may assuredly know with what charity you are to be reproved, with what love you are to be shielded, with what long-suffering and considerate kindness exhorted to relinquish your folly, I have selected for my proposed theme the words of the text."

The speaker then proceeded to state what had been the guilt of Wickliffe and Huss. Jerome likewise had come under the same condemnation. His unbelief, which had led to heresy and perfidy, was bad, but the hardness of his heart was worse by far. "Those who defend their error without stubbornness or obstinacy, and are still ready to be set right, are by no means to be reckoned heretics. But they who, despising the decisions of the fathers, endeavor, with all their might, to defend their perfidy, are more fit to die than to be corrected. . . . Error and unbelief are alike to be reproved, but stubbornness of heart is to be condemned. . . . Evils that might grow with time are at once to be met. Due correction should instruct ignorance, and severe discipline control obstinacy and hardness of heart. It is better, says Isidore, that one guilty one be punished for the good of many, than that many be endangered by the impunity of one. Wherefore, heretics are to be publicly extirpated, lest they ruin others by their evil example, false doctrine, and contagious influence. Unbelief, when it submits to correction, merits pardon; but stubbornness and obstinacy are only to be dealt with by exterminating them. Let no one then be presumptuously stubborn and contumacious in heart; let no one be confident in his own vain fancy. He is too hasty who resolves to enter where he has seen others fall, and he too reckless who is not struck with fear when others perish. When a fault is defended, it is repeated, and he adds sin to sin who shamelessly and obstinately defends his evil deeds. Hardness of heart is therefore to be detested, especially that which is not healed by contrition, controlled by devotion, or moved by prayers, which does not yield to threatenings, and is confirmed by blows. Hence he is inexcusably criminal who refuses to repent, and retains his pride.

"There are two things among human errors too hard to be tolerated: presumption before truth is discovered, and a presumptuous defence of what is false, afterward. No presumptuous man will confess his fault, because he does not believe himself guilty. If he sees it, he will not suffer himself to be convinced, or be regarded as delinquent. Most damnable, therefore, is a presumptuous pride, and a proud presumption, which, in the absence of truth, would arrogate to itself a fictitious justice, and ceases not to be proud of its own knowledge." Applying these principles in the case of Jerome, the bishop expresses his fear lest presumption should prove his ruin. Here was the hidden precipice; here, in this, the labyrinth of his errors. "This obstinacy of yours has procured your doom. Though you are a learned man, and have been a teacher, you have been deceived, as I think, by your excessive presumption. Error has led, step by step, to further error.

"I have purposed to smite you, Jerome, upon both cheeks, though ever with that fitting charity which heals while it wounds, and soothes while it pierces. Wherefore, turn not your face upon me like a flinty rock. But rather, according to the gospel, when you are smitten on one cheek, turn the other also. I will smite you, therefore, and would that I might heal. You ought to be softened in spirit by the memory of the crimes you have committed, and in view of the excessive benignity of your judges."

Premising that he does not throw another's filth in Jerome's face, but his own, that he may see and repent his crimes, the speaker proceeds to set forth the mischiefs done in Bohemia by Jerome and Huss. "Happy kingdom," he exclaims, "if this man had not been born! . . . . Of how great evils was the presumption of these two men the root! What violence, exiles, robberies, desolations, have sprung from it!"

Such, according to the bishop, was the blow on the one cheek. The other is, to say the least, hypocritically odious, though the tender mercies of the Bishop of Lodi were, beyond doubt, conscientiously cruel.

He proceeds to contrast the way in which a heretic deserved to be treated, with the gentleness used in Jerome's case. "Heretics ought to be carefully sought after, arrested, and committed to close prison. Articles of accusation should be received against them, and in their case, all sorts of persons, the infamous, usurers, the ribalds, or even public prostitutes, should be allowed to testify. Heretics, moreover, should be adjured and required under oath to declare the truth. On their refusal to do this, they are to be put to the torture, which should be severe and varied. None should be allowed admittance to them, except in extraordinary cases. They ought not to be allowed a public hearing. If they renounce their folly, they are to be mercifully pardoned; if they persist in it, they are to be condemned,

and given over to the secular arm." Such was the
theory, and such should be the practice, in dealing
with heretics, according to the Bishop of Lodi ; and
no voice in the council was ever heard to contradict
or even question this public announcement. The
background of his picture, thus prepared, was certainly black enough to make even the dark forms he
was to place upon it, seem light in comparison.

Addressing Jerome, he said, " You certainly have
not been treated with such rigor as this, although in
the worst repute for your heresies. In this respect
you surpass Arius, Sabellius, Faustus, Nestorius, and
all others, at least during their lifetime. The story
of your heresy has spread through England, Bohemia, France, Hungary, Poland, Lithuania, Russia,
Italy, and all Germany. You were arrested, as all
like you should be, and brought to the council, and,
through urgent necessity alone, shut up in prison.
And in regard to this imprisonment, the most reverend my lord cardinals, De Ursinis, Aquileia, Cambray, and Florence, personally interested themselves
to see if you could not be removed to some more
commodious place. And if they had not been apprehensive of your flight—a thing you had often
practised—each of them would have been willing to
receive you kindly to his house, and even to his
table and his chamber.

" Against you none but respectable witnesses were
admitted to testify—such as masters of theology,
doctors, bachelors, curates, and other venerable men,
in whom you could find no fault. The articles adduced against you were mostly proved to be true.

"You were not subjected to torture. Would that you had been! In this case, you might have been humbled and led to give up your errors. Pain would have opened your eyes, which your guilt had closed. Those, moreover, who chose to visit you, were allowed. Remember how kindly, how gently the most reverend lord cardinals, as well as many others, exhorted you, while they heartily pitied you also. A public audience has several times been granted to you, as you wished. Would that you had not been allowed it! I fear lest it have increased your daring presumption."

The bishop then enumerated six evils or mischiefs that had befallen, through the public audience allowed. "In the first place, you put it out of the power of those who kindly wished to apologize for you, to do so. It was their affection for you that made them speak of you as delirious, demented, foolish, or insane. Who, I ask, would say you were mad and delirious, unless he were delirious himself! What! of a man who could speak with such elegance, and plead with such precision! Those that excused you must now be silent. They can say no more. Your speech has closed their lips."

The bishop enumerated other things of an unfortunate nature, to be attributed to the same cause. In his speech Jerome had overlooked some of the numerous charges, directing his attention mainly to those which designated the real offences. His silence in regard to others was interpreted as a confession of guilt. His attempt, moreover, to show that the witnesses against him had testified falsely, was inter-

preted to his prejudice.   Again, he had insisted that
the testimony against him was not necessarily conclusive, and had employed the word *demonstrative.*
The bishop reproves him for imagining that the
rules of mathematics could apply to evidence, or
that there was no distinction between logic and
rhetoric.   "Who," asked the bishop, "could *demonstrate* more against you than you have yourself *demonstrated?* You alone are your own enemy.   You
alone are your own adversary.   You alone are most
inconsistent with, and opposed to yourself.   All of
us sympathize with you; you alone deal cruelly with
yourself.   All these regard you with kindly feeling,
but you alone cherish malice against yourself."

A fifth evil of Jerome's public audience was the
praise of Huss, whom he had previously anathema-
tized on oath.   The bishop did not pretend to deny
the virtuous life of Huss, but he made his heresy an
offset for the lack of other sins.   Though chaste in
life, his heresy was fornication.   Though never intoxicated with wine, yet he was intoxicated with
pride and contention.

But the crowning mischief of all to Jerome was,
that in his public audience he had condemned himself by his own testimony.   "Would that you had
been silent!   What could have been so forcibly
urged against you, as your own confession that you
had spoken falsely, perjured yourself, and in your
perjury relapsed into heresy?   you recalled what you
had solemnly sworn, and fell back in an error worse
than the first.   Wherefore, this sacred council, upon
which all authority upon earth has been conferred,

will judge you according to your ways . . . . In judgment or rebuke, the law has three objects which the
judge should regard: the reformation of the one
punished; the effect of the punishment on others;
and their security from the evil removed. Having
regard to these, this holy council purposes to proceed
to give judgment. And would that you would renounce your folly, and break down the stubbornness
of your heart! But you will be judged according to
the rules of equity, and the sanctions of the sacred
canons. And although you will not be converted,
yet the council must judge in such a way as to convert the unbelieving to wisdom,—that is, to prepare,
through the holy knowledge of faith, a people perfect for God. Which may He grant who is the just
Judge of living and dead, Jesus Christ, blessed forever." [1]

With this prayer the bishop closed his discourse,
and Jerome was permitted to speak previous to passing sentence. He took his stand in the midst of the
assembly, upon a bench, by which he was so elevated
as to be seen and heard by all. Addressing himself
to the council, and specifying as he did so the several classes that composed it, he preceded the statement of his case by a reference to the sermon that
had been so directly addressed to himself. In what
spirit the bishop had sermonized, Jerome confessed
he could not tell. For he had throughout perverted
all that could possibly be perverted into a wrong
sense, and one that he himself had never intended.
He besought the council, by the blood of Christ by

_____
[1] Van der Hardt, iii. 60.

which all were redeemed, to allow him to repel the charge implied in the words of the sermon, that he scorned and spurned the clergy. He was confident, moreover, that in his discussions in the schools, and elsewhere, and in his various speeches and disputations, as a loyal citizen he had sought the good and prosperity of the Bohemian realm. Yet his enemies had perversely interpreted his course and conduct. The sermon he condemned as false, and, under the eye of God, a fiction."[1]

He then entered directly upon his own case. He attributed his first recantation to the persuasions of the Cardinal of Florence, by whom he had been induced to write to that effect back to Bohemia. Judges had been appointed in his cause, with whom he was satisfied; but they had been changed for others,—after which he would no longer answer under oath, when questioned as to his opinions, although he had no wish to conceal them. He said, that all the charges last presented had not been read by the commission deputed for the purpose. He protested, however, that he did not say this through any stubbornness or obstinacy. He quoted the example of Paul, persecuted by the Jews, and said, that for himself it was not strange if he too must suffer for Christian faith and doctrine. He professed his belief in One holy Catholic church. This he defined as composed of the whole multitude of those that should be saved. He recognized also the church triumphant, as well as the church militant upon earth. There was, moreover, the Catholic church—embracing all

[1] Mon. Hus., ii. 353, 357.   L'Enfant, 395.   Also, Van der Hardt, ii. 458.

that professed the Christian faith. He recognized the authority, moreover, of prelates and rectors, enjoining the law of God upon men. He said that he held to the articles of faith. He spoke approvingly of the mass, of the sacred offices, and of fasts, when all these were kept free from the rites and ceremonies with which they were sometimes connected. He said, moreover, that the extravagance of the clergy, their pomp and pride, should be put off. They were not to convert the patrimony of Christ, which was meant for the poor, into excessive parade, as houses, horses, rich garments, or into means to feed their lust.

He recalled also the letter which he had written to Prague, containing his recantation which he had made in public session. He said that he was unwilling to occasion the mischief he must, by consenting to the condemnation of John Huss. If he had ever said anything wickedly, it was when he recanted and spoke against his conscience. He had done it, he said, through fear of the fire and its torturing and cruel heat. This had induced him to write as he had done to Prague. Here, by the direction of the council, Jerome's abjuration of the views was read, and his own subscription to it exhibited. Jerome confessed that it was his signature, but the fear of the fire had extorted it. He had acted a false and foolish part in writing out his recantation, and for this act he was overwhelmed with bitter grief. Especially did he condemn himself for recanting the doctrine of Huss and Wickliffe, and consenting to the condemnation of the former, whom he believed to have been a just and holy man. In all this, he had done most wickedly.[1]

Jerome repeated that he should die a Catholic, as he had lived. He defied the council to cite any point of his doctrine which was erroneous or heretical. His offence was his fidelity to the memory of his friend. "You wish to see me die," said he, "because I honor upright men who have stigmatized the pride and avarice of priests. Yet is that a sufficient cause to warrant my death? Why! before you found in me any evil whatever, you had resolved that I should die. Courage, therefore, and proceed! But believe me, that in dying I will leave you a sting in your hearts, and a gnawing worm in your consciences. I appeal to the sacred tribunal of Jesus Christ, and within a hundred years you shall answer there for your conduct to me."[2]

The providence of God turned these words of Jerome almost into a prophecy. Their remarkable utterance is attested by their stamp upon a coin of the age. Jerome, however, in all probability, had no idea at the time of any reformer that was to succeed him in his task. He merely meant, as he had said on a previous speech of his trial, that Heaven's unerring judgments would reverse the decisions of the council. Less than a hundred years would bring all his accusers and judges together at the bar of God.

The Patriarch of Constantinople now read Jerome's sentence.[3] It began by making a strange application of the words of Christ in regard to the un-

---

[1] Van der Hardt, iv. 768.
[2] Mon. Hus., ii. 357.
[3] Mansi Coun. xxvii. 784; also, Mon. Hus., ii. 353.

fruitful branch to be cast out and left to wither. It
was based on the violation of his abjuration by Jerome, and his approval of Wickliffe and Huss. "He
has turned like a dog to his vomit," said the sentence,
" and therefore the sacred council orders that he shall
be torn from the vine as a barren and rotten branch."
It declared him heretical, backsliding, and excommunicated. It condemned him as such, and cursed
him. It finally abandoned him to the secular arm,
in order to receive the just punishment due to so
great a crime; and, although this punishment was
capital, the council expressed its confident assurance
that it was not too great.

Then it was, if some accounts are to be received,
that the emperor's chancellor, Caspar Schlick, advanced
into the midst of the assembly, and protested in his
master's name against the condemnation of Jerome,
threatening all the persons engaged in it with the
anger of Sigismund. This tardy interposition was
not attended to, and "the chancellor retired without
gaining anything."[1]

Jerome was now given over into the hands of the
civil magistrates. It was still an early hour of the
morning; and on this Sabbath, while the crowds
should have been gathering to the churches, the outraged victim of the council's bigotry was on his way
to pass through the gates of flame, as he believed,
to the communion of the church triumphant in
heaven. Before he left the council, a high paper
crown, like the one which Huss in similar circumstances had worn, was brought in;[2] upon it were

---

[1] Van der Hardt, iv. 765.   [2] Mon. Hus., ii. 357.

pictures of demons surrounded by the flames. Jerome saw it, and throwing down his own hat on the floor, in the midst of the prelates, placed this on his head with his own hands, repeating the words which Huss had used before him on the like occasion,—"Jesus Christ, who died for me, a sinner, wore a crown of thorns. I will cheerfully wear this for Him." The soldiers then took charge of him, and led him away to execution.

As he turned to leave the cathedral, he chanted the creed in a firm voice, with eyes uplifted to heaven, and a face radiant with joy.[1] On his way to the stake he chanted, first, the Litany, and then, as he passed outside the Gottlieben gate of the city, a hymn in honor of the Virgin. The last commenced with the words, "Blessed art thou among women." As he reached the place of execution—the same where Huss had been burned—he knelt down, with his face to the stake, and spent some time in prayer. The executioners raised him up while still engaged in his devotions, and stripped him of his garments. They then bound him to the stake, first about the loins with a linen bandage, after which other parts of the body were made fast with cords and chains. As they piled the wood around the stake, mingling bundles of straw to kindle the conflagration, Jerome sang the hymn, "Hail, Festal Day"—"*Salve, feste dies.*" He then, in a loud voice that all might hear him, chanted the Nicene creed. When this was done, he turned and addressed the crowd in the German language: "Beloved youth, as I have now chanted, so,

[1] Mon. Hus., ii. 354–357.

and not otherwise, do I believe. This is the symbol of my faith. Yet for this I die, because I would not assent to and approve the decision of the council, and hold and assert with them that John Huss was holily and justly condemned by the council. For I knew him well, and I knew him as a true preacher of the gospel of Jesus Christ."

He saw among his executioners a poor man, bringing a fagot to heap upon the pile. It did not excite him to anger. He smiled and said, "O holy simplicity! a thousand times more guilty is he who abuses thee."

When the fagots had been piled to a level with his head, his garments were thrown upon them, and fire was applied by a lighted torch. But the executioner who bore the torch approached from behind, unwilling to be seen. "Come forward boldly," said Jerome; "apply the fire before my face. Had I been afraid, I should not have been here." As the flames began to spread, he exclaimed aloud, "Into thy hands, O Lord, I commit my spirit." When the fire began to penetrate to his flesh, he prayed again, "O Lord God, Almighty Father, have compassion on me, and forgive my sins. Thou knowest that I have ever delighted in thy truth." His voice was now lost, for the smoke and flame had become suffocating; but though no words were heard, all could see by the motion of the lips that he was still engaged in prayer. The agony of his martyrdom was protracted; it was unusually long before life was extinct. Blisters of water of the size of an egg might be seen over his whole body. "One might have gone," says a spectator, "from the St. Clement Church at Prague to the bridge over the Moldau, before he ceased to breathe."[1]

At last, all that belonged to him,—his bed, cap, clothing, shoes, and whatever he had had with him in prison,—was brought and thrown upon the blazing pile, to be consumed with him. His ashes, like those of Huss, were carefully gathered up, borne away, and cast into the Rhine. The council were apprehensive lest some fragment or relic of their victim should find its way back to Prague, and be cherished as the memorial of a condemned heretic. The least particle that could be associated with the names of either of the sufferers was sought out and carefully burned, lest it should become an object of veneration. But all their precautions were vain. The soil which their dying feet had pressed—in lack of other objects—became the prized memorial, and was borne to Prague to be guarded with religious care.[2] But more than the portraits even of the departed, was the image of themselves which these men had enstamped upon the minds and hearts of their countrymen. When the last surviving member of the council that sentenced them to execution should have been laid in his grave, the memory of these two Bohemian martyrs would still bloom fresh and green upon their natal soil.

[1] Mon. Hus., ii. 854.   [2] Æneas Sylvius.

CHAPTER IX.

INEFFICIENCY AND TUMULTS OF THE COUNCIL.   ILL-SUCCESS
AND RETURN OF THE EMPEROR.

MAY 31, 1416—JAN. 27, 1417.

THE execution of Jerome, amid the clashing
schemes and conflicting interests which marked the
progress of the council, was passed lightly by. A
gallant ship had gone down upon a stormy sea, and
the wild waves of passion rolled on as madly and
fiercely as if there had been no human victim of their
murderous play. No expression of regret or remorse
bubbles up visibly to the surface, to speak, in the
actors, any bitter memory of the deed. No doubt it
was remembered,—no doubt, in later years, minds
like Gerson's recurred to it sadly,—but the death of
Jerome, at the time, produced scarcely a pause in
the struggle of conflicting parties and interests.

On the next day after the execution, (May 31,) a decree of the council was issued, summoning its absent members to return, under penalty, in case of disobedience, of incurring the indignation of Almighty God, and St. Peter and St. Paul, his apostles.[1] The council felt that it was now incumbent upon it to prosecute with energy the matter of the union of the church. This was manifest in the congregations held upon the following days. In spite of a letter of Sigismund, urging upon them the business of reform, the members showed themselves more inclined to remove the difficulties that stood in the way of the deposition of Benedict and the election of a new pope.

The case of the Bohemians, moreover, called for the notice of the council. The execution of Jerome was not calculated to soothe the feelings or repress the indignation of his countrymen. Their letter of remonstrance had reached the council at the close of the previous year. Their citation for their presumption and suspicion of heretical pravity in adhering to Huss, had been demanded by the prosecuting officers of the council, in its name, on the twentieth of February, 1416. This citation was issued on the fifth of May, and was publicly affixed to the church doors and gates of Constance. A commission to attend to the process of trial—which was to be summary in the case of those cited—was appointed on the third of June. It was now, upon the non-appearance of the Bohemians summoned to answer before the council, that they were to be de-

[1] Van der Hardt, iv. 775.

clared guilty of contumacy. The number of these is variously stated from four hundred and fifty to five hundred and fifty.[1] They embraced, as we have already seen, some of the most powerful and distinguished members of the Bohemian nobility. To them the threats of the council were a mere *brutum fulmen.* They treated them with contempt. Secure in their distance from Constance and the consciousness of their own strength, they were driven into a more defiant attitude by the steps taken to awe them into submission. The execution of Jerome, following upon that of Huss, was in their eyes a new outrage, tending to destroy the last vestige of respect which they could ever have entertained for the body by whose order the deed was done.

A different course from theirs was the one pursued by one of their countrymen at Constance, the Knight De Latzembock.[2] He had gradually risen till he stood high in the emperor's favor. He it was who bore the news of the emperor's coronation at Aix la Chapelle to Constance, on the opening of the council. Since that time he had been employed in high positions, and had had charge of important matters. But still, in spite of all this, the stain of heretical leprosy clung to him. It was not forgotten that he was one of those whom the Bohemian king had commissioned to escort Huss to Constance. Although he had since had but little to do with him, and showed in his character and life more of the courtier than the friend, he yet fell under suspicion. The

---

[1] Probably all who had signed the letters of remonstrance to the council.

[2] L'Enfant, 406. Van der Hardt, iv. 795–6.

council felt that it was at least dangerous that such
a man should not be committed with themselves to
the guilt of their own deed.   There was something
ominous in his silence.   It could not be tolerated.
He must speak out.   He must seem at least to endorse the condemnation of his countrymen, or he
could not be trusted about the person of the emperor.   He was cited—according to a historian hostile to Huss—and required to abjure the doctrine
and approve the condemnation of Huss and Jerome.
With this requisition he complied.   Doubtless his
conscience excused him for the crime under the plea
of necessity; but the suspicion of his sincerity which
was still entertained, while it commends his intellectual convictions, suggests the policy and pliability of
the courtier.   To this man—this new convert—
letters were given by the council to be carried into
Bohemia and delivered to his countrymen; but we
hear no more of them, and it is doubtful whether he
who would abjure his convictions for fear of the
council, would be forward to thrust before the eyes
of his own countrymen the provocation of his infamy
not unattended by danger.

Never was the difference between preaching and
practice better illustrated than in the history and
proceedings of the council.   We have seen how loud
had been the cry of remonstrance and the complaint
of corruption.   It was notorious that the most
simoniacal arts had raised many of the prelates of
the council to the position they occupied.   The
channels of promotion were not through merit, but
money.   Again and again this crying infamy of the

church had been exposed. Except the deposition of John XXIII. no noticeable steps had been taken in the direction of reform. Two men had been put to death, upon whose characters there rested not a stain of corruption or impurity, and who were angels by the side of their judges. At last a victim was found—a poor insignificant copyist—of prelatical and pontifical simony. A scapegoat was wanted, and John Creith of Liege was the one selected.[1] He had —unfortunately for himself, though to his great pecuniary advantage—been one of the minions of John XXIII. Acting as his secretary, he had employed his knowledge and skill to his own emolument, counterfeiting, to this end, apostolic letters and documents. He was accused of having sold thirty benefices, and of having reserved in his own hands others, which were incompatible in the hands of one man. Upon this victim, punishment, therefore, must alight. He, at least, will be made a signal example. But what is his sentence? *Suspension from office!* No wonder the preacher of two or three days later, (June 7,) should remark—when speaking on the text, "They were filled with the Holy Ghost,"—that instead of the seven graces which were bestowed on the apostles at the day of Pentecost, he feared that the devil had had his Pentecost in the hearts of most of the clergy, and had inspired them with vices directly contrary to the graces of the apostles.[2]

But little, however, was accomplished by the council after Jerome's death, for several months. They were reluctant to enter upon any measures of reform.

---

[1] Niem apud Van der Hardt, ii. 444, 457.   [2] L'Enfant, 405.

The emperor was absent, and private interests and party purposes acknowledged no supreme authority to over-awe them. The council assumed the character for the most part of a great debating club, except as party policy mingled with the intrigues of the caucus. The affair of Petit was still warmly controverted, yet little if any progress was made toward its settlement. The Cardinal of Cambray issued his treatise on ecclesiastical power, some portions of which contain sentiments in advance of his age, and strongly savoring of a protestant character. Yet this very treatise gave rise, by the doubts which he threw out in its concluding chapter, to some of the most agitating and angry controversies. Should the English, or the union of Spain with the council, be recognized still as a separate and independent nation composing it? It was a firebrand thrown in among a mass of inflammable materials, and the conflagration at once burst forth. The pride of England, fresh from the glorious field of Agincourt, resented the doubt as an insult. Yet the French could not look with complacency upon the exaltation of their great rivals. The Spaniards, who had now arrived with a view to join the council, found their place preoccupied by the English, who had always heretofore been recognized as an integral portion of the German nation in the councils of the church. The controversy kindled to a flame. Fierce passions were indulged, and fierce words spoken. The Cardinal of Cambray was not allowed to touch upon the subject, as he had proposed, in a public discourse. He complained of this restriction upon his liberty. It was but a poor satis-

faction to be informed that he must be careful how
he appeared in the streets, for armed Englishmen
sought his life.   More than once the matter threatened to proceed to open violence, but by the intervention of the princes, and a mass of national protests
against present privileges being allowed as precedents,
passion was cooled and the danger deferred.

The council meanwhile had received new and large
accessions to its numbers.   England was more numerously represented.   Among others came Robert
Clifford, bishop of London, the two chancellors of
Oxford and Cambridge, and twelve doctors, ostensibly to maintain the rights of the English nation.

The kingdoms of Portugal, Aragon, Castile, Navarre, and Scotland sent delegates to Constance, who
were, most of them, successively received with similar
formalities to those upon which the representatives
of Gregory XII. had insisted.   Some of them were
quite leisurely in making their appearance.   Months
passed, bringing from them to the council only letters
and promises.   Nothing could be done, meanwhile,
that could be regarded as final and conclusive in regard to Benedict XIII.   His trial and deposition, in
order to be acknowledged legitimate, must be par-
ticipated in by all the nations.

It was during this period, previous to taking further and more decisive measures against Benedict,
that the council presented a most singular scene of
turmoil and recrimination.   Questions of national
precedence and representation—the complaints of
the cardinals that they were not notified previously
of the subjects of discussion—the affair of John Petit

still dragging its slow length along—vain and futile attempts to draw up plans on the subject of reform, which the emperor still urged upon the attention of the council—all conspired to render that body the scene of angry and bitter controversy. It was during this period, also, that Gerson signalized himself, not only by his zeal in controverted matters, but by peculiar manifestations of what at the present day might be regarded as ultra orthodoxy. We have recently seen the doctrine of "The immaculate conception of the Virgin Mary" solemnly adopted by the Roman Catholic church as one of the integral elements of its creed. Gerson, on this subject, was in advance of his times. At Paris he had manfully contended in behalf of the doctrine, and had classed its principal opponent with Huss himself. But now his devotion went still further.[1] He urged publicly upon the council the immaculate conception of St. Joseph, and, opposed as he was to the multiplication of saints'-days, went so far as to insist that to this rule of restriction St. Joseph should be excepted. But the council were not ready to endorse the suggestion. More than four hundred years more were destined to pass away, before the question in regard to the Virgin Mary could be put at rest. Another century may yet honor the logical consistency of Gerson, that ranks Mary and Joseph together as to their claim on this point.

It was near the close of the year (1416) that the council replied to a letter of Sigismund, informing him of the state of affairs at Constance. He had

---

[1] See his treatise in his works, iii. 1346.

ever a horror for all that tended to civil commotion.
His hostility to the doctrines of Petit was aggravated
by what he saw in the anarchy and violence of France
—results as he regarded them of his incendiary principles. His prejudice against Huss had been skilfully aggravated by the enemies of the reformer,
when they imputed to his views and preaching similar tendencies. For this reason, he was urgent that the
council should prosecute the Bohemian heresy to its
extinction. But this was a task beyond their power.
They wrote to the emperor now to implore his aid.[1]

There was good reason for doing so. The council
found themselves contemned by heretics. Their
threats were despised; their authority was disregarded; their own conduct was arraigned, and the
Bohemian nation boldly declared its purpose to persist in the course upon which it had entered. In
these circumstances their only hope of help was in
the emperor. He must enforce the authority of the
council by his imperial power. The letter which the
council wrote him is important for the picture which
it gives of the state of things in Bohemia, as well as
on other accounts. It commences with a statement of
the daily complaints made to the council of evils that
prevailed in Bohemia; the scandalous dangers, and
dangerous scandals, through errors, heresies, seditions,
and persecutions, which had given disturbance to the
clergy, and which were spread over a country inflamed
by "more than material fire." It speaks of the disciples of Wickliffe, Huss, and Jerome as the followers
of Belial, and abounding in impiety and perfidy. The

[1] Van der Hardt, iv. 1079.

two former, condemned by the council, were represented as saints in the churches, were spoken of as
such in sermons, were honored in the divine offices,
and had masses celebrated for them as martyrs.
Their followers sought to disseminate and perpetuate
their errors, drawing off to themselves all classes of
persons, learned and ignorant, and of both sexes.
They are spoken of as treating lightly holy mother
church, and holding sentences and censures in contempt. The evil was rising to an alarming height.
The intelligence of the council's proceedings had only
urged them to new and more detestable excesses.

The council then sets forth in a more specific form
the evils of which they complain; members of the
university, and other priests infected by them, continued to preach the errors of Wickliffe and Huss,
which the council had condemned. They had been
cherished, defended, and protected by certain barons
and nobles of the kingdom, who, in letters to the
council with their seals affixed, had avowed their
acts. The communion of the cup was preached and
practised in the cities and villages, notwithstanding
the decision of the council upon the subject, and the
threatened penalty of eternal damnation. The clergy
were ill treated and abused, and even the Jews enjoyed a greater liberty than was allowed to them.
The interdict was still continued in many monasteries
and churches, on account of the presence among them
of that wretch, John Jessenitz, by which means many
hundreds of masses are every day omitted. The
metropolitan church had been long unoccupied, both
on acount of the interdict, and the robbery of its

revenues, out of which three hundred ecclesiastics had formerly been sustained. The relics which had been deposited there, which the people had been accustomed to visit daily, had been plundered for years. Some of the barons were defaming the holy council, and preventing the clergy from complying with its commands. Such as had obeyed had been plundered and expelled from their posts.

The letter then sets forth the sad condition of the university, once foremost in rank among all of the German nation, now almost a deserted habitation, and driving from it those who are unwilling to be polluted by its errors. The nation, too, once submissive to its prelates, and religiously faithful to the divine worship, and to all things required by ecclesiastical obedience, is now disgraced throughout the world by perfidy and error.

Against these evils the council declares that it has done what it could. Convoked to exterminate heresy and reform the world, it has by the grace of God proceeded to the task assigned. One of the leaders of heresy it has given over by sentence to the secular court, the other remains in custody,[1] while processes have been fulminated against their favorers and adherents. Yet, in the need of more ample resources of defence, the council invokes, and pressingly demands, through its venerable and eminent bishops, doctors, masters, and ambassadors, the arm of his imperial majesty. It calls upon him as the

---

[1] This letter, in my judgment, belongs to an earlier date than the one which is here—on the authority of Van der Hardt—ascribed to it. Evidently Jerome was still in custody when it was written, thus requiring the letter to date some months previous. See Van der Hardt, iv. 1077.

defender and advocate of the church, to destroy the
perfidious, defend the holy church itself and its faithful members, no less than restrain the enemies of the
Christian name. It incites him against the Bohemians as errorists and persecutors of the church of
God, urging him to expel the seditious, and drive
out intruders. It then sets forth the character of
Wenzel, king of Bohemia, in language which his
brother Sigismund could appreciate. These excesses
never disturbed him. He dissembles in every thing.
He lets every thing take its course. The evils which
he should resist even to blood, and at the risk of his
life, he tolerates in the heart of his kingdom, or even,
as was more lamentably reported, cherishes and supports. " Proceed, therefore," the council say, " with
all dispatch; all lingering is dangerous; all delay
does mischief. Act for the salvation of all who are
like to perish before the eyes of the council, before
your own, and the eyes of all beholders. Act at
once, while any hope of safety remains. If the disease continues, and the time to arrest it is neglected,
there is fear that the evil will become irreparable.
Faith and the church, spiritualities and temporalities,
souls and bodies, are threatened with a like ruin.
Act heartily, glorious in the triumph of virtue, noble
worshipper of justice and merit, so as to reign for ever
with the Saviour of the world, of whom you are the
type. Your exalted piety may aspire to such merit." [1]

It was indeed time to call upon the emperor
for aid. To calm the storm it had raised was
beyond the power of the council. The letters

[1] Van der Hardt, iv. 1077; also, L'Enfant, 430.

of the Bohemian nobles already noticed, were not the only ones that reached them of the same tenor. Some less numerously signed, some written by individuals, attested the strength of the indignation excited by the provocations which had been offered. The absence of the emperor in Spain left them for a while to feel the bitterness of that contempt to which they were exposed by their own deeds, while unprotected by the imperial sword.

But the emperor's method of quieting the insurrectionary spirit was by far the wisest. He sought to reform the clergy, and urged the subject with repeated importunity upon the attention of the council. Successive failures to secure any advance in this direction might have satisfied him that moral suasion is a poor and ineffectual motive to arrest a party like that with which he had to deal, in a course where their own interest is at stake. He employed, however, one of his ministers to draw up for the council a plan of reform; but all the reward of the servant for speaking out his master's views, as he undoubtedly did, was to be called "a Hussite rather than a Christian."[1] "There must first," said these grandees of the council—to put off the evil day, and prevent their own exposure,—"There must first be a pope to authorize the reform." There were those who urged Sigismund to take the matter into his own hand, to fix the yearly salary of the popes and bishops, reserving what remained of the treasures of the church to further his darling project of a crusade against the Turks. But from such a step as this even the empe-

[1] L'Enfant, 503

ror shrunk. It would be committing the unpardon-
able sin with which Luther stood charged a century
later, of " attacking the monks' bellies."

The well known views of the emperor contributed
undoubtedly to secure for those who ventured to
express them, freedom of speech in the council. The
sermons preached abounded, as we have seen, with
most unpalatable statements of the corruption of the
clergy. These public discourses were the safety-
valve by which the pent up convictions of the necessity of reform were allowed harmlessly to escape.
Yet sometimes the truth must have stung deeply.
Just before the emperor's return, at the beginning
of the year 1417, a sermon was preached before the
council, which gives a fearful picture of the state of
the clergy.[1] Their vices are coolly and philosophi-
cally classed. The first of these classifications represents the ostentation and luxury of the clergy grasping at the goods of the poor and the revenues of the
church, for selfish indulgence. " In our pride," says
the preacher, " we surpass the princes of the world :
scorning the example and command of Jesus Christ,
we would set up as kings ; we march at the head of
armies ; we make ourselves terrible and inaccessible,
especially to the poor." Other crimes recounted
were—the ill-disposal of benefices, by bestowing
them on the incapable and vile—the mal-adminis-
tration of the sacrament, extended to the notoriously
impure, unjust, and excommunicate—neglect of scriptural study and gospel preaching—unjust decisions
by ecclesiastical judges, who make them a matter of

[1] L'Enfant, 436.

traffic—and similar charges in abundance. The picture of ecclesiastical manners or morals is too foul for the modern page. Yet it was presented in all its fearful colors in full council, and no one called it a slander. Each one knew only too well that it was drawn to the life.

The time was now drawing near for Sigismund's return to Constance. He had promised in one of his letters to the council to hasten his return, if in their judgment his presence should be deemed necessary. But it was a year and a half that his absence had been protracted. He left Constance on the twentieth of July, 1415, and entered its gates, upon his return, on the twenty-seventh of January, 1417. The success of his mission could not have been very flattering to his imperial pride. Benedict XIII. had virtually defied him, and still assumed the full exercise of papal prerogative. His attempt to negotiate a peace between France and England would have been utterly futile, had not the policy of Henry V. led him to adopt the purpose of leaving France to wear out its strength in intestine conflict. The Duke of Burgundy and the Constable d'Armagnac were sworn foes. Henry favored the duke, and even contracted with him a conditional alliance, while in a seeming compliance with the emperor's persuasions he entered into a truce with France for the space of a few months.

Yet Sigismund must have sorely felt that his influence would have been altogether in vain but for other causes, more effective than his personal influence. As the vessel that bore him across the channel approached the English coast, several English lords, headed by the Duke of Gloucester, stepped into the water, with their drawn swords in their hands, and stopped the boat. The emperor, surprised at such a reception, asked the reason of it. The duke replied, that if he came to challenge any authority in England, he had orders to forbid his landing; but if he came only as a mediator of peace, he should be treated with all the respect due to his imperial dignity.[1] Henry V. had the spirit of an independent sovereign. The proceedings of the emperor in France, in his assumption of authority, were not to be repeated on the shores of England. Sigismund showed his regard for the spirit of the English monarch, when, after months of useless negotiation to secure for France a short and worthless truce, he concluded himself, like the Duke of Burgundy, an alliance with Henry V.

The only result of his journey northward seems to have been the strengthening the hands of the ally of the Duke of Burgundy, and increasing the improbability that the doctrines of Petit would be condemned at the council. A slight which he offered to William of Bavaria, while in England, led that prince indignantly to withdraw from the English coast with all his ships. Sigismund was left a sort of state prisoner in London, unable, till he had signed the treaty with England, to reach the continent, and then only in English ships. On one occasion the mob rose against the emperor, and he was obliged to flee for refuge to Canterbury.

Rapin, i. 516.

All this was humiliating enough. Undoubtedly English manliness, that spurned the perjury of Sigismund in giving up Huss to the flames, had something to do with the threatened violence. But there was still another dreg in his bitter cup. To defray the expenses of his journey he had sold the whole of Brandenburg, together with the electorate, to Frederic of Zollern for 300,000 ducats,[1] and for a smaller sum created the Truchsesses of Waldburg governors of Swabia. Thus he had alienated instead of adding to his dominions, and in some respects his journey was a marked failure. He had indeed induced Spain to withdraw from Benedict, but the obstinate old pope was not to be cajoled or terrified even by an emperor. He still maintained his state, and fulminated his terrors in all the pride of his prerogative.

It was now time for the council to try their hand at a task which the emperor had left incomplete— the removal of Benedict as the lingering obstacle which obstructed the union of the church. At the twenty-third session, Nov. 5, 1416, a commission was appointed to draw up charges and hear testimony against the "schismatic, heretical, and tyrant" pontiff. This commission proceeded to business, and were ready to report at the next session, (Nov. 28,) when the citation of Benedict was decreed.[2] He was summoned to appear at Constance within one hundred days from the present session, or within seventy days from the issuing of the citation. The citation was decreed by edict, through apprehension that the criminal could not be personally reached. But two

---

[1] Schmidt's Gesch. der Deutsch., iv. 101.   [2] L'Enfant, 428.

monks were found bold enough to bear the summons to Peniscola, and into the presence of Benedict himself. These monks belonged to the Benedictine order, and their names were Lambert Stipiltz and Bernard Plancha.[1] The recital which they gave of their mission, showed that the idea of its danger was scarcely exaggerated.

As they drew near to Peniscola, accompanied by two nobles and several notaries, they were met by a doctor despatched by Benedict to request them to defer their entrance till the next day, under the pretext that they might be greeted then by a more honorable reception. With this request they refused to comply. "These devils," said they, "imagine they have gained everything if they can postpone the union a single hour." As they entered the town, a nephew of Benedict, escorted by two hundred well-armed soldiers, came to meet them. Their reception had every appearance of a welcome, the value of which, however, they could well appreciate. They amused themselves at the fright which the presence of two unarmed monks had created in Benedict.

The next day they were admitted to an audience. Benedict had with him three cardinals, several bishops and other ecclesiastics, and about three hundred laymen. These monks then read the decree of citation, which Benedict heard with extreme impatience. When they came the passage which spoke of him as schismatic and heretical, he could contain himself no longer. "It is not true," he cried out at one time; and again, "They slander me." At length,

[1] L'Enfant, 449.

in a more formal reply, he declared that the matter
was one of great importance, and his answer should
be given the next day, after deliberation with his
cardinals. He improved the occasion, however, to
go into a lengthened defence of his own course, more,
probably, for the ears of his auditors, than the satisfaction or conviction of the monks. "The church,"
said he, "is not at Constance, but at Peniscola.
Here," he exclaimed, striking his hand upon the
chair he occupied,—"Here is the Noah's ark, the true
church. These people of Constance call me schismatic and heretic, because I will not put the church
into their hands; a thing I will take good care not
to do. Already there would have been peace for
six months but for them. On their heads rests the
guilt of heresy and schism." The monks thought
such an answer enough. They demanded a copy of
it, which the pope was reluctant to grant. But
leaving behind them a notary of the king to take
charge of the document after it should be drawn up,
they withdrew to Tortosa.

Serious as the business was, it is connected with
some amusing incidents. It is said that as the monks
approached, dressed in black, according to the statutes of their order, in order to cite Benedict, the latter said to those around him, "Let us hear the ravens
of the council." But monkish repartee was equal to
pontifical wit. "There is nothing surprising," said
one of the monks boldly, "that ravens should come
near a dead body!" One historian ludicrously represents the monks as dressed in black, the devil's
color, entering into hell to cite Beelzebub, the great

devil, to come to judgment. Undoubtedly the sincerity was about equal on both sides. The monks
themselves considered the whole affair, notwithstanding their indignation against Benedict, as a good
joke.

The letter, in which they gave to the council an
account of their expedition, is dated Tortosa, Jan. 22,
1417. Five days later, on the 27th of the month,
Sigismund returned to Constance.

The announcement of his approach was enthusias-
tically received.[1] He was met several miles distant
from Constance by an imposing procession of princes,
nobles, and ecclesiastical dignitaries. He entered the
city amid the discharge of cannon, the ringing of
bells, and applauding shouts of welcome. The English saw with exultation that he proudly wore the
decoration of the Order of the Garter, which he had
received from the hands of Henry V. They were
themselves treated with distinguished honor. The
Bishop of Sarum greeted the emperor in the name
of the council. Sacred comedies, previously acted
in the presence of the authorities of the city, were
repeated by the English in the presence of Sigismund, and to his great delight and satisfaction. A
sermon was preached before him in the highest strain
of eulogy. If anything could compensate the emperor for the hardships of his journey, it was the
welcome he received, as well as the presence of the
Spanish nation joining in the deliberations of the
council.

[1] Van der Hardt, iv. 1089, 1091.

CHAPTER X.

BENEDICT DEPOSED. PROGRESS OF REFORM. MARTIN V. ELECTED.

Jan. 27, 1417—Nov. 21, 1418.

The presence of the emperor infused new life and energy into the proceedings of the council. The more arduous matters, which in his absence had been deferred, almost of necessity, might now be disposed of. The first in order of these, if not the most important, was that which concerned the depo-

(278)

sition of Benedict. His answer to the citation sent
him by the hands of the two monks, was read,
(March 7, 1417,) but only confirmed the impression
that he was obstinately resolved not to cede. He
had indeed sent the Bishop of Cuenza to Constance,
ostensibly to make propositions which should be a
basis of negotiation, but only, as his enemies asserted,
to sow division in the council. His representative
manifested a temper and spirit worthy of his master.
An English ambassador disputed with him the question of precedence. The Bishop of Cuenza, prefer-
ring to use the most decisive arguments, seized his
adversary, who was a small man, about the body, and
taking him from his seat, carried him out of the
church, and threw him into one of the vaults, which
chanced to be open. Resuming his place, he quietly
remarked to his colleague, Martin Fernandez of Cor-
dova, " As a priest, I bury the English ambassador ;
as a man of the sword, and a cavalier by birth, do
you perform what remains to be done."

But no arts or measures that Benedict could now
take would enable him to evade the purpose of the
council. He had been repeatedly cited, but did not
appear. He had deigned no reply, and no one appeared for him. He refused steadfastly and consistently to recognize, in any manner, the authority of
the council as more than that of a mere assembly.
The charges against him, as finally drawn up, had
been read as early as November 5, 1416. They were
supported by multitudes of witnesses, most of them
of high ecclesiastical or secular rank. Among these
witnesses was the emperor himself, as well as some

of the bishops of Benedict. He was charged with obstinate perseverance in schism. His various obnoxious acts,—regarded as fatally prejudicial to the peace of the church,—were attested, and he was again cited to answer. This was the last citation. The period allowed was extended, at the instance of the Spanish nation, and in order that the proceedings of the council might not be open to the charge of harshness or precipitation.[1] The blow was merely suspended.

Meanwhile the council itself was not secure from dangers within its own body. The incongruous elements of which it was composed, and the incongruous interests which it represented, made it repeatedly a scene of the wildest discord. More than once its warmest friends had reason to fear that its only achievement would be to render itself the Babel of Christendom. The English composed by themselves an entire nation in the council. Other nations were jealous of the influence which they were thus enabled to exert. The Spaniards, moreover, who had only of late joined the body, disputed with them the question of precedence.[2] The French seemed to resent the increasing importance of a nation which had given them reason to remember their own lasting disgrace, as well as inferiority, at Agincourt. The dispute waxed warm. All order was at an end. The consultations of the council more than once were characterized by the violent clamors of a mob. The English indeed carried their point at last, conceding to the Spaniards, on the question of precedence, a

[1] L'Enfant, 424.   Van der Hardt, iv. 969.   [2] L'Enfant, 424, 447.

right which they were willing to surrender only for the occasion, and for the sake of peace.

But another matter soon gave occasion for the renewal of similar scenes. The emperor and the German and English nations were earnest in favor of ecclesiastical reform. With them this was the first and most important measure to be initiated. Germany, especially, complained of the simony of the clergy, and the abuses of pontifical and prelatical prerogative. Maurice of Prague preached a sermon at this period, (May 9, 1417,) in which he exposed the disorders of the clergy to unsparing rebuke.[1] Huss could not have exceeded his former associate, and one of his late judges, in the freedom of invective. Maurice spoke of the prevailing opinion—which he declared, however, that he regarded as a heresy—that Huss had been put to death mainly because he had spoken so energetically upon this very point. His friend and associate, Stephen of Prague,[2] a few days later, did not hesitate to add his testimony. He exposed in like manner "the horrible simony" of the clergy, which had filled the highest posts of the church with incapable and unworthy occupants. "Is it right,"[3] he asks, "that fools should rule, and the wise obey them; that the young should give orders, and the old be their servitors; that the ignorant should have charge of what calls for the most discriminating management; that the learned should not dare to open their mouths; and that grooms should be preferred to doctors, and to

---

[1] Van der Hardt, i. 860; iv. 1287.   [2] Probably Stephen Paletz.   [3] Van der Hardt, i. 823.

preachers of the word of God?" Nor did he hesitate to declare in his sermon, in language indirectly
condemnatory of the council, that this matter of
reform was more essential to promote the interests
of the Christian faith, than the union of the different
obediences. The election of the pope he did not hesitate to pronounce a matter of secondary importance.

He could have said nothing more seriously in conflict with the cherished purposes and avowed policy
of the cardinals, and of many prelates of the different nations. These contended that the election of a
pope should precede all measures of reform.[1] Their
plea was, that in order to be valid these must have
the sanction of the pope. The plea was specious,
but self-interest was at the bottom of it. The emperor and the German nation were fully aware that
the hope of a reform in the abuses of the church was
only warranted, while the pontificate was vacant.
Let it be filled, and the pride of prerogative would
deny the right of the council to proceed in the matter, or would restrain and control its action. The
event justified this fear. For a while the emperor,
with the English and German nations, stood firm.
The others were irritated. The French even complained that their rights of free deliberation were
encroached upon by the emperor.

But none were more aggrieved than the college
of cardinals. They went so far as to demand of the
Elector of Brandenburg safe-conducts, that they might
withdraw from the council.[2] But the Elector of
Brandenburg was not the man to confer such a favor.

---

[1] Van der Hardt, iv. 1354.   [2] Van der Hardt, iv. 1416.

He shared himself with the German nation their convictions of the paramount and urgent necessity of reform. His long experience of public life had made him fully acquainted with the disorders of the ecclesiastical state. "The clergy," said he, "push themselves into secular matters; they use their revenues merely for their own selfish purposes. They are ever making new acquisitions, and already they have usurped a large part of the empire." Such language could serve only as a still greater provocation to the cardinals. But their passports could not be had. The elector not only refused their request, but told them plainly that the dissolution and transfer of the council belonged not to them, but to the emperor, as advocate and defender of the church.

Compelled to remain at Constance, the college of cardinals could speak of nothing, could think of nothing, but the election of a new pope. They had frequent consultations by themselves on the subject. They were apprehensive lest the prerogative of election should be wrested from their hands by the authority of the council. A contest which had arisen between the Castilians and Aragonese in regard to the representation of the Spanish nation, and the union of the former to the council, aided them in their projects. The Cardinal of Cambray, in a public discourse, urged that immediate steps should be taken for an election. He would not allow any measure of reform to take precedence of this. But, firm as the cardinals might be in their purpose, their opponents were not less decided. The contest grew more and more desperate. Fierce passions were excited. Harsh

words were spoken. At a congregation held on the
16th of June, there seemed no possible alternative
but the dissolution of the council.[1] The position of
the Castilians aggravated matters. They were secretly
in favor of Benedict, or apprehensive at least of the
result, if another pope was not soon elected. They
refused to unite with the council—though they had
already been long at Constance—till some order
should be taken on the subject. It was not without
the greatest difficulty that their resolution was overcome, and the storm weathered for the present.

It was, however, soon seen to which side the scale
must eventually incline. The Italian, Spanish, and
French nations sided already with the cardinals.
The English and German nations were in the minority, and only sustained their position by the aid
of the emperor. Against Sigismund, therefore, the
measures of the cardinals, and three nations, were
now directed. "Had he," they asked, "any right to
mix himself up in ecclesiastical matters?" While
he favored them, the strength of the imperial arm
was a welcome ally. Now that he opposed their
measures, he must be rebuked and kept within his
own sphere.[2]

It was in these circumstances, and after vainly
seeking a decree of the council prescribing the manner of a new election, that the cardinals adopted a
line of policy which did much to promote their
plans. They petitioned the emperor to appoint a
season of public devotion, to obtain from Heaven an
election favorable to the welfare of the church. Sigis-

---

[1] Van der Hardt, iv. 1435.　　　[2] L'Enfant, 475.

mund could scarcely refuse the request.   He ordered
their devotions to be publicly announced for a day
of the following week.   Why did he not order, first
of all, prayers for reform?   It was a sad mistake, as
he found at last.   Popular feeling was now changing
in favor of the cardinals.   Sigismund had virtually
signed the death warrant of his most cherished purpose.   The question of all questions, which Germany
demanded should be met—which she redemanded
in more imperative tones a century later, and before
which cardinals and prelates turned pale and trem-
bled—was put by for the time, and, to all practical
purposes so far as this council was concerned, finally.

During all this time the case of the Bohemians,
though overshadowed by matters of more pressing
importance, had not been altogether overlooked.
New commissioners to attend to their case were appointed to replace such as had not been able to serve.
But there was no danger of their being overbur-
dened with business.   None appeared before them
in answer to the citation of the council.   Huss and
Jerome had at Prague a greater power than ever.
Living, they were but men.   The council had rashly
promoted them to that of martyrs.   They had canonized them as unhesitatingly as John XXIII. did
the Swedish Bridget, and, although against their intentions, far more effectually in the esteem of the
Bohemian nation.   Respect for the memory of these
martyrs, and indignation at the injustice that doomed
them to the stake, blazed up out of the smouldering
grief of their recent loss into flames of fierce defiance.

At this moment, when the national spirit was

roused to desperation, when the passions of men were in a ferment, when the violence of antagonistic parties and opinions demanded a sharp eye and a strong arm to control them, Bohemia found itself practically without a ruler. The drunken wretch who occupied the throne was the laughing-stock of the world, and a disgrace to the nation over whom he pretended to reign. None feared him as a king. None respected him as a man. Nothing could show this better than the manner in which the question of deposing him was discussed. Nicholas of Hussinitz, the friend and patron of Huss, was the principal leader of the Hussite party. By his position as well as by his ability—for he was one of the most powerful of the Bohemian barons—he commanded great influence. But his course had excited the apprehensions of the dissolute monarch. Wenzel suspected him of aspiring to the throne, and banished him from Prague. He withdrew to his own district, where his authority was great, and gathered around him a powerful army of near forty thousand men. To these, animated with the enthusiasm of their new faith, and terrible in the desperateness of their resolves to avenge their wrongs, or at least to maintain what they regarded as their rights, he proposed the election of a new king who should be of their own belief.[1] Whether Nicholas himself aspired to the post is not entirely clear, but his proposition was subsequently rejected on the ground that they had now a king who answered their purpose well enough. The priest Coranda, who was a popular and power-

---

[1] See L'Enfant, Guerre des Hussites, i. 88.

ful speaker among the Hussites, maintained before the armed assembly, that the spectre of a king now occupying the throne—though a mere mockery of royalty—was far better for them than one who, in bearing their name, would only produce division in the nation, or excite prejudice against their cause. Never would Wenzel be any thing but a tool; and when so ready at hand, why not use him?

Into such contempt had the royal authority fallen. There was no government, except the self-restraint of infuriated parties. The Hussites were stung to vengeance by the mad and imbecile bigotry of the council, who had given back wrong and outrage in answer to their demand for truth and justice. But if they had asked for an egg and had received a scorpion, they were not like to forget the gift or its sting, any more than the giver. The apologists of the council at Prague represented to them the council itself, and thus volunteered to make themselves objects of a vengeance not always restrained within the limits of the law. The absence of a real executive power gave the country over into the hands of the Hussites. Many of their leaders were men of strong passions, and more impelled by party zeal than the spirit of him they reverenced as a martyr. Some joined them more for their own selfish advancement than from notions of sincere anxiety for the public cause.

In these circumstances, scenes of violence were almost a necessary result. Deeds were committed, which the great majority could only view with ill-dissembled regret. Some of the priests, who adhered

to the council, and who refused to regard the edict
which allowed, or perhaps was construed to require,
the administration of the cup, were driven from their
parishes. Churches were pillaged. Monasteries were
plundered and burned. The stern spirit of John
Knox might have smiled to see the *rookeries* torn
down, but Huss himself could never have approved
the violence which the vengeance of the council had
provoked. And yet the war-cry was in his name.
Vive Wickliffe et Huss was answered feebly by the
party cry, *Vive le Pape*.

The withdrawal of Zisca and Nicholas de Hussinitz to their estates, was for Wenzel a fatal policy.
Zisca was already the hero of many a hard-fought
field. His name alone was a tower of strength.
While Nicholas de Hussinitz was gathering his thousands on Mount Tabor—as a scriptural enthusiasm
had named the height he had selected for his fortress [1]—Zisca was not less successful in gathering
around him bold and daring spirits kindred to his
own. Resistance was completely overawed. The
communion under both kinds became the common
practice throughout Bohemia. The violent opposition of the clergy and the anathemas of the council
were laughed to scorn.

The University of Prague, already almost to a
man on the side of Huss, could hesitate no longer in
its choice of parties. Like the universities of England in the time of Cromwell, it allowed itself to be
swept along in the popular current. On the tenth

---

[1] Some derive the name from Thabor — in Bohemian, a camp — thus
making Tabor signify merely an en-
campment.

of March, (1417,) it issued a public declaration in
favor of the communion of the cup.[1] John Cardinal, now rector, who had shown himself the secret
friend of Huss at Constance, was employed to draw
it up. The university first of all protests, that it
does not presume to introduce any novelty of custom
or doctrine in opposition to the Catholic, Apostolic,
and Roman church. Its only aim is to enlighten
the faithful upon the subject of the eucharist. It
then expresses its greater readiness to decide in favor
of the communion under both kinds, as the council
of Constance had itself already declared that Christ
had so appointed in his institution of the ordinance
of the Holy Supper, and for many centuries the
church had practised its observance.

The university then exhorts all the faithful to
maintain with religious fidelity the institution of our
Saviour, notwithstanding opposing customs and constitutions, however venerable. Whether Christ entire was present in each kind, as the council maintained, the university does not decide. This is
spoken of merely as a tradition which may or may
not be true. And yet the language of the university is by no means harsh toward its opponents. It
urges indulgence in behalf of such as through past
observances, or ignorance and simplicity, had never
adopted their own opinion in regard to the cup.

There is reason to believe that many took this occasion to change their position on the great question
before the nation—some through policy doubtless,
others through conviction. Peter of Umetzow, a

[1] Mon. Hus., ii. 364.

theological professor, who had been one of the most determined opponents of Huss and his doctrines, in a full meeting of the university publicly avowed the change that had taken place in his views.[1]   He asked pardon of God and the king for having persecuted so holy a man and so orthodox a teacher as John Huss.   He declared that, rejecting the decision of the council of Constance, he could hold no other view in regard to the use of the cup than the one which the university had approved.

Wenzel, at this period, had himself withdrawn from Prague.   The absence of the principal Hussite nobles did not reassure him.   Either they might return, or others might visit him with complaints that would sadly disturb his easy and drunken indolence.   He had taken refuge in a fortress called Tossenicz, where he refused to see any one.   On one occasion, the Bohemian nobility, in large numbers, went to visit him; but he saw them coming, redoubled his guards, and refused them admittance.   They consulted together, and resolved to send a deputation who might be more readily received.   Two of their number, venerable with their grey hair and long beards, were sent to demand audience.   Their request was granted, but they were directed to go to another fortress, where the king promised to meet them.   He kept his word, and treated them to a magnificent entertainment.   After the repast was finished, one of the nobility addressed the king: "Sire," said he, "the lords and all the nobility of the Bohemian nation most humbly ask to be informed why you do not,

[1] Mon. Hus., ii. 365

like the king your father, of blessed memory, and like previous kings of Bohemia, reside at Prague, the capital of your kingdom, to the welfare and peace of your subjects. They are surprised at the indifference shown by your majesty, while the kingdom is exposed to violence and desolated by plunderers. They therefore pray you to return to Prague, promising you all fidelity and affection."

The king, who knew how to use plain language, and who had no pride to be wounded by a frank confession, replied in this manner: "My dear William"—William of Rosenberg was the one who had addressed him—"you say that the grandees of Bohemia are surprised, that instead of remaining at Prague I keep myself here among these rocks; but you must know that I am afraid of Spinca.[1] You must not think it strange that I keep away from you, when I could not be even safe, either in the monastery of Konigsaal, near Beraun, nor in the royal palace. I find myself much more comfortably situated here in Ziebrak, than I could be in the tower of Vienna."[1]

The nobility at once pledged their honor to Wenzel for his security, if he would return. At last he yielded, and took up his residence once more in the royal palace. But a few days after, the magistrates of the city, accompanied by nobles and barons, visited him with the request that certain churches might be allowed them in which to worship after their own manner, and celebrate the Holy Supper

[1] The name of a prison for criminals, at Prague, where he had been shut up for a year.   [2] Mon. Hus., ii. 359.

according to Christ's institution. The request was granted, and from this time the memory of Huss and Jerome was celebrated at each anniversary of the sixth of July.

We have some light on the progress of the reformation at Prague, in a sermon preached in the Bethlehem chapel at some time during this month, and, more than possibly, on this very day (July 6).[1] It is introduced by no *Ave Maria*, as till then had been the uniform practice, adopted usually even by Huss. The preacher invokes only the aid of Jesus Christ. Scriptural simplicity and usage were evidently gaining ground in other things than the use of the cup. The preacher fitly takes occasion to speak of the "blessedness of those who are persecuted for righteousness' sake." He dwells upon the character of Huss, confidently appealing to the assembly for the truth of what he uttered. He sets forth in language of eulogy—yet not extravagant—the holiness and purity of his life. "God gave him," he adds, "a tongue discreet to speak, or to be silent. Like a second Elias, his zeal was inflamed against Antichrist, and a simoniacal clergy. His life was spent in preaching or writing, hearing confessions, converting sinners, consoling the afflicted. He was chaste, grave, God-fearing, without avarice, envy, pride, or hypocrisy; listening with equal readiness to rich and poor, and giving counsel to one and aid to the other. After enduring protracted persecution in Bohemia, he was kept near six months in harsh imprisonment at Constance, where he suffered hunger, thirst, and innu-

[1] Mon. Hus., ii. 358.

merable vexations from his enemies, beside all the sickness and disease produced by his harsh treatment. At last, regardless of his replies, he was condemned, degraded from the priesthood, given over to the secular arm, on the testimony of his enemies and false extracts from his works.   As his life ended so piously —while he besought God for pardon, and prayed for his enemies—we are constrained to believe that his spirit, like that of Elias, mounted to heaven in a chariot of fire, to be received into the company of the angels."

The preacher passes hastily over Jerome, briefly reciting the main facts of his trial, imprisonment, and execution.   He speaks, however, of five other martyrs to the same cause who had suffered death. Three of these were those who had been decapitated at Prague: two had been burned at Olmutz.   He urges his hearers to imitate the patience and unworldliness of these men, and do it in hope to attain like them to a martyr's crown.

It is easy to see in what light the Hussites regarded their fallen leaders.   They did not bestow upon them the honors that Rome paid to her saints.   They did not pray in their name.   They cherished (*pie credimus*) the fond hope of their salvation.

We have seen that William of Rosenberg was spokesman for the Bohemian nobility in addressing the king at Ziebrak.   He, with all his vassals, joined during this year the party of reform.   If the method of conversion which he adopted was not unexceptionable, it was at least decisive.   All the clergy belonging to his dependence were assembled in one of his cities, and summoned to the church. A dea-con, John Biscupec, (or the little bishop, as he was called, and whom we meet again at the council of Basle,) mounted the pulpit from which it had been the custom to exhibit the sacred relics, and addressed the assembly. "The Lords of Rosenberg will and ordain," said he, " that all pastors in their jurisdiction adopt the communion of the cup, and teach and practice all that John Huss preached against the pope. Such as refuse to obey, will be driven from their churches after the space of six weeks." The announcement was listened to in silence, and silence was favorably construed. Invited to a great dinner, the priests were asked to explain their views. They demanded a month to deliberate. The result was, that from two priests only were their parishes taken and given to the Hussites. Undoubtedly numerous instances of a similar kind must have occurred, where the favor-ite arguments of the papal party were retorted upon themselves, and force was substituted for reason. Such a result was almost inevitable. The rights of the individual conscience were too little understood even by the Hussites. But, as if to show the vanity and fruitlessness of such methods of conversion, we find the Lord of Rosenberg himself, a few months later, returning to the imperio-papal party with as little scruple as he now abandoned it. Doubtless his vassal priests—with the exception of Biscupec—proved as pliant then as they were now. Yet the adherence to the Hussites at the present juncture, of such a man as the Lord of Rosenberg, was significant of the strong current of national feeling. Each day

what the council accounted heresy was growing
stronger in Bohemia.

Among the measures which the council found it
necessary to adopt, were some in its own defence.
Europe, notwithstanding all that Sigismund had
accomplished, was yet in a most lamentable condition of civil anarchy. Scenes of violence, revolution, revolt, and conflict were of daily occurrence.
Cities were at war with their bishops or feudal lords.
Princes seized the occasion to plunder one another
of exposed provinces. Armed banditti, sometimes
with strong fortresses as places of refuge, infested
the travelled routes, and, reckless alike of law and
justice, plundered the unarmed and defenceless.
Members of the council, coming to Constance or
returning to their homes, were arrested and imprisoned till ransom was exacted.

The emperor, with the princes and lords present
at Constance, held frequent consultations with a view
to restrain and correct the prevalent disorders. Much
was indeed effected toward restoring the amicable
relations of cities and provinces, but the council
found itself constrained to exercise also its authority.
Such as interfered with the liberty of its members,
in coming or returning, were threatened with excommunication. Yet instances of violent arrest were
repeatedly occurring, and had to be met as they
arose.

But the enemies from whom the council had most
to fear, were not the banditti, or the temporal lords.
Its weakness was in itself—in its own corruption.
Its own acts had stripped it of its true defence, and

exposed it to the shafts of opprobrium and ridicule. It had made itself a subject for satire, and satires were not wanting. The conduct of the council and the condition of the church were freely exposed in anonymous writings extensively circulated, and which the council chose to regard as libels. The evident disinclination of the majority of the body to engage in measures of reform, provoked the indignation of many, who found at last that they had built their hopes upon the sand. This indignation found vent in writings which a decree of the council stamped as defamatory. One of these was torn up unread, at the time of the reading of the decree. We cannot fully determine what were its contents, but it is not improbable that it was a paper drawn up under the guise of a petition addressed to the emperor in behalf of reform, and which has been preserved in the pages of Van der Hardt. Its irony is keen and bitter. Its exposure of the abuses and corruptions of the church is unsparing, yet fully warranted by the testimony of many, themselves members of the council.

" Most serene prince,"—so it commences,—" to secure the welfare of the commonwealth, each faithful and honest man should put forth his exertions:

> For I, Henry Move-About, [1]
> Bishop of no diocese,
> Vagrant of vagrants,
> Although least among the other servants of our congregation,
> Deputed for this purpose, legate or special messenger,
> Sent into the whole world, to observe all things,
> Coming to visit the portals of Saints Peter and Paul,

---

[1] Ego enim Henricus mobilis, Episcopus nullius dioceseos, Vagorum vagus —

The last line intended to parody the assumed title of the pope, *servus servorum.*

saw there such things as it is indecent for a man to speak, and specially the truth of that—*Dum caput ægrotat cætera membra dolent.*[1] For I saw there a crowd which no man could number, and, among the rest, the very head of holy mother church, diseased in all her members, even to the sole of the foot; for the whole head was sick."

The writer then ingeniously carries out this scriptural figure in its application. Various complicated diseases had seized upon the body and affected the brain. The fever of schism, the morbid appetite of simony, the threatened apoplexy from accumulating the life-blood of the church on an oppressed brain, the corruption of the entire body, represented by cardinals, patriarchs, prelates, etc., who were its internal organs, yet all diseased, are vividly and forcibly presented. The gross corruptions of the court of Rome are portrayed in such a manner as still further to carry out the figure. The abuses to be corrected, are classified by their reference to the different parts of the body. The writer gives a sketch of what he observed at Rome—"the archbishops and bishops, disorderly in life, setting no good example—promoting the least worthy—making their relatives bishops—performing no spiritual duties canonically—walking as proud worldlings. "O holy church, how wilt thou sink away in decline! I saw princes and laymen assuming the care of souls—religious persons deserting their regular life —the physicians themselves destroying and putting to death—Benedictines adhering to worldly things,

---

[1] When the head is sick, the other members suffer.

lurking about at taverns, plays, illegal shows, in slovenly habit—professors of canon law unjustly holding a plurality of benefices, without charity, thanksgiving, or devotion."

After an extended picture of the prevalent corruption, the writer addresses the emperor. " Now then it belongs to thee to assemble Hippocrates, Avicenna, Galen, and the doctors of every healing art, that they may give energy to the exhausted, heal the sick, and prescribe effectual remedies. And direct them to make ointments to cure the head, pills that may serve to regulate the system, clysters that may be applied. Invincible king, summon with thy holy and sacred council now at Constance, the physicians themselves of the world, but only the just and holy lights of the sacred council, fearing God, and heal and cause to be healed the aforesaid sick one, not only through the whole head, but in hands and feet which are full of ulcers, and send the dogs to lick the sores."

" I came into the world to look after that which holy mother church long had lost; I found it not, but rather all kinds of iniquity." He then exhorts the emperor to contend against the evil, and merit thereby eternal praise. For himself the writer expresses his freedom from all apprehension as to being questioned, " Friend, how camest thou in hither ? " although he confesses that he had not on the wedding garment.

Each passing day gave new force and appropriateness to the language of this strange petition. The hopes of speedy and prompt reform were fast dying out. The emperor's purpose, in spite of all his authority and his influence over the council, was destined to defeat, while the latter thereby was aggravating its own infamy. It was policy therefore to shut the mouths and stop the pens of those who assumed to judge its infallibility. This was attempted; but if men wrote with more caution, they were not disposed to think the less boldly. The Hussites had really allies in the council itself, who spoke their sentiments with a force and precision which, in many respects, could not have been exceeded at Prague.

During the summer of this year, the attention of the council had been drawn to the sect of the Flagellants, or Brothers of the Cross. The French Abbé de Boileau,[1] has attempted to trace their history. He ascribes their origin to Peter Damien, an Italian ecclesiastic of the eleventh century; but it is easy to see that the germ of the sect was planted in that principle so long at work in the church of the early centuries, which approved the self-imposed austerities and mortifications of the body, in order to promote the welfare of the soul. The views of the abbé are altogether too scriptural to accord fully with that monkish superstition in which the sect found full patronage for many of its excesses.

It was not, however, till about the year 1260, that the Flagellants began to attract much attention. Italy at that period presented a sad picture of commingled vice, crime, and superstition.[2] It was there that the sect first sprang up, spreading from city to

---

[1] Boileau, His. des Flag.   [2] Justin of Padua, as quoted by Boileau.

city, and province to province. The general belief
that the end of the world was approaching, excited
and sustained their enthusiasm. The apprehension
of the approaching advent of the Saviour, and of the
final judgment, took so strong a hold upon the minds
of the community, that nobles and peasants, the aged
and young, were affected by it. They formed themselves into processions, marching two by two through
the streets, exposing their naked limbs and almost
naked bodies to the blows of the lash which each
bore with him, and employed to lacerate his own
flesh. All were deeply affected by the general conviction that their sin must be expiated by self-inflicted torture. Their appearance was at once pitiable and affecting. With groans and tears and un-
dissembled grief, they endured the suffering administered by their own hands, till the blood flowed in
streams from their bodies.

Yet it was their spiritual condition, and not their
bodily sufferings, which occupied their thoughts.
They cried aloud to God for mercy, and prayed for
his pardon and grace. It was not enough that these
practises were followed by day. By night also, in
the cold of winter as well as in summer's heat, they
continued their processions. Priests might often be
seen at their head, bearing with them crosses and
standards. They went from village to village, and from
church to church, bowing down before the altars in
deep humility. The excitement became general—almost universal. A great change was wrought in the
aspect of society. Instruments of music and songs
of gladness were no more heard. Penitential moans,

and cries of grief and self-accusation, took their place. Nor was the change merely external. It affected the convictions and conduct of men. Enemies were reconciled. Usurers and extortioners restored what had been unjustly acquired. Criminals confessed their guilty deeds, and gave evidence of reform. Prisoners were enlarged, slaves were set at liberty, exiles were recalled. Deeds of charity and kindness were performed, while the fear of some near approaching and terrible judgment awed all spirits. Men were astonished at the strange phenomenon. Philosophers could not explain it. The pope had not authorized it. It had not been excited by the eloquence of popular orators. It had no acknowledged leader. Shut out from other countries, it was for a long time mostly confined to Italy, and after a short time its fanatical zeal appeared to be on the decline.

But the scenes of the pestilence, about the middle of the fourteenth century, seemed to kindle it anew. It crossed the Alps, and appeared in Germany with renewed vigor. Two hundred of the sect visited Spires, where their evident devotion secured them a welcome entertainment. At Strasbourg and Aix la Chapelle their appearance is recorded. But, with the progress of things, corruptions had begun to spread among them. They were joined by hypocrites and knaves, who would cloak their deeds under the mantle of the Flagellants. The most grievous charges were made against them. It was said that they accounted it no sin to lie; that they indulged in acts of grossest vice and crime. The tide now turned against them. Popes fulminated bulls, and

the emperor published edicts denouncing the sect.
They were driven out of Bohemia, Bavaria, and
Poland, and the University of Paris urged, and not
without effect, that they should not be tolerated in
France. But in vain were they persecuted. Their
numbers continued to increase. The Inquisition was
glutted with victims; and in the very year when the
council of Constance was opened, many were burnt
at Sangerhausen by the authority of the Inquisitor
of the Faith.

Undoubtedly they had by this time become, many
of them, confirmed fanatics. Their leader, a Conrad
Smith, is said to have pretended to be the prophet
Enoch, and to have been authorized by God to judge
the world. He is reported to have annulled the
sacraments, and to have put the self-inflicted flagel-
lation of his followers in their place. Some of the
reputed doctrines of the sect were far from compli-
mentary to the church. They maintained that God
had deposed the entire clergy, from pope to monk,
for their corruption, as Christ of old drove the money-
changers from the temple; that since their own institution, churches, cemeteries, and places and objects
reputed holy, were such no longer; the churches
were but dens of robbers; holy water was poisonous
because mingled with sparks of hell; and the offices
of the priests, ministering death to themselves and
others, were no more sacred than the howling of
dogs. Baptism of blood had taken the place of
baptism by water; confirmation was a cheat and a
mockery; the real presence was a figment; the sacrament of the altar, a mummery of the priests; and

confession to a priest, useless and vain. They rejected the doctrine of indulgences, the worship of the Virgin and the saints, fasts, and purgatory. Some of these doctrines, however, were replaced, according to the charges of their enemies, with others more excessively fanatical and extravagant.

These charges, however, evidently were applicable to but a small portion of the sect. But what to do with them was a question that puzzled the wisdom of the council. Severity had already been employed. The arm of the Inquisition had grown weary in its work. Kings and popes had attempted to crush them, but it was all in vain. The trampled seed sprang up under the feet that bruised its shell and pressed it to the earth. Gerson was now for trying more lenient measures. He urged this policy upon the council. They should pity these poor misguided men. Would he have said this, if the whole sect had been represented by its leader, chained fast, as Huss had been, in a Constance dungeon? It seems doubtful. But one thing may have turned the scale. The celebrated Vincent of Ferrara was reported to favor the sect of the Flagellants. We have no reason to believe that he ever joined them, but they at least claimed the sanction of his name. Vincent was a man not to be lightly dealt with. He wielded a power over the masses at that day, unrivalled by any other man in Europe. With all the peculiarities of his order,—the Dominican,—that still clung to him, he was the great popular preacher of his age. He was the John the Baptist of the European wilderness. It would not do, even for the council, to

deal harshly with such a man. It could not afford
to alienate him. It would only condemn itself in
arraigning him. Gerson endeavored to draw him to
Constance. He and D'Ailly both wrote to him, urging him to come. They undoubtedly believed that
if he were once with them they could bring him
over to their views. But he declined their overture.
What his reasons were we may surmise. He deemed,
undoubtedly, that his presence elsewhere would be
more useful, and Constance evidently had no attrac-
tion for one whose life is a sort of oasis in the corruption of his age.

But would Vincent have been safe at Constance?
If the question of the Flagellants had come before
the council, and he, though not of their number, had
defended their conduct in many things, as he had
enjoyed a full opportunity of inspecting it, would he
have left Constance as he entered it—with a reputation and character untarnished? For the sake of
our poor weak nature, we may be thankful that he
was spared a trial that might not have spared even
him.

Gerson's treatise on the sect is, on the whole, a
most just and sensible examination of the case. He
condemns the immodesty and cruelty which it occasioned, while he places penitence of spirit before God
far above all self-imposed austerities. He urges upon
those who belonged to it, submission to the council,
and prescribes as a remedy for the mental hallucina-
tions of the Flagellants, that they should be required
to labor, instead of running from place to place.

This was for the most part sound and sensible ad-

vice, and the council seems to have acceded to its
wisdom. But where was its consistency? If the
Hussites were heretics, much more were the Flagellants. Why should Vincent of Ferrara be dealt with
so gently, while Huss and Jerome are sent to the
funeral pile? Let the assumed infallibility of the
council answer.

The fate of Benedict XIII. was at length decided.
After all necessary formalities of process and citation, he was deposed by the council, in its thirty
seventh session, held July 26th, 1417.[1] The Cardinal of St. Mark read the sentence. It declared Benedict perjured, a scandal to the Catholic church, a
favorer of schism, a disturber of the peace and union
of the church, an obstinate and incorrigible schismatic, a heretic devoid of faith; in a word, a man
reprobate of God, and unworthy of every dignity,
specially of the pontifical. Of such, the council de-
grades, deposes, and deprives him, and forbids any
one to recognize him as pope under the severest penalties.

Thus at last the council might consider the union
of the church restored. After nearly three years
of study and effort, the work seemed accomplished.
But the deposition of Benedict, though uniting the
church, more effectively than ever divided the council. The question as to whether measures for reform
or the election of a new pontiff should be allowed
precedence, acquired a new and pressing importance.
The emperor persisted in his efforts for an immediate
reform. The cardinals were equally determined in

---

[1] Van der Hardt, iv. 1374.

their purpose to postpone it. The month of August was spent in intrigues by each party to carry its point. The Italians sought to win over the Germans, but these still stood firm by the emperor. Some of the Italian and French prelates also might be reckoned—although in the minority of their nations—the partisans of reform.

The sermons that were preached before the council became pleas in behalf of the one or the other party. Those that urged the importance of reform were startling in their exposures of corruption, and terrible in their invective. One preacher declared—no doubt truly—"that almost the entire clergy were under the dominion of the devil."[1] He represents the council as an assembly of Pharisees, who play the game of religion and the church, under the mask of devotion. "In the world, falsehood is king; among the clergy, avarice is law. In the prelates are found only malice, iniquity, negligence, ignorance, vanity, pride, avarice, simony, lust, pomp, hypocrisy. At the court of the pope there is no holiness. It is a diabolic court." Another preacher is scarcely less severe. He declares that the clergy spend their money on buffoons, dancing girls, dogs, and birds, rather than in charity to the poor. They frequent taverns and brothels, and go from their concubines and prostitutes to mass without any scruple. It has passed, he says, into a proverb, that "the prelates have as many mistresses as domestics." The convents are not spared. "It is a shame," he says "to speak of what is done in them; more a shame to do it. In

---

[1] L'Enfant, 494.

all these abominations, the court of Rome sets the example, even in the place where it is assembled for the reformation of manners." Other preachers spoke in the same strain.

But the partisans of a new election had their orators. The Cardinal of Cambray preached before the council. He did not attempt to controvert the statements that had already been made,—he rather confirmed them,—but urged that it was monstrous to think of reforming the body of the church while it was without a head.

The English nation remained as yet firmly attached to the emperor's project of giving precedence to the matter of reform. The king of England wrote to his bishops, urging unanimity in the matter, for he had heard that some of the English members of the council were inclining to the side of the cardinals. Such persons were to be commanded in his name to desist from their course, and, in case of refusal, were to be sent back to England to answer for their conduct.

The cardinals, however, did not fail to urge their favorite project, more and more strenuously. They presented a protest (Aug. 4) against the course of their opponents. Nor was this enough; they endeavored to overwhelm them, or at least weaken their influence, by exciting against them suspicion of heresy. A paper was adroitly drawn up in the form of queries, suggesting the various ways in which they seemed to favor the opinions of Huss. The whole document betrays malice and impudence. The English and Germans had been the most forward in con demning, or securing the condemnation, of Huss. They could not justly be accused of complicity with his cause. But they felt, for all this, only the more deeply the pressing necessity of reform. They would have all the arguments of men like Huss—drawn from the indisputable and gross corruption of the church—taken out of their mouths. This was the extent of their heresy, at least before the council. But the cardinals, and the three nations that held with them, became more bold and daring with each successive day. The former, on the ninth of September, renewed their protest, and now in stronger language.

Sigismund was present when its reading was commenced. It stung him to indignation. He rose at once, ere the reading was finished, and left the assembly. As he went out, accompanied by the Patriarch of Antioch, among others, some one cried out, "Let the heretics go!" This was reported to Sigismund, and did not tend to soothe his irritation. It was reported, probably on good grounds, that he meant to arrest some of the cardinals under pretence that they were engaged in consultations deleterious to the interests of the council. He forbade them the use of the cathedral church and the episcopal palace, in which they had been accustomed to meet. But such measures, failing to overawe, could only irritate. The Germans, meanwhile, were restive under the imputations of heresy which were cast upon them. They drew up their defence, in which they took occasion to argue anew the necessity of reform, and pointed out some of the gross abuses of which they complained.

The condition of the council was one exceedingly critical. It was divided into two great parties—on one side the English and Germans, headed by the emperor; on the other, the Italians, French, and Spaniards, led by the cardinals. What would have been the result had neither party yielded, it is diffi- cult to say; we can scarcely doubt that it would have led to the dissolution of the council.

But at this critical period the emperor lost his *fidem Achaten*, as the historian calls him. On the 4th of September, Robert Hallam, Bishop of Salis- bury, died.[1] He had been from the outset a strenu- ous supporter of the emperor's project. Previous to the council of Pisa, Richard Ullerston had writ- ten, at his instance, his celebrated work on the neces- sity and methods of reform. While the bishop lived, the English nation stood firm by the emperor. But now they could no longer be depended on. The solicitations and intrigues of the other party were working wonders. Even the German nation began to waver. The Archbishop of Riga, who cruelly and harshly had taken charge of the imprisonment of Huss, was won over by a bribe. He was promised, in place of his present dignity—which had become unaccept- able, through the hostility of the Teutonic order which he had incurred—the diocese of Liege. An- other leader of the German nation, John Abundi, Bishop of Coire, was won by the promise of being placed in the vacant See.[2]

The result could no longer remain in doubt. The desertion from the emperor had commenced. Some

[1] Van der Hardt, iv. 1414.   [2] L'Enfant, 511.

of the Italian and French bishops, who had resisted
hitherto the decisions of their nations, made haste to
leave the sinking ship. The question was now only
one of time. The emperor could not long hold out.
He at length capitulated, on the condition that the
council should initiate the measures of reform, by a
public decree, before the election should take place.
Vain condition! Some of the cardinals even now
did not hesitate to say, that such a decree could not
bind the future pope. Yet the condition was assent-
ed to. The cause of reform had made hitherto but
slow progress. Difficulty after difficulty had blocked
up its way. The council now, however, resolved that
on certain points a reform should be perfected. Two
months had passed away in party negotiation and
intrigue, when at length another (the twenty-ninth)
session was held (Oct. 9th).[1] The measures which
were declared to be settled by public decree, related
to the frequent and regular convocation of general
councils—precautions against the renewal of schism
—the profession of faith and duty to be made by
the pope on his election—the translation of benefices, and exactions from vacant bishoprics. It is
easy to see that all this implied but an external
and insufficient reform, while the disease was too
deep to be reached by any such appliance. It was
equally in vain that it was determined, a few days
later, to enlarge the project, and add new measures
tending to the check of ecclesiastical abuses. They
all had respect merely to that which belonged to the
externals of the church, its dignities, offices, reve-

[1] Van der Hardt, iv. 1432.

nues.[1] Germany vainly demanded reform now ; a century later she would demand it in more emphatic
tones.   The very point on which nearly all the nations had insisted most strenuously, and in regard to
which there seemed most hope of success, that of
annates—the first year's income when a benefice was
vacant, and which was claimed for its support by the
court of Rome—was the one about which great difficulties were now raised.   The emperor and others
would have the officers of the court of Rome provided with a fixed annual salary.   Doubtful of so uncertain a provision, the cardinals could not relinquish
the annates, and the whole question must of necessity be left to the future pope.

Who he would be, was now the question of most
engrossing interest.   On the thirtieth of October,
the council decreed to proceed to his election.[2]   The
cardinals had at first somewhat humbly dared to put
forward their claims to the right of sole electors as
their prerogative.   Some of their opponents, in view
of the manner in which they had previously exercised it, would have excluded them altogether from
the conclave.   A compromise was at length effected,
by which six prelates or persons of distinction from
each of the five nations should be joined to the
college of cardinals, in order to form the body of
the electors.   The number of these, including the
twenty-three cardinals, was therefore fifty-three.   For
each of these a chamber was provided in the Merchants' Exchange, where the sessions of the conclave
were to be held.   Every precaution was taken to

<hr>

[1] L'Enfant, 521.   [2] Van der Hardt, iv. 1449.

prevent any communication between them and others outside the building. Persons of high state and authority were to guard all the passages, and all were warned by sound of trumpet not to approach within a certain distance of the place where the conclave was in session. Even the food of the electors and their servants—for each was allowed two—was to some extent prescribed, and was passed into the building, not by the door, but by a window, in order that none might have a pretext or opportunity to enter. Even after the food had been passed in, it was to be examined before it was sent to the electors, lest some letter or line should be enclosed in it by which some communication or information should be conveyed to them.

The electors entered the conclave Nov. 2, 1417.[1] For some time there seemed no prospect of their effecting a choice, as two-thirds of the votes must be given to the successful candidate. Each nation would undoubtedly have been glad to have had for pope one of its own countrymen. But the Germans were the first to yield their preference. The Archbishop of Riga, who seems by this time to have acquired the art of seizing upon and improving occasions that could favor his own interests, led the way. At length the other nations so far consented to yield their claims, that the necessary vote was cast for Otho de Colonna, an Italian cardinal. He had been one of the cardinals of John XXIII., and had borne a reputation as free from stain as it was perhaps possible for a member of a college with such a head.

[1] L'Enfant, 529.

He was undoubtedly less able than many of the
others. The cardinals of Cambray and St. Mark
were by far his superiors, but they had made themselves offensively conspicuous; and their compeer,
Zabarella of Florence, had gone out a few days
before from one of the assemblies—exhausted by the
effort of a speech which he truly said at the time
might be called his dying testimony—never to return. He died on the twenty-sixth of September,
the most dangerous competitor—had he survived—
for the pontifical dignity.[1]

Otho de Colonna took the title of Martin V.
Different estimates were formed of his character.[2]
But whatever he might have been before his election, he was, after it, but a wheel in the ecclesiastical
machine, and was governed by laws that would have
overruled his own will had he not chosen to submit.
The news of his election spread at once through the
city. Through a breach made in the walls of the
building where the conclave was assembled, the fact
had been first announced, and was received with
loud acclamations. The people, gathered by thousands, could not restrain their enthusiasm as they
shouted the name of the new pope. The emperor,
regardless, as some say, of his dignity, hasted to
prostrate himself before him, kissing his feet, and
thanking the electors for the excellent choice they
had made. The pope replied with a fraternal embrace, and with thanks to the emperor for his zeal
for the peace of the church.

The enthroning of the newly elected pope pre-

---

[1] L'Enfant, 513.   [2] Ib. 538, 539.

sented a scene of imposing splendor. The emperor, princes and nobility, the clergy of all ranks, beside men of every civil office and station, formed the escort which accompanied him from the conclave to the cathedral. His ordination as deacon took place November 12th, his consecration and coronation as pope, Nov. 21st.[1] These were marked by scenes of scarcely less splendor and magnificence. As the procession on this last occasion moved through the streets of the city, it was met by the Jews, who assured the new pope of their obedience, and besought of him a confirmation of their privileges, while presenting him at the same time a copy of the Old Testament. The pope paused a moment, received the volume—according to some—but handed it back with the remark, "You have the law, but do not understand it. Behold, old things have passed away, all has become new."

According to another account, the pope refused to receive the volume. Sigismund took it for a moment, however, remarking as he handed it back, "The laws of Moses are just and good—let no one reject them; but as to you, you keep none of them as you ought." Upon this the pope, turning toward them, said, "May Almighty God take away the veil from your eyes, and grant that you may behold the light of eternal life;" then adding the apostolic benediction.

The power and intrigue of the cardinals had thus secured their triumph. With a pope to head them, they could do more than they had done already—

---

[1] L'Enfant, 547.

they could safely defy the emperor. Each party now strove to gain the favor and patronage of the pope. The imperial power occupied but a secondary place. All measures of reform must be such as to be acceptable to the court of Rome. It was as much as a defeat already, of projects for which the best men of the age had toiled, and written, and plead. The work of reformation was in reality postponed. The heart of the emperor was sickened within him. The French urged him to promote their measures of reform. His reply was bitter: "You would have a pope first. You have one now. Go to him. It is his business, not mine."

CHAPTER XI.

MEASURES OF THE POPE AND COUNCIL AGAINST THE BOHEMIANS.

State of Bohemia. — Alarm of the Clergy who Adhered to the Council. — Disorder. — Flight of Wenzel. — Apprehensions of the Council. — Gerson's Treatise on the Eucharist. — Maurice of Prague. — Sigismund's Letter to Launa. — Threatens a Crusade. — His Letters to His Brother, Wenzel. — Their Insolence and Duplicity. — Letter of Martin V. to Bohemia. — Demands of the Council. — Process Against Such as are Suspected of Heresy. — The Bull of Martin V. — Its Contents. — Its Severity. — Points of Examination for the Suspected. — How the Trial was to be Conducted. — Execution of Lord Cobham. — Terror of a Crusade. — Crusade Against the Moors. — Indignation of the Bohemians. — Nicholas de Hussinitz. — Boldness of Zisca. — Course of John Dominic. — He is Convinced that Arms are Necessary to Subdue the Bohemians.

Nov. 22, 1417 — April 15, 1418.

WHILE the council at Constance was rent into factions by intrigues to elect a pope, Bohemia became more than ever a scene of civil discord. The Hussites were steadily increasing in numbers and in confidence. The course of the council, instead of regaining its lost adherents, alienated many who might otherwise have sustained it. Nothing was done to restore to that body the respect and confidence which had been destroyed by the execution of Huss and Jerome. The action of the university carried with it many who, until that time, had remained wavering and undecided. The clergy who adhered to the council became more thoroughly alarmed. They had

exhausted all their energies in attempting to breast
the storm; but their very efforts only recoiled upon
themselves.   They provoked and exasperated where
conciliation would have been policy.   Justifying, as
they did, the execution of Huss, and invoking the
interference of the secular power, they forfeited that
respect and security which they might have claimed
had they quietly attended to their own duties.

They by no means limited their demands to being
left unmolested in their own persons and spheres of
labor. The storm which they invoked upon the heads
of others, was thus brought down upon their own.
Refusing toleration, it is not strange that the measure which they meted should have been measured to
them again.   They occupied the position, and were
regarded in the light, of allies to an invading army—
designed to oppress, crush, and extirpate the followers of Huss.   They were not merely misguided men
and teachers of error, but—in the circumstances of
the kingdom—revolutionists in principle, and traitors
in fact; and so the Hussites, on repeated occasions,
felt constrained to deal with them.   Stripped of a
large part of their revenues, the edge of their orthodoxy was sharpened by the exasperation of their
feelings.   Some of their churches—we may presume
already vacated by them, or perhaps closed by interdict—were given up by Wenzel to the services of
the new worship.   Amid the civil disorder, it was
not surprising that men destitute of principle, and
fond of fishing in troubled waters, should abound.
Robbers and bandits gladly seized the occasion to
commit deeds of violence, which could be charged

to the persecuting zeal of the Hussites, but of which the latter were innocent.

The craven and timid monarch, who would sooner see both parties overthrown and his kingdom a desert than have his own indolence or gluttony disturbed, abandoned at this moment the duties of his post. Unwilling to commit himself fully to either party, fearful on the one side of being accounted a heretic, and on the other of offending the partisans and followers of Huss, who were overwhelmingly in the ascendant, he withdrew from Prague, and left it the spoil and prey of conflicting parties—torn by faction, or private malice and violence, now loosened from restraint. We are only surprised that the party of reform should have exhibited so much self-control. The king, intent only upon his own ease and indulgence, had fled to his castle in the country, leaving his whole kingdom to the mercy of insurrection and anarchy. The presence and authority of the more powerful Bohemian nobles, sometimes perhaps encouraging revolution and violence, were generally the best security for peace and order. Each controlled his own vassals; and the overwhelming majority of this nobility on the side of the reformers, overawed all organized opposition.

The council had good reason for anxiety as to the effect of their own proceedings upon the Bohemian people. They saw themselves virtually defied. Their authority was contemned, and their spiritual claims were openly derided. Not one of the four hundred nobles whom they had summoned before them had shown regard enough for their commands or threat-

enings to appear before the commissioners appointed
to sit in judgment upon their case. In the present
state of affairs, it was vain to think of subduing them
by violent measures. The forces necessary for such
an attempt could not easily be got together. In
these circumstances the council did what it should
have done first and only—employed the weapons of
reason and argument. Gerson was employed to
draw up a treatise on the communion of the cup, in
order to refute the positions and opinions of the Bohemian heretics.[1] His work is a strange mixture of
sound sense and absurd assumption, of indisputable
truth and unwarranted inference. He concedes
nearly, if not quite, all upon which Jacobel based his
argument—the plain command of scripture, the practice of the early church, and the authority of the
Christian fathers. He admits the scriptures moreover to be the supreme authority, paramount to all
else, whether traditions, or decrees of councils, or papal
bulls, or canon law, and, in face of all this, places the
authority of the church, and the dangers of desecrat-
ing the sacred symbols, over against the clear authority of the word of God. It was the doctrine of
transubstantiation that blinded him. His work is a
psychological curiosity. The intellectual giant of
his age is caught in his own toils; he is the dupe of
his own logic.

His treatise was a mere waste of ink and labor. It
proved to be perfectly harmless and ineffectual in
Bohemia. Jacobel could afford to leave it unanswered,
or rather, he had answered it before it was written.

---

[1] Van der Hardt, iii. 766.

Nor could the difficulty of the council have been much relieved, when, at its instance, Maurice of Prague took up the pen against the Calixtines—as the advocates of the communion of the cup now began to be called. His treatise was brought out towards the close of the year (1417).

But more forcible arguments were needed to convert to the views of the council those whose innate sense of justice had been so outraged by the execution of Huss. The emperor exerted himself to check the torrent of innovation that was sweeping over the land. Some of his letters have been preserved, but however they may attest the strength of his feelings, or the energy of his will, they do little credit either to his head or heart. One of them is addressed to the inhabitants of Launa,[1] a city on the Eger, among whom the views of Huss had made such progress before he left Prague for Constance, that he addressed them words of counsel and exhortation. In this letter Sigismund speaks of the urgency with which his brother and some of the Bohemian nobles had prayed him to unite with the council, in order to put an end to the troubles introduced into the kingdom by pernicious innovations; he makes mention of his brother, whom he despised and at this very time was accusing of heresy, in terms of fraternal and affectionate regard—as though he had never robbed him of the imperial crown, or thrust him in prison—and declares the deep anxiety he feels that nothing may occur to the prejudice of him or his kingdom.

After this exordium, in which the hypocrite stands

---

[1] Mon. Hus. i., Epis. xiv. Launa is sometimes written Launy.

confessed beneath his too transparent mask, he proceeds to picture the state of the country, subject to
the violence and rapine which had been reported to
him. The council, he says, had resolved to proceed
against Wenzel as a favorer of heresy, and consequently of these disorders, but by his interposition
had been dissuaded from their purpose. This state
of things had continued now for the space of three
years, but how much longer he should be able to
hold back the bolts of vengeance which the council
were ready to launch against his brother if he refused to change his course, it was impossible to say.
He exhorts the Bohemians to resist the innovating
opinions, declaring that he who failed to prosecute
their defenders, denying them all rest, was guilty of
cherishing them. He directs them not only to abstain from what he calls the persecutions of the
church and clergy, but diligently to promote the
cause of faith, than which no object could be more
precious or important. If these his counsels and
commands are rejected, the council of Constance will
proceed against them, and, if ecclesiastical censures
are insufficient, will invoke the aid of the secular
arm.[1] Why this letter should have been addressed
to the citizens of Launa instead of Prague, is somewhat doubtful. Launa might be more easily overawed, or possibly the emperor might have apprehended that the magistrates of Prague would have
returned a reply in a tone too bold and defiant.

But his correspondence, both with his brother and
with the Bohemians, was of the most indiscreet and

[1] Van der Hardt, iv. 1408.

haughty kind. The Jesuit historian, Balbinus, who saw the emperor's letters in the archives of Prague, was at first disposed to regard them as a forgery, devised by the disciples of Huss to cast odium on their reputed author. He could not believe that Sigismund would have written in such a style of bitter and exasperating severity. But the evidence of the manuscripts before him was so thoroughly confirmed by the after-writings and conduct of the emperor, as to leave no room for doubt. If the council had acted an unwise part, the letters of Sigismund betrayed equal folly. The tendency of the whole treatment of the Bohemian nation was to alienate them from all sympathy with the council, and force them to assume the attitude of open rebellion.

One of the emperor's letters to Wenzel shows the policy employed to overawe the royal imbecile. Sigismund sets before him the hazard which he incurs of provoking the publication of a crusade against him, in which it would be necessary that the German emperor should march against his own brother. Sigismund well knew that the strength of Wenzel's orthodoxy was to be measured by his terror of an invading army, and, to strengthen his faith, adopted this measure of playing upon his fears.

In another of Sigismund's letters, written to the Bohemian nobles sometime during the year 1417, he attempts his own vindication, especially in regard to the fate of Huss. He candidly acknowledges that he was overpowered by the council. They threatened him with its dissolution, unless he would accede to their demands. The question was at once reduced to this: should he, for the sake of one man's life, defeat all the hopes of Christendom which centred in the fate and proceedings of the council? Sigismund reproves the Bohemians for presuming to take up the defence of a man whom the council had condemned, and threatens them with a crusade unless they shall desist from their purpose. At the result which must necessarily follow, he professes to shudder, as well he might. He beseeches them to consider the consequences of persisting in what he denominates their leagues and conspiracies; urges them to abide—if one has anything against another—by the decision of his brother, the king of Bohemia; assures them that if his own intervention is necessary to the quieting of the disputes, it shall not be found wanting. He interposes in behalf of the clergy, intimating unwarrantably, so far as the action or authority of the council were concerned, that they would be guided by scripture, the profoundity of which he confessed himself too uninstructed to investigate.

In this letter he is not wanting in expressions of affection and regard for the besotted Wenzel. At one time we see him employing terms of respect toward a brother whom he detested—for he is speaking of him to the Bohemians. Anon, he treats him with the contempt he deserves—for he is speaking where there is no need of disguise. He threatens him, as he had just threatened his subjects, with the terrors of a crusade. Truly he attempted to carry out his maxim in regard to dissimulation, a maxim which, translated into plain words, is that—no man is

fit to rule who cannot play the hypocrite. But the
Bohemians were discovering very plainly already the
difference between pretence and purpose, the mantle
and the man. We shall soon see the emperor, conscious of detection, speaking with an irony in which
the sneer was only too transparent.

At the close of the year 1417, safe-conducts had
been sent into Bohemia to those who had been cited
to appear and answer before the council.[1] But the
friends of Huss, warned by his fate, had no desire to
involve the council in new perfidy on their account.
We have no knowledge of so much as a single Bohemian accepting the safe-conduct sent him, or improving the opportunity which it afforded. Even
when the new pontiff subsequently wrote (March,
1418) to the Bohemians, exhorting them to submission, and threatening them with the secular arm if
they refused compliance, nothing was effected.[2] That
violent measures had not been already resorted to,
he attributes, and probably with truth, to the interposition of the emperor, who had already too much
on his hands to venture upon a rash conflict with the
Bohemian nation. In February, 1418, when those
who had been cited did not appear, the council passed
a decree,[3] consisting of twenty-four articles, setting
forth authentically its demands. These were, in substance, that the king should swear to maintain invio-
late the rights and prerogatives of the Roman and
other churches, unrestricted by the impositions of the
Hussites ; that all who hath taught the doctrines of
Huss and Wickliffe should abjure them, and approve

¹ L'Enfant, 580.   ² Ib., 589.   ³ Ib., 580, 583.

the sentence of the council pronounced against these men and their writings; that such as refused, in contempt of the keys, to obey this command, should be condignly punished; that the priests and clergy who had been driven from their benefices should be restored, and left unmolested; that the relics and treasures that had been taken from the churches should be replaced; that the university should be reformed, and that the followers of Huss and Wickliffe should be excluded therefrom; that the principal heresiarchs, nine of whom are mentioned by name,[1] should be compelled to appear before the council; that all who had communed under both kinds should abjure the heresy of Jacobel; that the treatises of Wickliffe, Huss, and Jacobel should all of them be surrendered and burned; that the songs sung in derision of the council, and in praise of Huss and Jerome, should be suppressed under the severest penalties; that none should be allowed to preach unless by the authority of the ordinary; that the latter with other prelates should be allowed full liberty in the exercise of their office, and whosoever should interfere to prevent it should thereby incur sentence of excommunication; that all who should favor or promote any measure tending to the spread of the opinions of Huss or Wickliffe should be proceeded against, according to the canons; that every league or compact having this for its object should be dissolved; that the former rites of worship should be all restored, and that all who should be convicted of

---

[1] Jessenitz, Simon of Tisnow, Jacobel, John Cardinal, Christiann of Prachatitz, Zdenko of Labaun, and others.

teaching the doctrines of Huss or Wickliffe, or maintaining the sanctity of these men, should be committed to the flames. The laity were required, under pain of being regarded as favorers of heresy, to aid in the execution of these injunctions.[1]

Such a decree was directly calculated to defeat every purpose for which it was framed. It was the exhibition of senile malice and bare authority, and was conceived in the very spirit that had sent Huss and Jerome to the stake. Its violent tone awed less than it provoked. Its demands, moreover, were exorbitant. Many might have been disinclined to break altogether with the council, who would scorn compliance with terms like these. The circumstances of the case, indeed, rendered compliance impossible. A nation could not be bridled by a word. The convictions of years were not to be mastered by the sentence of a body of men, whose notoriety for intrigue and corruption, according to testimony above impeachment, had scandalized the world, and forfeited for themselves all respect.

Nearly at this same time (Feb. 22, 1418) Martin V. issued his bull against the followers and favorers of Wickliffe and Huss.[2] It is addressed to all archbishops, bishops, and inquisitors throughout the world, and is a model from which bigoted intolerance and persecution might copy. It exhausts the odium of language in describing the character of the objects of its vengeance. They are "schismatic, seditious, impelled by Luciferian pride and wolfish rage, duped by devilish tricks, tied together by the tail, how-

---

[1] Van der Hardt, iv. 1514.   [2] Ib., iv. 1518.

ever scattered over the world, and thus leagued in
favor of Wickliffe, Huss, and Jerome. These pestilent persons had obstinately sown their perverse
dogmas, while at first the prelates and ecclesiastical
authority had shown themselves to be only dumb
dogs, unwilling to bark or to restrain, according to
the canons, these deceitful and pestiferous heresiarchs." The bull then proceeds to describe the wide
spread of the mischief, lamenting it in the most lugu-
brious tones. It recites what had been done by the
council to check the growing heresy, and ordains
that all archbishops, bishops, and ecclesiastical authorities shall hasten to the rescue. They were to
try and adjudge as heretics all who should be found
" to think or teach otherwise than as the holy Roman
and Catholic church thinks or teaches "—all who
held the doctrines or defended the character of Huss
or Wickliffe, and they to deliver such over to the
secular arm. Such as received or favored these persons were to be exemplarily and severely punished
for their " enormous crime," that others might take
warning. All kings, princes, lords, nobles, knights,
cities, universities, etc., were to be admonished, and
required to banish all such persons as bore this character for heresy from their territories, and all places
subject to their dominion. They were not to suffer
such persons to preach, dwell, possess property, engage in business, or have any thing to do in common
with the faithful, in any place subject to their control. If they died heretics, even though the church
had not formally declared them such, they were to
be denied Christian burial. No masses should be

said for them. Their property should be confiscated and withheld from those to whom it would otherwise descend, at least until competent ecclesiastical authority had pronounced sentence in the case. Such as were suspected of heresy were to purge themselves under oath. If they refused or neglected to do it, they were to " be struck with the sword of anathema," and after a year's lapse condemned as heretics. All lay lords, magistrates, and judges, of what name or dignity soever, were required and commanded, as they prized the Christian name, to afford all necessary aid, whenever they should be called upon for it by the inquisitors or ecclesiastical authorities, for the arrest, restraint, or imprisonment of heretics, or their favorers. These last were to be carefully secured by "iron handcuffs and fetters," till their case had been carried through the ecclesiastical court; and any one who should be neglectful in guarding them while under his charge, was to be condignly punished. The bull then requires the archbishops, bishops, commissaries, inquisitors, etc., diligently to search out, in all places subject to their jurisdiction, all that are guilty of heresy, or of showing it favor; to pronounce against them sentence of excommunication, suspension, or interdict, as the case may require. All who should refuse or neglect to obey this command, should be deposed and deprived, and punished with other and more severe penalties, according to the enormity of their crime.

But even this was not enough. To aid the slow wit of any less facile persecutor, he was furnished in the bull itself with a full list of the points on which those suspected of heresy were to be examined, and from which they were to purge themselves on oath. These points embraced the forty-five articles of Wickliffe, and the thirty charged against Huss which the council had condemned, beside thirty-nine others, extending to subjects not included in the former. Of these thirty-nine the first eleven pertained to the persons and works of Wickliffe, Huss, and Jerome.[1] The person arraigned was asked whether he had known them, or had conversed with them, knowing them to be excommunicate; whether he had prayed for them, had spoken of them, or accounted them as holy; whether he approved their condemnation, and the acts and authority of the council; whether he possessed any of their works, or knew any that did possess them; and whether he condemned the articles of the heretics aforesaid, in the words of the council.

Of the other points of examination, some had reference to various sects that had arisen in that, or the previous age; some represented a peculiar phase of the opinions of Wickliffe, or Huss, and some had reference to ecclesiastical authority, the legitimate election of the pontiff, or the infallibility of the council. One had respect to the venial nature of perjury, a subject which the perjured violators of the safe-conduct of Huss had better have let alone. One had reference to the subject of lay preaching; another to the right of a priest to preach out of his own parish.

On these points the suspected heretic was to be

[1] L'Enfant, 585.

examined under oath. He was to appear in person
before the bishop or inquisitor, and give answer as he
should be asked. No attorney or advocate was to be
allowed him. The whole trial was to be conducted
in the manner which the judge should deem most
expedient. The sentence might extend to excommunication, suspension, or interdict; to deprivation
of dignity or office; to fine and confiscation of property; to deposition from rank or professorships in
universities; to imprisonment, and such corporeal
inflictions as were allowable in the case of heretics.
The judgment was to be summary and without
appeal, and the delinquent, if it was found necessary, was to be given over to the secular arm. All
these processes were made obligatory on the bishops
and inquisitors, and their neglect would be accounted
a crime.[1]

Such was the document by which the new pontiff
signalized his zeal against the Bohemian heresy.
Every line and letter of it breathed the spirit that
sent Huss to the stake. Nor was it meant to remain
a dead letter. The news of Lord Cobham's death
in England followed, in Bohemia, with scarce a day's
interval, the announcement of the bull. That great
and noble man, once the bosom friend of the king,
had been hung in iron chains and roasted alive, as
a sacrifice to the bigoted zeal of the church. His
death by fire showed that he died, not as a traitor
to the state, but as the victim of ecclesiastical intolerance. Such an event was all that was necessary to
fill to overflowing the odious cup which had been

[1] Van der Hardt, iv. 1518.

put to the lips of the Bohemians by the bull of
Martin V. If the council had studied measures of
exasperation instead of conciliation, they could not
more wisely have calculated on the result. They
were continually strengthening the party whom they
sought to defeat.

The threat of a crusade, thrown out by the council, as well as the pope and emperor, and employed
alike to overawe Wenzel and his subjects, however
exasperating it might be, was by no means to be
lightly treated. If sincere zealots for the papacy
had become more rare than in a former age, their
place in the ranks of invasion could be well supplied
by the banditti and soldiers of fortune, who stood
ready to engage in any feasible work of plunder,—
none the less prompt that a pontiff lent them the
sanction of his authority, and covered their violence
with his absolution.

Indeed, at this very juncture the pope published
a crusade against the Moors, at the solicitation of
the king of Portugal. John XXIII. had employed
similar measures against his enemy Ladislaus, king
of Naples. Europe had not yet forgotten—was not
likely soon to forget—the merciless cruelties of the
crusade against the Albigenses. Ruthless havoc and
indiscriminating massacre had changed the garden of
Southern France into an uninhabited desert. The
very name of crusade—notwithstanding the schism
and decline of the papacy—was still terrible. But
even the danger of its fulmination against the Bohemians, did not shake their purpose, or their steadfast adherence to their convictions. Its only effect

was to aggravate their indignation—already glowing
with scorn and defiance—against the council.

It was to no purpose that Martin V. sent John
Dominic, one of his cardinals, as legate into Bohemia.[1] The legate could effect nothing. The bull
that had preceded him had done its work. Dominic threw up his mission in despair, and returned to
report his ill success. He wrote to Sigismund and
the pope that the Bohemians could only be brought
back and reduced by force of arms. Tongue and
pen were no longer weapons with which to vanquish
them.[2] Instead of receding from their position, they
had only assumed its responsibilities more boldly.
The churches they demanded were granted them by
the feeble monarch. It would not have been safe to
refuse. His half-threatening remark to Nicholas of
Hussinitz—who spoke on this occasion in the name
of his countrymen—that he was twisting a rope for
his own neck, had only served to cause him to with
draw from Prague to his own estates, where he could
strengthen himself and his party in all security.
Zisca (April 15) soon after appeared before the king,
at his summons addressed to the Hussite leaders to
meet him unarmed; but he came with a body of
men fully equipped for battle.[3] "Here we are, all
armed, sire," said he, "according to your orders, to
shed the last drop of our blood against your enemies, if we may but know who they are." Zisca's

---

[1] L'Enfant, 590. Bower says (iii.
204) that John Dominic was sent as
legate to Bohemia, by Martin V.,
after the arrival of the latter at Geneva. The pope reached this city June

11, 1418, so that Dominic's mission
could not have been discharged before
July or August of that year.

[2] Fleury, xxvi. 359.

[3] L'Enfant, 591. Fleury, xxvi. 391.

boldness secured his impunity. If the king had cherished hostile intentions, they were for the time abandoned. He did not care to confront such resolution and energy as the Hussite leader had shown.

But this course, pursued by the reform party—wise as it was in its very boldness—was induced in part, undoubtedly, by the manner in which Dominic had discharged his mission. Instead of gentle measures, which alone could have succeeded, he showed himself true to the spirit which had dictated the papal bull. At Slany, a few leagues from Prague, he entered one of the churches of the Hussites, and finding upon the altar a box, which probably contained the cups used by them in the celebration of the eucharist, he dashed it to the earth, and ordained that the former methods of worship should all be resumed. Not content with this, he is said, in conjunction with the Archbishop Conrad, to have burned a preacher and a layman at the same place. Nothing more was necessary to drive the Hussites to desperation. Such a premonition of the significance of the bull, was not lost upon them. Zisca knew well how to take advantage of it. No personal violence was offered to the legate, but he was everywhere greeted with doggerel songs, reproaches, invectives, ridicule, and insult. Threats were made against his life, unless he withdrew at once from the kingdom. It is more than possible that if he had not taken so plain a hint, they would have been executed. One thing, however, he had learned, that nothing short of the imperial power could bring the Bohemians back to their allegiance to the pope. It remained to be seen

whether even this would suffice. Dominic himself
returned from Bohemia to accompany the emperor
into Hungary, where his efforts against the opinions
of the reformers are said to have been more successful.

CHAPTER XII.

FUTILE ISSUE OF THE COUNCIL. ITS DISSOLUTION.

Jan. 1, 1418 — April 28, 1418.

The council was now approaching the close of its proceedings. With the election of Martin V. the interest in its continuance at once began to decline. The prospects of reform were more hopeless than ever; for it was soon seen that the election had only given a head to its enemies.

The new pontiff showed much alacrity in the announcement of his election.[1] He wrote to the universities, and the different states and kingdoms, a circular letter, in which he attributes the choice that had been made to the inspiration of the Holy Ghost. The reception of his letter was not everywhere

[1] L'Enfant, 599.

(335)

equally welcome. Pontifical nature had, for more than forty years, excited deep distrust throughout Christendom. Otho de Colonna as cardinal had been highly spoken of; but what would he be as Martin V.? His family was a noble one.[1] For centuries it had abounded in great men. Kings, pontiffs, and, as some said, even emperors had sprung from it. Its importance, if nothing more, was attested by the fact that Boniface VIII. had excommunicated the whole family, even to the fourth generation. But Boniface VIII. had secured his election as pontiff by "terrifying his predecessor at midnight, and threatening him with eternal damnation if he did not immediately resign." Beside, more than a century had passed away, and the curse of excommunication had well-nigh spent its force. Succeeding pontiffs, moreover, guided by a wisdom equally infallible with that of their predecessor, had cancelled the decree of his pious vengeance.

The Colonnas, moreover, had shown themselves men not lightly to be assailed. Martin V. had grown old in the discharge of important ecclesiastical offices connected with the papacy. He was one of the electors of Alexander V., and helped give him a successor in the person of the notorious John XXIII. When the latter fled from Constance, Otho de Colonna accompanied him. Some might have asked what light this fact threw upon his character. He was certainly a learned man—at least in canon law, which he had taught in his youth as a professor at Perusia. Platina praises him as prudent, gentle,

[1] L'Enfant, 538.

temperate, just, and dexterous in the management of
affairs. Whatever he may have been as cardinal, as
pope he was the author of the bull against the Hussites, and disappointed the hopes of all that earnestly
longed for reform. But the office was greater than
the man. His position mastered him. He trod in
the footsteps of his predecessors, because he did not
fancy the thorns he must meet in diverging from the
beaten path. " As cardinal," says Windeck, the emperor's prime minister, " he was poor and modest ;
but as pope, Martin V. was greedy of gain, and made
himself very rich."

His election as cardinal ranged the greater part
of Christendom on his side. Congratulations came
in upon him from almost every direction. Some,
however, were inclined to hesitate in the declaration
of their allegiance. France resented the part which
the emperor had taken in his election. Sigismund
had leagued himself with England, and was regarded
as an enemy. Should France accept as pope the
creature of his choice ? He had governed the council, and had not left it free to act. Martin V. was
but a tool of the emperor. The French parliament
declined to recognize any one as pope till the deputation at the council had returned safe.

Other matters soon conspired to aggravate the
difficulty. The king of Aragon had not entirely recovered from his leanings toward Benedict XIII.
If he threw aside his old friend, he demanded some
equivalent in return. Money was needed, and he
cast a greedy eye on the property of the church.
He, as well as his father, had been at considerable

expense and trouble to bring about the measures
which had ranged Aragon on the side of the council,
and which had resulted in the election of Martin V.
This was the ground of his claim. He had demanded
the right to dispose of benefices in Sicily and Sardinia, independent of the pontiff, with a share of
tithes on ecclesiastical property in Aragon belonging to the Roman See.[1] Martin V. thought the
18,000 florins which he could draw yearly from Sicily
and Sardinia, too much to surrender for a good-will
now no longer necessary, and he refused the terms,
offering in their stead others, which the king of Aragon treated with scorn. The result was that Benedict
XIII. received thenceforth, first the secret, and then
the open support of the king. Thus was he enabled
to defy the bull of excommunication launched against
him by Martin V., on his refusal to lay down the
pontifical dignity.

But this was not all. Benedict was not content
to act merely on the defensive. When he heard, at
Peniscola, of the election of Martin V., he assembled
the four cardinals and the few clerks he had with
him, and calling his assembly a general council and
the Catholic church, he solemnly excommunicated as
schismatics all who had shared in the election of
Martin V., and all who should acknowledge or obey
him.[2] It was in vain that many of the Spanish
bishops repaired to Peniscola, and entreated Benedict to yield, and not any longer oppose himself to all
Christendom. It was in vain that some of his cardinals seconded the request. To all alike he made

---

[1] Fleury, xxvi. 377.   L'Enfant, 574.   [2] Bower, iii. 203.

the same answer, that Christ had entrusted him, as
his vicar on earth, with the care of his church, and
he would never betray the trust, or yield the See of
St. Peter to a usurper.   At last, finding himself
almost entirely deserted, he declared that if he must
treat, it should be with Martin V. alone.

"If Martin is so reasonable a man as you say," so
answered Benedict to the ambassador who announced
to him the new election, "I am quite willing to have
a conference with him in regard to the means of giving peace to the church." This was all the submission that could be wrung out of the old hero, calmly
defying the world from his fortress of Peniscola, and
resolved to live and to die—a pope.   Even the council of Constance must leave the church to some extent divided by allegiance to two heads.

But it was when measures of reform, so long
promised and so long delayed, were at last taken
up by Martin V., that the dissatisfaction of the nations began to manifest itself in a marked manner.
The grave complaints and urgent demands which
issued in the appointment by the council of the reformatory college, could not be altogether ignored.
The schemes of this latter body were laid before the
pope, and he found that something must be done.
But he showed himself equal to the emergency, the
needed Fabius of corruption.   Although he had
sworn to the article of the reformatory college, by
which he bound himself to suppress the most crying
abuses of the court of Rome, one of his first acts as
pope betrayed his real purpose to evade the obligation.   The rules of the Roman chancery had been

regarded, and to a great extent justly, as the source
of simony and papal usurpations. It was necessary,
therefore, that these should first of all be set right.
The pope examined and corrected them. They
were at length published; but only a skilful critic
could have discovered any marked difference between these, and those that had been issued by
John XXIII. Scarce a single abuse was given up.
Reservations, vacancies, dispensations, tithes, annates,
indulgences—all was in fact retained.

Other abuses were complained of. The five nations demanded of the pope, a few days after his
election, that he should fulfil his promise.[1] He told
them each to draw up a list of their grievances. He
then proposed to treat with each nation by itself,
and instead of a general reform, adopt the measure
of *concordats* with each.[2] There was wisdom in this.
It was easier to deal with them singly. They were
less formidable when thus divided. Beside, from
one nation terms could be secured to which another
would not consent. England had a terrible statute
of *prœmunire*, which Martin V. would not choose to
see thrown in his way as a barrier in dealing with
the French or Germans.

Concordats were accordingly arranged. In these
the pope managed with great prudence. He gave
up only what it was impossible to retain, nor did he
yield even this without seeking to secure in return
some equivalent. On some points he was met with
direct and persistent opposition. England, for eight
years, would not receive his cardinal legate. The

[1] L'Enfant, 553.   [2] Van der Hardt, iv. 1512.

Archbishop Chichely would not consent to a step
that infringed the prerogatives of his primacy, or
contemned, as he maintained, the laws of England.[1]
France was strengthened in her aversion to the concordat offered her, by her jealousy of papal prerogative threatening to encroach on the liberties of the
Gallican church, and by her hatred of England and
the emperor.

But in truth the concordats were of small account.
They met some of the complaints of the nations, but
betrayed throughout an entire aversion to any real
or thorough reform. One article limited the cardinals to twenty-four;[2] but of what avail was this,
except for the moment? Another was on the subject of the abuse of indulgences; and yet, in less
than a single century, this was to be the exciting
cause of a revolt that would rend the church in
twain. Others still were directed to the subjects of
dispensations, plurality of benefices, restrictions upon
the monks, and matters of order and ecclesiastical
regulation, attempting to remedy the more gross and
crying evils, lopping off limbs indeed from the tree
of corruption, mutilating its fair proportions, but in
fact only pruning it for a more vigorous and luxuri-
ant growth.[3] It needed a Luther to lay the axe at
the root of the tree, but no Luther was to be found
at Constance after the death of Huss.

There were some regulations adopted by the council generally, with the sanction of the pope, beside
the concordats, that were intended to answer the
purpose of reform. But the whole movement was

---

[1] L'Enfant, 559.   [2] Ib., 569.   [3] Fleury, xxvi. 372, 394. L'Enfant, 597–600.

regarded by many members of the council as a mere
feint to ward off the charge that might be made
against that body of neglecting its appropriate work.
The pope himself knew what he was about. He
conceded just what he might safely yield, or what he
could not safely retain. Provincial councils should
be held every three years, to last eight or ten days.
The pope should decide nothing important without
the advice of his cardinals. He should not take the
title of *Most Holy*, unless in his life and conduct he
showed himself worthy of it. The cardinals were to
be distinguished for their learning, morals, and experience, and none could be elected at an age short
of thirty years. The officers of the chancellor's
court were to be of a fixed number, and the charges
allowed them were specified. Reservations were to
be abolished; dispensations to be granted only with
the concurrence of a majority of the college of cardinals. The pope should no longer impede the course
of justice. He should not protract suits, or annul
them after sentence, unless for legitimate causes. He
should not impose tenths unless authorized by a general council. Restrictions were imposed upon ex-
emptions and translations. Simony was to be punished by deprivation in an ecclesiastic, and by excommunication in a layman.[1]

Such were the measures for the reform of the papal
court. In matters pertaining to episcopal jurisdiction, the council pronounced on the subject of benefices and the right of patronage, church property,
matrimonial suits, dowries, the estates of widows and

---

[1] L'Enfant, 658, *et seq.*

wards, heresies, schisms, legacies, donations, the conflict of civil and ecclesiastical jurisdiction. The duty
of provincial synods was .declared. They were to
maintain ecclesiastical liberty and union; nor were
they to make war, except when commanded by the
sovereign, or on the failure of ecclesiastical censures
to attain their object.

The priesthood is next looked after. The bishops
must exercise a sharp surveillance over it. If one
lived with a concubine, he was to lose his benefice
unless within a month he sent her away. The children of priests could not be admitted to orders, or
allowed to hold a benefice, without a dispensation
from Rome.[1] Residence, on curates, was rendered
imperative. They were always to wear the ecclesiastical habit. None was to serve in a parish where
he could not speak the language. The age, the revenues, and the mode of electing canons were prescribed. Unjust oaths, imposed as a condition of
choice, were null. Bishops were allowed a similar
release. On a bishop's death, the canons were not
allowed to despoil his house or property. The monks
also were bound more strictly to regard their vows
of obedience, charity, and poverty.[2] The nuns were
required to conform to certain rules prescribing age
and conduct. If a man presented himself to be
received into holy orders, he was strictly to be questioned whether his father or grandfather had not
treated ecclesiastics with violence, in their persons or
goods. Civil interference with ecclesiastical courts
was to be repelled, and punished by interdict. The

---

[1] L'Enfant, 681.   [2] Ib., 686.

consecration of chapels, the observance of festivals, the exposure of relics to public view, afforded matter of deliberation for the grave wisdom of the reforming college acting in concert with the pope. The last article can speak for itself. It mildly decrees, in regard to that much-abused people whom Martin V. at his coronation had treated with insult, "that when a Jew is converted, and adheres to Christianity, he shall give up only half his property, whether landed or personal, in restitution of usury practised on Christians, and shall charitably be allowed to retain the other half, for his own support and that of his family." [1]

Such were in substance the acts of the reformatory college. The church had asked for bread: the council gave her a stone. She asked for an egg: the council gave her a scorpion. The decrees of reform read like a libel on the ecclesiastical order of the age. Could the hierarchy have become so corrupt, we ask, that these prohibitions of gross indecency and injustice could assume the name of an organized reform? There were some who regarded them in their true significance—as a plaster to cover up the sore which they could not heal. In fact, they deceived no one. The pope wished merely to save appearances. In regard to the article proposed by the reformatory college bearing upon the circumstances in which a pope might be deposed by the council, he avoided giving any answer. He would not allow of a decree which might trench on his own prerogative. What the council had done

[1] L'Enfant, 707.

in declaring its supremacy over the Papal See, he
chose to ignore. There was a significance in the fact,
that in the questions to be proposed to the Hussites,
and enumerated in his bull, there was one on this
very point.

Thus, nearly four years had passed away, and
nothing of importance had been accomplished in
regard to one of the chief objects for which the
council had been convoked. The result was ridiculous — humiliating. The nations were dissatisfied.
They were loud in their complaints. But Martin
V., secure in his seat, met them all with philosophical
equanimity. The council had served his purpose,
and he wished now to get rid of it. Unless it was
speedily dissolved, he feared its activity. It might
do mischief. It was only too easy to see whither-
ward things were tending. The emperor was disappointed, disheartened, disgusted. He had been foiled
and beaten at his own game of dissimulation. The
pope could do all that he had done, and *not blush*.

The Spanish nation, especially, was indignant. They
wished to carry back from Constance some equivalent for having thrown Benedict XIII. overboard.
How were they now better off than before, if there
was to be no reform worthy of the name? In personal merit, Benedict XIII. might claim to be at
least equal to Martin V. Why should the former
be given up, if the papal court was to continue what
it was before?

The indignation of the Spaniards found vent in
satire.[1] "A mass against simony"—such was the

[1] L'Enfant, 567.

singular name of the article in which their scorn for papal corruption was expressed. A man dreams of going as a pilgrim to the Church of the Holy Cross at Rome. As he approaches it, he sees the house of a peasant, Simon by name, rising higher than the church itself, though the house was yet without a roof. While gazing with surprise at its height, a certain person meets him and says, "A truce to your surprise : take a seat here now, and write out a new mass, or a new office touching simony ; for the house you see represents the estate of Simon Magus, who is ever at work to raise it above the church." The pilgrim obeys the direction, and seats himself to write.

" INTRODUCTION.—We deplore, all of us in the Lord, the sad times in which we live. We groan over the horrible simony that prevails at present. For this, poor human wretches mourn and grieve, according to the saying, *My heart utters forth one word*, that is, *Simony*, a word hard to be heard. *Gloria Patri*.

"O God, who for the sins of men, and by the little care shown to distinguish the good and bad, hast permitted simony to make such great progress, insomuch that where the more holiness should abound, there the more simony reigns, so that churches are taxed, benefices are reserved, elections are abolished, sacraments are sold and bought,—we pray thee to purify the church from these pollutions, granting to those guilty of simony, converting grace, or, if they refuse to be converted, smiting them as Peter smote Simon Magus, or as Elisha smote Gehazi, those traffickers in sacred things. *Per Dominum*.

" (Scripture to be read—Revelation of St. John, chap. xvii.)

" In those days came one of the seven angels and spake with me, saying, Come, and I will show thee the judgment of the great whore that sitteth upon many waters, with whom the kings of the earth have committed fornication, and the inhabitants of the earth have been made drunk with the wine of her prostitution. So he carried me away in the spirit into the wilderness; and I saw a woman sit upon a scarlet-covered beast, full of names of blasphemy, having seven heads and ten horns. And the woman was arrayed in purple and scarlet color, and decked with gold and precious stones and pearls, having a golden cup in her hand full of abominations, and the filthiness of her fornication.

" GRAD.[1] Lord, who shall abide in thy tabernacle; who shall dwell in thy holy mountain?

" VER. He that hath clean hands and a pure heart, uncontaminated with simony, who does according to the righteousness of God. Hallelujah.

" He hath grown fat, he hath become gross, his heart is lifted up, and he hath forsaken the Lord his Maker, and hath given himself up to the iniquity of simony. Hallelujah.

" SEQ. Matt. x. Jesus said to his disciple, Go ye, and preach, The kingdom of heaven is at hand. Heal the sick, raise the dead, recover the lepers, drive out demons, freely give as ye have freely received. Take neither gold nor silver in your purse.

---

[1] The successive offices of the mass are indicated by the abbreviated headings.

" OFFERT. All seek their own, not the things that are Jesus Christ's.

" SECRET. O God, who of the abundance of thy mercy hast commanded to bestow the sacraments and the benefits of the church gratuitously, grant converting grace to those who buy and sell. And if they will not be converted, do to them according to their iniquity, that others better than they may take their bishopric. *Per Dominum nostrum.*

" COMMUN. If my children shall not play the master in benefices wickedly acquired, then shall I be without spot, and I shall be pure from the great sin of simony.

" POST COMMUN. O Lord, who hast freely bestowed thyself upon us, we pray thee that those who sell and those who buy these same gifts of thine, may ever receive the portion of Judas, who sold thee— thee who livest and reignest with God the Father, in the unity of the Holy Spirit.

" (This mass to be chanted immediately after the festival of the See of St. Peter.)"

When the mass had thus been written, the one who had dictated it said to the pilgrim, " In the name of the true spouse of the church of Jesus Christ, I command you promptly to inform King Alfonso what is therein written, that he may present it to the pope, boldly and without delay, praying him, in the name of God, and as pastor and head of the church, that he himself pray, and cause others to pray, that this cursed sin of simony may be removed from the church. For I know that the smoke thereof hath risen up to heaven, and that divine Justice is so provoked, that if this pope does not provide some remedy, he may be assured that he shall soon be smitten by a great plague, so that he shall fall and be reduced to nothing. While, if he shall correct abuses, he shall reign upon the throne of the church, and triumph over his enemies. Yet, let him know that he has not been raised to the See of St. Peter through his own merit, but by God's permission, to reform the church in all humility and fidelity, while exercising his power against such as refuse to obey its commands."

Nothing could more plainly manifest the deep discontent that prevailed, than the appearance of such a document in spite of the decree of the council against all defamatory and libellous compositions. Undoubtedly the dissatisfaction of the king of Aragon with Martin V. was mainly due to the fact that the latter would not alienate in his favor the possessions of the church. But the utter neglect of the council, through the pope's management, to initiate any thorough reform, gave, in the eyes of many, a pretext for his course. Nor did those who sided with him fail to impeach the character of the council as legitimate, on the ground that it was not properly convoked, and that the church was not properly represented.

Other nations had complaints to offer. But all were vain. They had to devour their grief in silence. The pope was master of the council, and they who had placed him over them, had to mourn—like the Israelites when a king had been granted at their request—the impolicy and folly of a course that had made them the slaves of another's will.

In the little that had been now accomplished, more than three months had been spent, and the pope was eager to return to Italy, and recover from the grasp of his enemies the ravaged states of the church. It was in vain that Sigismund urged him to delay. Every thing was expedited to secure the speedy dissolution of the council. Even an embassy from the Greek church, which reached Constance at the beginning of the year, (1418,) and which proposed the important subject of the union of the Greek and Latin churches, could not retard the arrangements of Martin V. for closing the council. Something indeed was done to encourage the union, which the Greeks, pressed as they were by the Turks, manifested an unusual readiness to promote. Latin women—some of princely houses—were sent back as brides for Greek husbands ;[1] and perhaps this was the best argument for union which the council had to offer.

Meanwhile the emperor was busy with civil as well as ecclesiastical affairs. He was anxious to harmonize his distracted and turbulent provinces and princes. Frederic of Austria had been received back to the imperial favor.[2] The Duke of Milan was constrained to acknowledge his feudal allegiance, and was urged on by the emperor to attack Genoa, thus endangering the peace of Italy, and especially the safety of Florence.[3] But the perfidious wretch, Philippo Maria, stained with blood and crime, fought for the promo tion of his own selfish interests, and Sigismund had too many matters on hand to impose upon him—had

---

[1] L'Enfant, 577.   [2] Ib., 605.   [3] Ib., 572.

he been so disposed—any restraint. He was anxious
above all to replenish his exhausted treasury. More
complaisant to him than to the king of Aragon,
Martin V. allowed him, in consideration of what he
had done for the church, a share of the ecclesiastical revenues of Germany for the space of a year.[1]

It was in vain that the several dioceses which were
affected by this project, uttered their complaints; in
vain that they appealed to the bull of the pope,
which they had regarded as protecting them from
such an imposition. The logic of their skilful advocate, Dominic de Geminiano, might expose the papal
inconsistency and injustice, but it was powerless
against interest armed with imperial patronage, especially when the pope, by express reservation, had
secured all pontifical revenues from being touched.

From the Duke of Austria, Sigismund wrung out
50,000 florins, as the condition of peace and a ransom for his states. He was ready enough to accept
the money, and recover to his allegiance one of his
rebellious subjects, of whom he had too many on his
hands already. The Swiss had seized the occasion
of the duke's being put under the ban of the empire,
to rob him of several of the cities which he had
held of the empire. Sigismund now demanded them
back. The Swiss refused compliance with the demand, and the emperor accepted in place of them—
what he most needed—money. The cities of Mayence, Spires, and Worms, anxious to secure privileges
for themselves, found all negotiations vain without—
money. The emperor's coffers were replenished—

[1] L'Enfant, 615.

only again to be exhausted. Something of a satisfaction to him it must have been to be recognized as
emperor—as he now was in solemn ceremony—by the
newly elected pontiff. The golden rose was bestowed upon him;[1] but the still unsettled state of the empire, the futile measures of reform in the council,
the growing strength of the Hussites in Bohemia, all
tended to provoke and irritate him. He was continually busy, ever anxious, going from and suddenly
returning to Constance, none could tell why. The
Turk threatened him in Hungary. He anxiously
awaited intelligence from the embassadors sent by
the council to restore peace between France and
England. He sympathized with Gerson in his disappointment that the writings of Petit and Falkenberg had never been condemned in full council, and
when he saw Martin V. about to leave the city of
Constance, he must have reviewed with saddened
heart the labors and anxieties of the last four years.

It was certainly a most significant fact that, in
spite of Gerson's eloquence and logic, the urgency of
the French monarch, the deep feeling and anxious
effort of the emperor, as well as the letters of the
king of Poland and the arguments of his embassadors, the pope and council could not be induced to
touch the books of Petit and Falkenberg. Gerson
was indignant. " Why," he asked—and the council
would have been at a loss for an answer—" Why condemn the writings of Huss and Wickliffe, and leave
writings far more pernicious unsentenced ? Well may
the Bohemians accuse the council—and with justice

[1] L'Enfant, 592.

—of a most criminal partiality, in judging with such severity heresies far less criminal than those of Petit and Falkenberg, which it treats with indifference. The authority of the council is made cheap; its acts become null and void; it is made a laughing-stock for schismatics, infidels, and especially Peter de Luna and such as favor him, when they see so little accomplished on the election of a pope from whom so much was expected."[1]

But the ambassadors of the king of Poland were resolved to make one more effort, full as much characterized by the spirit of humanity and justice, as that of which Gerson was the champion against Petit. Is brutal violence the proper instrument for converting infidels to Christianity?—that was the question. Protesting against the violence and carnage of the Teutonic knights, the king of Poland, and Voladimir, his ambassador, plead the cause of reason and truth. Should their plea be heard? It was in advance of the age. It was a gleam of light from a brighter future. Should it be quenched in the darkness of papal bigotry? Should it yield to the prejudices against which it clashed? Let us see.

Otho de Colonna had signed, while yet cardinal, the condemnation of Falkenberg's as well as Petit's writings. He now wore the tiara, and presided over the council at this its forty-fifth and last session, (April 22, 1418.) At the fitting moment the advocate of the Polish ambassadors arose, and presented to the council the book of Falkenberg.[2] It had been

[1] Gers. Op., v. 1014.   [2] Van der Hardt, iv. 1549.

condemned by the commission appointed to examine
it, by the nations severally, by the college of cardinals, and all this with perfect unanimity. He therefore submitted humbly that it should also be condemned in full council, otherwise the ambassadors
of Poland and Lithuania would protest against this
denial of justice, and would appeal to a future council. The statement of the advocate was disputed.
The patriarchs of Constantinople and Antioch maintained that the book had not been unanimously condemned. Two notaries pronounced the assertion
false. In the midst of the confusion consequent,
Paul Voladimir arose and demanded audience. His
advocate had omitted some things that should have
been spoken. As he reached his hand, however, to
take from the advocate the paper which he wished
to read, the pope imposed silence, and declared by
the mouth of one of his officers, that what had been
passed in full council in matters of faith, he regarded
as inviolably binding—but nothing more.

This declaration was meant to be final. But Voladimir was not thus to be put off. He went on with
his reading. Again the pope silenced him, threatening excommunication unless he should desist.[1] He
then presented his protest in the names of the king
of Poland and the duke of Lithuania, solemnly appealed to the next general council, and demanded
the certification of his protest and appeal. The
language employed is bold and manly. The chief
purpose for which the council was convoked—the
extirpation of heresy—had been neglected. Desir-

[1] L'Enfant, 609.

ing to obey God rather than man, he declares that
if sentence is not pronounced against the book of
Falkenberg, and justice done in the premises, he appeals to a future council.

All was in vain. Martin did not wish to provoke
the vengeance or risk the allegiance of the Teutonic
knights. Strangely enough, moreover, at the close
of the council the Duke of Burgundy is his fast
friend. Shall he be alienated by the condemnation
of his advocate, Petit? Surely Martin V. was, as
Platina says, "a prudent man." But before the
council's close, he gave evidence of it. John of
Bavaria, Bishop of Liege—the See by which the
Archbishop of Riga had been bought over—was
merely a worldly prince. He wished to resign his
bishopric, and marry a fortune in the person of the
widow of the Duke of Brabant, a near relative.
For this, a dispensation from the pope was necessary.
A thousand crowns bought the dispensation, and
Martin V. pocketed the fruits of his simony. What
a fit commentary on the reforms he had initiated, as
well as on his "prudence!" Such conduct confounded the emperor.[1] He went to the pope, and
met him with the blunt, but significant question,
"Holy Father, why are we here at Constance?"
"To reform the church," replied the pope. "One
would not be apt to say so," rejoined the emperor,
"when you allow cousins-german to marry. Pardon
sins you may, perhaps, but not grant a permit for
them." The emperor, however, could go no further.
His own robes were far from being free of stain. He

[1] L'Enfant, 608.

had already used the pope to perform a similar
service for some friends of his own. Thus many
seemed to see in Martin V. a John XXIII. *redevi-
vus*. The man might die, but the system lived.
The name of pope was but the new dial-plate to
cover the same mechanism working out the same
results.

Futile as the results of the council appeared, there
was no hope of mending them, and most of the members were as ready as Martin V. to depart. Some
would haste away, in order to enjoy at leisure the
fruits of their treason or intrigue; some to remedy
the mischiefs occasioned by their absence; some, like
Gerson, to weep in solitude over the disappointment
of their fondest hopes. What must have been the
reflections of sincere, enlightened, and earnest men,
like Voladimir, as they retraced their steps from the
council to their homes? The Polish ambassador saw
the cause of sacred and Christian charity trampled
under foot. The head of the church himself had
silenced the voice of justice—had virtually condemned a just cause unheard. Nay, more, he had
taken "prudent" precautions that it never should be
heard. He had published a constitution, *ad perpet-
uam rei memoriam*, by which he declared that "it
is not permissible for any one to appeal from the
sovereign judge, (*i. e.*, the supreme pontiff,) who is
vicar of Jesus Christ, on earth, neither to decline his
judgment in matters of faith." Well might Gerson
declare, and Voladimir feel, that "it tended to overthrow the authority not only of the council of Pisa,
but of Constance also, and to annul all that they had

done, whether in electing a new pope, or deposing
such as had intruded into the pontificate.

The council in fact lay at the mercy of a terrible
contradiction that bereft it of all moral power. It
had begun by asserting its supremacy, and deposing
a pope. It ended by giving itself a master, and bend-
ing its neck to his yoke. It was far more independent when it assembled, than when the time of its
dissolution approached. Cromwell, dismissing the
Long Parliament with a " Get you gone," could have
humbled them, not more than the council was humbled by the assumed authority of the pontiff. They
had become his tools merely, and when he had done
with them he flung them away. The terrible question had been started, Which is supreme, pope or
council?—but the issue at Constance foreboded sadly,
to thoughtful minds, that future when popes should
rule, independent of councils, summoning, or leaving
them unsummoned, at their pleasure. The tyranny
of the monarchical principle was already, in fact, en-
throned in the church, by the weakness of a council
that had presumed to bind it in fetters of iron.

We follow the better minds of the council with a
sad sympathy, as they withdraw to their homes or to
their places of exile. They feel that they have acted a
humiliating part in the great tragedy of the church.
The catastrophe has thrown its dark shadow on all
their future years, and on the future of Christendom.
They have learned what they would have been hap-
pier, if not wiser, never to have known. They have
fathomed around them depths of depravity that
fill them with foreboding and despair. Bohemia

had no such ally against the council as the council itself.

But before the final leaves-taking, the pope wished to manifest his generosity. He could do it easily, and, what was more, cheaply. If money was scarce, and piety a thing still more rare, the bank of Papal Indulgences could discount to meet any demand. In the latter part of March, (1418,) his bounty was signalized by an invitation addressed to the people, by heralds, to assemble at the episcopal palace to receive indulgences.[1] A great multitude was soon collected, in the midst of whom the pope exercised a liberality that cost him—nothing. The ceremonies of the occasion occupied most of the afternoon, and closed with a more substantial and expensive tribute to the emperor, princes, and cardinals, of a public dinner; at the close of which, the pontifical humility was manifested in washing the feet of his guests. Day after day the treasury of Indulgence was drawn upon, and the graciousness of the pontiff expressively signalized.

But all this was nothing to what took place on the dissolution of the council. As the pope declared its sessions closed, he "accorded, by the authority of God Almighty, the blessed apostles Peter and Paul, as well as by his own, full absolution to all the members of the council, for all their sins,"[2] and extended his favors to the members of their families, on condition of their "fasting every Friday for the space of a year." To make the matter more easy, fasting might be dispensed with, in some cases, by the substitution of good works.

[1] L'Enfant, 600.   [2] L'Enfant, 610.

The emperor, by the mouth of his advocate, returned thanks to the several members of the council for what they had done, promising, on his part, an inviolable allegiance to the Roman church and the pope, and declaring that in whatever respects the council had come short, it had not been through his fault.[1]

Such language plainly intimated the dissatisfaction of the emperor; nor did he stand alone in this feeling, as we have already seen. But the king of Poland felt most deeply aggrieved. He seems to have shown great zeal, as well as humanity, in seeking the conversion of the infidels bordering upon his states, and his efforts had been eminently successful. The violence and rapine of the Teutonic knights were most odious and reprehensible. The king of Poland now saw them shielded by the action of the pontiff, and himself left exposed to the shafts of Falkenberg's malice. He wrote to the pope a letter of complaint[2] which seems to have been not without effect, although Falkenberg was still uncondemned. Some of the friends of the king of Poland counselled him, as the wisest and most effectual measure, to select some monk, as violent, virulent, and able as Falkenberg, and set him, with his pen, to maul and demolish his adversary. If such a one could have been found, the counsel might not have been unwise.

The French concordat, on its arrival at Paris, was any thing but welcome. The parliament refused to receive it, and even drew up reasons against it, to be presented to the pope. Years passed before France would accept it. The nuncios, whom the pope sent

[1] L'Enfant, 611.   [2] Ib., 613.

to urge its approval, were driven to maintain the
desperate position that a sentence of the pope was
to be obeyed, even though it was unjust. Such a
maxim roused the spirit of Gerson in his exile, and
he met it with a bold and manly refutation.

The Germans felt that they had been cheated by
the council. The dioceses, whose revenues had been
given over to the emperor, were loud in their complaints. The Archbishop of England, in a spirit
worthy of the nation, met the demands of the pope
on the privileges of his primacy and the laws of England, in an attitude of defiance. Spain was already
almost in open revolt against Martin, and ready to
league with Benedict XIII. Bohemia was, for the
present, hopelessly lost to the papacy,—volcanic in its
indignation and resentment at the proceedings of the
council. Italy was too much absorbed in the wretched conflicts that tore her into parties and factions, to
have any thought left except for her own misery.
In the midst of all this widespread dissatisfaction, it
is a most significant fact that the only hearty support-
ers of the pontiff were the Duke of Burgundy and
the Teutonic knights—the patrons respectively of
Petit and Falkenberg. Well might Gerson, in his
sad and lonely meditations over the doings and
results of the council, lament that he had toiled and
worn himself out to no purpose. The bright hopes
he had cherished were but dreams. The ideal of his
life, the image he had worshipped, had vanished. A
Gorgon's head, that he dared not look upon, had
taken its place. Where a temple should have been,
he saw a Babel. Rome was not to be reformed.

Reform would annihilate her. Her disease was past
cure.

And now all were intent upon quitting the scene
where so much of good and bad, of learning and
power, of eloquence and intrigue, of integrity and
corruption, had mingled and fermented together.
The pope was in most haste to leave. The emperor
begged him, with all earnestness, to stay a few months
longer. He represented to him that many things
yet remained to claim his attention. But these entreaties were vain. The pope wished to see Rome;
he wished to snatch it from the grasp of its invaders.
On the sixteenth of May (1418) he left Constance
for Geneva. The procession that accompanied him
was splendid and imposing. The "servant of servants" went forth as the prince of the kings of the
earth. Ten horses, caparisoned in scarlet and led by
hand, preceded. Four horsemen, with pikes, each
surmounted by a cardinal's hat, followed them. Then
came two priests, one bearing a cross of gold, another
the sacrament. The cardinals, in their red caps, with
priests, theologians, senators of the city, and canons,
bearing wax tapers, made way for the pope, who followed, mounted on a white horse and dressed in pontifical habits. The tiara which he wore shone brill-
iant with precious stones, while four princes supported
the dais above his head that shielded him from the
sun. The emperor was on his right, and held the
bridle of his horse. The electors and princes of the
empire stood near to render their assistance. Then
followed the clergy, the nobility, and the various
orders, till the procession swelled in number to forty

thousand men. In such state the pope passed the
gate of the city. The emperor and princes accompanied him to Gottlieben, where he embarked upon the
Rhine, to finish, by water, his journey to Geneva.
The emperor himself did not long linger at Constance, and in a short time its former glory had
departed.

CHAPTER XIII.[1]

VIOLENCE OF PARTIES IN BOHEMIA. SIGISMUND'S ARMY
BEFORE PRAGUE.

Reception of the Decree of the Council in Bohemia. — The Reply of the Hussites. — Its Propositions. — Doctrines. — The Celebrated Four Articles. —
Zisca. — His Tact and Energy. — His Letter to Tausch. — Popular Indigna-
tion. — Communion of the Cup on Tabor. — Plan for Attacking Prague. —
Wenzel Absent from the City. — Attack on the New City. — Acts of Vio-
lence. — Release of Prisoners Demanded at the Town House. — Tumult. —
Assault. — Germans Thrown out the Windows. — New Magistrates Appoint-
ed. — Continued Attack upon the New City. — Zisca Withdraws to Pilsen. —
Danger of the Citizens. — The Queen Seeks Aid of the Emperor. — Death of
Wenzel. — Its Circumstances. — Projects of the Emperor. — Citizens Call on
Zisca for Aid. — Scenes of Violence. — Conflicts at Prague. — Fight at the
Bridge. — Conflict Renewed the Next Day. — Continued Skirmishes. — A
Truce Effected. — Movements Elsewhere. — Negligent Observance of the
Truce. — John Naakuasa Burned. — Gurim Assaulted. — The Succession to
the Crown. — Convention Summoned by Sigismund at Beraun. — His Promises.
— Presence of the Bohemians at Beraun. — Their Submission. — Conditions
Imposed by Sigismund. — His Letter to Prague. — Compliance of the Huss-
ites. — Insults Offered Them. — Proceedings of Sigismund at Breslau. —
Hussites Divided into Calixtines and Taborites. — Policy and Views of
Each. — The Adamites. — The Fanaticism of the Taborites in Regard to the
Advent of Christ. — Its Effects. — Danger of Dissensions.

April 15, 1418—Jan. 9, 1420.

The dissolution of the council of Constance, and
the effort necessary on the part of Sigismund to restore the peace of his empire, gave a short respite to

[1] The authorities which have been
mainly relied upon for this and the
two following chapters, are Cochleius'
History of the Hussites, Æneas Syl-
vius' History of Bohemia, L'Enfant's
Guerre des Hussites, Diarium Belli
Hussitici, by a Calixtine author, Life
of Zisca, and Life of Procopius,
(Prague, 1789,) and the general
Church Histories during this period.

the Bohemians,—if respite that condition could be
called, in which the exterminating and persecuting
bull of Martin V. was continually suspended over
them. This fulmination was to them the parting word
of the council, its farewell of bitter malediction. It
showed plainly enough on what terms alone peace
could be made. Unable to secure the persons of
the Bohemian countrymen of Huss, whom they
might subject to a similar treatment, the council
translated the act of his execution into words, and,
in the bull itself, despatched into Germany a written
auto de fè, a legible funeral pile, every line aglow
with the spirit of the inquisitor.

But the logic of this document was a two-edged
sword. It cut both ways. Jacobel's treatises on the
cup did not contain arguments half so effectual to
strengthen the faith of his party, as were contained
in the decrees of the council and the bull of the
pope. No conclusion is more firmly held than that
which is reached by a *reductio ad absurdum*. The
papal fulmination might have been headed by the
creed of the Hussites, and followed by a Q. E. D.,
to signalize the fact that the truth of the theorem
was demonstrated. At least this must have been so
to many minds.

But the Bohemians did not choose to pass over in
silence so extraordinary a document as this bull of a
pope, elected for the purpose of evangelical reform.
They answered it, and circulated the reply far and
wide through the land. Although it does not appear
to have been issued until some months after the publication of the bull, it may as well be given here, as

showing the spirit in which the bull was received.
It is entitled "A faithful and Christian exhortation
of the Bohemians to kings and princes, to stir them
up to the zeal of the gospel." It speaks of the in-
dustrious efforts that had been made in certain quarters to excite hostility and persecution against the
Bohemians.[1] "As well on your part as on ours, many
men, both noble and untitled, have foolishly lost
their lives. Yet never hitherto have ye in any part
understood our faith by our own confession; neither
whether we be able to prove the same out of the
scriptures or not, and yet in the mean time kings,
princes, lords, and cities have sustained great damage.
And hereof we do greatly marvel, that you do so
much trust and believe the pope and his priests,
which give you drink full of poison, and such comfort as no man can understand, in that they say they
will give you forgiveness of sins, and grant grace
and pardon to this end, that you should war upon us
and destroy us, whereas their graces and pardons are
none other than great lies, and a great seducing of
the body and soul of all them that believe them, and
put their trust in them. This we would prove to
them, and convince them by the Holy Scripture; and
we would suffer that whoever is desirous to hear, the
same should hear it. For the pope and all his priests
herein deal with you as the devil would have dealt
with our Lord Jesus Christ. . . .

"So the devil deceiveth the pope and all his priests
with the riches of the world, and with worldly

[1] I have preferred to retain the language of the early English trans- lator, rather than change it to more modern phraseology.

power; and they think they can give grace and pardon when they will; and they themselves shall never find favor before Almighty God, except they repent, and make amends for their great deceiving of Christendom. And how can they give to others that which they themselves have not? So did the devil, who was rich in promising and poor in giving. And like as the devil is not ashamed to tell a lie, so all they are not ashamed to speak that which shall never be found true, nor be proved by the Holy Scriptures; because, for no cause they stir up kings, princes, lords, and citizens to make war against us, not to the end that the Christian faith should thereby be defended, but because they fear their secret vices and heresies shall be disclosed and made manifest. For if they had a true cause, and a godly love to the Christian faith, they would then take the books of the Holy Scripture, and would come to us, and confute us with the weapons of God's word; and that is our chief desire. For so did the apostles of our Lord Jesus Christ, who came to the pagans and the Jews, and brought them from their infidelity to the true faith of our Lord Jesus Christ; and this they did in the spirit of meekness. . . . So ought they also to do, if they perceived that they were just and we unjust. . . . The truth ought not to be afraid of falsehood. . . . Zerobabel declareth that the truth is of all things the most mighty, and overcometh all things. For Christ is the truth. John xiv. . . . Therefore, if the pope and his priests have the truth, let them overcome us by the word of God. But if they have lies, then they cannot long abide in their presumption.

" Wherefore we beseech and exhort all the imperial
cities, all kings, princes, noblemen, rich and poor, for
God's sake, and for his righteousness, that one of
them write hereof to another, and that there may be
some means devised by which we may commune
with you, safely and friendly, at some such place as
shall be fit for both you and us; and do you bring
with you your bishops and teachers, and let them
and our teachers fight together with the word of
God, and let us hear them; and let not the one overcome the other by violence or false subtlety, but
only by the word of God.   And if your bishops
and teachers have better proofs of their faith out of
the Holy Scripture than we, and our faith be found
untrue, we will receive penance and satisfaction according to the gospel.   But if your bishops and
teachers be overcome of ours by the Holy Scripture, then do ye repent and hearken to us, and hold
with us.   And if your bishops and teachers will cease
from their spiritual pride, and repent and make satisfaction, then will we help you according to our
power. . . .

" And if ye will not determine to do any other
thing than to fight against us, then will we take the
Lord to our help, and his truth; and we will defend
it to the death, and we will not be afraid for the
excommunication or curse of the pope, or his cardinals, or of the bishops, because we know that the
pope is not God, as he maketh himself, so that he
may curse and excommunicate when he will, or bless
when he will; who has now these many years cursed
and excommunicated us, and yet, notwithstanding,

God and his gracious blessing hath been our help." To the objection supposed to be made, that they could not do without priests and bishops to baptize, hear confessions, and minister the holy mysteries, and that even though they should be evil and wicked, it was impossible to do without them, the Bohemians reply, that "when wicked bishops and priests shall be banished, then place shall be made for good priests and bishops."

As to the charge that they did not believe in purgatory, the Virgin Mary, or the saints, they claim that they will prove by Holy Scripture how they ought to believe in regard to these things, better than the bishops or priests could tell them. As to obedience to the pope, they declare that they will render him obedience when he should be holy and just. In regard to their overthrow of public worship, " destroying monasteries, and banishing thence the wicked monks and nuns," as was charged upon them by their enemies, they reply, "Truly we did it, thinking once that they were holy, that they did the reverend service of God; but after that we well observed and considered their life and works, then we perceived that they were hypocrites, falsely aping humility, and wicked builders on high, and sellers of pardons and masses for the dead, and such as devoured in themselves the sins of the people. . . . Forasmuch as their selling of their prayers and masses for the dead for gifts, is no better than hypocrisy and heresy,—therefore if we do speak against them, and destroy their monasteries, we do not therein destroy the service of God, but rather the service of the devil, and the school of heretics. And if ye knew them as we know them, ye would as diligently destroy them as we do. For Christ our Lord did not ordain any such order . . . . and he said, Every plant which my Heavenly Father hath not planted, shall be rooted up."

In the close of their apology, the Bohemians bring forward several subjects to be considered. They are disposed in sixteen articles, intended mainly to expose the corruptions of the church, the avarice, extortion, lewdness, and hypocrisy of the clergy. Their articles are then stated, which they declare they will strive for and maintain unto the death. These are, the prohibition of gross public sins, whether in laity or clergy; the inconsistency of large revenues and pomp with the simplicity of ministers of Jesus Christ; the freedom of the word of God to be read and preached in all places, "without any inhibition of either spiritual or earthly power;" and the communion of the body and blood of Christ as he ordained.

This apology of the Bohemians is signed by four of their leading captains, Procopius, Conrad, Samssmolich, and Smahors. It is honorable at once to their courage, their prudence, their Christian intelligence, and their regard for the supreme authority of the word of God. It undoubtedly expressed the general feeling and conviction of the nation.

To attempt to confute them by the logic of an armed invasion was but madness. Persecution would only exasperate. Nor were they wanting in men who dared, and who were competent, to place them-

selves at their head. Years before, Zisca had won
high renown as a bold and able general. His promptitude and energy in dispelling the storm that threatened the Hussites when they had been summoned
to appear unarmed before Wenzel, had secured the
confidence and respect of the Bohemians. He was
finally acknowledged their leader by an indisputable
preëminence, and he was worthy of the post. His
abilities, attested by subsequent campaigns, rank
him as the greatest general of the age.

Never did any man unite in himself qualities more
eminently fitting him to be at once the head of a
party, and the leader of an army. His genius for
planning a campaign or assault, was only equalled
by his prompt energy in putting his plan in execution. He understood perfectly the art of rendering
himself the master of the minds of the multitude.
Bohemia was in arms for the communion of the cup.
He holds up a sacramental cup before the army, and
tells them to behold their standard. He has no
troops but infantry. By an unexpected assault he
surprises the army of the emperor, and carries off a
thousand horses, thus at once providing himself with
cavalry. He is without a fortified town to afford
security for his troops. He ascends a high mountain
with his soldiers, and there addresses them: "Do
you want houses ? Set up your tents here, and make
your camp your city." The thing is done, and Tabor is at once a fortress. From its impregnable
heights Zisca can defy his foe. Thither, moreover,
he may always securely retreat. Cromwell's Ironsides could not surpass Zisca's soldiers. The latter

also felt the inspiration of their leader's words—
words derived from scripture, and glowing with the
enthusiasm which it inspired.   To the inhabitants of
Tausch he writes:[1] "May God grant, dear brethren,
that performing good works, like the true children
of your Heavenly Father, you may remain steadfast
in his fear; if he has visited you, let not affliction
abate your courage; think of those who labor for
the faith, and who suffer on account of the name of
Jesus Christ.   Imitate the old Bohemians, your ancestors, always ready to defend the cause of God and
their own.   Let us constantly have before our eyes
the divine law, and the good of the common weal;
let us be vigilant; and let whoever knows how to
handle a knife, or to throw a stone, or to brandish
a club, be ready to march. . . . Let your preachers
encourage your people to war against Antichrist; let
every one, young and old, prepare for it.   When I
shall arrive among you, let there be no want of
bread, or beer, or forage ; lay up a store also of good
works.   Behold, the time is now come to arm yourselves, not only against your outward enemies, but
also against those that you have within yourselves.
Remember your first combat when you were few in
number against many, and without arms against
those that were well-provided.   The hand of God
is not shortened: courage, therefore, and be ready.
ZISCA *of the Cup.*"

This letter shows at once the spirit of Zisca, his
skill in touching the chords of popular feeling, and
his watchfulness over the cause which he had taken

[1] L'Enfant's Guerre des Hus., i. 93.

in hand. Cromwell, before the battle of Dunbar, charging his soldiers to "trust in God and keep their powder dry," was manifesting the same exquisite combination of religious enthusiasm and good sense that Zisca did, when he urged the people in the same breath, to "let there be no want of bread, beer, and forage," and to "lay up also a store of good works." The soldiers of Zisca were trained by him as the great Englishman trained his Ironsides. The laity as well as clergy preached for both. The camp was a church, the army a religious assembly. Tabor was, in a new sense, the Mount of Transfiguration. From all parts of Bohemia throngs came flocking thither, and there—as a kind of national covenant— the communion of the cup as well as of bread was freely administered.

The intelligence of what was taking place at Tabor spread over Bohemia. The friends of Huss and of the cup were encouraged. The popular tide, directed by such a man as Zisca, was certain to bear down all before it. His army was not composed of mere soldiers of fortune. They were men of deep religious convictions—some of them, indeed, driven well-nigh mad by persecution—reckless of life in their indignant defiance of Martin's bull, which seemed to combine in it the cruelty of the inquisition, the brutality of the dragoon, and the malice of the fiend. Many, undoubtedly, like Zisca himself, could speak of their own private wrongs. The image of an outraged sister, or of a friend bound in chains to the stake about which the flames raged, rose up before them at the sight of a monk or priest, and led them to

those acts of resentment and vengeance with which
they were so heavily charged. "If ye knew them
as we know them," said they in their apology for
destroying the monasteries, "ye would as diligently
destroy them as we do."

These institutions were undoubtedly excessively
corrupt, and so far as their friends at the council and
the approvers of the violence of the bull were concerned, there could be no ground for reproof. Even
for us, who regret the violence, it is difficult to say
how far circumstances justified it, or how far, as John
Knox urged, it was necessary to destroy the rookeries in order to drive out the foul birds, the harpies,
from their roosts. As favorers of the bull, they were
public persecutors, and their urgent application for
foreign intervention and invasion, justly led to their
being regarded as traitors.

It was on the twenty-second of July (1419) that
the grand communion of the multitude was held at
Tabor.[1] Undesignedly, the priests in many places
had contributed to favor the plans of Zisca. They
had refused the communion of the cup to the laity
in their own neighborhoods, and had thus forced
them, in order to enjoy a privilege which they most
highly prized, to swell the ranks of the Hussite
leader. They would, of course, in the state in which
things then were, go armed, and thus, beyond his
expectations, the multitude of his followers was
swelled by thousands. It is not surprising, when we
consider the feelings with which they were inflamed,
and the confidence which their visible strength and

---

[1] Guerre des Hus., i. 91.   Diari. Bel. Hus., 143.

numbers must have inspired, that a plan should have been adopted for seizing or assaulting the city of Prague. The multitude could not all remain long together. Many of them doubtless belonged in Prague itself, or its neighborhood, and a march upon the city might be made as they returned to their own homes. The elements of disaffection were abundant within the walls, and on the thirtieth of July they broke out into open violence.[1]

The king himself had withdrawn from Prague to one of his castles, some miles distant; but already the fear of his brother, the terrors of a crusade, or the levelling principles of some of the reformers, who imagined that monarchy might be superseded by a republic, had driven him over toward the side of the papal party. His officers and soldiers who were left behind, showed themselves similarly disposed with their master. Violent assaults were made, and individuals were seized and imprisoned. The citizens of Prague could not therefore feel themselves safe while the soldiers of the king possessed within the walls a fortified position like that of the castle or royal palace, from which they might at any moment be assaulted. The host of Zisca, by his training, had now assumed the aspect of a regular army. He led them on to the attack of the new city—the part of Prague occupied by the party which was opposed to the reformers, and supported by the court. The inhabitants of the city joined in the assault. Zisca seems however to have been content for the present merely to intimidate the papal party.

[1] Guerre des Hus., i., 92, 93.   Diari. Bel Hus., 143.

Some of his army—more intent on observing their
religious rite, and improving the occasion for regaining the places of public worship, from which, in the
absence of their advocate, Nicholas de Hussinitz,
they had probably been again excluded by Wenzel's
orders—sought to enter St. Stephen's church. They
found it locked. Indignant at this exclusion, they
assaulted it, and burst open the doors. The priest,
who had ventured to resist them, became the object
of their vengeance. They broke open his parsonage,
and hung him from one of the windows.

After having enjoyed the freedom of the church
and performed their favorite ceremonies, the party
withdrew, and proceeded to the Carmelite monastery.
Here they resolved to array themselves in proper
order, and, forming themselves into a procession,
march to the council-house of the new city,[1] demanding that those of their friends who had been imprisoned should be released. The demand was presented.
The council hesitated to grant it. Some were for
holding out to the last. The people stood without,
quietly awaiting an answer to their demand. At
this moment, some one from one of the upper windows threw a stone, which struck the Hussite priest
who bore the host. The people were enraged.
Their patience was exhausted by delay, and they
regarded the act as a signal for an assault. Resistance was vain. The indignant vengeance of the
people, led on by Zisca, swept all before it. The
council-house was taken by storm. Eleven of the
councillors escaped; but the seven others, all Ger-

[1] Diar. Bel. Hus., 14.

mans, and, as such, hateful to the Bohemians, were
thrown from the upper windows as they were seized,
and impaled on the spears and lances of the multitude below.[1]   The prisoners were of course released.[2]

It is a singular but instructive fact, that at this
moment, when violence seemed to rule, when the
attack of the royal garrison had been foiled, and
when some of the council had been put to death, and
others had fled, no thought of lawless license or ravage was allowed a place in the minds of the triumph-
ing party.   Their first care was to restore the forms
of civil government.   Proclamation was made, and,
under pain of death or exile, all citizens were summoned to meet together at the council-house, to elect
four magistrates, to whom the authority and seal of
the city should be committed till the time for the
next regular election of councilmen should substitute
others in their place.

Meanwhile the assault upon the new city was continued.   For five days, scenes of violence were constantly occurring.   The court, it was now known, had
taken an open stand against the Hussites.   It was
resolved that the leaders of the reform party should
all be put to death.   The attacks which had been
made upon the Hussite processions by the officers
and soldiers of the king, and which had aggravated
difficulties, had evidently been by the king's order,
or at least his connivance.   The people saw nothing
before them but victory on the one hand, and, on the
other, persecution with a suppression of their worship.

---

[1] Æneas Sylvius, ch. xxxvii.   [2] Life of Zisca, p. 9.

They therefore pursued the siege with ardor. But the queen with the royal party had retired to the castle in the upper city, and while they resisted the assault, despatched, for the second time, messages to Sigismund for aid.

Zisca at this moment withdrew from the city. His biographer[1] informs us that the excesses of the citizens, which he could not approve, was the reason of his departure. It is more probable that he foresaw the storm about to burst upon the city in response to the summons of Wenzel, and wished to be prepared for it. He withdrew to Pilsen, gathering his troops around him. The place was at the safe distance of fifty or sixty miles from Prague, and secured its defence from the direction of Nuremberg. Here Zisca quietly watched the progress of affairs, ready to suppress any attempt that might be made to carry into execution the designs of the enemy. He was sufficiently strong and secure to defy any probable assault.

Meanwhile the citizens of Prague bore with the greatest impatience the presence of the royal garrison within the walls. There it was, perched upon the lofty heights of the hill upon which the castle stood, ready at once to swoop down upon its victims. Though they had been forced to give over their assault upon it, the garrison was exposed to continued molestations. Efforts were made to secure a truce or a compromise, but the citizens would consent to none which did not allow them free liberty of worship. Thus negotiations were protracted. The cas-

---

[1] Life of Zisca, p. 11, 12.

tle was in fact in a state of siege, with little prospect of relief.

But at this juncture, and while Sigismund, who had been appealed to for aid, was busily engaged in Hungary in protecting the rights of his hereditary states, a summons, more effectual than any that had been sent him hitherto, roused him to prompt and energetic action. This was the announcement of the death of his brother, the king of Bohemia. He died in a manner worthy of his life. Upon being informed of the commotion that had taken place at Prague on the thirtieth of July, he broke out in a torrent of passionate invective against its authors. Several of the courtiers who were present expressed their detestation of the enormities that had been perpetrated. One of his attendants, however, ventured to say that he had foreseen what was about to take place; probably intending to attribute it to Wenzel's withdrawal from Prague. Such freedom of language aroused the tiger in the heart of the irascible and passionate king. He sprang upon the bold attendant who had dared to speak words so uncourteous to royal ears, and dashing him to the ground, was about to consummate his violence by plunging his dagger into the bosom of his prostrate victim. From this he was withheld by his attendants, and could scarcely be persuaded not to order the bold speaker at once to be executed. The excitement and frenzy which had thus been produced were too much for a frame already worn out by dissipation. He was struck with paralysis,[1] and after

[1] Guerre des Huss., 99. Æneas Sylvius, ch. xxxvii.

lingering eighteen days, expired. He had marked the names of several Hussites whom he had doomed to death, but the blow that smote him rescued and delivered them.[1]

The death of Wenzel (Aug. 16, 1419) left the kingdom of Bohemia, in default of other heirs, to his brother Sigismund. The queen, Sophia,[2] sought, on her husband's death, not only to secure the aid of Sigismund, but to engage the citizens of Prague to conditions of peace, by which the emperor should be at once adopted as their king. But they refused to acknowledge him. His whole course had been such as to commend him only to the abhorrence of all who cherished the memory of Huss.

Meanwhile Sigismund himself was making preparations for taking possession of the kingdom, which he claimed to inherit from his brother. The citizens of Prague became alarmed. Their enemies still held the royal castle, as well as the Vissehrad, and anxiously awaited the emperor's approach, to retaliate upon the citizens for the assaults they had endured. The only security of the latter was in a speedy reduction of the castle. They at once applied for aid to their allies. Zisca saw the importance of the enterprise. Accompanied by Coranda and Nicholas de Hussinitz, he hastened to the rescue. The new city, with the Vissehrad, was taken by the combined forces, on November 4, 1419. The castle hardly escaped.

---

[1] The body of Wenzel, according to some authorities, was first deposited in its tomb, and afterward taken up and flung into the Moldau. Here it was found by a fisherman, of whom it was purchased by Sigismund, who had it properly entombed. Godeau, xxxvii. 26. Also, Æneas Sylvius, ch. xxxvii. Diar. Bel. Hus., 145.

[2] Æneas Sylvius, ch. xxxviii.

In order to understand fully the apprehension, on
the part of the citizens of Prague, which led them to
invite Zisca to their aid, we must recur to what had
taken place since his first assault of the new city. The
writer of the "Diary of the Hussite War" gives us a
version of what transpired, which, though it differs in
some respects from the statements of other historians, commends itself to our confidence by its superior credibility. The rage of the king on the announcement of what took place on the 30th of July
was due, not so much to the scenes of violence which
then transpired, as to the presumption of the citizens
in electing their own magistrates, without waiting for
his sanction. The fear that haunted him, was that
of being deposed from the throne. He watched with
intense jealousy every movement which seemed to
indicate the least disposition to put any other in his
place. His threat, addressed to Nicholas de Hussinitz,[1] grew out of this extreme sensitiveness to a
dreaded danger. These fears were fully understood
by the members of his court, some of whom favored
the Hussite party. By their means a temporary
peace was negotiated, the conditions of which were,
that the citizens should humbly submit themselves
to the king, while he, on his part, and in maintenance
of his authority, should acknowledge the four magistrates elected by the people, and give them his sanction. The Hussites, moreover, were to be allowed
liberty of worship. On these conditions, peace was
restored, and the commotion subsided. But is was

---

[1] This threat was, that in leading
the citizens who came with the demand for some of the churches in
which Hussite worship might be held,
he was spinning a cord for his own
neck.

only till the intelligence of Wenzel's death excited
new distrust. On the next day scenes of violence
again occurred.

The fury of the populace was directed, chiefly,
against those churches in which the communion of
the cup was not allowed.[1] The organs and images
were broken and destroyed. The clergy, apprehensive of danger, fled. As night drew on, the violence
increased. The Carthusian monastery was attacked,
and the wine found there was freely drunk, until
many were intoxicated. The monastery itself was
plundered, and the monks within were borne off to
the council-house, to be restrained of their liberty,
and perhaps otherwise punished for having consented
to the death of Huss, and opposed the communion
of the cup. On the next day the Carthusian monastery was taken anew by assault, and burned, leaving
only its walls standing. The tomb of Archbishop
Albic, in the Church of the Holy Virgin, was broken
open, and the images dashed in pieces. The commotion spread to the neighboring cities and villages.
The monastery of the preaching friars at Piska was
completely sacked. A great multitude, drawn from
various parts of the kingdom, assembled on a mountain[2] near Ladwy, and after listening to various exhortations to love God, and abide by the truth, and
enjoying the communion of the cup, marched in procession to Prague, and were hospitably welcomed by
the citizens. Torches were carried and drums beaten
as they entered the gates, and the multitude took
possession of the Ambrosian monastery, where they

[1] Diar. Bel. Hus., 145.   [2] Diar. Bel. Hus., 146.

were supplied with food for several days by the inhabitants of the city. The presence of the multitude had doubtless been sought, and it contributed effectually to expedite a second truce between the two parties. Upon this, the strangers, who had also tried their skill at image breaking, withdrew from Prague.[1]

For several weeks the city continued quiet. The queen, however,—and certain barons of the kingdom, the principal of whom were Czenko de Wartenberg, the governor of the castle, William of Hazmburgk, and John Chudoba, availing themselves of the treasures which Wenzel left behind him,—called in the aid of the German forces, and began to act upon the aggressive.[2] The citizens of Prague, asking for freedom of worship only, were too well aware of the vengeance which had been provoked by the violence of some among them, nor did they fail to arm themselves against the enemy. The city was thus in a state of insurrection. Its inhabitants felt that, with Sigismund advancing against them, there could be no security while the castle held out.

In these circumstances Zisca was appealed to. The cause in many respects was a common one, and he hastened to comply with the summons. Probably but a small part of his forces accompanied him. The report was spread in Prague that his enemies were disputing with him access to the city. The great drums[3] were beaten. Multitudes obeyed the signal. The forces were joined, and the assault commenced. At first the royal party had the advantage. They

---

[1] Diar. Bel. Hus., 146, 147. [2] Æneas Sylvius, ch. xxxviii.
[3] Magnæ Companæ pro concursu populi.

disputed the passage of the bridge, and were able to
do it by the strong positions which they held in the
royal castle, the archiepiscopal palace, and the house
of the Duke of Saxony. They were armed, moreover, with mortars,[1]—though these did but little execution, whether from want of skill in their management, or from their imperfect structure. The passage
to the Kleine-Seite, (*parvam partam*,) though hotly
disputed, was at length secured by breaking open a
gate adjoining the house of the Duke of Saxony,
although numbers were slain on both sides. The
royal party at once commenced their retreat to the
castle. Horses, arms, and various spoils left behind
them, were eagerly seized and appropriated.[2]

The whole night long the uproar continued. The
bells were rung as if in defiance, and in order to continue the alarm. At midnight the queen fled, accompanied by but a small number, among whom was
the Baron Ulric de Rosenberg. There was great
danger that the castle itself would be forced to yield.
During the night, however, the invading party had
largely withdrawn to their homes. The royalists
improved the occasion, and sallying forth from the
castle, seized upon the council-house of the Kleine-
Seite, and bearing off the treasures and records, set
the building itself on fire. The flames spread to the
adjoining houses, which were rapidly consumed.

These events took place at an early hour in the
morning (Nov. 5, 1419). The attack of the citizens
was not resumed till a late hour of the day. The
strength of each party—one favored by position, and

---

[1] Bombardis.   [2] Diar. Bel. Hus., 148, 149.

the other by numbers—was nearly equal. The royal
party burned several houses and dwellings, some of
them of great value, among them the School of St.
Nicholas. They bore off moreover to the castle a
number of prisoners. The citizens on their part
plundered and sacked the archiepiscopal palace
and other buildings. Thus each party seemed to
aspire to exceed the other in vandalism. Those of
the castle could command, from their high position,
an extensive view, and, among other means of offence,
sought to prevent the entrance of provisions within
the walls of the city.

Thus the contest lingered on undecisive. For
several days there were frequent skirmishes. The
citizens were reinforced by four thousand Taborites,
who cut their way through the enemy and succeeded
in making good their entrance into Prague, where
they were received with acclamation. The royalist
party saw themselves again forced to offer terms of
peace. This was effected by the promise that the Bohemians should be allowed the communion of the cup,
and that the law of God and the truth of the gospel
should be maintained throughout the kingdom. On
the other hand, the citizens bound themselves to
refrain from any further violence toward the churches,
and any further breaking of images. The Vissehrad
also was to be no further molested.[1] This truce was
doubtless unacceptable to Zisca, who, with the Taborites, withdrew at once from the city. Subsequent events made its impolicy manifest. It left
their enemies a stronghold, from which they could

---

[1] Diar. Bel. Hus., 150.

at their pleasure commence to act upon the aggressive.

Meanwhile the enemies of the Taborites, who had opposed them on their march to Prague, had not been idle. They were encouraged and directed by the emperor. Led on by Peter von Sternberg, they had begun to act upon the offensive. They had assaulted those cities which had contributed men to aid the citizens of Prague. At Ausch[1] they had taken a number of prisoners; but when, encouraged by success, they had ventured an attack upon the heights of Knin, they were completely routed. As Zisca, dissatisfied with the results at Prague, had now rejoined his army, the enemy were constrained to limit their operations to mere skirmishes of little importance.

The truce agreed upon was to continue from Nov. 12, 1419, to April 21, 1420. It was destined, however, soon to be broken. The Hussite szealously improved it, while it lasted, in preachings, communions, and lamentations over the death of Huss. They were, however, subject to continual molestations. Wherever their enemies prevailed, they were forced to undergo the greatest vexations and sufferings. Such of them as had been taken captive, were treated with great harshness. Some were cruelly imprisoned, and left in their dungeons to endure hunger and thirst. Some were sold[2] for money, or subjected to every species of abuse. A favorite mode of disposing of them was to throw them, sometimes alive, and sometimes after being beheaded, into deep wells or

[1] Frequently written Aussig.   [2] Pescheck., i. 14.

pits, a barbarity which was generally practised in the
night-time.   It was estimated that those who were
thus destroyed amounted to the number of sixteen
hundred persons.   But such inhuman cruelty was as
impolitic as it was inhuman.   It only tended to inflame the Hussites to indignation and vengeance.   In
some cases it forced them to desperation.[1]

It was but a few days after the commencement of
the truce, that a Hussite priest, John Naakuasa, engaged in visiting the sick, was taken on the highway
near Glatow.[2]   He was sold for a large sum to the
Germans of Bavaria, who had come to join Raczko
in his assault upon that place.   He was required by
them to abjure the doctrine of the communion of
the cup.   This he refused to do.   After insults and
reproaches had been exhausted upon him in vain, he
was bound to a tree for a stake.   Cords were drawn
through his hands first perforated by swords, and
thus secured, he was burned, a martyr to his faith.

At about the same time, an assault was made upon
a neighboring city Gurim.   The magistrates and
several of the prominent citizens, among whom was
John Chodk, (or Chodek,) a former officer of the
king, and several priests, all adherents of the communion of the cup, were seized and borne off as
captives.   They were subjected to the most bitter
wrongs and insults.   Blazing torches were thrown at
them, and they were cast into prison, where the severity and harshness of their treatment were aggravated by their being bound with iron chains and
fetters.

---

[1] Diar. Bel. Hus., 151.   [2] Ib.

In the midst of these transactions, a question arose demanding a practical answer, and as to which the minds of the Bohemians were much divided. This was in regard to the succession of Sigismund to the vacant throne. His complicity in the death of Huss had alienated from him the good-will of a large part of the Bohemian nation. Some of the Hussites were altogether in favor of having no king. They preferred a republic. Among these Zisca must probably be reckoned, although his preferences appear to have been far less decided than those of many of his compatriots.

When the emperor's proclamation was published, summoning the states to meet him at Beraun,[1] (Dec. 25, 1419,) and to acknowledge him as rightful sovereign, some were for compliance, while others were for treating the proclamation and summons with contempt. The only promise which Sigismund had hitherto made, served only to excite distrust. It was an evident cover for duplicity. He declared that he would govern the kingdom as it had been governed under his father Charles IV.[2] What did this mean? The Hussites had then no existence as a religious body. They could not well confide in a promise which simply ignored their existence. In spite, how-

[1] L'Enfant gives Beraun as the place of conference, although Brünn would seem to have been more appropriate, situated as it was in Moravia, and between Hungary and Bohemia. The emperor's departure to Breslau is thus more easily explained. Had the conference been at Beraun, near Prague, it seems strange that he should not have visited the latter place. The only difficulty in the way is, that the distance of Brünn from Prague seems too great for the deputation to have visited it, discharged their mission, and returned in eight days. The author of the *Diarium* speaks of the place by its Latin name, as *Bruna*.

[2] Guerre des Hus., i. 117. Æneas Sylvius, ch. xxxix.

ever, of all distrust, the citizens of Prague were present by deputation at Beraun. The barons of the kingdom of Bohemia and the march of Moravia, as well as the magistrates of the royal cities and the officials of the kingdom generally, were present. The Queen Sophia, the legate of the pope, with many princes and magistrates, accompanied the emperor. The embassy from Prague reached Beraun on the twenty-seventh of December [1] (1419). They entered the city with sound of trumpets, and in somewhat imposing array. The emperor, with the magnates of his court, and many of the clergy as well as laity, witnessed the entrance of the procession, and gazed with surprise at its numbers and array. It was hospitably received, in quarters set apart specially for its entertainment. Priests from Prague accompanied it, and performed their favorite rites of worship free from all molestation. The priests of the other party refused, however, to perform any of the sacred offices pertaining to their function, while the citizens of Prague remained within the walls. Beraun should suffer for permitting the entrance of the heretics. Such was the spirit in which the Hussites were still regarded.[2]

On the third day the embassy presented itself before the emperor. On bended knees they saluted him in the name of their city, and accepted him as their hereditary king and master. Sigismund upbraided them with great severity, and imposed the conditions on which he was willing to receive them into favor. His feelings toward them were exceed-

---

[1] Guerre des Hus., i. 117.   [2] Diar. Bel. Hus., 153.

ingly embittered. The conduct of the clergy and legates of the papal party had increased his exasperation. The events that had taken place at Prague had aggravated his purpose of vengeance, and the disappointments which he had elsewhere experienced had only soured his spirit, till he was ready to sanction any measures, however atrocious, that might be necessary, in order to subdue his rebellious subjects. Several weeks before the meeting of this convention at Beraun, he had written to the magistrates at Prague a letter, in which, forgetful of the imperial dignity, he had indulged in a tone of sarcasm which was only calculated to irritate rather than conciliate revolt.[1]

Addressing the magistrates, he says, in bitter irony, " Especially are we anxious that you should not give up your Wickliffite sanctity. Oh! what pleasure must it give a prince to have so large a number of such rulers and such subjects! He will establish his throne, and his glory will spread from the East to the West. Therefore, most dear and loyal, our heart is cheered to learn what is your prudence, wisdom, union! Indeed, you are a mirror for other lands, the light of the ignorant and such as wander in darkness, and the council of Constance is nothing but obscurity compared with your wisdom. Have you not illuminated Prague and all Bohemia

---

[1] The author of the Diary of the Hussite war (p. 157) says, that Sigismund wrote letters, which were sent throughout the kingdom, in which he commanded all the barons, and especially all the magistrates of the kingdom, including the governors of the royal castle, burgomasters, and judges, to constrain, persecute, and exterminate from the kingdom all Wickliffites, Hussites, and favorers of the cup."

by the fame of your learning? You may pass for pope, or even king, since you are so wise." The emperor then reproaches them for the manner in which they had dealt with monasteries, convents, and parishes from which they had expelled the curates, because, as they said, they would not receive the law of God. Their treatment of the senators and judges—their iconoclastic propensities, which they indulged by breaking to pieces the images of the saints as useless idols—their disrespect for the relics of the saints, while they exalted Huss and Jerome to the rank of martyrs—their refusal to bow before the host—their neglect of the festivals of the saints—their readiness to hear preachers of both sexes—are the crimes which the emperor charges upon them. In view of these, he asks, " Who can suffice to chant your praises, if you are every day to make new progress in these holy innovations? Certainly the kings and princes of Christendom have admired, now do, and ever will admire, the extraordinary wisdom that has been infused into you, and of which the ancient fathers knew nothing. Thus, most beloved, if in time past we have written to you not to renounce the obedience of the Roman church, we have done it through ignorance, unaware of your exquisite discernment." He then ironically praises their conduct on the occasion of the death of Wenzel, when, armed with various weapons, they ran through the city, in cloisters, churches, and chapels, singing their fine funeral songs. " It only remains," he adds, " for us urgently to beseech you to associate us with *your college*, and employ all your means to fit us for the government of Bohemia. But do not go about to say, as in the gospel, 'We will not have this man to reign over us,' or, 'This is the heir—let us kill him,' for we wish to profit by your counsels, and to be governed by your lights."

Such a letter gave little assurance of favorable conditions for the citizens of Prague. Nothing but the emperor's weakness forced him to temporize. Yet even under the pressure to which he was subjected by the state of his affairs, and notwithstanding the evident strength of the Hussite party, the conditions he imposed were sufficiently onerous. They were such as might most effectually promote any measures for completely subduing and suppressing the Hussite party. The citizens, as a pledge of their submission to his power and authority, were to remove all the chains from the streets of the city, as well as the statues which they had set up. They were to level and destroy all the entrenchments and fortifications which had been constructed since the death of Wenzel, for the siege or the storming of the castle. The monks and priests should no longer be molested in any respect, and the citizens should make all ready for the coming of the emperor himself.[1]

Not content with this, Sigismund deposed from office all those magistrates who adhered to the communion of the cup, substituting in their place such as were distinguished for having opposed this innovation. Several forts and strong places were at the same time to be given into the hands of the emperor, who stationed in them faithful partisans. Some

---

[1] Guerre des Hus., i. 117.

of these contained large treasures, which were afterward employed to sustain the imperial arms.

After little more than a week's absence, the embassy of the citizens returned to Prague[1] (Jan. 4,
1420.) Hard as the conditions imposed were, and
although accompanied by the act that substituted
enemies in place of magistrates of their own choice,
there seemed to prevail a sincere disposition to submit to Sigismund's authority. The chains and statues were taken down from the streets and deposited
in the council-house. The fortifications erected
against the castle were levelled, even amid the derision of the Germans of the garrison and the royal
party. "Now," cried they, as they saw the works
demolished by the hands of the builders,—"Now
these Wickliffite and Hussite heretics will be destroyed, and we shall have an end of them." At
the same time many of the royal party, who had
fled the city, returned. Priests, monks, canons, and
common people, who had withdrawn upon the violence that took place on occasion of the death of
Wenzel, boldly appeared. Proclamation was made
through the city, in the name of the king and magistrates, that all persons who had left the city might
now freely and safely reoccupy their dwellings. It
was forbidden, morever, to offer insult to priests or
monks, as had been the practice of men as well as
boys, when any passed them along the street.

The enemies of the Hussites, however, showed no
disposition to relax their persecuting spirit and zeal.
On the ninth of January (1420) John Chodk, of

[1] Diar. Bel. Hus., 154.

Gurim, who had been taken prisoner some weeks before by the enemy, and who had hitherto been kept a close prisoner, was put to death. He admonished his murderers of the guilt which they were committing in the cruelties which they practised upon Christian believers, warning them to repent of these and their other sins. He, with three others, who were priests of the Hussite party, was thrown into a deep well (*ad foveam profundam seu Sachtam.*) On the same night many laymen were put to death in a similar manner. [1]

But the emperor himself more than approved—he encouraged, by word and example, this persecuting and barbarous treatment of the Hussites. From the conference at Beraun, he had withdrawn to Breslau. Here he had manifested such a disposition to proceed against the followers of Huss, as to destroy the last vestige of confidence in his character or promise. He could not have pursued a course more directly calculated to defeat his own projects. The Hussites were already divided in sentiment upon many points. Some of them up to this time had been in favor of Sigismund for king, while others were bitterly opposed to him, and preferred a republic, or at least another person for their monarch. Persecution, too, had had its usual effect. Many had become wild enthusiasts. Driven to desperation, they had compared themselves to the ancient Israelites, and, as God's chosen people, dealt out threatenings and denunciations against their foes as impious Canaanites and heathen. Political and religious interests, vari-

---

[1] Diar. Bel. Hus., 154, 155.

ously combined, had served to widen the divisions
that already existed in the views and sentiments of
such as bore the common name of Huss.   The three
principal parties were the Catholics, the Utraquists
or Calixtines, so called from their devotion to the
communion of the *chalice* or cup, and the Taborites.
The first had lost much of their influence, or had
become merged in the party of the Calixtines.   These
last were called the *limping* Hussites, by those who
were more radical than themselves in their views of
reform.   And yet they were the most consistent and
intelligent in their demands.   They held to the communion of the cup, the free preaching of the word
of God, the severe repression of public sins, as well
of clergy as of laity, and the wrong of allowing to
the priests landed property, or a share in the civil
administration.   The Calixtines were, in fact, the
moderate or conservative party.   They numbered
among them the most influential men of Bohemia,
and it was not long before they were joined by
Archbishop Conrad himself.

The Taborites were so called, as composing mainly
the army which founded the city of Tabor, of which
they continued to retain possession.   They were the
soldiers of reform, and shared a deeper enthusiasm
in the cause for which they bled, than their more
peaceful brethren.   They had lost, far more than their
compatriots, all regard for the authority of popes,
councils, or the church of Rome.   They rejected altogether a hierarchy of priests, nor would they allow
any mere outward symbol or external ceremonial,
as a spot upon the purity of a scriptural worship.

Many of them went beyond the views of Huss, Jerome, and Jacobel, whom they still reverenced, and
rejected entirely the doctrine of transubstantiation.
A great majority of the Taborites belonged to the
lower classes, and some of them were excessively
ignorant. Some doubtless, in rejecting priestly rule,
gave themselves over to wholesale license. Contempt
for the horrid vices and cupidity of the sacerdotal
order would naturally smooth the way to violence
and outrage, especially when that order became the
aggressors. In this terrible reaction, the lower and
more ignorant class would act a prominent part.
Their leaders would almost insensibly be forced to
conform to their tastes and yield to their prejudices.
These were the men, some wild and raving in their
vengeance, some more scriptural and even evangelical in their sentiments, who composed that terrible
force that supplied Zisca with his armies, and made
the name of Hussite terrible over all Europe.[1]

Among the Taborites, and enjoying the liberty
which they allowed, were mingled persons of other
sects from which they must be carefully distinguished. The freedom which was vindicated in Bohemia,
drew to it the free-thinkers and heretics of other
lands. Some of these were possessed of a spirit, and
adopted sentiments, utterly discordant with those
of the Hussites. Among them were the Adamites,[2]
whose views of clothing much resembled those of
the more fanatical of the early Quakers, who exposed
themselves half naked to the public gaze. On other
points they rendered themselves still more obnoxious.

[1] Diar. Bel. Hus. [2] Æneas Sylvius, ch. xli.

They carried the doctrine of modern free-love to a most licentious extreme. They do not seem at any time to have actually united themselves with the Taborites, nor do their views appear to have been adopted by the latter. Zisca considered them so criminal and dangerous, that he slew and exterminated them almost to a man.

The Taborites themselves were fanatical mainly in their forced interpretation of the prophecies. They made abundant use of the obscurities of the book of Revelation, yet, like some of the preachers of the council of Constance, applied them mainly to the harlotry of the Roman church. They held and preached the speedy coming of our Lord, to judge and to punish the world. The destruction of Sodom was a favorite figure, with them, of the approaching judgment of the nations. They went so far as to specify the cities of refuge—the Zoar of the purified church. These were five in number—Pilsen, Saatz, Launa, Slany, and Laatowia. The first of these they called the city of the Sun, and to it was conceded a preëminence above the others.[1] The preachers of the Taborites scattered through Bohemia, propagated their peculiar views with great effect. Multitudes sold their possessions, no longer valuable to them, for a small sum, and hastened to take up their residence in the five cities of refuge. Letters were written and dispersed abroad, in which the doctrine of the coming of Christ was supported by prophecies ill understood and falsely applied. Whole families would come, bringing the proceeds of their property

[1] Diar. Bel. Hus.

with them, to swell the numbers of the Taborite
hosts. Their money was freely devoted to promote
the cause which they had espoused. Nothing could
have been more favorable to the plans and measures
of Zisca. The ranks of his army were kept full, and
he was careful to train it to the most exact discipline.
The enthusiasm of his soldiers, and their religious
ardor, fitted them to follow the command of one
whose genius as a General was combined with a devotion that made him, as a leader of armies, the
Cromwell of his age.

There was obvious danger of a serious division
among the Hussites, some favoring the Calixtines,
some joining themselves to the Taborites. In fact,
so strongly had the prejudices of men already taken
root, that strong jealousies and rivalries had even
now sprung up at Prague. The Calixtines prevailed
in the old town, and the Taborites in the new—
where their battles had been fought and their victories won. For twenty years there was a state of ri-
valry, sometimes approaching to open war, between
the two parts of the city. It was owing to this fact
undoubtedly in part, and the consequent jealousy
produced by the presence of Zisca, that he was prevented from making a longer stay when he marched
at different times to the relief of the city. The folly
of Sigismund was manifest in adopting measures of
severity which united, even temporarily, the discordant elements of opposition.

CHAPTER XIV.

DEFEAT AND RETREAT OF THE EMPEROR.

JAN. 9, 1420–JULY 28, 1420.

ON the side of the Calixtines was ranged the larger portion of the Bohemian nobility. Among the Ta-

borites, the common people almost exclusively were
to be found. The former inclined to accept Sigismund as their king. The latter preferred, if not a
republic, at least some other monarch than the emperor. Had the two parties been left to themselves,
the issue might have been somewhat doubtful. Bohemia might have shared the fate of England in the
seventeenth century, for Zisca manifested a signal
ability, and a tact for managing popular enthusiasm
and religious impulses equal to that of the Lord
Protector of England. But the folly of Sigismund
only tended to band together the repugnant elements into one common rebellion. The proceedings
of the royal party had already alarmed the citizens
of Prague. They were so far excited by their fears,
as once more to lay aside their party aversions in
presence of a common foe. Zisca was, by conceded
ability, if not by general consent, acknowledged as
the champion of the nation, although there were
some, not enough perhaps to be called a party, who
were in favor of placing Nicholas de Hussinitz upon
the throne.

Mutual animosities, however, were for the time
suppressed by the cruel policy pursued by the imperialists. The pretext for this was found in the excesses of the Taborites. The latter were fierce and
relentless in the vengeance which they meted out to
priests and monks. Their violence at Prague was
copied throughout Bohemia. In some places their
devastations were terrible. In the course of a few
months, several hundred monasteries were sacked
and burned. In Prague alone, during the year

1419, forty are said to have been destroyed by the Hussites.[1]

But the imperialists needed no example from which to copy. They reduced cruelty to an art, and practised their barbarities on system. If any one was found, priest or layman, young or old, male or female, who refused to abjure the doctrine of the cup, the fate of such a one was sealed. No pity was shown, and no entreaty could rescue them from the flames, drowning, or the pits. The mines of Cuttemberg were pestilent with the stench of victims. The convention at Beraun did not stay the rage of the imperialists, who seemed to regard it as merely binding their enemies, and giving them over to their hands in unresisting submission. Some of Sigismund's letters fell into the hands of the Hussites, and betrayed his bitter purpose of vengeance. To Czenko of Wartemberg, governor of the royal castle, he wrote,—" Exterminate the Horebites." At Breslau, the Hussites in a tumult had killed a magistrate. Sigismund took ample vengeance by putting twelve of them to death.[2]

The passions of the Taborites were inflamed almost to madness by the studied cruelties and insults to which all those who adhered to the communion of the cup—whenever occasion offered—were subjected. In the early part of March, John Krasa, a merchant, or, according to others, a Calixtine priest of Prague, had visited Breslau whither Sigismund had withdrawn from the conference of Beraun on matters of business. In conversation, he happened to speak

[1] Guerre des Hus., 104.   [2] Ib., 120. Æneas Sylvius, xxxix. Godeau, xxxvii. 30.

with disapproval of the burning of Huss, and in
favor of the practice of the communion of the cup.
For this crime he was seized and thrown into prison.
On the following day, Nicolas of Bethlehem, who
had been deputed from Prague to the emperor to
inform him that he would be recognized as king of
Bohemia only when he had declared himself in favor
of the Calixtine dogma, was also seized and cast into
the same prison with Kraza. The indignation of
Sigismund against Nicolas was extreme. He was
condemned to be burned. Krasa cheered him in the
prison, reminding him of the sufferings of the old
martyrs, and of the everlasting joy that would follow their momentary pains. On the 14th of March,
1420, Nicolas was led out to die; but when the
ropes were fastened to his feet by which a horse
was to drag him to the place of execution, he was
seized with a panic fear, and, yielding to the fair
promises of the legate, who was then present, he
renounced the doctrines of Huss.[1] But Krasa, notwithstanding the fate of his companion, and the
promises and terrors by which it was attempted
to shake his own constancy, continued immovable.
He refused all the terms of pardon offered him. He
was then slowly dragged through the streets. The
legate, who would have preferred his recantation to
his execution, followed him, several times ordering
the procession to halt, and exhorting Krasa to recant and save his life. But his steadfast reply was,
"I am ready to die for the gospel of Jesus." He
was already half dead when he reached the place of

[1] Pescheck's Reformation and Anti-reformation in Bohemia, i. 12.

execution, where he was devoted to the flames. It was on the next day that the papal bull of excommunication and crusade against the Bohemians was published from the pulpits, and placarded on the walls of the churches.

Every where the most barbarous cruelties were practised against the followers of Huss. A price was set upon the heads of the Taborites.[1] For a priest, the sum paid was five guilders; for a layman, one. The most horrid butcheries were the result of this barbarous measure.

In May the burgomaster of Leitmeritz, Pichel by name, a cruel and deceitful wretch, seized in one night twenty-four respectable citizens, among whom was his own son-in-law, and threw them into a deep dungeon near St. Michael's gate.[2] When they were almost inanimate with cold and hunger, he took them out, with the assistance of some of the imperial officers, and, attended by a guard, pronounced upon them the sentence of death. They were then chained, borne in wagons to the banks of the Elbe, and thrown into the river. A great crowd, embracing the wives, children, and friends of the prisoners, witnessed the murderous spectacle, and could not restrain the utterance of their grief. The Burgomaster's daughter—his only child—cast herself with clasped hands at his feet, interceding for the life of her husband. "Spare your tears," was the stern and merciless reply; "you know not what you desire. Can you not have a better husband than he?" The father was inexorable, and the daughter, driven to

desperation, exclaimed, " Father, you shall not give
me in marriage again." Smiting her breast, and tear-
ing her hair, she followed her husband with the rest.
The victims, as they were cast into the river, protested their innocence, and, bidding their friends
farewell, exhorted them to constancy and obedience
to the word of God, rather than the commandments
of men. They then prayed for their enemies, and
commended their spirits to Heaven. With their
hands and feet bound together, they were conveyed
in boats to the middle of the river and then cast
into the stream. Lest any should escape, the banks
were lined with executioners armed with pikes, who
stood ready to stab and force back any that floated
toward the shore. All perished. The burgomaster's
daughter, after a vain struggle to save her husband,
perished with him. The next day both were found,
clasped in one another's arms, and buried in the same
grave.

Such violence produced a powerful reaction. At
Prague it was like a spark falling on tinder. The
passions of the Calixtines as well as the Taborites were
inflamed anew. A violent leader, John, a Premonstrant priest of the Monastery of St. Mary, formerly
a monk of Zelew, put himself at the head of the
popular movement. He harangued the citizens,
taking for his text the barbarous cruelty of the imperialists. He pronounced Sigismund the red horse
of Apocalyptic vision—the sworn enemy of the cup
—the author of the terrible excommunication which
had overtaken the great body of the nation.[1]   " Will

[1] Diar. Bel. Hus., 161.

he treat you better," he asked, "than he has those of Breslau?"

The excitement produced was intense. The populace swore never to receive Sigismund as their king. Circular letters were sent out to the several cities which the convention had agreed to give up to Sigismund, exhorting them never to admit him or his forces.[1] He was pronounced an enemy of the Sclavonian language, and responsible for the execution of Huss. He was charged with alienating portions of Bohemia for his own selfish interests, and with laboring for the excommunication and death of all the Hussite teachers.[2]

In such circumstances, any further attempt to fulfil the terms of the convention was scarcely to be expected. Many of the Taborites of Prague, apprehensive of the result of the measure agreed upon at Beraun, had already left the city, and indignantly withdrawn to Tabor, or joined the forces under the command of John of Hussinitz. Wherever they went, they imparted to others their own indignation, and encouraged an open violation of the terms of the convention.

Zisca saw no prospect of peace for the kingdom if Sigismund was allowed the undisputed succession to the crown. With several Hussite knights, he foreswore obedience to a man who had allowed his safe-conduct to be violated with impunity in the case of Huss, and who already was appearing at the head of armies to subdue the kingdom, and trample upon its freedom of worship. This league, thus com-

[1] Æneas Sylvius, ch. xxxix.　　[2] Guerre des Hus., i. 120.

menced, grew rapidly. Barons, knights, and cities
joined it. They swore never to receive Sigismund
as their king. With the increasing danger from
abroad, the prospects of a fierce resistance from the
union of the Hussites against the emperor brightened.
His own cruelties, and the perfidy and violence of the
royal party, were taking effect.

The Taborite preachers had been instrumental in
filling the five " cities of refuge," but especially Pilsen, full to overflowing.[1] It became therefore an object for the enemy to gain possession of it. Indeed,
it had been pledged to the emperor by the terms
agreed upon by the convention ; but to defeat them
in this purpose, Zisca threw himself with his forces
into the place, and held it for a time, refusing all
conditions of surrender. He declined all negotiation
with an enemy whom he dared not trust. He had
with him in the city several eminent barons of the
kingdom ; among them Brzenko de Sswihow and
Walkun de Adlar. Of the party opposed to the
communion of the cup, many were driven without
the walls. Several monasteries and palaces adjoining
the city were destroyed, at the instance of Wenzel de
Coranda, one of the Hussite priests.

But Zisca was not suffered to remain unmolested.
The royal party, led by Bohwslaus de Swamberg,
made an assault with a view to recover the city. He
was defeated in his attempt, and put to flight, though
the loss was considerable upon both sides.[2] But the
anxiety of the queen and the royal party to regain
the place, led them promptly to reinforce the army

---

[1] Diar. Bel. Hus., 155. Guerre des Hus., i. 119.   [2] Diar. Bel. Hus., 150.

of the siege. Skirmishes between the hostile armies were frequent, and the captives on both sides were treated with great cruelty.

Unable to make much progress, the royal party proposed to negotiate for the evacuation of the city by the Hussites. The latter declined all terms with a party in whose pledges they could place no confidence. At length, urged by a deputation sent to them from Prague, who still wished to conciliate the emperor by surrendering this as one of the cities claimed, they consented to treat for an evacuation of the place. The conditions were, that the city should enjoy the freedom of the communion of the cup, and that such as wished to leave the city might withdraw unmolested to Hradisch, with their wives and children. To these conditions the royal party obligated themselves, under severe penalties. But, like the members of the council of Constance in the case of Huss, they seem to have fully imbibed the doctrine that no faith is to be kept with heretics. Several of their generals with a large force of cavalry lay at Pisek, to whom information of the capitulation of the city was dispatched, with directions to attack the Hussites on their march to Hradisch, or Tabor. The necessary march of twenty miles in order to reach the latter place, would naturally afford the enemy many opportunities for assaulting them by a sudden and unexpected attack.

The advice was not neglected. The royal party overtook the Hussites near Sudomertz, and a battle was there fought. The Taborites, destitute of cavalry, were in danger of being surrounded. They protected their flanks by drawing their baggage-wagons in a circle around them, and thus were enabled for several hours to repel assault. The enemy, foiled in their purpose, at length withdrew from the field, bearing off thirty of the Taborites prisoners. The army of Zisca, leaving its wounded to the care of the villagers, resumed its march unmolested to Tabor, where they received a hearty welcome, with rejoicings over their escape. The battle of Sudomertz was fought on March 25, 1420.

While these events were occurring at Pilsen, affairs were assuming at Prague a more threatening aspect. The Hussites became alarmed at the denunciations and threats of the royal party. Pilsen had been surrendered at their suggestion, partly, doubtless, in order to fulfil their promise to the emperor, as well as that Zisca might be left free to march, when necessity should require it, to their rescue. The zeal of the Hussite preachers was enkindled as their fears were excited. John, the Premonstrant priest, distinguished himself by his fervid declamations. Though possessed of no great learning, his eloquence was most effective. He was at this time expounding the revelation of St. John, and took occasion to apply its predictions to the events of the day. He was especially severe upon the emperor— the great *red dragon* of the Apocalyptic vision. The fact that he had allowed his courtiers to wear as a badge upon their breasts a dragon of gold, made the application more striking. The ardor of the people was aroused to a higher pitch than ever. In the cause which they had espoused many of them were ready to risk at once property and life.

Other causes, however, beside the fervid eloquence of their preachers, contributed to animate the spirit of the Hussites, and rouse them from their desponding submission to Sigismund to an attitude of bold defiance. The emperor's violence at Breslau in Silesia, whither he had withdrawn from Beraun, was a great political blunder as well as crime. The cruel treatment of Krasa furnished an inexhaustible theme for fervid declamation. The emperor had consented to his execution. The grounds of his condemnation were,[1] "that he would not hold, believe, affirm, and approve the following articles: that the council of Constance was legitimately congregated in the Holy Spirit; that whatsoever the aforesaid council enacted, decreed, and defined, was just, holy, and to be held by all Christian believers, under pain of mortal sin; that in whatever it reprobated and condemned, it acted justly, holily, and well; that the aforesaid council, in condemning John Huss to a most cruel death, proceeded in accordance with justice and holiness; and that its condemnation of the communing of the people under both kinds was just." These articles Krasa refused to approve, and his cruel death renewed and aggravated among the Hussites the bitter memories of Constance, and stimulated the thirst for vengeance.

This execution took place on the fifteenth of March, 1420. On the seventeenth, a crusade against the Bohemians who favored the communion of the cup

---

[1] Diar. Bel. Hus., 158.

was published by the papal legate.[1]   On his ill-success in attempting to bring back Bohemia to the
obedience of the pope, he had withdrawn to Hungary.   Soured with disappointment and disgust, he
declared that nothing but force would subdue the
spirit of the rebels.   His representations, undoubtedly enforced by Sigismund, had so much weight
with Martin V., that the latter was induced to proclaim throughout Christendom (March 1, 1420) a
crusade against the heretics of Bohemia.[2]   They were
to be proceeded against as " rebels against the Roman
church, and as heretics."   The crusade was announced
in the cathedral of Breslau, at the preaching of the
sermon, while the emperor was present; and he exerted himself for the publication of the bull throughout the whole of his dominions.

This Bull of the crusade is a most remarkable
document for the age in which it was published.[3]   It
shows the same blind zeal and persecuting bigotry
which characterized similar measures of preceding
centuries.   A Christian instead of a Mohammedan
people were now, however, the objects of its vengeance—a people whose great heresy was, that they
made the word God their supreme authority, and
contended for the institutions of the gospel in their
primitive simplicity and integrity.

The pope addresses the bull " To the venerable
brethren, patriarchs, archbishops, bishops; to his beloved children the administrators, abbots, priors, and
other officers of churches and of monasteries, as well

---

[1] Cochleii. Hist. Hus., p. 187.   [2] Godeau, xxxvii. 23.   Fleury, xxvi. 289.
[3] Diar. Bel. Hus., 159.

as to all professing the Christian religion, in what place
soever, to whom these presents shall come." After
speaking of his duty and anxiety to recover the
wandering sheep of the fold of that Lord of all, whose
vicar he is on earth, he declares his purpose, "by the
coöperating grace of God," to restrain, by due severity, the minds of those who had cast off the divine
fear. By the counsel of his venerable brethren, the
cardinals of the holy Roman church, he had resolved,
"by the treasures of the mystic dispensation," to excite the soldiers and athletes of Christ more fervently
to pursue this object. He praises the celebrated
faith of his most dearly beloved son in Christ, the
Emperor Sigismund, who, as it were by a divine inspiration, strove with great effort, and at great cost,
to restore the church to its integrity. The zeal of
his faith, the ardor of his devotion, the gentleness of
his compassion, had led him to seek the wider diffu-
sion of the Christian religion, in opposition to those
reprobate men of profane malignity and iniquity, the
followers of Wickliffe and Huss, as well as others,
the eyes of whose understanding had been blinded;
children of darkness, who by their superstitious doctrines and crude dogmas would put the Catholic
church under restraint, overthrow the orthodox faith,
and give over the flock, led astray by error, to the
bondage of hell. These men, their favorers, abettors,
and defenders, unless they give up their errors, and
submit themselves to the traditions of the holy fathers, were to be exterminated from among the faithful, and the deadly virus of souls was to be eradicated
even by the destruction of the body. So happy a

consummation is earnestly besought by the emperor, of the pope and of the Catholic church. Extolling the purpose of the emperor with the most emphatic eulogy, with eyes directed to heaven in prayer for his success, he exhorts "all kings, dukes, margraves, princes, barons, counts, lords, captains, magistrates, and all officials; states, free cities, universities, and villages, by the sprinkling of the blood of their most glorious Redeemer, and in hope of the remission of their sins, to the extermination of the followers of Wickliffe, Huss, and other heretics, with their favorers and abettors; and to this end they should mightily exert themselves in whatever should be necessary to the prosecution of this work." He therefore charges and commands all ecclesiastical officers to whom the bull is directed, "to contribute all their power and influence to promote the purpose of the emperor, even to the raising and equipping of armies, if they are called upon to do it, in order to proceed against heretics and all who favor them." They were to act as valiant heralds, lifting their voices loud in all states, dioceses, and regions where it should be found fit. They were to select such persons as they should deem proper, to extend the proclamation to all Christian believers as they might chance to be met, and who could be led to volunteer in the crusade. These were to be allowed, by the apostolic authority, relaxation for a hundred days of imposed penance, in consideration of their enlistment. By the preaching of the word of the cross, and by setting forth the symbol publicly, by exhortations and fitting admonitions, they were to be urged to put forth all their efforts for the overthrow of the heretics. The ecclesiastics were themselves to bestow the cross freely upon those who volunteered, and were to fasten it to their shoulders with their own hands. To animate them to greater fervor, the pope himself, " by the mercy of Almighty God, and the authority of the holy apostles St. Peter and St. Paul, as well as by the power of binding and loosing bestowed by God upon himself, grants to those who shall enter upon the crusade, or to such even as should die upon the road, plenary pardon of their sins, if repented of and confessed, and, in the retribution of the just, eternal salvation. Such as could not go in person, but contributed to the cause by sending others, and equipping them according to their ability, should have full remission of their sins. Even such as had laid violent hands upon the clergy, or had been guilty of arson or sacrilege, might hope to fight their way to heaven by warring against the followers of Wickliffe and Huss." The ecclesiastics were to take special care to have this bull circulated as widely as possible.

The long dreaded blow was thus struck at last. All Christendom, with its generals and armies, was summoned to crush out the heresies of men whom the council chose to burn rather than refute. The affairs of the Bohemians presented indeed an ominous aspect. The imperial and papal powers leagued together, and summoned all bearing the Christian name to aid them in suppressing and exterminating a people, numbering at the most not more than three or four millions, who were at the same time beset by domestic foes, and who were far from unanimous among themselves in religious and political views. But the result disappointed all human expectations. The forces of the empire dashed and shattered themselves against the invincible resolution and desperate courage of a band of men sustained by religious enthusiasm, and conducted by able generals.

In fact, previous to the publication of the crusade, the tide had begun to set strongly in Bohemia against the pretensions of Sigismund. He had himself anticipated its fuller announcement, by an edict characterized by cruelty and injustice. He sent written orders through the land to all barons, and to all the magistrates, to the chief governor of the nation, (Czenko,) to the governors of royal towns, the officers and judges, to drive out, persecute, and as far as possible utterly exterminate the followers of Wickliffe and Huss, as well as the adherents to the communion of the cup.[1]

This was enough to satisfy any that had hitherto been hesitating and doubtful in their allegiance, that Sigismund was the last man that should be allowed to ascend the vacant throne. Zisca's league against him grew rapidly. Zatec, Slany, Launy, and other cities formed mutual alliance to resist him.[2] Multitudes, driven to desperation, banded themselves together for security, or aggression in their own neighborhood.

It was in this way that the city of Ausch was taken. The governors had driven out of it all the Hussite citizens. A band of men composed of these, with Taborites and rustics from the villages, and led

---

[1] Diar. Bel. Hus., 157.   [2] Guerre des Hus., i. 123.

on by Zisca, lay hid in ambush in the woods for
several days and nights, till, aided by friends within
the walls, they seized upon an occasion when the city
was given up to feasting and drunkenness, and were
enabled successfully to assault it.   (Feb. 2, 1420.)
Driving out their enemies, they took possession of
the city, and were at once rendered secure in retaining it by the crowd of their friends who rushed
thither as to a place of safety.   It was shortly after
this that the fortified town of Hradisch, in the immediate vicinity of Tabor, fell into their hands, and
was delivered over into the charge of Procopius of
Kamenitz, one of the ablest of the Hussite generals.
On the destruction of Ausch by fire shortly afterward, its inhabitants transferred themselves with
their wives and children to Hradisch of Tabor,
whither Zisca and his forces directed their steps on
withdrawing from Pilsen.[1]

But at Prague the announcement of the crusade
produced a most marked effect.   Men could not but
tremble at the thought of what that terrible word
meant—with its signification written out in the havoc
and carnage of past centuries, when the innocent
and guilty, Catholic and heretic, were swept indiscriminately to one common doom.   Indecision was
allowable no longer.   Even the moderate and non-
committal must take their side, and choose the party
by which they would abide.   The enemies of the
Hussites were full of exultation.   " These heretical
wretches," said they, " will now be burned at last, or
they, with their wives and children, will perish by

[1] Diar. Bel. Hus., 162.

the sword of the emperor.   Let us fly from among
them, to the most secure places, lest we miserably
perish along with them." [1]

This was a wise precaution.   There was certainly
danger of indiscriminate massacre, when all alike
were exposed to the blind fanaticism of a crusading
army—at least judging by the precedent of the last
crusade against the Albigenses; and however consol-
atory to the blind actor in the tragedy it might be
to know that in slaying all " God would know his
own," it did not present to the one in danger of becoming a victim, any very soothing reflections.   The
enemies of the Hussites in Prague were able fully
to appreciate such considerations as these, and fearful
of losing life and property together, they took refuge
with their families and effects in the castle and Vis-
schrad.   Seven hundred of the wealthiest citizens
of Old Prague, and as many more of the New city—
a large number of them Germans, and cherishing a
national hostility against the Bohemians—were received within the fortified district, on condition of
obligating themselves, under oath, on the expiration
of the truce, (Apr. 23,) to render their assistance in
subduing the city, and, on the destruction or extirpation of the adherents of the cup, to return to their
dwellings. [2]

The citizens, alarmed at the intelligence of the
crusade, and the measures and vaunts of their enemies, were not idle.   Incited by their preachers, and
especially by John, the Premonstrant monk, of whom
mention has been already made, they assembled at

[1] Diar. Bel. Hus., 160.   [2] Ib., 161.

the council-house of the Old city in order to deliberate on what it was most expedient for them to do.
The assembly was large, and their priests and magistrates were present. They bound themselves together,
in a covenant or league of mutual defence, against all
persons whomsoever who should presume to impugn
the communion of the cup. They swore to be faithful in defence of the truth, and the oath was administered to them by the magistrates who still remained
in office.

Four captains were elected for the Old, and four
for the New city,[1] to whose charge the keys of the
council-house and gates were entrusted, and to whom
an authority was committed, limited only by their
discretion, for promoting or devising measures of
defence. Beside these, forty persons were appointed
from the Old, and forty from the New city, who were
to act as officers or leaders, upon any emergency
that might arise. After drawing up in a public act
the doings of their assembly, and depositing the
written document in safe hands, the people withdrew
peaceably to their dwellings. Calixtine and Taborite were ready to join hands in a league of mutual
defence. The Old city and the New forgot temporarily their aversions, and united to resist a common
foe.

The prospects of the Hussites were dark indeed.
Sigismund had already gathered a large army, constantly recruited from all parts of the empire. It
was said to amount from 140,000 to 150,000 men.
He moved on somewhat slowly, allowing the differ-

[1] Diar. Bel. Hus., 162.

ent reinforcements to overtake him, and endeavoring to make sure of the fortified places which he passed. Zisca was not unmindful of the threatening danger. He saw the necessity of having some secure place upon which he might fall back in case of reverse. None appeared more favorable for his project than Tabor itself. Its natural position was such as to render it almost impregnable to the foe. It was almost a peninsula in shape, bounded on one side by the river Luznice, and on the other by a tributary stream of deep and rapid current. The place itself was lofty and precipitous. It was girt about by steep and almost inaccessible rocks. The only passage to it was by a narrow neck of land, which a few valiant men could make a posse of Thermopylæ. Even this was defended by a deep fosse which Zisca caused to be dug, and by a triple wall, of such strength as to defy the assault of the most powerful engines. The walls were protected by numerous towers fitly located, and means of defence were devised by men who had rendered themselves already masters in the art of taking cities.[1] Here Zisca directed his followers to build houses on the place where their tents stood, and at once the camp of the Taborites became a fortified city.

These precautions taken, Zisca listened to the urgent request of the citizens of Prague to aid them in the siege of the royal castle. Leaving Tabor itself to the hazard of an attack, he hastened to their aid. The Vissehrad was closely besieged, and subjected to great extremity. The garrison were reduced to

Æneas Sylvius, ch. xl.

the necessity of subsisting on the most loathsome food. Dogs, cats, and rats were ravenously devoured. At last the garrison agreed to surrender unless they were relieved by the emperor within fifteen days.

Meanwhile, the emperor was making his way to Prague. Czenko had sent him word of the danger to which the Vissehrad was exposed. He despatched at once a force of cavalry, in order to raise the siege. Nor did he neglect other means for the relief of his friends at Prague. In order to draw off a portion of the besieging army, an attack upon Tabor was resolved upon. The Lord of Rosenberg, who had embraced the party of the Hussites, but who was now inspired by terror at the report of the invading army, was willing to make his peace with the emperor by turning his arms against his late allies. In proof of his sincerity, he prohibited, in his own district, the communion of the cup, and declared his readiness to assist the emperor in the prosecution of the war. To him, therefore, the attack upon Tabor was entrusted. The occasion was the most favorable, while so many of its inhabitants were absent at Prague. Accompanied by a powerful force, he advanced to the assault.

But intelligence of his movements was communicated to Zisca, who at once despatched a force of three hundred and fifty cavalry, under Nicholas de Hussinitz, to the relief of Tabor. This force left Prague on the night of June 25, (1420.) On the thirtieth of the month a severe and decisive battle was fought. The Taborites came down from the mountain, and made an attack upon the enemy on

one side, while Nicholas de Hussinitz, of whose coming the Taborites had been made aware, assaulted
them upon the other. The terror of the enemy was
such that, after standing their ground for a short
time, they turned and fled. Never was there a more
signal rout. The imperial forces outnumbered those
of the Taborites, it is said,[1] twenty to one. They
were pursued in their flight, and large numbers were
slain or taken captive. An immense booty was left
behind. Gold and silver goblets, ornaments and
vestures of the most costly kind, warlike weapons
and engines, provisions for the sustenance of the
army, in great abundance and variety, rewarded the
valor of the Taborites. Songs of thanksgiving to
the God who had given them the victory, succeeded
to the clash of resounding arms, and the conquering
host, laden with spoil, exulted, as they retraced their
steps, over the enemies of their faith.

The result of this attack was sadly ominous of the
fate of the whole campaign. The Lord of Rosenberg was stung with shame at his ignominious defeat.
In his resentment he sought to wreak a weak and
unmanly vengeance upon the adherents of the cup.
He hunted them out wherever they could be found,
took them captive, and, shutting them up in prison,
vainly endeavored to force them to abjure the doctrine which he himself had once avowed. Several
of his castles were filled with these unfortunate men.
Most of them were subjected to the severest and harshest treatment for many months. Some of them were
put to death. But the Hussites did not forget the

[1] Diar. Bel. Hus., 163.

traitor. They exacted a severe penalty for his treason and his cruelty, in the ravage of his estates.

Other victories were won by the Hussites. At Voticz, between Tabor and Prague, a battle was fought, in which an imperial army of four thousand cavalry was routed.[1] The walled town of Hradisch had been taken by surprise. A band of rustics and colliers, led by three zealous Hussites, and accompanied by a priest who encouraged them, secured possession of it on the night of June 25. The enemies of the communion of the cup were driven out of the city, of which the Hussites maintained possession, forming themselves at the same time into a military organization, and choosing themselves leaders.

The fall of Hradisch was a sore blow to the imperial cause. Sigismund sent at once an army of ten thousand men to retake the place. These were composed of the *élite* of his army. But they did not choose to make any assault. They contented themselves with seeking to regain the city under false pretences of negotiations; but the Hussites were not to be duped by them, and they were forced to return without accomplishing their object.

But all eyes were now directed anxiously toward Prague. As the capital of the kingdom, its possession was of the greatest importance to each party. On the twelfth of June the news arrived that the emperor was on his march, accompanied with an overwhelming force of more than 100,000 men. The citizens of Prague pressed the siege of the Vissehrad, and endeavored to increase the number of their

[1] Guerre des Hus., i. 121.

allies. Among these came Hinko Krussina, with his
Horebites.[1] These were the most fierce and cruel of
all the Hussite forces. They breathed vengeance
against all priests and monks, and seemed to find
no satisfaction equal to that of torturing, mangling,
insulting, and murdering them. Merciless as they
were desperate, Prague needed them, with all their
fanatic thirst of blood, to defend her against the
hosts of the crusading army. They were received
with congratulations and shouts of welcome. Krussina was made one of the chief commanders of the
city.

The emperor had sent forward a body of eleven
thousand men to the relief of his party in Prague.
He stopped himself for a short time at Koniggratz,[2]
where he had met a friendly reception, and sent an
embassy to Prague, reminding the city of its promise
of fealty, and requiring it to keep its word. He demanded that the citizens should give up their arms,
and deposit them in the Vissehrad.

This message was delivered on the twenty-fourth
of June, the emperor meanwhile resuming his march,
and advancing toward Prague. His conduct was
marked by a vindictive cruelty. Under pretence of
retaliation, he drowned twenty-four Hussites in the
Elbe.[3] The monasteries fared little better in his
hands than in those of Zisca. He plundered them to
pay his troops. Some of them were immensely
wealthy, and invited spoliation. The Hussites might
rob them as enemies, but it was hard that they

[1] Godeau, xxxvii. 31.
[2] Guerre des Hus., i. 126.
[3] Godeau (xxxviii. 33) says seventeen were drowned.

should experience the same fate from the hands of one who came as their avenger. Yet the pillage of churches and convents was the resource of both parties, and the immense wealth of the church furnished fuel for the fire that consumed it.

The number of monasteries destroyed by Zisca has been reckoned by historians at more than five hundred.[1] None had manifested a more bigoted hostility to reform and to the communion of the cup, no class had become more corrupt, and none could be more properly regarded as implicated in compassing the death of Huss, by invective and false accusation, than the monks; and Zisca's memory treasured the affront that had been offered to his own sister—an affront to be expiated by blood alone. His vengeance was terrible. By flying marches he swept the country, and spread on every side the terror of his name. Convents and monasteries were sacked and burned, sometimes with all who resided within the walls. Krussina, with his Horebites, did not yield to Zisca in the promptitude and energy of a cruel vengeance. The Cistercian monastery of Graditz fell into their hands, and was utterly destroyed. The monastery of Cromau was possessed of such wealth and splendor as to be an object of attractive curiosity to travellers. They turned aside to behold it. The Taborites paid it a visit—curious also in their way to see what it contained—and only its ruins were left to invite the curiosity of the pilgrim. At Prague, the Cistercian monastery of the royal court was doomed to a similar fate. One of its

[1] Guerre des Hus., i. 127.

inmates, James, a scholastic of wonderful eloquence, and former rector of the university, was spared by Zisca only at the earnest intercession of the senate. Truly it might be still said, as it had been months before, that "the cart drew the horse." Laws were silent in the midst of arms. Zisca was the dictator of Prague.

The emperor's army in all recklessness and cruelty was fully equal to that of Zisca. It was only inferior in strong religious conviction, fanatic feeling, and desperate courage. It was a conglomerate of all the refuse of Christendom, though led by kings, margraves, dukes, barons, princes, and knights, and accompanied by archbishops, bishops, doctors, prelates, and a host of ecclesiastics. Some twenty years before, Cardinal D'Ailly had expressed his wish that the pope would proclaim a crusade as a means of drawing off the festering masses of corruption, and relieving the church by the *Sangrado* prescription of letting of blood. His wish was now realized. With all the splendor of the empire, the scum of the nations accompanied and mainly composed the imperial armies. Almost every tribe and nation of Europe was represented in the motley host. [1] Bohemians and Moravians in arms against their countrymen, Hungarians and Croatians, Dalmatians and Bulgarians, Wallachians and Servians, Sclavonians and Thuringians, Bavarians and Austrians, met in

[1] Ibi diversarum nationum fuere tribus et linguæ, Bohemi et Moravi, Hungari et Croati, Dalmati et Bulgari, Walachi et Siculi, Cuni Iasi, Ruteni, Rasi, Slavi, Pruteni, Suevi, Turingi, Styrii, Misnenses, Bavari, Australes, Franci, Francones, Angli, Brabanti, Vestphali, Holandi, Helvetii, Lusatii, Silesii, Carinthii, Arragonii, Hispani, Poloni, Teutonici, de Rheno, et alii quam plurimi.—*Diar. Bel. Hus.*, 167.

the same host with inhabitants of England, France, Brabant, Westphalia, Holland, Switzerland, Aragon, Spain, Portugal, Poland, and Italy. The East and West joined hands for the plunder and the vengeance of a crusade. There was a Babel of nations and of tongues. If the council of Constance could claim to be Œcumenical, much more might Sigismund's army. Such was the host which had been marshalled to maintain the cause of the papacy, and put down a cause that vainly had challenged the council to confute it from scripture. How well it performed its task the sequel will show.

Bohemia presented, certainly, between the two contending parties, a strange picture of anarchy, rapine, cruelty, and sacrilege. Here we shall find the tombs of kings profaned, their dust no longer protected by coffins, the golden plates of which could pay the wages of a ruffian soldiery. There the fragments of marble altars, and pavements on which the knees of devout pilgrims had rested, are used to charge the catapults of the invading host. The carcasses of the slain putrefy and poison the air, or are flung piecemeal into besieged towns, till pestilence helps famine to do its work. Indiscriminate massacre involves the innocent and guilty, friend and foe, in one common doom. Retaliation and vengeance, sometimes, though rarely, conducted under legal forms, supply each party with its hosts of martyrs. " Dreadful traditions have perpetuated the memory of so many frightful scenes : near Toplitz, it was said, might be seen a pear-tree, which blossomed every year, and never yielded fruit—a tree accursed from the streams of blood that had saturated its roots. At Commotau, near a church where thousands of victims perished, slaughtered by Zisca, it was asserted that the soil was formed of the remains of bones, and that at whatever depth search was made, nothing could be found but human teeth." [1]

Sigismund himself acted as if he considered Bohemia a land doomed and accursed. The progress of his march was signalized by new atrocities, and deeds of reckless cruelty. He, as well as Zisca, would inspire terror. But in his case the project failed. There was alarm, but there was resentment and desperation also. The soldiers of Zisca were ready to be martyrs. The soldiers of Sigismund showed but a feeble faith, and a weak desire for that eternal glory awarded to those that fell, by the bull of the pope. The heterogeneous mass of plunderers and robbers lacked the spirit that animated the terrible soldiers who took the cup for a banner.

It was on the thirtieth of June, that the emperor with the body of his army approached the neighborhood of Prague.[2] He was fortunate in finding any part of the city still retaining its allegiance. Czenko, by a double treason—or perhaps, and more probably, by stratagem—had preserved for him the castle of Wenzel. He had pretended to surrender it to the demands of the citizens who closely besieged it, and who offered him his choice, to proclaim the freedom of the communion of the cup, or withdraw from the castle. He assumed to yield to the last demand, and, it was said, withdrew with a large treas-

<hr>

[1] Bonnechose.   [2] Guerre des Hus., i. 128.

ure to his own chateau. He had however secretly informed the emperor of the step which he had taken, urging his speedy advance, and by his connivance or treachery the castle was still held; or, if it had been surrendered, was regained for the emperor. The first step therefore of the latter was, if possible, to raise the siege of the Vissehrad. A single day only remained for the term of its surrender to expire. The approach of the imperial army to its relief was announced by drums and trumpets and bells, while strains of martial music mingled with the hymns and songs of the clergy, as they accompanied the emperor in grand procession to the royal castle.[1] The army itself encamped on the wide plain about Bruska and Owenecz, ready to commence the siege of the city. Its numbers, if not its strength, received continually new accessions, till the pride of superiority, and the taunts of bigotry, found vent in insults that would more wisely have been reserved for a vanquished foe.

From day to day the soldiers of the imperial army, from a height on the bank of the river overlooking the city, and over against the Monastery of the Holy Cross and the Church of St. Valentine, uttered their howls and barkings like dogs, accompanied by sneers and taunting words, and cries of " Huss, Huss ! Heretic, Heretic ! "[2] If a Bohemian fell into their hands, unless speedily rescued by parties of his friends who still maintained themselves in roving about the precincts of the imperial army, he was mercilessly burned, without regard to the fact of his favoring

[1] Diar. Bel. Hus., 166.   [2] Ib., 168.

the doctrine of the communion of the cup. His
nationality was accounted a sufficient crime. Skirmishes were of frequent occurrence. Small bands
of Taborites, issuing from the city, would sometimes
rout great numbers of the foe. With their favorite
weapon, an iron flail, they threshed down the invaders, armed in all the pride and pomp of war. The
enemy attempted to take or burn the machines by
which the citizens hurled masses of stone upon those
who approached the walls, but all their attempts
were vain. They were repulsed with loss upon all
occasions.

Sigismund soon perceived that in order to reduce the city, the only method which promised success was to starve it to surrender. For this purpose
it was necessary for him to occupy some position
which would command the Moldau, by which provisions were still brought into the city. He determined therefore to take possession with a strong
force of the high steep hill Witkow, or Galgenberg,[1] (Gibbet-hill,) as it is called. Zisca had either
had some intimation of his purpose, or discerned the
danger to which the city was evidently exposed.
Sigismund in possession of Witkow would moreover
be able to invest Prague upon three sides at once.

Anticipating his movements, the Hussite general
promptly seized upon the height, and fortified it, by
wooden entrenchments, a fosse, and walls of stone
and earth.[2] The extreme promptitude with which
Zisca acted, prevented any measures of opposition
from the imperial forces being taken till his en-

---

[1] Godeau, xxxvii. 35.   [2] Guerre des Hus., i. 129.

trenchments were nearly complete. An assault was
made upon the city, (July 13,) in which the citizens,
although they repulsed the enemy, suffered some
loss. But on the next day (July 14) preparations
were made for an attack upon the Galgenberg, which
it was determined to carry by storm. The city,
moreover, was to be assaulted at the same time from
three different directions, mainly with the purpose
of rendering any measure of sending aid from the
city to Zisca impracticable. From the castle it was
ordered that there should be a sortie against the
palace of the Duke of Saxony, which the citizens
had strongly fortified, and 16,000 men were detailed
for this purpose. From the Vissehrad a like sortie
was to be made against the New city, while from the
plain on which the army lay encamped, a force was
to march to the assault of the Old city.

While these arrangements were taking effect, eight
thousand calvary of Misnia, led by their margrave,
and strengthened by a large force from the imperial
army, marched to storm the Galgenberg. They ascended the hill at quick step and with sound of trumpets,
and took possession of some of the advanced works.
A defensive roofed tower was taken, which was abandoned by all but twenty-six men and three women,
who emulated one another in the courage and energy
with which for a time they repelled the assailants.
They defended themselves with stones and pikes.
One of the women, though herself destitute of defensive armor, encouraged her associates by refusing
to fly, and exhorting them not to yield. " A Christian believer," she said, " ought not to give ground

to Antichrist." She fell fighting at her post. Zisca himself was at one time in great danger. He had lost his footing and had fallen to the ground, when his friends with their flails rushed to his rescue, and saved him from being captured by the enemy.

The city itself was meanwhile full of alarm. All human help seemed vain, and the greatest apprehension was felt lest the combined assault should prove successful. At this moment a strange sight presented itself. The citizens gathered with the women and children in sad groups, and with tears and groans supplicated aid from Heaven. While fathers and brothers stood by the walls or marched to the terrible encounter, those who were left behind commended them to the God of armies. The voice of prayer mingled with the clash of arms, and at the critical moment a priest, filled with enthusiastic courage, and bearing with him the holy sacrament, rushed forth from the gates, followed by only fifty bowmen and a crowd of peasants armed with flails. The bells rang, and the shouts of the people echoed far beyond the walls, as the little band issued from the gate of the city to face thousands of the invading host. A sudden panic seized the imperialists, who probably imagined that the whole force of the city was marching out against them. Zisca and his soldiers were inspirited by this opportune aid. The enemy were driven back from the entrenchments, and hurled headlong down the steep rocks. Horse and rider perished alike by the fall, and in a single hour several hundred were slain, beside many fatally wounded, or carried off as captives. The rout was complete. The emperor, from a high point on the banks of the Moldau, witnessed the defeat of his most cherished hopes. Overwhelmed with grief, indignation, and shame, he withdrew from the field, and led the army back to the camp.

The citizens regarded their success as a deliverance wrought out for them by the hand of God. They knelt down upon the field of battle, and sang their *Te Deum* with grateful joy. In long processions they marched through the streets of the city, ascribing their success to the interposition of Heaven. It was not by their own strength, but by the wonderful power of God, (*miraculose,*) that a small band had won such a victory over a numerous host. Hymns and songs filled the air with the music of triumph. Grief was turned into joy, and the whole city echoed with exultant praise. The little children sang hymns which were composed on the occasion, and which breathed the spirit of the song of Moses over the defeat of the Egyptian host. The scene of the battle was made memorable by the name of the great general whose skill and courage had foiled the power and designs of the emperor. The hill, formerly known as Galgenberg, or Witkow, was now known as Ziscaberg.

The results of the battle were made more manifest in the imperial camp than in the rout of the army. National animosities were awakened among the soldiers, composed in large part of Bohemians and Germans. Many things conspired to aggravate these dissensions. The very name of Bohemia became a term of reproach. If a Bohemian fell into the hands

of the Germans, it made little difference whether he
was Hussite, Calixtine, or Catholic, so far as the treatment which he received was concerned. The cruelties
which were perpetrated upon their countrymen aroused the indignation of those Bohemians in whose
bosoms a spark of nationality yet glowed. Deeds
of atrocity were committed, the recital of which
could awaken only horror or a spirit of vengeance—
such vengeance as Zisca took, in ample measure.

On the sixth of July, a few days previous to the
assault upon the city, while the Duke of Austria
with a large reinforcement for the imperial army was
on his march from Militcz to Prague, a band of
sixty calvary turned aside to the neighboring village
of Arnosstowitsch, and at the treacherous suggestion
of certain priests, seized upon the Calixtine preacher
of the place, and his vicar, and placing both upon
one horse, brought them to the Duke at Bystizitsch,[1]
presenting them as heretics to be punished for their
stubborn pertinacity. The preacher, whose name was
Wenzel, was a man greatly respected and beloved. He
and his vicar had become known as decided Calixtines.
The duke sent them to the bishop of the place, that
he might determine how they should be dealt with.
The bishop sent them back again to the duke—thus
from Caiaphas to Pilate, says the old historian.
They were insulted and abused, and threatened with
the flames unless they would recant. Calmly but
firmly they resisted all the efforts made to induce
them to yield. " It is the gospel," [2] said Wenzel,
" and the practice of the primitive church, and thus

---

[1] Pescheck, 1. 16.   [2] Diar. Bel. Hus., 169.

it is in your missal : blot out the scripture, and destroy this gospel." At this, one of the knights who stood by, struck Wenzel with his iron glove. The blood flowed in streams from his face. At last, as night wore on, the soldiers, wearied in their insults, left them. The next morning they were led out to be burned. But the number of the victims was now increased by three old men, peasants of the neighborhood, and four children,—one of seven, one of eight, and another of eleven years,—who had been found guilty of the same crime of holding the doctrine of the cup. When all had been brought near to the funeral pile, they were urged, if they had any wish to live, to abjure. " Far be it from us," replied Wenzel,—" far be it from us to yield to your persuasions ; sooner would we undergo not one, but a hundred deaths, rather than deny so plain a doctrine of the gospel." Upon this the executioners lighted the fagots. The children, leaning upon Wenzel's bosom, sang aloud as the flames rose around them. One after another yielded up his life, and at last Wenzel himself expired.

At Budweis a similar scene was witnessed. Two Hussite preachers, after a harsh and tedious imprisonment, were burned, on their refusal to abjure the communion of the cup.[1] Similar occurrences, which took place in various parts of the kingdom, could only aggravate the existing divisions, and excite anew the thirst for vengeance. Their frequency, and the odium which at the same time rested upon all that bore the Bohemian name, or whose national spirit

[1] Diar. Bel. Hus., 170.

resented the barbarous cruelties and unjust prejudice of the Germans, aroused the most excited passions in the camp of the imperial army. There was
great danger that the mighty host would dissolve
and melt away. It was evident that further assault upon the city would be for the present utterly
futile.

It was at this moment, in itself critical, that another event came to fill to overflowing the cup of the
emperor's disappointment and humiliation. On the
nineteenth of July the tents of the imperial army
caught fire and were utterly consumed. The loss in
other respects was great. The high wind which prevailed prevented the success of all the efforts made
to quench the conflagration. The fire was attributed,
although there seems no valid ground for the charge,
to the malice of a Hussite.[1]

The Taborites, envenomed against the Germans,
who slew all the Bohemians indiscriminately that
fell into their hands, insisted that such of them as
had been taken captive should be dealt with as they
had dealt with others. National animosity strengthened, or at least combined with fanatic passions, to
demand these victims. A rush was made upon the
council-house where the prisoners were confined, and
the demand was made that they should be given up
to be burned.[2] The authorities unwillingly yielded,
for they had no power to resist. Sixteen prisoners

---

[1] Godeau (xxxvii. 35) states that
the camp of the imperial army was
set on fire at the instigation of the
Hussites, by a woman of Prague, who
found the opportunity to apply the
brand. A strong wind prevailed at
the time, and it was found impossible
to stay the progress of the flames.
L'Enfant gives the story as a mere
rumor, but seems not to put much
faith in it.

[2] Diar. Bel. Hus., 184.

were led forth without the walls, and all, with one
exception, were burned in sight of the Germans of
the imperial army.   The one who was spared was a
monk, who promised that he would administer the
communion to the people under both kinds.

The citizens of Prague, exulting in their present
deliverance, were not unmindful of future danger,
when the imperial army might be reinforced or
equipped anew.   They were ready to treat with the
emperor on the basis of the four famous articles,
which may be said to have composed their creed.
They were the more ready to do it from the aversion
which was generally felt toward the the Taborites,
and their peculiar opinions and practises.   The followers of Zisca had little taste for hierarchical pomp.
The simple letter of the gospel was their supreme
authority.   Traditions and ceremonies were with
them like images and statues—only the rags of superstition, the flaunting robes of Rome's harlotry.   The
splendor and magnificence of churches and monasteries they deemed to be libels upon the simplicity
of the gospel.   Scarcely had the imperial army fall-
en back from the walls of the city, when the priest
Coranda, accompanied by a multitude of Taborites,
many of them women, among whom were "the sis-
ters of Pilsen," rushed into the Church of St. Michael,
and tore up the seats of the priests as well as the laity,
asserting that their best use and true value was to
strengthen the entrenchments and fortifications of
Zisca on the Galgenberg.   The issue showed, however, that his aim was more to rebuke the vanity
of superstitious worship, as he would undoubtedly

have phrased it, than use the plundered materials
for the purpose which he avowed. Most of them
were carried off and burned. Few at least ever
reached the Galgenberg, although Zisca did not neglect to provide for the defence of a fortress that now
bore his name—though by some it was called "the
mountain of the cup."

The well-known disposition of the Taborites,
which threatened ruin to some of the most splendid
structures of the city, combined with the daily
ravages of the enemy to urge the barons of the
kingdom, most of whom were Calixtines, to propose
negotiations for peace. The emperor showed himself not altogether disinclined to see what could be
done by treaty, now that force had failed. He saw
the sad divisions and dissensions of his army, which
had now risen to such a pitch that there were continual broils between the Bohemian and the German
soldiers, the latter charging the former with treason,
and declaring that if they had been left alone to
fight the battle, they would have won the victory.
The German soldiers had, moreover, learned of
their superiors at Constance the art of burning human beings, and their taste for it had become so
strong that it was difficult to restrain its indulgence.
The whole region about Prague was ravaged with a
merciless ferocity. Villages and castles were sacked
and burned. Women and children, with indiscriminate cruelty, were thrown into the flames.

In such a work of desolation and atrocious crime,
the pride and ferocity found vent which had at first
insulted the citizens, but now, leaving them unmo-

lested, turned to wreak its vengeance upon the help-
less and unoffending.   The barons sighed for peace.
The citizens of Prague were equally anxious to be
relieved of the presence of the imperialists and Taborites—the first, terrible enemies, the last, unwel-
come guests.   But these could not be dismissed till
those had withdrawn.

The Bohemian barons, Calixtines and Catholics,
held a conference to consider what measures could
be taken in order to secure a cessation of hostilities.
Those who represented Prague declined to enter
into any compact, without the knowledge and consent of other cities with which they were in league.
Anxious, however, for peace, they besought, for their
own sake and for that of the kingdom, that with
their teachers and priests they might obtain an audience of the king, at which they might in the four
languages,—Bohemian, Hungarian, German, and Latin,—publicly declare the truth of their four articles,
which were the ground of dispute—might be allowed
to sustain them clearly by scripture before the whole
army, and thus vindicate the nation from the slanders which had covered it with infamy.   If it was
thought necessary, the doctors on the emperor's side
might answer, as they saw fit, whatever was presented.   These terms seem at first to have proved
acceptable, as a basis for initating negotiation, to the
Bohemian barons of the imperial party.   A question
was raised at this point in regard to an exchange of
hostages pending the negotiation, in which the imperial party were allowed their own terms.   But when
the whole matter was submitted to Sigismund, he

refused to approve the proposed measures. His disinclination to do so was doubtless strengthened by the bigoted refusal of the papal legate, Ferdinand of Lucca, to sanction any such step as the one which the citizens of Prague desired to have taken.

Foiled in their purpose therefore, the latter resolved to publish, in their defence, the four articles on which they mainly insisted, and with this end in view drew them up, and addressed them " to all Christian believers," prefacing them with the expression of their purpose to abide by them, living or dying, and to maintain them to the utmost of their power. The four articles as thus drawn up were, (1) The full and unrestricted freedom of the preaching of the gospel throughout Bohemia; (2) the freedom of the communion of the cup; (3) the exclusion of the clergy from large temporal possessions or civil authority; and (4) the strict repression and punishment of gross public sins, whether in clergy or laity.[1]

Embodied in the articles are the complaints which the Calixtine party, represented by the citizens, have to make of the more reprehensible abuses of the church, and of the more grievous corruptions of the clergy—their pride, sensuality, tyranny, the sale of indulgences, simony in the disposal of ecclesiastical benefices, etc. Each article is fortified with a mass of scriptural quotations, and under the one on the subject of the communion of the cup, figure the names of popes, councils, and fathers. We shall soon have

[1] Godeau, xxxvii. 36. They are to be found in full in Diar. Bel. Hus., 176, 180.

occasion to notice these articles—the formal manifesto of the Calixtine party—more at length, and pause here only to remark, that any compromise which did not concede them freely, on the part of the emperor, was out of the question.

His whole course, from the outset, was one continuous blunder. The very measures adopted by him to regain his authority in Bohemia, led to results the direct reverse of what he had intended and expected. He had forced those who had hitherto wavered, to a decision. The invading army must be welcomed, or resisted; and many, who would have preferred to have remained in the old communion, were under the necessity of doing so, if at all, at the expense of their patriotism, and in face of the manifest injustice and horrors of the crusade.

In these circumstances, it is not surprising that the more moderate portion of the nation, averse alike to the excesses of the Taborites and the atrocities of the imperialists, should incline to take sides with the Calixtines. We shall soon see Czenko, governor of the castle, as well as Archbishop Conrad himself,[1] open and avowed advocates of the communion of the cup.

Sigismund's present campaign, notwithstanding the mighty host which the publication of the crusade had ranged under his banner, had proved a total failure. The only object for which he still lingered at Prague, after all hope of conciliation had vanished, was his coronation. This took place at mid-day, July 28, in

[1] The letter of Archbishop Conrad to Sigismund, in which he renounces allegiance to him, and declares his adherence to the four Calixtine arti cles, is to be found in Mon. Hus., i. 84. His adherence to the cup dates July 7, 1420.—*Pescheck.*

the castle of Wenzel.[1] Few of the barons of the
kingdom were present; and the knights whom he
created upon the occasion only disgraced the ceremonial by which it was attempted to honor them.[2]
Most of them were unacquainted with war. Some had
never shared in a battle. The coronation scene was
a mockery. Those who should have been present
were regarded as rebels, and Sigismund only assumed
the crown to fly before the terror of their triumphant arms.

[1] Æneas Sylvius, ch. xlii.   [2] Diar. Bel. Hus,. 181.

CHAPTER XV.

TABORITES AND CALIXTINES.[1]

JULY 28, 1420–AUG. 5, 1420.

THE retreat of the imperial army from Prague withdrew that external pressure which had constrained the Calixtines and the Taborites, notwithstanding their mutual repugnance, and diversity of taste and opinion, to unite in league against a common foe. With the proposal for a truce, by the barons of the kingdom, one of the conditions of which, of course, was, that Sigismund should be

---

[1] As the differences which arose among the followers of Huss after his death, and which divided them into two ultimately distinct parties, have been passed over so lightly by the general church historians, I have thought it important to present them here somewhat more in detail. I have given their *articles* and their *practice*, as noted by those who were eye-witnesses and capable observers. The substance of the chapter was first published in an article in the columns of the "Presbyterian Quarterly Review" for June, 1856.

(440)

acknowledged as king, Zisca had nothing to do. The Taborites almost unanimously preferred a republic, at least an elected king; the citizens of Prague, with the barons of the kingdom, were willing, and even anxious, to receive Sigismund as their monarch, on the sole condition that their demands in regard to the four articles should be granted.

These diverse views of public policy, although held by some on the bare ground of their fitness and expediency, were yet, as a general thing, rooted in a diversity of religious sentiment. The citizens of Old Prague, and the Bohemian barons, were mostly Calixtines, and they were confirmed in their conservatism by what they regarded as the insane fancies, the barbarous taste, and radical views of the Taborites. Although there was unquestionably great diversity, even among them, some leaning to the most radical reformers, and others scarcely differing, except on the single point of the cup, from the Roman Catholic church, yet as a body they stood, from the first, committed to the four articles already referred to, in which the peculiarities of their creed were substantially embodied. For a full century at least, these articles were uniformly and consistently maintained.

They were drawn up with great care and deliberation, and after full conference of the Calixtine nobles and citizens of Prague. They were introduced by the declaration, " Be it known to all Christian believers, that the faithful in the kingdom of Bohemia insist, and by the help of God, propose to insist, in life or death, as far as may be, in behalf of the following articles:

" 1. That the word of God be preached orderly, without let or hinderance, throughout the kingdom of Bohemia, by the priests of the Lord, according the charge of Christ in the last of Mark, ' Go ye into all the world, and preach the gospel to every creature ;' for, according to the apostle, ' The word of the Lord is not bound,' but is to be declared, so that ' the word of the Lord shall run and be glorified.' 2 Thess. iii. ' And no one shall be prohibited from speaking with tongues in the church of God.' 1 Cor. xiv.

" 2. That the sacrament of the divine eucharist under each kind, viz., of bread and wine, be freely administered to all the faithful of Christ, not disqualified to receive it by reason of mortal sin, according to the sentence and institution of the Saviour, who said, ' Take, eat; this is my body,' and ' Drink ye all, from this; for this is my blood of the New Testament, which is shed for many.' "

This article is sustained at length by large citations from the scriptures and the Christian fathers. The council of Carthage, the twenty-sixth canon, and the authorities of Gregory, Augustine, Jerome, Dionysius, Cyprian, Ambrose, Origen, Beda, Fulgentius, Remigius, Innocent, Paschasius, Lyra, and Albertus Magnus, are adduced in support of this article.

" 3. That the secular dominion which the clergy exercise, against the precept of Christ, over worldly goods and possessions, to the prejudice of their office and the damage of civil rule, be taken away and withdrawn from them, and the clergy itself be brought back to the evangelical rule and the apostolic practice, as Christ lived with his disciples, ac-

cording to the charge of the Saviour, Mat. x., saying,
'Possess neither gold nor silver nor money in your
purse.' And Mat. xx., 'The princes of the Gentiles
exercise lordship over them, and they who have authority over them are called benefactors; but it shall
not be so among you; but whoever is greatest among
you, let him be your servant; and whoever is pre-
eminent, let him be your minister.' So also Mark x."

Numerous other passages from scripture are cited
to the same purport, beside the authority of Jerome,
Augustine, Ambrose, and Boniface, in his letter to
Pope Eugenius.

"4. That all mortal sins, especially such as are
public, and other disorders contrary to the law of
God, in each estate soever, be prohibited and prevented, by those to whom it pertains. For not only
those who do these things, but those who consent to
them, are worthy of death, occasioning among the
people fornications, revels, thefts, homicides, falsehoods, perjuries; vain, knavish, or superstitious arts;
avaricious gains, usury, and the like. Among the
clergy, moreover, are simoniacal heresies, exactions of
money for baptism, confirmation, confession, the sacrament of the eucharist, holy oil, marriage, wafers,
prayers for the dead, festivals, preachings, burials,
consecrations of churches, altars, and chapels, pre-
bends, benefices, prelatic dignities, episcopal acts, sale
of indulgences, beside many other heresies which
arise from these and pollute the church of Christ.

"Moreover, there are impious and unjust practices,
as unchastity of concubinage, and other fornications;
anger, strife, contentions; frivolous citations, and vex-

ations and spoliations of simple men, according to caprice; exactions of assessments, and innumerable deceptions of the simple by false promises. Each and all of these, every Christian believer and true son of mother church is bound to exterminate, in himself and others, even as he should hate and detest the devil himself, the order and estate of his calling being ever observed.

" And if any one ascribe to us, beyond this our pious and holy intent, any thing that is unchaste and scandalous, let him be held by Christian believers as a false and unjust witness, since we have this only in our hearts, with all our strength and according to our entire ability, to please the Lord Jesus Christ, and to follow and fulfil his law and precepts, and these four catholic articles, with all fidelity."

They then declare their purpose to stand firmly in defence of the truth of the gospel, and to oppose all that shall impugn it, with such means as they can command, withstanding them to the last as the most cruel tyrant and Antichrist. And if, by any that adhere to them, anything should be done of a scandalous nature, they protest that it is against their intention, and their earnest purpose to prevent it, and that they hold themselves ever ready to be better instructed from Holy Scripture.

Such were the articles of the Calixtines, deliberately adopted and firmly maintained. The authors of them did not seem to perceive that their appeal to scripture was inconsistent with their assumed conservative position, and with some practices which they still retained. They were still in bondage to the ancient usages of the church, and revolted from the greater liberty of their Taborite brethren.

But if the former were superior in education, refinement, and the general moderation of their views, the last were immensely superior in deep feeling, earnest conviction, and that desperate and fanatical courage which made them terrible on the battle-field. Without them, Prague lay at the mercy of the emperor. Zisca's soldiers alone had earned the epithet of *invincible.* They could not be vanquished till the last man was slain. Nor were they altogether unconscious of their power, although under Zisca's generalship they were not inclined to employ it to secure any undue advantage. As occasion demanded, or the pressure of external attack was applied, the Calixtines asked and received the aid of their terrible allies, the Taborites.

The distinction betwen them, however, was already marked, and was continually widening, as the sentiments and tastes of each became more fully developed. Each party naturally desired that its own views might prevail. On Aug. 5, 1420, less than a week after the imperialists had withdrawn, the Taborites presented their articles to the city, with the alternative that if not accepted they would leave the city at once. The New city, where the Taborites were in the majority, accepted them without hesitation. The Old city demanded time for deliberation; and one of the masters of the university, an Englishman named Peter, discussed the articles, each in its order, in presence of the magistrates and the citizens, showing how far and in what sense they

might be approved or rejected "with a safe conscience." The articles thus discussed pertained rather
to moral conduct and rules of life, than to points of
faith. They condemn gross public sins among laity
and clergy; require the severe repression and punishment of all forms of licentiousness, tavern-drink-
ing, luxury and extravagance of dress, fraud, robbery,
and usury. They demand that laws, which they
describe as "Pagan and Teutonic," inconsistent with
the law of God, shall be repealed, and all things be
ordered and arranged according to the rules of divine
justice; that the priests shall observe an apostolic
simplicity, in keeping with the divine command;
that the magistrates be held subject to the law of
God, and that their enactments be registered in the
council-house, where they may be read by all the
people; that such enemies of *the truth of God* as
had shown themselves faithless to God and man,
should be banished the city and no favor shown
them ; that *heretical monasteries* be broken up and
destroyed, as well as unnecessary churches and altars,
with their images, robes, gold and silver chalices,
and every antichristian abomination savoring of
idolatry or simony, all which are not from God our
Heavenly Father.

In the defence of the truths expressed by these
articles, the Taborites declare that they have already,
in obedience to the divine will, risked property and
life, while many of their brethren had shed their
blood to maintain them. They declare their own
purpose, whether the articles shall be received or
rejected, to stand by them to the last. But these

articles were not accepted or approved by the magistrates and citizens of Old Prague, who were for the
most part Calixtines.   The last article, on the subject
of destroying monasteries and unnecessary churches,
which the Taborites would have called rookeries of
superstition, was especially objectionable.   Nor was
the conduct of the Taborites such as to smooth the
difficulties which lay in their way.   On the next
day after the articles had been presented, a portion
of the Taborites made an assault on the St. Clement
monastery, and a few days later, sacked and burned
the cloisters of the Royal Court, thus reducing—as
they had often done already—the theory of their
articles to practice.   They bore off with them fragments of the broken images and tables of the monasteries, and, forgetful of their wonted sobriety, made
a large and free use of the wine found in the vaults
of the cloisters.   As evening approached, some of
them projected an attack upon the Vissehrad, which
still held out for Sigismund; but the tumultuous and
disorderly assault was repulsed with great loss, by
the garrison.

The Taborites of New Prague wished still to retain their brethren within its walls.   The only condition on which this wish could be realized was the
acceptance by the Old city of the articles of the
Taborites.   But the magistrates opposed them.   It
was therefore resolved to call a meeting of the citizens, depose the present magistracy, and elect a new,
who should be known to favor the Taborite articles.
This project was executed on August 18th.   In spite
of this measure, however, Zisca, with his followers,

left the city a few days after. He did not, however,
abandon his project for bringing Prague over to his
views. As he left the city, his followers pledged
themselves not to rest till they had routed or destroyed the enemies of the cup.[1] His plan was, to
conquer the Calixtines by annihilating their allies
throughout Bohemia. As it was, he saw clearly the
impolicy of attempting at present to force upon the
citizens the objectionable articles.

The articles themselves, not excepting the last,
expressed the sincere convictions of the Taborites.
While terrible on the battle-field, and signal in their
vengeance, even their enemies are, to a remarkable
degree, unanimous in testifying to their sobriety, and
their exemplary freedom from the gross vices of the
age. A Puritanic severity characterized their demeanor. The corruptions of the priesthood, as well
as persecuting edicts, repelled them from the communion of the Roman church. With a stern and
inexorable justice they repressed whatever they
deemed inconsistent with the truth of the gospel.
If Zisca took exemplary vengeance upon the Adamites, with their free-love doctrine and licentious practices, it was because, whatever their heresy, their
teachings and proceedings struck at the root of all
purity, and of social order and morals.

At first the views of the Taborites had coincided
almost entirely with those of the Calixtines.[2] They

[1] Godeau, xxxvii. 38.

[2] One of the principal authorities
upon which the account of the Taborites and Calixtines, with their doc-
trinal views and relative position
toward each other is based, is " Lau-
rentii de Byzan Cancellarii Regalis,
Belli Hussitici, ab anno, 1414, ad an.
1423." The author, although a Calixtine, evidently aims to give an impartial account of the Taborites. The
Diarium is to be found in the sixth

had no distinct name except as they held it in common with all who were known as Hussites. They were brought together in one community, as the Presbyterians of Scotland were under Charles II., that they might enjoy the privilege of worship without molestation. It was during the year 1419 that their assemblies were first held in the neighborhood of Bechin, not far from Tabor, some twenty leagues distant from Prague. The people gathered, reared their tents, and for several days engaged in religious services, enjoying also the communion of the cup. The vast multitudes, on some occasions, numbered more than forty thousand people.[1] Everything was conducted with the utmost decorum. Some of the Taborite priests preached, some heard confessions, and others administered the communion under both kinds. Different groups were formed, which were severally addressed by speakers or preachers selected for the purpose. The men, the women, and the children formed each a body by themselves. These days, thus observed, were a sort of pentecostal season, and from far and near came the multitudes who thronged to the sacred festivity. Peaceably they came, and peaceably they returned. Songs of praise and joy lightened the tedium of the journey, as the processions moved

volume of " Reliquiæ Manusciptorum Omnis Ævi Diplomatum ac Monumentorum ineditorum adhuc," by J. P. de Ludwig. Balbinus—a Roman Catholic historian — speaks highly (*laudat sepius ac iterum*) of the work. The author was chancellor of New Prague.

[1] Sacerdotes Evangelii (A. D. 1419)

magistro Joh. Hus. faventes . . . cum populo sexus utriusque, ex diversis regni Bohemia partibus, civitatibus et villis, cum sacramento Eucharistiæ, in montem quendam prope castrum Bechian, quem montem *Thabor* appellanerunt, frequentare cæperunt . . . . Ultra quam 40,000 communicaverunt cum devotione.—*Diarium*, p. 143.

along their way.   Nothing was allowed inconsistent
with the objects of the assemblage.

No wantonness or levity, no dancing or drunkenness, was to be witnessed.   Everything which could
tend to disturb the seriousness, or interfere with the
devotion proper to the occasion, was carefully repressed.[1]   Even the sportiveness of childhood was
checked, and no sound of musical instruments was
allowed to break in upon the quiet of the place and
the solemnity of the worship.   At the close of the
religious exercises, each partook of a moderate repast
which they had brought with them from their homes.
All outward distinctions were neglected, or forgotten.
The rich and the poor sat down together, and priest
and layman were undistinguished by garb.   They
addressed one another by the appellation of brother
and sister, each sharing his portion with such as
were more needy than himself.   As in the apostolic
and primitive church—says the Calixtine narrative
—there was but one heart, one will.   Nothing was
thought of, nothing was transacted, save what pertained to the welfare of souls, or concerned the
restoration of the church to its primitive model.
Their humble repast was concluded by a solemn
thanksgiving to God; and the exercises of the day
closed with a procession of the vast multitude around
Tabor—where the assemblies were usually held—in
which all united in singing psalms of praise to God.
They then bade one another farewell—strangers
before, but brethren now—and each returned by the
way he came, back to his own dwelling.   They were

[1] Diar. Bel. Hus., 188.

even careful in this respect, that they might not unnecessarily trample down the harvest fields.

As these seasons continued to be observed, the multitudes who assembled increased. From the most distant parts of Bohemia—from Pisek, Wodnian, Necolicz, Heyman, Ausch, Janovicz, Ledlezan, Pilsen; from Prague itself, and from many parts of Moravia—they came, some with horses, others on foot, pilgrims to that spot, precious above every other, because there they might enjoy, unmolested, their peculiar worship and the communion of the cup. Undoubtedly many were drawn thither by curiosity. Nor would it always be as easy as at first, to restrain and repress the tendencies to excess or unwarranted indulgence. Sharp things would naturally be spoken of a corrupt clergy, opposed to what these Taborites believed the authentic and authoritative command of Christ in the institution of the Supper. With all the general quietness of their demeanor, the Taborites had bitter enemies; and Wenzel himself, taught by experience how easy it was for him to pass from a throne to a prison, grew suspicious. He feared lest the report, industriously spread by their enemies, that such a multitude would soon choose their own king and their own archbishop, might be true. An effort was therefore made to suppress these assemblies. The barons forbade their vassals and subjects to visit Tabor, under penalty of death or confiscation of their goods.[1]

But all these measures were vain. The current

---

[1] Diar. Bel. Hus., 189.

of popular religious feeling had acquired a force and fervor that defied resistance. Sooner than forego his privilege, the peasant chose to abandon his home altogether, and, disposing of his property, escape at once the oppression of priest and baron. Tabor attracted them, says the old annalist, as the magnet attracts iron. Thus the very attempt to repress the popular enthusiasm defeated its own object. The people were taught rebellion by unwise restrictions; and Tabor, from a camping-ground of religious assemblies, became at once a populous city. The opportune death of Wenzel favored this movement. Zisca, with his rare combination of sagacity, enthusiastic devotion, and military genius, found the materials of an army already at hand. They needed only to be moulded by that discipline of which he was so perfect a master, and inspired with confidence in their cause as the cause of truth, and in the indisputable ability of their leader, to become well-nigh invincible.

Tabor thus became the refuge and the fortress of the Hussites. But already many had advanced beyond the point that had been reached by him whom they still honored as a martyr. He had bequeathed to them, with his dying breath, and amid the fires of the stake, the invaluable principle of the sole authority of the word of God. With this as their starting-point, they went beyond him. Even Jacobel and the Calixtines generally were laggards in their views of reform. Not only a single sacrament, but all the institutions, doctrines, and rites of the church were to be subjected to a scripture test. Ambrose,

Jerome, Augustine, and Gregory, they said, were but men. There was no need of consulting the sentences of the schools, or giving heed to learned doctors, when all things essential to salvation were to be found in scripture.

On the basis of these principles, they maintained that no sayings or writings of learned men were to be held or believed as catholic by the faithful, unless they were contained explicitly in the canon of the Bible;[1] that every one who pursues the study of the liberal arts or accepts degrees in them is vain and heathenish, and sins against the gospel of Christ; that no decrees of the holy fathers, no institutions of the ancients, no rites or traditions of human invention, were to be held, but all such were to be abolished and destroyed as works of Antichrist, since Christ and his apostles had nowhere enjoined them in the New Testament. On this ground they rejected chrism, the anointing with oil, and sprinkling with holy water; the exorcising, blessing, hallowing of the chalice, church furniture, and robes; the observing of canonical hours; the dress, ceremonies, and order of the mass; the chanting of the priests, and the baptizing of children with exorcisms, holy water, and sponsors, instead of the simple rite by the application of pure water. For books of missals, or chants, gold and silver chalices, priestly vestments, etc., they felt equal aversion. All these things were to be destroyed or burned, and it was more proper for the laity to wear the priestly robes, or cut them up for their own apparel, than for the priests themselves

---

[1] These articles are to be found in full in Diar. Bel. Hus., 191, 193.

to perform in them the divine offices. Auricular
confession, the fast of Lent, vigils, festivals of saints,
or other seasons of special devotion, except the Lord's
day, were treated with no more respect. A priest,
tricked out in his robes with their useless ornaments,
and celebrating mass in the customary manner, was
but like the harlot of the Apocalypse, to be despised
by the faithful. The sacrament of the eucharist should
be celebrated in the manner practised by Christ and
his apostles, in the ordinary garb, without an altar,
and in any place that might fitly serve. The
bread was not itself to be lifted up for the adoration of the worshippers, but was to be administered
in a plain and audible tone of voice. The clergy,
moreover, were to be like the Levites of the Old
Testament in regard to the possession of property;
they were to be directly dependent on the contribu-
tions of the people. As to purgatory, and prayers
for the dead, or works of piety in their behalf, all
these were rejected as silly and inane superstitions.
Invocation of the saints was condemned as savoring
either of heresy or idolatry. All images, or the
likeness of anything as an object of worship, stood
charged with savoring of idolatry, and all such, as
idols, were to be destroyed and burned.

These articles were published in the year 1420,
soon after the Taborites had withdrawn from Prague.
They gave great scandal to the Calixtines, who appealed to the world for testimony to the moderation
of their views.[1] It is evident that from the time

---

[1] The author of the *Diarium Bel.*   Taborites led to the report, through-
Hus. says that the practices of the   out the kingdom and foreign lands,

when the Taborites first commenced their assemblies
during the previous year, there had been great progress made in breaking away from the ceremonies,
institutions, and doctrines of the Roman church.
The explanation of this is to be found in the free
and friendly conferences enjoyed at Tabor by men
who interchanged their views on religious subjects,
with the open Bible before them as their only supreme authority.   Tabor was the one asylum for the
persecuted in the kingdom, where perfect freedom
of religious opinion was allowed.   "You may think
as you like here," wrote an orthodox Roman Catholic,
on a visit to Tabor, to one of his friends.

Thus persecution abroad drove into a single community the men who were foremost in their views
of reform, and most advanced in apprehending the
true spirit of the gospel, and the simplicity of its
ritual.   With the scriptures acknowledged, on all
sides, as the only supreme authority in matters of
faith, it was no difficult or tedious work to adduce
ample testimony of the superfluous ceremonies and
false doctrines with which the purity of the gospel
had been overlaid by a corrupt church.

With the views of the Taborites on religious sub-

that the Hussites had abolished the
distinction between laity and clergy; that shoemakers and mechanics
performed the divine offices; that
mass was celebrated by the unshorn,
without priestly vestments; that the
Taborite priests ordered the destruction of all ornaments and musical instruments in the churches, requiring
all, willing or unwilling, to accept
their own rites; that books, chalices,
missals etc., were sold for a mere
trifle; and that relics of the saints
were taken from the altars or show-
cases, and thrown into nooks and
corners. By such reports Bohemia
was defamed in other lands. The
Calixtines were provoked and exasperated at the Taborites for giving
occasion for such stories, and wished
to vindicate themselves from all complicity in such excesses.—P. 196.

jects, some of a peculiar cast, in regard to social and political matters, were naturally allied. They were all anti-imperialists, and nearly all republicans, or at least in favor of an elective king. Their experience of a corrupt priesthood had produced in them an aversion to the learning of schools and colleges, whose degrees they treated with contempt as heathenish and antichristian innovations. Their study of the Apocalypse—a favorite book of the Bible, from its denunciations of the Great Apostasy—led them into many extravagances of belief and practice.

All however did not go to the same extreme with Martin Loqui, one of their preachers, who derived his name from his eminence as a speaker, and whose principal associates were John Oilezin, Marcold, Coranda, and a certain Wenzel of Prague.[1] These men, with a large portion of the Taborites, held the doctrine of the speedy advent of Christ, and the approaching mission of "the seven last plagues," by which all Christ's enemies should be destroyed. In this vengeance the faithful of Christ are to bear a part: all who shall hear the word of Christ, are to receive the warning to "flee to the mountains," where the Taborites were already assembled; and whoever neglects to do this, shall perish by the plagues. At this time, the Taborites should be the holy angels sent out to rescue the faithful and bring them to a place of safety, as Lot was rescued from Sodom; they should be the executioners of God's justice upon the guilty nations, while only the five cities, which they named "places of refuge," should

[1] Diar. Bel. Hus., 203.

be spared.[1] The riches of the Gentiles, or the property of Christ's enemies, should be taken from them
by the faithful, and destroyed or burned. In this
consummation of all things, Christ will himself visibly descend to earth and assume the government of
the world; and all who have not on the wedding-
garment, will be cast into outer darkness.[2] All the
kingdoms of the world will come to an end. There
will be no more exaction, no more paying of tribute.
Sin will be destroyed. There will be no more
scandal, abomination, and falsehood; no more
persecution or suffering, for all will be the elect
children of God. The glory of this kingdom, thus
restored, will be greater—before the resurrection of
the dead—than that of the primitive church. The
sun of human intelligence will no longer shine; none
will need to teach another to know the Lord, for all
shall be taught of God. The law of grace will then
no longer have place; it will be done away. The use
of churches will be dispensed with, for God himself
will be the temple, and, like hope and faith, lost in
sight and fruition, all outward structures will disap-
pear. Then shall come the resurrection of the dead
—the first resurrection, in which the dead in Christ
shall be raised, among whom John Huss shall appear;
and thus for his elect's sake God would hasten the
final destiny of the world.

In this renovation of all things, man will be restored to the state of innocence enjoyed by Adam
before his fall. There will no longer be pains attend-
ing childbirth, no such thing as original sin, no neces-

---

[1] Diar. Bel. Hus., 155, 204.   [2] Ib. 205.

sity for the waters of baptism, no more need of the
sacrament of the eucharist, for men shall eat angels'
food, and never die.[1]

These peculiar views were an excrescence upon the
religious system of the Taborites, and were shortly
modified very essentially by succeeding events. The
prophecy in regard to the five cities of refuge was
effectually defeated, and many of the peculiar teachings in regard to Christ's advent were abandoned.
They were all based upon an unwarranted interpretation of obscure texts; and when their novelty wore
off, they were for the most part cast aside.

The Taborites however clung fondly to the notion
that they were God's peculiar people, and were specially designated by him for the reformation of the
church and the defence of the faithful. This belief
led them to interpose for the destruction of what they
regarded as idolatry, superstition, and Antichrist.
Their creed on these points was not a dead letter,
and they went about their work with an energy and
a courage which might challenge the reproach, but
was too serious and earnest for the derision of their
foes. They did not shrink—however it might scandalize their Calixtine brethren, or the so-called Catholic church—from carrying the theory of a creed
which they embraced with all the fervor of their
spirits, to a practical application. Wherever they
went, they observed with all fidelity the simple rites
of their worship. Their priests ministered the communion under both kinds, without the aid of rubric,
missal, priest's robe, or the Latin tongue. They spoke

---

[1] Diar. Bel. Hus., 206, 207.

and prayed in their own vernacular.   They were not careful to use a gold or silver chalice for the wine of the communion.   An iron, earthen, or wooden cup answered their purpose full as well.   If they declared the churches and altars, which had been desecrated by " the mammon of unrighteousness " and the simony of the priests, to be churches and altars " of the devil and of idols," or spoke of monasteries as dens of robbers, sties where the swine of lazy and useless monks were fattened, they sometimes suited the action to the speech, sacked the church, shivered the altar, and burned the monastery.   If some unfortunate monk attempted to remonstrate—" Go ye into all the world, and preach the gospel," was the prompt reply. "Christ never told men to serve him by shutting themselves up in indolence,"—such was the argument by which the Taborites answered all objections. Monasteries thus became the special objects of their vengeance.   Hundreds of them were sacked and burned.   Some of the nuns, whom the terror of the Taborites had effectually converted to the communion of the cup, married—to the horror and scandal of the Calixtines.

The Taborites treated many of the reputed holy things of the age with the most sacrilegious disrespect.   Relics of the saints were ruthlessly flung out of the churches, like common earth.   The holy oil was unceremoniously applied to a most profane use, unless it was emptied, like the chrism and holy water, upon the ground.   The vessels that contained these liquids were broken, or polluted; for the Taborites held in contempt holy sprinklings and extreme unc-

tion. Their form of baptism was the application of
water, with the simple formula of administration in
the name of the Father, the Son, and the Holy Ghost.[1]
Auricular confession they dismissed with the brief
logic of adopting the formal division of sins by the
church, and declaring that if venial—by this probably
meaning sins of the heart—it was enough to confess
them to God; if mortal, (public and gross,) they
should be confessed in presence of the brethren.
As to purgatory, they maintained that by the discipline of probation God prepares such as will be saved,
to enter upon their reward and their eternal immunity from sin with the close of their earthly existence. They who die in mortal sin go at once to their
retribution of eternal justice in hell. Consequently
prayer for the dead is vain and futile.[2] The Taborites neither prayed to the saints, nor paid regard to
their images and pictures in the churches. "What
was Peter, or Paul, or any other of the saints?" they
asked. "Were they not men, saved like us by the
help of God alone, and in prayer to him, by the intercession of no saint, but of Christ only?" They
resented the superstitious worship which the pictures
and statues of the saints received. The sternness
of the prophet on Carmel, while he mocked the worshippers of Baal, seemed to relax into a grim smile;
and we can imagine with what cool derision the Taborite could look up, in the presence of his gaping

[1] The author of the *Diar. Bel. Hus.*
says the rite of baptism was performed by a flowing stream, or with water
brought from any place indiscriminately. Sponsors were rejected in
the rite. Even the infant, after baptism, was required to commune *sub
utraque specie.* P. 199.

[2] Ib., 255.

and credulous enemies, to the gouged eye or slit nose (*erutis oculis et nasis abscissis*) of some mangled image, crying out, in his so-called blasphemy, "If you are God or his saint, defend yourself, and we will believe you." (*Si Deus aut ejus sanctus es, tunc te defende, et credimus tibi.*) The place of His worship was to be disfigured by no image, desecrated by no sculpture. A handful of filth, or a thrust of his sword, or a blow of his terrible flail, relieved him from all the apprehension which a beautiful painting might excite as to his worshipping in a desecrated place. Monasteries were "dens of robbers," and wickedly founded against the law of Christ. The disciples were commanded to go forth into all the world, and not shut themselves up as hermits; hence the cloisters and monasteries were to be utterly overthrown and destroyed.[1] The fasts of the Roman church were unhesitatingly rejected. Only such days were observed as the Taborite preachers directed. On these occasions no one ate or drank, from morning till night, or even till the following day.

As to naming churches after particular saints, the views of the Taborite would have fully accorded with the sentiments of the most rigid Puritan of the Commonwealth. Even Jerome and Augustine, whom Huss and Jacobel loved to quote as authority, did not pass unquestioned by the Taborites. By confirming or multiplying ecclesiastical rites, it was possible —they maintained—that these men had done the church more evil than good. To give churches their

[1] Diar. Bel. Hus., 197.

names, or the names of others who were merely men, was an impious and accursed thing, and such churches, with the splendid dwellings of their pastors, ought to be burned and destroyed. The apostles never consecrated churches by such titles, or dwelt in such houses; they were content with alms, and went about all over the world, preaching the gospel, without tithes or endowed churches.

The leaders of the Taborites laid it down as a fundamental principle, that the law of Christ was sufficient for the government of his church. All that was necessary to salvation, he had declared in the New Testament.[1] Human institutions and ceremonies were of no account. As Christ said to the scribes and Pharisees, "ye have nullified the law by your traditions," so also might modern scribes and Pharisees be addressed. Unless they desisted from their error, they might expect all the plagues of the Apocalyse to light upon them.

In consistency with these views, the Taborite priests endeavored to reduce the ordinances of worship to the simplicity of the primitive church. They rejected the use of sacerdotal vestments, declined observance of canonical hours, administered the divine rites, not from the altar, but from a simple table, in the open air, or in houses where they might be assembled. First of all, the priests knelt, with heads bowed toward the earth, while one repeated the Lord's prayer. He that was selected to solemnize the sacrament then rose, uttered in a clear voice the words of consecration, and broke and administered the

[1] Diar. Bel. Hus., 194.

bread; afterward the wine, in a vessel of iron, clay, wood, or other material, as might happen to be convenient.

The Taborites evidently knew how to defend their doctrines by word; but their most effectual logic resided in their terrible flails, that threshed down all opposition that dared to lift its head. Councils, and crusades, and denunciations of all kinds, were ineffectual to put them down. They relinquished none of their peculiar tenets, except those which they derived from the study of the Apocalypse. Time showed the futility of many of the interpretations which some of their preachers gave to the prophecies of this book. Others seem to have been generally abandoned, insomuch that the Roman Catholic historian, Natalis Alexander, in giving account of their doctrines, makes no mention of those which are said to have originated with Martin Loqui. The only tenets which he ascribes to them, beside those of which the Calixtine author of "The Diary of the Hussite War" makes mention, and which have been already given, are such as we might naturally suppose would be associated with them. He speaks of their denial of the supremacy of the Papal See, their doctrine of the parity of the clergy, their maintaining that whoever was guilty of mortal sin was, *ipso facto*, deprived of all secular and ecclesiastical authority, and was not to be obeyed. According to him, they held, that prayer for the dead was an invention of the avarice of the priesthood; that there was no need of consecrated cemeteries, for it made no difference with what kind of earth human bodies

were covered; and that the religious orders of the
monks were a device of devils.

It is easy to perceive, that notwithstanding some
fanatical views, and some opinions which were nurtured by the ignorance and prejudice of many among
them, their sincere as well as avowed purpose was to
restore the church, as near as possible, to its primitive model. Most of their doctrines were based
clearly upon the authority of scripture; and we are
only surprised to find them, within so short a period
after the death of Huss, so far in advance of what
Huss and Jerome, or even Jacobel, had taught. Many
of them—not all, however—utterly rejected the doctrine of transubstantiation, which Huss and Jerome
had avowed to the last, and which Jacobel had maintained in his peculiar sense, by distinguishing between
Christ's material and his spiritual body, the latter of
which only was present in the sacrament of the altar.
The doctrine of justification by faith alone, so distinctly apprehended and taught by Luther, does not
appear to have attracted their special attention.
Their circumstances and position ranged them on the
negative side of most of the questions between them
and the Roman church, and their principal work was
more to tear down than construct, more to refute a
false system than to build up a new theology. They
had little leisure and little learning, or intellectual
discipline, to apply themselves to the philosophy of
their own belief, or study the order and harmony of
doctrines which they derived from the simple word
of scripture, and adopted with an unquestioning faith.

The doctrines of the Taborites proved especially

disastrous to the monasteries. These were regarded as nuisances to be abated. Monks and nuns were dispersed, or forced to accept the communion of the cup. Refusal to comply was met with violence. This was the case even in Prague. The Monastery of the Holy Spirit was given up to the Germans for the preaching of the word of God. Those of St. Francis and St. James were stored with warlike machines and implements. The cups and furniture were sold for money. The sacred chrism and holy water were emptied on the earth.

Zisca carried out these principles, in letter and in spirit. As city after city came into the hands of the Taborites, the monasteries were devoted to destruction, and their inmates scattered. In the spirit of the ancient Israelites invading Canaan, the idolatrous rites of the Roman church were all to be suppressed.

This picture of the Taborites would be incomplete, without adding to it the features preserved to us by a letter of Æneas Sylvius to the Cardinal de Carvajal, in which he gives an account of the visit paid them by himself, in company with others, at a date some years after the siege of Prague.[1] As ambassadors, sent to treat with the Taborites, they demanded and received their hospitality. They were cheerfully welcomed by the Taborites, who went out to meet them; and they were entertained with cordiality and respect. "A most remarkable spectacle was now witnessed—an indiscriminate rabble, mostly composed

[1] The date of this letter is 1451. Æneas Sylvius, sent by the pope to see what could be done to bring back the Calixtines to the church, gives this account in his narrative of his conference with George Podiebrad.— *Guer. des Hus.*, ii. 224.

of peasants, who wished however to appear genteel
and refined. Although a cold rain-storm, such as
frequently occurs in Bohemia, prevailed at the time,
many had no other protection than a mere frock.
Some wore robes made of skins, some of their horsemen had no saddles, some had no bridle, and others
were without stirrups. One was booted, another not.
One had lost an eye, another a hand, so that, to
borrow the language of Virgil, it was a shame to see
*populataque tempora raptis auribus, et truncas inhon-
esto vulnere nares.* There was no order of proceeding,
no reserve in speech, and we were received in a
rough and peasant style. Yet presents were made
us of fish, wine, and beer. Having entered the
town, we took a view of it; and if I were not to call
it a town or asylum for heretics, I should be at a
loss for a name to give it. For whatever monsters
of impiety and of blasphemies are unmasked among
Christians, flock together here, and find security in a
place where there are as many heresies as there are
heads, and full liberty to believe what you like.
On the outer gate of the city there are two shields
suspended. On one of these is a picture of an angel
holding a cup, which he is represented as extending
to the people as if to invite them to the communion
of the cup. On the other there is a portrait of Zisca,
who is represented as an old man and entirely blind.
. . . What more fitting for such a people, who have
no understanding of divine things, no religion, no
apprehension of what is just and right, than a blind
leader! In this case that word of the Saviour is
fulfilled, 'If the blind lead the blind, both fall into

the ditch.' . . . These people have no greater anxiety
for anything, than to hear a sermon. If any one neglects this, and lies asleep at home, or busies himself
with work or play during the time of sermon, he is
beaten for it, and is compelled to obligate himself
to hear the word of God. Their place of worship
is built of wood, and is much like a barn; this they
call their temple. Here they preach to the people;
here they daily expound the law. They have here
but one altar, neither consecrated, nor to be consecrated, and from this they exhibit the sacrament to
the people. The priests neither wear crowns, nor
shave their beards. The Taborites voluntarily provide by gifts for their support. They offer nothing
upon the altar; they condemn tithes; of first fruits,
they hold neither to the name nor to the thing itself.
Yet they do not accord in one and the same belief.
One thinks in one way, and another in another; each
follows his own liking. Neither do they live by a
single rule."

It is to be borne in mind that we have no account
of the Taborites, except from persons who were either
their avowed enemies, or were strongly prejudiced
against them. They undoubtedly were guilty of
many imprudent acts, many deeds of violence, many
excesses utterly unwarrantable. Many elements of
fanaticism were mingled with their creed. Many
and strong prejudices, peculiar to the class of which
they were mostly composed, possessed their minds;
but when their circumstances are considered,—the
persecution that drove them from their dwellings;
the crusade that forced them in self-defence to take

the weapons of war into their hands; the contempt
and cruelty with which they were treated; and the
necessities of their outlawed condition,—the severe
measures which they dealt out to the monasteries,
whose inmates they regarded as accomplices of the
council that burned Huss, and the terrible examples
of vengeance, provoked by their own sufferings and
wrongs, and by which they made themselves formidable to their foes—these excesses of a ferocity fit only
to foil and frighten a crusading army—cease to wear
that aspect of utter and ruthless malignity which
they would otherwise bear.   The creed of the Taborites was in the main scriptural, and we cannot but
approve that wise policy by which they allowed all
the diversities of opinion which prevailed among
them, a full and perfect tolerance.   Centuries passed
away, and their representatives were seen spreading
themselves over the world in the persons of the
Moravian missionaries, to whose simple confidence in
God, John Wesley acknowledged himself indebted
for lessons of a faith wiser and stronger than his
own.

On the battle-field the Taborites maintained their
undisputed superiority and preëminence, even after
the death of Zisca.   They fought under the impulse
of the most powerful motives which can inspire the
soul.   Each soldier was a hero.   He was ready to be
a martyr.   His valor was not that of the soldier of
fortune, inspired by earthly ambitions and panting
for an earthly prize.   He was a champion of his
faith; and his firm belief was, that in pouring out his
blood, and laying down his life, he was rendering

but a poor and unworthy tribute to that "truth of God," in defence of which it was an honor to die.

The Calixtines formed—as they would wish to be regarded—the conservative reformers of the Bohemian nation. They remained steadfast in their regard for the memory of Huss, and in their attachment to the celebrated four articles which formed that portion of their creed in which they differed from the church of Rome. Once only they compromised matters with the Taborites, by declaring the wearing of priests' vestments a matter of indifference, a non-essential. They wished to preserve the order and the institutions of the church intact, except so far as they would be modified by the admission of the four articles. They declared themselves opposed to all unnecessary innovations. They wished to commend themselves to the Christian world as faithful adherents to the Catholic faith. They took pains therefore to distinguish their cause and views from those of the Taborites, in as marked a manner as possible.

In a council held at Prague, in the year 1421, they drew up twenty-three articles, which they set forth in a document intended to serve as the exponent of their faith. In these they maintained transubstantiation, the necessity of the seven sacraments, the Catholic forms and rites of baptism with sponsors, chrism, the holy oil, and triple immersion in holy water, auricular confession, episcopal authority, the exclusive power of the keys by the priesthood, extreme unction, the invocation of the saints, purgatory and prayer for the dead, the propriety of the priestly robes, and the offices connected with the mass, the observance of fast-days and the festivals of the saints, the consecration and sanctity of churches, the necessity of sacred vessels and ornaments, as well as a peculiar and distinctive dress for priests, the observance of canonical hours, and obedience to episcopal authority. On all these points, the Calixtines, however inconsistent or neglectful of the consequences flowing from their first article, as to the supreme authority of scripture, wished to abide by the rule and observance of the Roman church.

In reply to the twenty-three articles of the Calixtines, the Taborites drew up an equal number of an opposite tenor. But for a long time the two parties were so evenly balanced, that neither could claim a manifest preponderance. The great majority of the barons of the kingdom, with the citizens of Old Prague, were Calixtines, and Zisca himself, though the general of the Taborites, had evidently a strong leaning toward this party, at least on many points. The citizens of the New city, and the lower classes of the nation generally, composed the body of the Taborites. The danger of foreign invasion did not allow the two parties to risk their common security in fratricidal quarrels. It was evident, however, that only the power and wisdom of Zisca prevented an open division and hostility between them. If a compromise was ever to be affected with the so-called Catholic church, it could only be on a Calixtine basis.

CHAPTER XVI.

THE CAMPAIGNS OF ZISCA.

AUG. 5, 1420—OCT. 11, 1424.

ALTHOUGH the emperor had been forced to raise
the siege of Prague, he did not abandon his designs
against Bohemia. He determined to levy fresh
armies, and make another attempt to recover the
kingdom. His retreat from Prague was as desolating to the region through which he passed as his
invading march had been. With his hussars, he

(471)

stopped for a while at Kuttenberg, and the valor and
energies of his army were devoted to the work of
ravage and plunder.

His retreat allowed the differences that existed
between the Calixtines and Taborites to show themselves. The twelve articles of the latter, for which
they demanded the approval and sanction of the
city, and one of which threatened danger to the
churches and monasteries, were at first rejected, and
afterward approved only through a revolutionary
movement that secured new magistrates, whom the
Taborites nominated. In spite of this, however, they
determined to leave the city. Their friends in New
Prague strongly urged them to remain, but the
Calixtines of Old Prague were more than willing to
have them depart. Their radical views of reform,
and their unyielding hostility to images, statues,
pictures, the old church forms, and whatever savored
in their opinion of superstition and Antichrist, di-
verged so far from the moderation of the Calixtines,
who would be satisfied with securing the granting of
their four articles, that Zisca acted only a prudent
part in withdrawing his forces from Prague, (Aug.
22, 1420.)

But his object in doing this was not merely to
prevent a collision between the Taborites and Calixtines. He wished to keep his forces employed, and
suppress through Bohemia any movements in favor
of Sigismund. The monks and priests soon felt the
weight of his vengeance. With sword in hand, he
swore never to rest till the power of the papacy in
Bohemia was utterly prostrate. The cities which

resisted the freedom of the communion of the cup, but especially the monasteries, were marked for assault and pillage.[1] Kniczan, about a league from Prague, was the first to feel his vengeance. The castle was taken, the church destroyed, and seven priests burned. Zisca then directed his steps to the Circle of Prachin. Desolation marked his course. The city of Pisek fell into his hands. He presented himself before the walls of Prachatitz. It stood charged with having treated the Hussites with harsh cruelty. Zisca for once was disposed to be lenient. It was at Prachatitz that he had spent his early years as a student. He wished to spare the city, if possible, as a tribute to the memory of the happy days and the friendships he had enjoyed there. He summoned it to open its gates to him, promising it favorable and lenient terms, but was met by a blunt refusal. Upon this he stormed the city, (Nov. 12, 1420.) It was taken, and no mercy shown. Two hundred and thirty were left dead in the streets, and more than fourscore persons were burned. Even women and children were driven into exile. To the plea for mercy, Zisca's stern reply was, "We must fulfil the law of the Lord Christ in your blood."

Meanwhile Sigismund had gathered a new army, and advanced to resume the siege of Prague. During the past two months (September and October, 1420) he had amused the barons of the empire by frequent assemblies, which he summoned with the ostensible purpose of restoring peace and order throughout the kingdom. But all these efforts were

---

[1] Guerre des Hus., i. 180.

futile. His own character would not allow his subjects to trust him. His complicity in the death of
Huss could not easily be blotted from the memories
of men who regarded the victim of his perfidy as a
martyr for the truth.

By great exertions this second army had been
brought together. The march of the emperor was
expedited by intelligence of the danger which
threatened the garrison of the Vissehrad. With his
Moravian recruits, and all that he retained of his
former army, he reached Prague before the Vissehrad fell into the hands of the besiegers. But a letter
which he had written to the garrison, revealing his
plans, fell into the hands of the Hussites and put
them on their guard.[1] The arrangements which he
had made to raise the siege by an attack upon the
city simultaneous with a sortie by the garrison, were
frustrated. The latter remained quiet, whether they
had lost hope of successful resistance, or did not
understand the emperor's signals. The next day
they surrendered. Great was the rejoicing of the
citizens, and great the mortification of Sigismund.

Yet he was not disposed to abandon his purposes
without again trying the fortune of arms. He haz-
arded a battle, but it proved disastrous to his army.
In the absence of Zisca, the citizens of Prague had
called in Krussina, with his Horebites, to their assistance. They had the reputation of being full as
brave, and more merciless even than the Taborites.
The emperor saw his forces beaten and flying like
chaff[2] before the terrible blows dealt by the flails of

---

[1] Guerre des Hus., i. 134.   [2] Godeau, xxxvii. 40.

the undisciplined peasantry. "I want to come to blows," said he, "with those flail-bearers." "Sire," replied Plumlovisc, a Moravian nobleman, "I fear that we shall all perish; those iron flails are exceedingly formidable." "Oh! you Moravians," replied Sigismund,—"I know you; you are afraid!" The Moravians were stung to desperation by the rash and unworthy taunt. Flinging themselves from their horses, they rushed—where the emperor did not choose to venture—upon the entrenchments of the Hussites. But their assault was futile. A sortie from the city rushed to the rescue of its brave defenders. The besiegers were forced to give way. They fled on all sides, and fell by thousands before the swords and flails of their pursuers. A great part of the Moravian nobility were left on the field of battle. The rout of the army was complete; and again Sigismund was constrained to retire from before the walls of Prague.

The patience and hopes of the Hussites, who had relied upon Sigismund's disposition to conciliate and give peace to his kingdom, were alike exhausted. The Calixtines even, by the force of circumstances, found themselves brought to occupy the position, politically, of the Taborites. The pride of Sigismund, his haughty demeanor, and his intractable purpose to subdue Bohemia and dictate his own terms, had forced the great majority to the conviction that he was unfit to occupy the throne. It was finally determined to call a convention of the states of the kingdom, and elect a new king (Dec. 30, 1420.) An effort also was made to compromise the differences between the Calixtines and Taborites. This was a difficult matter. One main subject of controversy was, whether the priests should wear their robes in celebrating mass, according to the old rites of the church. Some favored and some opposed it, and each party was strenuous. In some places even the Bohemian women had interfered to prevent the priests wearing the robes. The difference was at last compromised, on the suggestion of Jacobel that the wearing of the robes should be accounted a matter of indifference. It was easier to frame the decree than to carry it into effect. It however answered its purpose of effecting a present conciliation in the convention. In regard to the choice of a king there was some division. Nicholas de Hussinitz had aspired to be a candidate. His claims, however, were set aside, and he withdrew in angry disappointment from the city, swearing never again to enter it. At a short distance from Prague his horse fell. He was seriously injured, and was brought back to the city to die. His followers, on the loss of their leader, went over to Zisca.[1]

The crown was offered to the king of Poland.[2] But the embassy, sent to announce the proceedings of the Bohemians, was captured by the emperor and thrown into prison. The pope, moreover, interfered to prevent the king of Poland from listening to the proposal, or accepting the offered crown.

In this measure of the states Zisca had taken part. Leaving most of his troops behind, he accepted the invitation, extended to himself and other barons, to

---

[1] Guerre des Hus., i. 137.   [2] Fleury, xxvi. 483.

be present at the convention which was held at the
council-house of Prague.[1]   On his entering the city
he was received with great honors, and his views
harmonized with those of the great majority of the
assembly.   The discords of the kingdom were now
for a time hushed, and Sigismund found himself
almost unanimously rejected by the nation.

Zisca again left Prague to pay visits to his "good
friends," the monks.   He marched in the direction
of Pilsen.   The rich cloisters of Choteschau and
Kladrub were seized, and fortified instead of being
destroyed.   Zisca had resolved to make his conquest
of permanent service to his cause.   Whatever he
could garrison and maintain as a Hussite fortress, was
seized and held for this purpose.   In fact, this method
of procedure was essential to the success of the plan
which he had projected, of driving his enemies out
of the kingdom.   Sigismund's third defeat was due
to the wisdom of this policy.

One of the emperor's generals was still maintaining his cause in Bohemia.   Bohuslaus von Schwamberg held himself secure in the strong fortress of
Kastikow.   Zisca surprised him by a night march,
and took the castle.   Bohuslaus was imprisoned at
the instance of the Taborites, who wished to have
him treated harshly; but Zisca, feigning compliance,
at length set him free.

Some of the soldiers who followed him, whether
from this or other causes, or both combined, left him.
They formed an army by themselves, and attempted
to prosecute their plans under leaders of their own

[1] Diar. Bel. Hus.

choice. But the imperial general, Flaschko, of Kuttenberg, fell upon and routed them. This partial
success encouraged Sigismund, and he expedited
measures, in order again to invade the kingdom. He
saw that Zisca was the great obstacle to his success.
His spirit seemed to diffuse itself throughout Bohemia,
and his name alone was a tower of strength. The
occasion seemed favorable, since the Hussite general
was weakened by the loss of a part of his army.
But the emperor's movements were too dilatory.
Allies from Prague and Tabor flocked at once to
Zisca's standards. The enemy who had ventured to
besiege Kladrub were suddenly confronted by the
Taborite hosts. A panic terror seized them, and
instead of a battle there was only a rout and pursuit. Sigismund fled first to Leitmeritz, then to
Kuttenberg, and at last to Moravia.

His defeat and absence from the kingdom left
room for divisions and jealousies to spring up anew.
Pilsen, in some way, had merited Zisca's displeasure.
He marched against it, but the city shut its gates.
Zisca besieged it for the space of seventeen days,
but it still resisted. At length a truce was effected.
The cities of Pilsen, Miess, Domatzlitz, and others
entered into a league with Prague, on the basis of
ratifying the four articles of the Calixtines. This
truce was effected in the early part of 1421, and
continued in force through the year. Zisca was not
idle, however. Commotau, Launy, and Slany fell
into his hands. Other places were threatened, and
some priests were burned.

The junction of the Calixtines and Taborites in

their measures for rejecting Sigismund and electing a new king, seems to have tended to restrain the excesses of the Taborites. Strange views had been adopted by some of them, especially by those who followed Martin Loqui. Beside his extravagant interpretations of the Apocalypse, he seems to have taught other doctrines peculiarly offensive. He denied transubstantiation—although on this point many of the Taborites agreed with him. He taught, that God was in man; that neither was He to be sought in heaven, nor the devil in hell; that all books, and forms of faith, and church ceremonies were needless and superfluous; that the marriage vow was not indissolubly binding. To these doctrines, of which we can only gather a general idea, he added others which he appears to have derived from the Adamites, or to have held in common with them. His followers, to whom he gave the promise of eternal life, became numerous. He was first banished from Tabor, but afterward pursued by Zisca, who heard of his proceedings at Beraun, where he was disseminating his views.

The Taborite general determined to put a stop to his course. Although a Calixtine himself, he had allowed a perfect toleration among his own soldiers; but when their doctrines were carried to licentiousness, or an excess which threatened dangerous results, he was prompt in putting a check upon them. At Beraun some of Loqui's followers were burned, and some recanted. Loqui himself was also put to death [1]—according to some, by Zisca, according to

---

[1] Guerre des Hus., i. 168.

others, by Archbishop Conrad. The probability is, that Zisca, who was a Calixtine, banished the unfortunate and misguided man from Tabor, or possibly sent him to Conrad, that he might determine what should be done with him.[1] It seems quite evident, at least, that he fell a victim to that jealousy which the Calixtines felt for their reputation.

It is fully evident, that although Zisca well understood how to manage the enthusiasm, not to say the fanaticism of his followers, his own good sense was not blinded by any fanatic views of his own. It was

[1] Pescheck (i. 19) gives quite another version of the case of Loqui. He says, "Martin Loquis was accused of introducing the errors of the Waldenses into the sacrament, and of teaching, 'with horrid profaneness,' that the bread and the cup should be handed to the communicants. At the intercession of the men of Tabor, he escaped; and to avoid the hatred and rage of his enemies, he fled to Moravia with another clergyman, Procopius Jednook. Passing through Chrudim, they were recognized, and put in irons. When examined as to their views of the holy supper, Martin said 'that the body of Christ is in heaven, and that he has one only, and no more.' Such a presumptuous blasphemy, the officer who had seized him could not bear. He struck the prisoner, and then sent for the executioner to commit the heretic to the flames. Ambrosius, curate of Hradek, who happened to be present, begged to have them given into his own charge. He took them to Hradek, kept them fifteen days, and took all imaginable pains to bring them to confess and renounce their errors. But finding them immovable, he sent them to Raudnitz, where they were detained two months in a dungeon, and tormented in various ways. There they were so tortured by fire, in order to force them to declare whence they learned their errors, and who were their accomplices, that their intestines came out.

"When admonished to return to the way of truth, they answered, smilingly, 'It is not for us, but for yourself to think of such a return; you have departed from the word of God to erroneous and antichristian opinions; ye worship the creature instead of the creator.' In consequence of this—on August 21, 1421—they were condemned to the flames. When the priest exhorted them to request the people's prayers in their behalf, they answered, 'We do not stand in need of their prayers; but you, Christians, pray for yourselves, and for those who mislead you, that the Father of mercies may deliver you from your darkness.' Having arrived at the place of execution, they were put into a barrel and burned."

If this narrative is correct, it relieves the memory of Zisca from a stain which was once regarded as his best title to honor.

the policy of the general, full as much as any taste for religious symbolism, that led him to adopt the plan of having a priest bearing a cup in his hand, lead the army in its attacks. At the crude fancies of some of his followers, he only smiled, except when he could employ them as his allies in the camp or on the battle-field. He even delighted oftentimes in seeing the would-be prophets of the army exposed to division. On one occasion, wishing to encamp upon a certain field, the prophets forbade it, with the assurance that the next day fire from heaven would descend to consume the harvests that covered it, and endanger the safety of the army. The next day, however, proved rainy, and the prophets found themselves exposed to the derision of those whom they had attempted to overrule. It became a proverb in the camp, that the prophecies of the priests and their fulfilment came as near together as fire and water. However Zisca and his soldiers might favor the pretended inspiration of some of their spiritual guides, no dreams, or impressions, or inspired fancies were allowed to prevent their assaults when they promised success, or induce the hazarding of a battle when good sense or military sagacity forbade it.

The alliance of the Bohemian cities on the basis of the articles of Prague, continued to extend. New accessions were continually made to this—which might now be called a national league. Chrudim, Mant, Polictzka, Leitomischel, Trautenau, and Konigshof joined it. Jaromirtz, which refused, was sacked, and many of its inhabitants were drowned or burned. Twenty-three priests fell victims to their

obstinacy in resisting the liberty of the communion
of the cup. Leitmeritz still held out against the
league. Zisca with his forces marched against it, but
the city refused to surrender to him. "Let them of
Prague come," said they, "and we will yield the
city up into their hands." Zisca chose to make
another assault, but it proved unsuccessful, and the
citizens had the satisfaction of capitulating to the
army of Prague, which hastened to receive their
surrender, and witness their oaths to maintain invio-
late the four articles.

Thus each day saw the hopes of Sigismund for
recovering the crown, becoming weaker and more
desperate. The castle of Wenzel still held out for
him in Prague; but it was now resolved that this
should be reduced. Zisca from Leitmeritz marched
to Prague, with this object in view. He built a fort
over against the city for the security of his own
soldiers, and from this he directed his attacks against
the castle. It surrendered after a resistance of fourteen days, and the last vestige of Sigismund's authority vanished from the capital of Bohemia.
Czenko, the governor, had now thrown off all reserve, and boldly united himself with the Calixtine
barons, with whom he was already agreed in religious
sentiment.

At this opportune moment, and after unprece-
dented successes against the enemy, the convention
of the states met at Czaslau, (July, 1421.) Representatives appeared in large numbers, not only from
every part of Bohemia, but also from Moravia. A
regency was appointed, of twenty members, taken

from the different orders of the nation. Zisca appeared in it, in the first rank of the nobles. It was resolved, with remarkable unanimity, that the four articles of Prague should be universally received; that they should be maintained and defended to the last extremity, to the risk of property and life. Some wished that to these, two others should be added—one, to the effect that Sigismund should be forever excluded from the throne; the other, that instead of a king, a commission should be appointed to discharge his duties. To these two, however, the Moravians objected. Much as they disliked Sigismund, they wished to leave the future policy of the kingdom open, to be modified by circumstances. They may, moreover, have been apprehensive—far more than the Bohemians—of the vengeance of the emperor upon such a step being taken. His ambassadors in fact appeared before the convention, and attempted by threats to overawe the body, and induce them to accept Sigismund as king. But it was all in vain.

The barons, however, were not content with a mere rejection of the demand. They replied by drawing up an apology and vindication, containing fourteen articles, in which they stated their reasons for solemnly refusing to Sigismund all allegiance.[1] They complain of the atrocious injuries, as well as slanderous calumnies of their enemies, the desolating and burning of their cities and villages, the inhuman and cruel massacres, not only of men, but of women and children, that had been perpetrated

[1] Guerre des Hus., i. 164.

by a foreign foe, and the loss and damage which
they had suffered from the invading army. They
then arraign the conduct of Sigismund for his complicity in the death of Huss ; for the various acts of
injustice from the council which he had sanctioned ;
for the publication of the crusade, his levying armies
against the kingdom, and studiously defaming it
abroad, in order to swell the league against it ; for
his acts at Breslau in burning a Calixtine, and putting many eminent citizens to death ; for the plunder
and devastation committed by his army ; for carrying off the crown of the kingdom, with its tables
and the treasures for the poor ; for giving away and
alienating the march of Brandenberg, which belonged to Bohemia ; for his slanders against the
barons of the kingdom, calling them all traitors, and
industriously circulating reports, far and near, prejudicial to the reputation of Bohemia, and tending to
its irreparable injury ; for his violation of the liberties and rights of the kingdom ; and his unjust exactions, cruelly enforced, to the ruin and desolation of
many cities.

On these grounds, they demand that reparation
be made, and that the freedom of their four articles
be granted them without reserve or limitation.

To these articles Sigismund attempted a reply,
but it made only a feeble impression. [1] It is amusing
to observe how the historian, or rather the carica-
turist of the Hussites, Cochleius, attempts to vindicate Sigismund from the charges of the barons.
He begins by assuming that the barons are all here-

[1] Guerre des Hus., i. 165.

tics; and, on the authority of Jerome, he defines the
heretic, in the language of scripture, as one in whose
mouth is no truth, whose heart is vain, whose throat
is an open sepulchre, and whose tongue is full of
deceit. He thence infers that the apology of the
barons, as the production of heretics, is false and vain,
and that Sigismund, whose faith and virtue have
been so highly praised, could not have been guilty
of the things laid to his charge. His carrying away
the crown and the archives of the kingdom, however, is defended on the plea of its necessity.

The convention had not yet dispersed, when news
arrived of an invasion on the borders of Silesia.
The barons at once made arrangements to repel the
enemy.   Czenko and Krussina—a strange alliance
of Horebite and Calixtine—marched against them.
The Silesians were awed by the opposing force, and
hastily retreated across the border.

Zisca, previous to this, had gone to Wodnian, near
Prachin.   Thence he marched to the siege of Raby.[1]
It was here that he met with the misfortune of the
loss of his other eye. He had mounted a tree in
order to inspect the entrenchments of the enemy,
when an arrow from the walls pierced it.   After he
had fully ascertained his danger, he consented to be
removed to Prague that he might have the aid of
the physicians of that city, in the hope that its sight
might possibly be restored. But his own impru-
dence and recklessness destroyed the last chance of
any such favorable result. The old hero was incura-
bly and hopelessly blind. Yet even now he could

---

[1] The date of this event is given by some authorities as March 15, 1421.

not forego his favorite employment. His friends
sought to retain him at Prague. But he withstood
all their entreaties. " Let me go," said he; " I have
blood yet to shed." A message from his army reached
him. It urgently pressed his return. The soldiers
would march under no other general. This determined the matter, and Zisca hastened to rejoin his army.

It was time for him to do it. The emperor had
made extensive though ill-advised preparations for another invasion of the kingdom. A large army from
Germany was to enter Bohemia from the west, while
he was at the same time to march against it from the
east. But his own dilatoriness defeated his plan.
The western army, soon after the time agreed upon
—the day of St. Bartholomew, destined to become
still more memorable in the annals of persecution—
crossed the Bohemian frontier and commenced the
siege of Sozium. But the resistance they met, together with their disappointment in hearing no tidings
of the emperor, disconcerted and disheartened them,
and leaving their work undone, they returned to Germany. Their immense force, estimated at 200,000
men, was dissolved and scattered.

The emperor at length appeared on the Bohemian
frontier toward the close of the year,[1] (Dec. 25,
1421.) Great efforts had been made to gather an
army capable of resisting him. It was agreed that
its officers should be appointed by the city of Prague.
But all would have been in vain probably, without
the aid of Zisca. The mere presence of the blind old
warrior was a terror to the foe.

[1] Æneas Sylvius, ch. xliv. Guerre des Hus., i. 172.

Sigismund with his powerful army was now approaching Prague. Several places had already been taken. Zisca, meanwhile, had been busy in suppressing all movements throughout Bohemia in favor of the emperor. At Pilsen, however, he was met with an obstinate resistance, and was forced to raise the siege and retreat before the foe, who had reassembled and resumed the offensive upon receiving intelligence of the emperor's invasion. Blind as he was, Zisca conducted a three days' retreat to Saatz in a most masterly manner. But already the emperor had collected his scattered forces, and was prepared to encircle, with his mighty host, the doomed city. Prague was alarmed, and summoned the blind old hero again to her aid. Zisca was received within her walls, almost with royal honors.[1]

Gathering his forces, he marched first to Kuttenberg, and then to Czaslau. But the citizens of Kuttenberg were ill-pleased with the visit of the Taborites. The occasion was not a favorable one. The invading army strengthened at once their fears and their orthodoxy. They saw for the first time the ceremonial, or rather the want of ceremonial, of Taborite worship. Scarcely had the soldiers entered the city, when they hasted to improve their privilege of the freedom of communion. With all their dusty clothing upon them, just as they were when they dismounted from their horses, they made their appearance in the sacred assembly. It seemed to the Kuttenbergers almost a sacrilege thus to hurry from their horses to the altar; and when they had wit-

---

[1] Guerre des Hus., i. 173.

nessed their communion with common bread, and the use of a tin or wooden cup for the wine, with the short prayer and simple words of consecration, they turned away in disgust. So strong was their aversion to such allies, so widely divergent was the practise of the Taborites in the communion from the old forms of the mass which the Kuttenbergers still retained, that scarcely had Zisca with his forces left the city, when they opened their gates to receive the army of the emperor.

Zisca strengthened the fortifications of Czaslau, and then returned to cope with the hostile army. Sigismund had already marched upon Humpoletz and Ludetz, when the antagonist forces approached each other, and the pickets of the two armies exchanged blows. At this critical moment the treason of the Kuttenbergers gave Sigismund the advantage. Putting their city in his rear to protect it, he prepared to confront Zisca. The Hussite general saw himself forced to retreat. The citizens of Prague, uncertain of the issue, fearful of incurring the vengeance of Sigismund, and encouraged by the example of Kuttenberg, began to drop away from Zisca's army. As the enemy approached, he fell back upon the hill Transkauk; and here it was that the emperor felt that he had his sure grasp upon his destined victim. He carefully spread out the wings of his army to enclose the Taborites. Night settled down in darkness over the scene, and the morning threatened to dawn upon a beleagured host, with no alternative but that of sure and hopeless defeat or unconditional surrender.

But the blind Zisca was not to be so easily caught.
He waited, indeed, another day, retaining his position
upon the hill, whence his enemies did not venture the
attempt to dislodge him; but on the second night his
plans were matured and ready for execution. Quietly
marshalling all his army, he led them, nearly without
loss, and with scarcely striking a blow, through the
camp of the enemy. The emperor saw himself again
defeated in his plans—completely outgeneralled by
an antagonist whom he regarded as already within
his toils.

Zisca marched first to Colin, thence to Giczin and
Turnau, recruiting his forces. Sigismund was not
prepared to attack him before he had recovered himself sufficiently to be able to turn and face his pur-
suer. He encamped on the banks of the Nebonid,
ready for battle. But Sigismund no longer thought
of attacking him. He withdrew to Moravia, laying
Kuttenberg—probably deeming its fidelity to him in
this time of his reverse utterly unreliable—in ashes.
Zisca followed him in his retreat. He overtook him
(Jan. 9, 1422) at Deutschbrod, where a fierce battle
was fought, which lasted for three hours. At length
victory declared in favor of the Taborites. The enemy fled, but their retreat proved more disastrous
than the battle-field. The crowd of fugitives was
such that, in attempting to cross the bridge of the
Sazanna, their progress was checked, and fifteen thousand cavalry, led by their general, Pipo of Florence,
attempted to cross the river on the ice.[1] But the
weight of men and horses proved too much for its

---

[1] Æneas Sylvius, ch. xliv.

strength to support. It gave way beneath them, and nearly all were drowned. Sigismund continued his retreat to Iglau. He left behind him seven standards, five hundred baggage-wagons, and an immense booty, which Zisca distributed to his soldiers.

Blind though he was, the Taborite general could not content himself with merely acting on the defensive. The loss of sight forced him to employ the eyes of others, and from their observations he formed his plans of attack or defence. His memory of localities was wonderful. His frequent campaigns had made him familiar with almost every part of Bohemia. The whole region was spread out before his mind's eye like a map, and his measures were taken with the utmost wisdom and precaution. In battle, he took his stand upon a baggage-wagon, near the standard, and, by the eyes of others, closely watched each stage of the conflict, and the necessities of his position. Nothing escaped him. He discerned as if by instinct, and by a military genius for which the age in which he lived could not furnish a parallel or a rival, the strong and the weak points of each army, and the measures by which they might be turned to his own advantage.

As a general, friends and enemies vie with one another in elevating him to the first rank. Scarce any history of Hebrews, Greeks, or Latins," says Cochleius,[1] "brings before us any leader of armies of such capacity as Zisca was." An undisciplined peasantry were trained by him to withstand and repel the shock of imperial cavalry. A restless

[1] Cochleius, p. 206.

energy in his iron frame defied fatigue, and scorned
to rest, and into his troops he infused his own activity
and daring.   But prudent sagacity supplied the
means of energy and courage, and new expedients
were devised as necessity required, till his soldiers
attained a perfect confidence in the almost magic
skill and enterprise of their leader.   Many of his
most signal and successful battles were fought after
he had become entirely blind; and never, till the
breath left his body, did the terror of his name cease
to make his foes tremble.

Returning from the pursuit of Sigismund, he found
some of his partisans still active in Bohemia.   The
Bishop of Leitomischel, the bitter enemy of Huss and
Jerome at Constance, and the persecutor of the Calixtines, now appears again upon the stage.[1]   He had
been promoted to the bishopric of Olmutz, and on
Conrad's secession to the Calixtines he was elevated
to the vacant archbishopric.   Sigismund had not a
more faithful and daring ally, nor the Bohemians a
more bitter or dangerous foe.   At the moment of
the threatened invasion, with a sword for his crosier
and an armed band for his flock, he attempted to
promote at once the cause of the emperor and his
own by violent methods.   He had deservedly earned
the epithet of "The Iron Bishop."   From the altar where
he celebrated mass, he would haste to the camp,
mount on horseback, with his helmet on his head
and his body cased in armor, and sink the church-
man in the warrior, the bishop in the general.   His
rage against the Hussites was almost fiendish.   He

[1] Guerre des Hus., i. 175.

boasted of the number he had slain with his own hand. But the defeat of Sigismund was the prelude to his own. His army was cut to pieces in the neighborhood of Broda, and completely annihilated. Zisca, assuming the authority which his victories assured him, seated upon the ruins of the fortress, and under the captured standards, knighted the bravest of his soldiers, and distributed among them an immense booty.

Not content with thus prostrating the enemy in Bohemia, Zisca extended his arms into Moravia. He had already reached the borders of the Austrian territory, when he was summoned back to Prague. Leaving behind him his ablest general, Procopius Magnus, or Rasus as he was called, to prosecute the war, he returned with a portion of his army into Bohemia.

Events at Prague had assumed, suddenly, an ominous aspect. On the refusal of the king of Poland to accept the crown, it had been offered to Withold, Grand Duke of Lithuania.[1] He also had declined to accept it, but had recommended to the Bohemian barons his near relative, Sigismund Corybut. Accompanying him to Prague, they had both sealed their Calixtine faith by partaking of the communion of the cup. But at this juncture, many of the nobility, disappointed, perhaps gladly, by the king of Poland's declinature of the crown, had fallen back upon their old preference for Sigismund. Doubtless they imagined that successive defeats had made him wiser, while freedom from foreign invasion allowed the antagonistic elements of the Taborites and Calixtines again to show themselves.

[1] Fleury, xxvi. 484.

At Prague the Calixtine party had recovered their supremacy, and had elected magistrates who favored their views. The old hostility against the Taborites was revived. They cited before them the bold Premonstrant monk, John, whom they accused of tyranny and sanguinary acts.[1] The monk obeyed the summons. With nine of his companions he presented himself at the council-house. He was at once arrested, and the whole number were summarily tried and executed. It was attempted to keep the deed secret; but the blood of the victims flowing out into the street, told their friends of their sad fate. This was the signal for vengeance. Jacobel, whom we now find on the side of the Taborites, encouraged the multitude. He held up to their view the head of the monk, whom he called a martyr. In their rage, the Taborites assaulted and massacred the magistrates who had ordered the execution. The council-house was taken, and the library destroyed.[2]

This event was the signal for hostilities to recommence. The presence of Corybut had no effect to repress passion or restore order. Although a Calixtine, there was a strong party opposed to him. When the coronation was to take place, it was found impossible to obtain the regalia. Some of these Sigismund had carried away with him. But for this, it is possible, as Cochleius suggests, that Sigismund would never have recovered his throne. At first Zisca favored the cause of Corybut. He urged the people generally to accept him as king. But the favorable moment had now passed. The nation was divided

---

[1] Guerre des Hus., i. 169.   [2] Æneas Sylvius, ch. xliv.

into fierce parties, embittered by prejudice and mutual aggressions. The old church party began again to raise its head,—and these at one extreme, and the Taborites at the other, were irreconcilably opposed to Corybut. It was in vain that Zisca, here differing from the Taborites, espoused his cause.

The diet that was held at Prague toward the close of the year (Nov., 1421) to determine the question in regard to the election of a king, was much divided. Zisca urged harmony, and the exercise of a kindly and forbearing spirit. "Forgive one another," said he, " that you may unite in saying ' Our Father.' " On the other hand, he did not fail to reprove the violence of the Taborites. He exhorted them to " honor the elders, and deal justly, not with violence, so that God may be with us." But his counsels and persuasions were vain. There was an utter lack of unanimity. Corybut, for the present at least, despaired of the election, and prepared to leave Prague.

It was not such words as those of Zisca that would heal the division. The vengeance of the Taborites for the murder of the Premonstrant monk had been signal, and had embittered their foes. They had unwittingly given the latter a great advantage. In their excitement the mob had proceeded to great lengths. They had plundered the library of the university, and destroyed the records of the council-house. They had sacked the houses of the councillors, and had even assaulted the dwellings of the Jews.

As if this provocation was not enough, the citizens of Prague were indignant and took offence at the

tone in which Zisca had addressed them. They complained of it as too authoritative. They disliked him
the more that, while on many points he differed from
the Taborites, he was still their general, and lent to
them the strength and sanction of his name. Against
him therefore their animosity was now directed.

But Zisca was not a man to be trampled upon by
those whom he had so often protected from invasion.
Their insults could not be directed against him with
impunity. He saw, moreover, that unless the present
movement in favor of Sigismund was checked, Bohemia would be subjected to his control, and not
only the Taborites, but the Calixtines would be given
over to the counsels of such men as the Bishop of
Leitomischel, who were living embodiments of the
spirit of the crusade. Even Corybut, favoring the
Calixtines as the stronger party, and the one from
whom he had the most to expect, was, however unwittingly, playing into the emperor's hands. Zisca
withdrew from Prague, brooding over his plans of
vengeance, which he was not slow to execute against
those barons whose counsels were betraying the
freedom and the interests of their country. He attacked their partisans and ravaged their estates.

The Calixtines promptly armed to repel his assaults,[1] and endeavored to crush him whom they
now regarded as an open enemy. All their former
jealousies were revived and embittered. He stood
in the way of their coming to terms with Sigismund
—terms which, however ignominious, they were willing to accept. Czenko of Wartemberg, former gov-

ernor of the castle, gathered an army, largely composed of the nobility, and marched against Zisca. But the Taborite general was victorious, and the Calixtines were severely beaten. Distributing the booty among his soldiers, Zisca with only three days' delay pushed on to Kozagedy, which he took by storm. Terror preceded him, and devastation marked his track. He mercilessly cut down all that opposed him, and laid castle and fortress, as well as all that offered resistance, in ashes.

But his incessant activity and unwearied energy were too much for his soldiers. When he ordered a night march upon Koniggratz, they began to complain. "Zisca," said they, "is blind, but we are not. We cannot fight like him in the dark." They threatened to halt upon their march, and the plans of their general against Koniggratz were in danger of being defeated. Zisca reasoned with them. He endeavored to overcome their reluctance to follow him. Himself a Calixtine in sentiment, though not in sympathy, his arguments were the more forcible. "It is for your sake," said he, "that I fight. It is no concern of mine, personally. I could make peace for myself if I chose. All is for your good."

Soothing their minds with these reasonings, he at once changed his course of remark, and surprised them by one of those strokes of policy which showed the inexhaustible resources of his mind. "Come, now," he added, "listen to counsel. In what neighborhood are we now?" "Between the hills Podmokly and Cziniswes," was the reply. Zisca, who in a moment apprehended the position of the army, was

ready with an expedient to meet their objection of
the darkness of the night. " Go with all dispatch,"
said he, " and light up the village of Miestecz, so that
we may see our way." The command was obeyed,
and the conflagration of that village lighted their
march to the walls of Koniggratz. The city fell into
Zisca's hands, with scarce the show of resistance. A
friendly party within aided the victors." [1]

But the Calixtines of Prague felt the loss of the
place too severely not to make strenuous efforts for
its recovery. Borzek, a former governor of Prague,
led out an army to attack Zisca and regain Koniggratz. The Taborite general did not decline the
offered battle. He marched out to meet the foe, and
a terrible conflict ensued. The Calixtines suffered a
complete and annihilating defeat.

The course of events had wrought a change in
Zisca's policy. Driven to desperation by the Calixtines, he now conformed to the Taborite ceremonial.
The priests before him no longer said mass in their
robes, according to the rites of the old church. He
had been willing and even anxious before, that
former differences between Calixtine and Taborite
should be compromised by uniting upon Corybut as
king. But this expedient failed to secure unanimity,
and Corybut, in throwing himself into the arms of
the Calixtines, had alienated himself more than ever
from the Taborites. Zisca now treated him as an
enemy. He had, in fact, introduced foreign troops
to the aid of the army of Prague, and stood ready
to lead them against the Taborites. At this aspect

[1] Guerre des Hus., i. 195.

of things Zisca felt the necessity of strengthening his army. Procopius, whom he had left behind him when summoned to meet the diet at Prague, and who had followed the enemy across the frontier, was probably recalled; at least he now rejoined Zisca with his forces (May, 1422.)

Borzek, on his defeat, in which he was badly wounded, withdrew to his castle. Zisca returned to Koniggratz, and, destroying its fortifications that it might be defenceless in case it was seized by the enemy, marched to Czaslau. Here he stengthened himself, and put the place in a state of defence against the new army which was marching against him from Prague. One of his generals, Lupak, with the force under his command, was cut off by the enemy. Zisca upon this seems to have withdrawn from Czaslau, willing probably to have it stand a siege and delay the foe, while he hastened to Moravia, [1] where the Archduke Albert, nephew of Sigismund, was recovering the cities which Procopius had taken. The archduke laid claim to Moravia as a gift from the emperor, and exerted all his energies to drive out the Hussites and subject it to his own dominion. He was engaged in beleaguering Suntenberg, when Procopius was dispatched to relieve it. At the news of the approach of Zisca's army, (Aug. 12, 1422,) the archduke consulted his safety by a hasty retreat. He was not anxious even to face the terrible army of the blind old Taborite general.

Zisca, taking summary vengeance upon all parties that had shown any inclination to favor the arch-

---

[1] Guerre des Hus., i. 196.

duke, followed him in his retreat. He advanced
into Austria as far as Stokerau, on the Danube, and
only four leagues from Vienna. The archduke, however, had escaped him, and lay upon the opposite
bank. Zisca turned aside for the siege of Kremsen,
when the army from Prague, which had followed on
his track, came up with him. Procopius promptly
marched to his relief; and the army of Prague, led
by John—possibly the archbishop—was foiled. Zisca,
secure for the present from the archduke, whom
he left to be looked after by his general Procopius,
returned to Bohemia.

Never had a harder task than the present one been
confided even to his hands. The Calixtines and the
imperialists were virtually in league together against
him. The one within, and the other without the
kingdom, attempted to crush him as the common
enemy of both. But the spirit of the blind hero
breathed defiance, and his genius and skill were
equal to the emergency. With Procopius left behind him to hold the foreign enemy in check, he
now turned to suppress internal hostilities. At Cka-
litz, in the neighborhood of Koniggratz, he fell in
with a body of troops from Prague, which he cut to
pieces and dispersed. Arnau, however, nine miles
north of Koniggratz, repulsed his assault, (Jan. 6,
1423.) The castle of Mlazowicza was less fortunate.
It fell into his hands, and he signalized his vengeance
by hewing its commander in pieces. For several
months he continued his ravages by flying marches,
increasing as much as possible the strength of his
army. Klattau was taken by storm; but when

Zisca reached Saatz, his whole force consisted of only 7,000 foot and 500 horse. Yet with this force he directed his marshal, John Bzdinka, to march in the direction of Czaslau and Prague. At Kostelez he fell in with the Calixtine army, under the command of Czenko. The Elbe now threatened to cut off all opportunity of retreat, and Czenko's army was too strong to be safely withstood. The Taborites, however, discovered a ford by which they were enabled to cross the Elbe, and for three days the army of Czenko followed in close pursuit. Zisca was overtaken near Kuttenberg, and finding the ground favorable, no longer declined battle. Corybut, who now made common cause with the Calixtine army of Prague, arrived with a reinforcement, and Zisca, who had animated his soldiers by a speech, in which he pointed them to the ruins of Kuttenberg as an illustration of imperial mercy, saw the opportunity of gaining a decisive victory unexpectedly snatched from his grasp. Feigning an apprehension of defeat, he slowly retreated, till by his manœuvres he had drawn the enemy into a position in which he could safely engage.

Again victorious, Zisca now commenced his march directly for Prague, which he reached on Sept. 11, (1423.) He had now thrice defeated the most powerful armies which his enemies at Prague could marshal, and the intelligence of his approach filled them with consternation.[1] They determined, however, to resist his attack, and closing the gates against him, forced him to the necessity of storming the

[1] Guerre des Hus., i. 202.

city. But here his soldiers began to hesitate and
murmur. They had too often fought to defend those
walls which they were now to assault, not to shrink
from an act, however necessary in their circumstances, which only the genius and the vengeance of
Zisca could have conceived and dared. Though
accustomed to blood, and hardened to all the atrocities of the battle-field, their hearts were affected,
and complaints were heard when Zisca proceeded
with his measures for storming the city.

But the blind old warrior could speak as well as
fight, and could marshal and guide the passions of
men with a skill equal to that with which he conducted armies. Standing on a cask, where he might be
seen of those whom he no longer saw, he harangued
his troops, and his powerful voice at once kindled
all hearts by its familiar yet stirring tones.[1] " Companions," said he, " why do you murmur ? I am not
your enemy, but your general. It is by me that you
have gained so many victories—by me that you have
won fame and wealth. And yet, for you I have
lost my sight, I am condemned to ceaseless darkness.
. . . For all my labors, what is my reward ? Nothing but a name ! It is then for you that I have
acted ; that I have conquered. It is not my own
interest that arms me against this city. It is not the
blood of a blind old man that it thirsts after, but it
dreads your intrepid hearts and your invincible arms.
When they shall have taken me in their nets, they
will lay snares for you, from which you will scarcely
escape. Let us therefore take Prague. Let us crush

[1] Guerre des Hus., i. 203.

the sedition before Sigismund is informed of it. A
few men, well united, will do more against the emperor than a vast multitude divided. Let no person
therefore accuse me, for I act in your interest. Now
make your choice. Will you have peace? Take
care that it does not cover some ambush! Will you
have war? Here I am!"

These words had the desired effect. There was
no more murmuring. The Taborites invested the
city, and suffered no one to issue forth from the
gates. Every thing was ready for the assault, but
Zisca delayed his order to storm the city. Perhaps
he had ever hoped, and still believed, that he would
be spared the terrible necessity. If he had laid his
plans to subdue the city by terror, he was not disappointed. The citizens had no wish to engage in conflict with the man who rarely lost a battle—never
succumbed under defeat—never abandoned his purpose. They could not bear to imagine what results
might follow the storming of the city, or the revival
within it of the spirit of the Premonstrant monk, a
spirit suppressed and almost stifled, but still ready to
show itself, if occasion permitted, as fierce and as terrible as ever. They met to deliberate, and determined
to send a deputation to Zisca to induce him to relent.

At the head of the deputation was John of Rokyzan, a Calixtine preacher of great credit and ability,
subsequently archbishop, who from the obscurity and
poverty of his birth had raised himself by his talents
to a high position. His representations were effectual
with Zisca, who in all probability was only too willing to listen to counsels which might at once spare

his own honor and the execution of his terrible
threat. To the entreaties of the deputation he lent
a favorable ear, and the terms of the treaty of peace
were at once settled. It was signed in the camp;
and, as a monument of the alliance, and from regard
for ancient customs, a pile of stones was raised upon
the spot, as if to intimate that the party which
should violate its provisions should perish beneath
the stones that formed the rude altar. Zisca then
made a public entry into Prague, where he was received with the greatest honors, and was allowed to
exercise a paramount authority.

The emperor's hopes, which he had based upon
the divisions of the Bohemian nation, were baffled
by the truce which restored to Zisca the control of
the kingdom. He saw that arms and counsels were
alike futile to regain it, while he had such a foe to
watch and counterwork his designs. He sought
therefore to win him over by the most liberal promises. "For himself," he said, "it was sufficient
that he should merely be *proclaimed* king of Bohemia. To Zisca should be left the government of the
kingdom." To all these honors Sigismund joined
the promise to Zisca of immense wealth.[1]

This was to the emperor a most humiliating pos-
ture of affairs. After all his efforts, supported by
the bull of the pope and successive crusading armies, he saw himself reduced to the ignominy of
offering to accept the aid and reward the valor of
the man who, in defence of what had been branded
as heresy, had demolished and annihilated all his

Guer. des Hus., i. 205.   Fleury, xxvi. 521.   Also, Cochleius, liv. v.

armies. Æneas Sylvius grows indignant in narra-
ting a proceeding which he condemns as a disgrace to
the emperor, and a stain upon his royal name.[1] That
a man whom all Christendom venerated, and of
whom heathen nations stood in awe—the son of an
emperor, and an emperor himself—in the vigor of his
years, should be reduced to treat upon such terms
with " a man hardly noble by birth, old, blind, heretical, sacrilegious, with audacity for any enormity;"
that he should offer him the government of the
kingdom, the command of its armies, and an immense
yearly revenue, in order to secure his alliance and
aid ; all this was indeed, in the eyes of the Roman
historian, as disgraceful as it was humiliating.   If
Huss had ever longed for revenge upon his murderers, if he had wished them an earthly retribution for
their crime, he could not have imagined anything
more bitter as a dreg in their cup, than that they
should see their chosen champion, supported by the
papal bull and immense armies, forced to bend the knee
to a man who was regarded at once as a rebel and a
heretic, and whose very blindness made the homage
paid him more bitterly if not ludicrously humiliating.

But the terms proposed were never executed.
We do not even know how they were regarded by
Zisca.   It is more than possible that he thought
favorably of them.   Specious pretexts were not
wanting for their acceptance.   He might have been
king himself in all but name, and none better than
he united a knowledge of the people with a capacity
to govern them.

---

[1] Æneas Sylvius, ch. xlvi.

But at this culminating point of Zisca's fortunes death overtook him. He lived to foil the purposes of Sigismund, and died at the moment when his death was in some respects another defeat to blast his hopes. Had he been longer spared to his country, it is reasonable to suppose that the nation would have been harmonized, if that were possible, and that under his government national prosperity and freedom of worship would have gone hand in hand. The plague, however, which was at the time ravaging Bohemia, numbered him among its victims. He died Oct. 11, 1424, while engaged in the siege of a small town on the Moravian border. Perhaps, with a foresight of the hostility that might hunt out his bones and drag them like Wickliffe's from their grave, he ordered his soldiers to abandon his body to the birds of prey, and to have his skin made into a drum, the mere sound of which would make their enemies tremble.[1]

The command of Zisca was not, however, obeyed. His body was interred with honors in the cathedral church at Czaslau, and his iron mace was suspended near his tomb. Upon his monument was placed, according to Theobald, in his history of the Hussite wars, the following inscription: "Here lies John Zisca, inferior to no other general in military science, the rigorous punisher of the pride and avarice of the priesthood, and the zealous defender of his country. What the blind Appius Claudius did for the Romans by his counsel, and Curius Camillus by his actions, I accomplished for the Bohemians. I never

---

[1] Fleury, xxvi. 522.   Guer. des Hus., i. 206.

failed fortune, nor she me; and although blind, I always perceived what ought to be done. I have fought eleven times with standards displayed, and I have always conquered. I was unceasingly seen defending the cause of the unfortunate and the poor, against sensual and bloated priests, and therefore did God sustain me. If their hatred did not oppose it, I should be reckoned among the most illustrious; and yet, in spite of the pope, my bones repose in this holy place."

In the biography of Zisca published at Prague,[1] another epitaph is given, more in keeping with the character of the man, and which may have been inscribed after the former was defaced. "Here rests John Zisca, the leader of oppressed freedom in the name and for the name of God." We are told, moreover, that not far from his tomb was engraved the inscription—"Huss, here reposes John Zisca, thy avenger; and the emperor himself has quailed before him."

Zisca's person was of middle stature, of a strong and muscular frame, especially in the shoulders and chest. His head was large, round, and closely shaven. His nose was aquiline, and his long moustaches added to the ferocity of a countenance that spoke out, in its bold and eagle eye, the penetration and the energy of the man. His complexion was dark and bilious, bespeaking his capacity for long and patient endurance; and his forehead presented that indenture, falling perpendicularly down it, which has been remarked in several famous war-

[1] Edition of 1789.

riors—and has in consequence been called the martial line.[1]

His outward aspect was no unworthy index of the spirit within. In all that pertained to war or strategy, Zisca was the man of his age, and it is even doubtful whether the world has ever presented any leaders of armies who might not be honored by being accounted rivals of Zisca in ability. With a kingdom rent by dissensions, and the weaker and less powerful class only on his side, he had to repel successive assaults from armies immensely superior, and led by able generals. He had to stand—single-handed as it were—against the hosts of Christendom animated by the spirit of religious bigotry, and breathing exterminating vengeance against all that bore the name of Huss, or expressed sympathy for him. But he met the tide successfully; he stemmed it and turned it back. In the most desperate circumstances, he never quailed or wavered. Unforeseen and overwhelming difficulties only brought out the inexhaustible resources of his genius and sagacity, and he never offered to capitulate, but always waited to accept terms of surrender from the foe. He did not make his suit to Prague, but Prague made its suit to him. He did not solicit the emperor's alliance; the emperor, however, solicited his. The tactics, equipage, and defences of his army, as well as their unshrinking courage and resolute energy, betrayed the impress, and manifested at once the sagacity and the inspiring power of Zisca's genius. His enemies might condemn him as a heretic. They

[1] Bonnechose.

might blacken his memory with charges of crimes that make us shudder, but his ability as a general, and his unapproachable mastery in the art of conducting battles and managing armies, were never questioned.

What his real character was as a man, is somewhat more doubtful. His enemies have drawn his portrait; and no friendly hand, unless that which inscribed his epitaph, has rescued it from their caricature. It is evident that his soul glowed with the deepest resentment and indignation at the wrongs of Huss, and the injustice of the council that ordered his execution. He saw a whole nation virtually condemned unheard, and hemmed around by a league of Christendom, marshalled by a papal crusade to carry out the sentence. He felt himself called to be an avenger of the wronged, and he fulfilled his mission with an inexorable severity. No tears flowed from his blind eyes. Pity was in his view a weakness, of which he was rarely known to be guilty. His system of army discipline was inflexibly rigid, and it extended to all the acts and circumstances of a state of war. It was truly a military code, and every infraction was punished with death.

Zisca was undoubtedly ambitious, as he was cruel, but grosser vices were foreign to his character. He distributed the plunder to the army, never anxious to retain it himself. Every soldier was a brother, and that was the epithet which he employed in his familiar intercourse with his army. He was moreover a Bohemian in heart and soul. He loved his country. He resented her wrongs, and burned to avenge her insulted honor. With too sound a mind to be carried away by fanaticism, he knew how to employ the fanaticism of others; and yet, in his own way he was scrupulously devout and religious. In spite of all his cruelty and his ambition, we must account him a great and an honest man, sincere in his convictions as he was terrible in his vengeance.

CHAPTER XVII.

THE LAST CRUSADE. DEFEAT OF THE IMPERIALISTS.

Oct. 11, 1424—Jan., 1432.

The success of the Taborites was largely due to the impolitic and cruel measures of the papal party. At the very time when Zisca was most closely pressed by the imperialists, he found a most effective, although involuntary, ally in an unexpected quarter. In its thirty-ninth session, the council of Constance had decreed that another council should be convoked, to prosecute still further the reform which it assumed to have initiated. It was to be convoked within the space of six years from the close of its own sessions.

The council thus decreed, was convoked by a bull of Martin V., and its opening session was held at Pavia early in May, 1423. But the thin attendance, and the dread of the plague, which had commenced its ravages in the city, led to its transfer to Sienna, whither the members were directed to repair by the

(510)

first of November of the same year. The first session was held upon the 25th, and the council proceeded to fulminate the most severe decrees against
the followers of Wickliffe and Huss. Temporal
princes were enjoined to drive them out of their dominions; spiritual rewards were promised to such as
should inform against them, or give them over into
the hands of the inquisitors. It was ordained, moreover, that the decree granting indulgences should be
read yearly to the people, in an audible voice. on the
first and fourth Sundays of Lent, and on several of
the festivals of the church. All intercourse with the
condemned heretics was forbidden. Such as furnished them with food, spices, salt, or weapons of
war, were to be subjected to severe penalties.[1] Secular princes were to spare no effort for their complete
extermination.

No measure could have been more unwise than
this of the council. It could not fail to strengthen
the prejudice, and exasperate anew the feelings of
the Bohemians against the papal party. Undoubtedly it strengthened the cause it was meant to crush,
and deferred for years the hope of compromise.

The death of Zisca left the Taborites without an
acknowledged leader. Some of them—to indicate
their deep sense of the loss which they had sustained
—called themselves, *The Orphans.* Zisca had been
a father to them, and his death was bewailed with
an unaffected grief. Others were absorbed by the
Horebites, while others still chose to retain their old
name.[2]

---

[1] Richerius, iii. 279, 282.   [2] Fleury, xxvi. 523.

Among the ablest generals who survived Zisca, were Procopius Magnus (or Rasus, for he had originally been a monk[1]) and Procopius Parvus, the former of whom had been thoroughly trained in Zisca's school, and had eminently justified the confidence which the latter reposed in his ability. The course of events soon elevated him to the position of virtual, if not acknowledged, leader of the party. But the death of Zisca had been equivalent to a sore defeat. It was impossible that some degree of disorganization should not follow upon the loss of a leader of such preëminence. Civil disorders again prevailed. Sigismund and Martin V. were not inattentive observers of events, and with renewed hope, determined to avail themselves of this favorable moment for the execution of their long-cherished but oft defeated designs. A renewal of the crusade was preached at the instigation of the pope, and an army 100,000 imperialists was gathered under the invading banners. They marched to the relief of the town of Ausch which had been besieged by the Hussites, but were repulsed with a severe loss of from nine to twelve thousand men. The battle was fought June 15, 1426, and the intelligence was speedily carried to Nuremberg, where a diet had been assembled, and where another invasion of Bohemia had been resolved upon, at the instigation of the papal legate, Pontanus Orsini. But the terror caused by this defeat was such, that all measures for executing this resolve of the diet were at once stayed.

A year was suffered to pass before the electoral and

[1] Life of Procopius. Prague, 1789.

other princes could unite on any further measures. A diet was then held at Frankfort, at which it was unanimously resolved that four distinct armies should be assembled for the invasion of Bohemia. Every soldier was required to confess and hear mass once a week. Nothing was neglected to secure, by ritual devotion, the divine favor. The Cardinal of Winchester assumed the chief command. Acting under the special directions of the pope, and authorized to use at discretion the spiritual or the temporal sword,[1] he urged forward the preparations for a decisive campaign. A numerous army was gathered, a portion of which proceeded to the siege of Miess, a small town on the western borders of Bohemia, in the circle of Pilsen.

Intelligence of the invasion soon reached the Taborites. All internal dissensions were immediately at an end. They marched with the utmost promptitude to the relief of the beleaguered city. Scarcely was the German army aware of their approach, when they appeared within sight of the walls. A panic terror seized the imperial host. Without waiting to meet a foe which their fears magnified, they broke and fled in confusion. Their terror was infectious. The next division of the imperial army was thrown into hopeless disorder, and the iron flails of the Horebites did fearful execution upon the broken ranks of the invaders. An immense booty, composed of almost every description of military stores, was the reward of Bohemian valor.[2]

The princes of the empire had learned a lesson

---

[1] Fleury, xxvi. 551.   [2] Æneas Sylvius, ch. xl.

which was not soon forgotten. Several years passed before the attempt to subdue Bohemia was renewed. The removal, however, of external danger, again allowed scope for internal dissension. The Calixtines and Taborites were soon at variance. No one showed himself more anxious to conciliate the opposing parties, and restore peace to the kingdom, than Procopius Magnus. By his able generalship and terrible victories, he had acquired a fame second only to that of Zisca. But he was less ambitious of military distinction than anxious to secure civil peace and order. As occasion required, he appeared by turns the theologian, the negotiator, the general.

At the commencement of the year 1428, a convention was held at Beraun to see what could be done toward a general pacification of the nation. The Taborites, Orphans, and Calixtines from Prague were present. But there was no possibility of bringing the different parties to stand upon a common platform. Procopius and his Taborites contended that sacerdotal habits were not necessary to the proper solemnization of the eucharist, and that there was no need of elevating or adoring the host. The Calixtine view of the seven sacraments was rejected by those whom he represented, while differences were also developed in regard to the doctrines of free-will, justification, and predestination.[1]

The convention broke up without accomplishing anything. Procopius, somewhat provoked at the course of the Calixtines, withdrew to Raudnitz, there to meet and welcome the Taborite Smirckzic, who

---

[1] Guerre des Hus., i. 267.

had been imprisoned at Prague for sedition, but who had managed to escape. The Orphans of Kuttenberg planned and executed an invasion of Silesia, marking their way by ravaged villages and desolated monasteries. At Nissa they were arrested by an obstinate resistance; and, even when Procopius had marched to their relief, were forced to retreat with loss. This was only the earnest of a more serious defeat suffered by the Taborites and Orphans at Brünn, in Moravia.

The imperialists prudently declined to pursue their advantage. They did not wish to confront men who might be goaded to desperate courage by another assault. The Taborites were suffered to withdraw to Austria, and the Orphans to Bohemia. They first extended their ravages to Cornenburg and Vienna; but, apprehensive of an attack from Hungary, withdrew to Tabor. The fortified town of Bechin had meanwhile begun to act upon the offensive. Procopius took it, after a siege of four months, and garrisoned it with Taborites.

The Orphans, at the same time, prosecuted the siege of Lichtenberg. In want of food, they marched into Silesia, leaving but a small portion of their forces behind them. The besieged did not fail to improve the occasion to make a sortie. A partial success encouraged them in their hopes of a successful resistance, but in December (1428) they were forced to surrender.

Assisted by a junction with a portion of the Taborites, the Orphans now executed their plan of a new invasion of Silesia. Every thing was put to fire or sword. Several of the nobility who offered resistance were slain. After a bloody conflict the Silesians were completely routed, and left to the Bohemians their wagons and baggage. The severity of the winter arrested the progress of the invaders, and they returned to Bohemia.

The emperor had been no inattentive spectator of what was taking place. While the different parties were vainly seeking a common basis of conciliation, he again proposed, by a deputation—which at Kutten-burg met the citizens of Prague, the Orphans, and the Taborites—that the Bohemians should accept him as king. He urged his rights to the kingdom, and seemed to be willing to make some concessions. But the Bohemians could not trust him. They replied, that Sigismund, by the effusion of blood which he had occasioned, and by his complicity in the death of Huss and Jerome, as well as in the crusades to the dishonor of the nation, had forfeited all right to the kingdom, since his whole conduct showed that he had sworn its destruction.

Procopius, who was still at Bechin, invited the ambassadors to visit him at Tabor. It is more than possible that he hoped to obtain for himself the same conditions which had been offered by the emperor to Zisca, and thus close the war with honor to himself, and restore peace and security to a desolated land. The ambassadors furnished him a safe-conduct, that he might visit Sigismund and confer with him in person. He did so, but the emperor spurned the terms which Procopius was disposed to offer; and the latter, irritated by such treatment, returned to Tabor "meditating vengeance."

The motives of Sigismund it is not difficult to surmise. Events throughout Bohemia, and especially
at Prague, showed that the division between the two
parties of the Bohemians was bitter and irreconcila-
ble. Early in the year (Jan. 30, 1429) the citizens
of Old and New Prague had come to an open rupture. Each party chose itself leaders, and the city
was for the whole day a scene of desperate and
deadly conflict. A truce for a few days was effected,
which was subsequently extended till the 25th of
July, when the states of the kingdom met at Prague,
to effect, if possible, a general pacification. Procopius
was present at the assembly. He proposed to receive
Sigismund as king, provided that he, with his Hungarian subjects, would receive and follow the Holy
Scripture, commune under both kinds, and grant such
requests as they should see fit to make.

These terms were laid before the diet which soon
met at Presburg. Procopius was at the head of the
Bohemian deputation, which consisted of several
nobles and Calixtines from Old Prague. For eight
days the deliberations were continued, without attain-
ing any satisfactory result. At length, after consulting with parties at Prague, it was determined to accept Sigismund as king. Deputies from the different
orders were named, to go and inform Sigismund of
the conclusion which had been reached. But the
Orphans boldly opposed the measure. "A free people,"
they said, "needed no king." This was the signal for
the recommencement of hostilities. At Prague, and
throughout Bohemia, the civil strife was immediately
renewed.

But the refusal of Sigismund to accept the terms offered by the Bohemians, had the effect of producing a conciliatory spirit between the opposing parties. Glorying in his orthodoxy as the patron of the church, he rejected alike the articles of the Calixtines and the Taborites. It was now quite evident that the acceptance of Sigismund by the nation would be the signal for the commencement of a bitter persecution against all who refused to return to the communion of the Roman church. Under the direction and by the management of Procopius, a plan of conciliation between the opposing parties of Calixtines and Taborites was agreed upon. An enormous fine was the penalty of infringing it; and Procopius, the principal author of this compact, was elected generalissimo.

Conscious of the difficulties of his position, aware of the necessity of still inspiring his foes with terror, and sagacious enough to perceive that the best security for internal peace was the employment abroad of an army accustomed to action, Procopius resolved to seize the occasion for punishing the presumption of the Misnians, from whose attacks the Bohemians had often suffered. "It is the moment to act," said he; "the hour of great things has arrived."[1] The words were greeted with loud acclamation. Procopius led forth his army, crossed the Elbe, and fell on Misnia, Saxony, Brandenburg, Bavaria, and Austria. Dreadful ravages marked his progress. Churches and monasteries were destroyed. Many towns were reduced to ashes, and their defenders perished with them. Over the smoking ruins the conquerors

[1] Guerre des Hus., i. 274.

shouted, "Behold the funeral obsequies of John Huss!"

Returning from this campaign, the Taborites distributed themselves into several bands in different places, adopting names according to their fancy. Some were known as *Collectors,* some as *Small-Caps,*[1] some as *Little Cousins,* others as *Wolf-bands.* The winter was no sooner passed than they were ready (1430) again to unite for a new campaign. With 20,000 cavalry, 30,000 infantry, and 3,000 chariots, and with Procopius the Great and other able generals at their head, they again renewed their invasion of Misnia. Continuing their march to Dresden, they left behind them, desolated or reduced to ashes, Kolditz, Mogeln, Dablen, Godelberg, and more than a hundred towns and villages. The Elector of Brandenberg vainly attempted to arrest their progress. John of Pollentz met with no better success. Several of the neighboring princes, impelled by a common apprehension lest their own turn for invasion should at last come, prepared to offer a united resistance; but divisions of feeling and opinion paralyzed their energies, and the Bohemians were left almost unmolested. In the region of Grim, Colditz, and Altemburg, the invaders successively spread their ravages. At Leipsig the news of their approach produced great apprehension. Verden, Reichembac, Averbach, and Olsnisch were laid in ashes. Germany took the alarm, and began to rouse itself to a sense of the necessity of measures to resist the terrible invaders. City after city had been forced to purchase immunity

---

[1] Petit chapeaus.   L'Enfant.

by pecuniary bribes. The Bishop of Bamberg ransomed the place by the payment of 9,000 golden ducats. Nuremberg paid a still larger sum.

The policy of Martin V. toward the Hussites was summed up in one word—a crusade. For twelve years this had been his uniform reply, when pressed for a solution of the Bohemian question. He exhorted the emperor and kings and princes to unite, and crush out forever the dangerous heresy. To the king of Poland he sent a master of the sacred palace, Andrew of Constantinople, as his ambassador to induce him to take active measures in concert with Sigismund. He represented, in a letter which the ambassador bore with him, that prudence as well as religion required the suppression of a people whose dogmas were fatal to all government, opposed to the authority of kings, and destructive of all human legislation. They favored, he said, many dangerous errors and superstitions, denied sovereigns their tribute, and held that all property was common and all men equal. The attempt to check and subdue them had been vain hitherto, and it seemed that providence had expressly reserved the work that the king of Poland might have this left him to crown his other conquests.

The pontiff, in a second letter, renewed his application, (Jan. 13, 1430,) representing to the king that he could do " nothing more acceptable to God, more useful to the world, or glorious to himself, than to turn all his thoughts and all his strength to the extirpation of the perfidious heresy" of the Bohemians. Help, however, was not to come from this

quarter.   Domestic dissensions—even had the king
of Poland been disposed—effectually prevented his
compliance with the exhortation of the pope.

Sigismund, meanwhile, had been diligently pur-
suing his own measures.   The untoward fortune of
his campaigns against the Turk had materially affected the energy with which he had prosecuted his
purpose to recover Bohemia to his allegiance.   But
the alarm excited by the Hussite invasions aided his
project, and a diet was summoned to meet at Vienna,
Nov. 1, 1429, before which the matter was to be
brought.   The delay of Sigismund in reaching the
place, led to a transfer of the diet to Presburg.   The
subject which invited attention was the course which
should be adopted to restore peace to the empire, so
that its entire strength might be concentrated upon
an invasion of Bohemia.   After some deliberation,
several of the princes urged a postponement of any
decisive action until after another diet, in which the
German states should be more fully represented, and
which should be held at Nuremberg or Frankfort.
Sigismund reluctantly acquiesced in the proposal to
meet at Nuremberg.   He spoke, in his indignation,
of throwing down the imperial sceptre, and relieving
himself of the burdensome and vexatious duties of
his position.   "Hungary," he said, "is enough to
furnish me with bread."   But his threats availed
nothing.   The German princes were resolved to hold
a diet on their own soil.

The object of the assembly was to find a solution
for the standing problem of the Bohemian heresy.
After many delays, enough were assembled to pro-

ceed to business. For eight months the deliberations were protracted; and at length nearly all the
prelates and princes of the empire were brought
together, either in person or by ambassadors. Martin
V. sent to the diet the Cardinal St. Angelo, Juliano
Cæsarini, who afterward presided at the council
of Basle. By his influence the reluctance of the
diet to act upon the offensive was overcome. It
was finally resolved to make still another invasion of
Bohemia. The papal legate came, provided for the
emergency. He had brought with him a bull of
Martin V. ordaining a crusade, which was now oppor-
tunely to be published. It exhorted all believers to
assume the cross, and set forth on this holy expedition. Indulgences were profusely promised to those
who should engage in the enterprise, or contribute to
its promotion. Those who should fast and pray for
its success, should have a remission of penance for
sixty days. From other vows interfering with enlistment in the holy war, a dispensation should be
freely bestowed.[1]

The greatest efforts were now put forth to secure
a successful issue for this, the sixth[2] invasion of
Bohemia by the imperialists. The time fixed for the
expedition was June 24, 1431. The princes and
prelates exerted themselves to assemble a powerful
army. To John Hoffman—the old opponent of Huss
doubtless, but now Bishop of Misnia[3]—the legate
wrote a letter, in which he exhorted him to unite
in "the holy league." "Alas!" he exclaims, "the

[1] Guerre des Hus., i. 299.

[2] It was only the third papal crusade published and proclaimed by
bulls of Martin V.   [3] Or, Miess.

abominable heresy of the Wickliffites and Hussites exceeds to-day in cruelty all the heresies of preceding ages. It has inspired them to a fierce obstinacy, so that, like the adder, they shut their ears to the voice and doctrine of the church their mother, reckless of all the methods which she may take to bring them back to reason. Not content with their poisonous dogmas and their blasphemies, they have despoiled all humanity and all piety, and have become like ferocious beasts, to be satisfied only with the blood of Catholics."

He then dwells indignantly upon the violence, plunderings, and sacrilege of the Hussites, vindicating the wisdom of the princes in arming for their extermination. He closes with the solemn and formal command to proclaim, or have proclaimed, without delay, in all cathedral and parish churches of his diocese, the bull of " Apostolic Indulgences."

The bishop rendered a prompt obedience. Similar measures doubtless were taken in most of the other dioceses of the empire. The emperor meanwhile, to test the spirit of the Bohemians, advanced to Egra, and sent two of his nobles forward to Prague, to propose terms upon which he should be received as king. The Taborites and Calixtines were engaged in warm disputes. At the opportune moment, the two nobles interposed their propositions. The citizens of Prague, and Procopius and Kerski, the leaders of the Taborites, favored them as a basis of negotiation. In spite of the opposition of the Orphans, a deputation of four, one of whom was a Taborite priest, were sent to confer with the emperor.

More than two weeks were spent in useless conference, when the deputation from Prague became satisfied that the only object of the emperor was to
amuse and deceive them till he was ready to strike
a decisive blow. Complaining of this to the emperor
himself, they protested that henceforth their enemies
alone were responsible for the continuance of this
terrible and bloody conflict. For themselves, they
were ready for peace, and the fault of preventing it
did not rest upon their heads.

The deputation returned to Prague. Their report
produced great consternation in the city. The magistrates took measures for publishing throughout
Bohemia the imminency of the threatened danger.
The populace were bitter in their maledictions and
curses of the emperor. The most moderate and
cautious were satisfied that he had attempted to
dupe and betray them, and that his proposed negotiations for peace were only intended to mislead them
into a false confidence.

Prompt measures were immediately taken. The
states of the kingdom were informed of the danger
of a new crusade, and the Taborites and Orphans
were recalled from foreign conquests to defend their
native land. In execution of their purpose at the
close of the previous campaign, they had gone abroad
spreading on every side the desolation of their ravages and the terror of their arms. Divided among
themselves, and not rarely at open variance, this
dread of a common foe was necessary to bring them
again together. The old leagues and confederations
were revived. Old feuds were forgotten. The

barons of Bohemia and Moravia, the Calixtines of
Prague and the indomitable Taborites and Orphans,
again united to repel the invader. In a few weeks
50,000 infantry, 7,000 cavalry, and 3,600 chariots
were gathered for review at Chotischau, in the circle
of Pilsen.

Meanwhile, with some unexpected delay, the crusading forces had been got together. They were
estimated to number 130,000 men. But they were
not ready to march until the month of August.
The Elector of Brandenberg was appointed to the
chief command. Amid scenes of the most imposing
ceremonial, the sword was placed in his hand by the
cardinal legate. The Count of Hohenlohe presented
him with the imperial banner, and the highest hopes
were entertained of the success of the campaign.

But before the invading army crossed the frontiers
of Bohemia, the cardinal determined to see what
could be accomplished by persuasion and argument.
He addressed a letter to the Bohemians, overflowing
with tenderness and anxiety for their spiritual welfare. He vaunted the tender mercies of the church,
and protested that the aim of the invaders was kind
and Christian, and that if the Bohemians would only
submit and return to the unity of the church, they
should be left entirely unharmed. In a tone of earnest entreaty, as if any act of violence or cruelty was
most remote from his thought, he urged and besought
them to give up their heresies, and accept the charity
which the church was ready to bestow.

The eloquence of the letter in other circumstances
might have been credited in part to sincerity and

affectionate anxiety, but the author of it must himself have felt that its success—if it met any—would be due to the armed legions who stood ready to enforce its application. No doubt a large number of the Bohemians were prepared to meet it with a favorable response; but as a general thing, Calixtine as well as Taborite had learned only too thoroughly to distrust the professions of the enemy and the good faith of Sigismund. The reply that was made was one in which all parties could unite, and one which betrayed no trace of variance between the different elements of opposition. While laying down the four Calixtine articles as the only basis upon which any measures of negotiation or conciliation were possible, it proceeds in an unsparing manner to expose the policy hitherto pursued by the imperialists and the enemies of Bohemia. It was a document well calculated to kindle anew the patriotic zeal of the nation, and fire it to fierce indignation against the arts and arms of the invader. Its closing paragraphs glowed with an indomitable and defiant spirit worthy of Zisca himself. It declared that the Bohemians would maintain their rights to the end, and repel force by force, by whomsoever offered. "Your trust," say the authors of the letter, addressing the party of the cardinal, "is in an arm of flesh; but our trust is in the God of armies."

This reply to the cardinal's letter was in reality the manifesto of the Bohemians, and it was sent not only to the cardinal, but to the different states of the kingdom. This correspondence took place during the months of June and July, (1431,) while the imperialists were marshalling their army, and the different parties in Bohemia were uniting their forces for a desperate resistance.

The cardinal legate attended in person the march of the main body of the imperialists. He sought, by all the ecclesiastical resources at his command, to enkindle the fanatic zeal of the crusaders. The son-in-law of the emperor, Albert of Austria, was prepared to make a diversion in favor of the imperialists on the side of Moravia, while 80,000 infantry, 40,000 cavalry, and a formidable artillery approached the western frontiers of Bohemia. The Elector of Saxony invested Taschau, while another corps proceeded to Ratisbon. At the entrance of the Frauenberg forest, the imperialists halted. A council of war was held, and scouts sent out to make explorations. Procopius, not unmindful of his danger, took pains to deceive them, and lead them into the belief that the Hussites were divided. The imperialists were duped, and in the confidence of security entered the forest near Tausch. Of a sudden the report spread that the Hussites were united, and were rapidly advancing in order of battle. The Archduke of Bavaria, and all his troops, seized with a panic, broke up in the night and fled. Abandoning all their stores, they hurried back in the greatest disorder to Riesensburg. The Elector of Brandenburg, with the division under his command, betrayed the same terror. His soldiers tore up their standards and fled.[1]

---

[1] Wenzel (History of Germany, ii. 177) says, " The free knights of the empire, filled with shame at this cowardly discomfiture, vowed to restore the honor of the empire, and to march against the Hussites, on condition of no prince being permitted to join their ranks. The nobility cast all the

The cardinal legate alone showed more presence of mind. He rallied the fugitives again at Riesenburg, a few miles distant from Tausch, and his glowing words restored shame if not enthusiasm to the soldiery. But the approach of the Bohemians renewed the old terror. The army was dispirited and disorganized. They fled, and the flight was a complete rout. The Bohemians met no resistance. They had nothing to do but massacre the fugitives and seize the booty. The mass of the imperialists obstructed their own escape. Eight thousand wagons full of military stores, with all the heavy artillery, fell into the hands of Procopius and his Hussite soldiers. The strong chest of the imperial army was seized, and the cardinal himself barely escaped, with the loss of his hat, cross, sacerdotal robes, and the bull of the crusade. The last was long preserved at Tausch as a glorious trophy of the Hussite victory.

So disastrous a defeat effectually crushed the hopes that had hitherto been cherished of subjecting the Bohemians by force of arms. Even the cardinal Julian, who had instigated the crusade so effectually, now declared himself in favor of adopting more conciliatory measures. The time was approaching for the assembling of the council summoned at Basle, and he wrote a letter to the Bohemians in the most gentle tone, inviting them to be present and discuss their grievances and present their demands, with the assurance that they should be allowed the fullest

blame on the cowardly or egotistical policy pursued by the princes: the flight, however, chiefly arose from the disinclination of the common soldiers to serve against the Hussites, whose cause was deemed by them both glorious and just."

freedom.   The council itself (which met Dec., 1431[1])
renewed the invitation.[2]   It was accompanied by a
safe-conduct, the substance of which declared that
they should have entire liberty to remain at Basle,
to act, decide, treat, and enter into arrangements
with the council; that they should celebrate with
perfect liberty, in their own houses, their peculiar
forms of worship; that in public and in private,
they should be allowed from scripture and the holy
doctors to advance proof of their *four articles*, against
which no preaching of the Catholics should be allowed
while they remained within the city; that any attempt at the violation of their safe-conduct should
be severely punished, and that on their return they
should be accompanied by a safe escort to the Bohemian frontier.   But even these conditions, favorable
as they were, could not at once overcome their deep
distrust.   In fact, the source from which they came
could not fail to excite suspicion.   They who but
just now breathed only a spirit of exterminating
invasion—who had incited all Christendom to engage
in a crusade to be marked by plunder and carnage—
assume a tone too gentle to accord with their former
threats.

[1] The council had been summoned
to meet at Basle at a much earlier
date, and was in fact opened at the
cathedral church of Basle, July 23,
1431; but the number of members
present was so small, that the first
session was not held till Dec. 24.

[2] Richerius, iii. 398.

CHAPTER XVIII.

THE COUNCIL OF BASLE. CALIXTINE ASCENDENCY.

1432—1467.

MEANWHILE, however, changes were taking place in the relative position of the parties hitherto combined against Bohemia—changes which enforced the policy of conciliation. Germany was loudly and urgently insisting upon her demand for ecclesiastical reform. The disappointment of her hopes at the council of Constance only made her more earnest that some measures should now be adopted, which should effectually check the corruption of the church. The cardinal legate, who had carefully surveyed the ground, and had received information which excited his alarm, felt that it would no longer answer to trifle with the demand. He boldly declared, that unless something was done it would be to no purpose to eradicate the Bohemian heresy. Other heresies would spring up to supply its place, and introduce new divisions into the church. Unless there was a reformation in the clergy, the result was inevitable.[1] The license and excesses of the German clergy—so he wrote to Pope Eugenius IV. (Gabriel Condulmer, who had succeeded to the tiara on the death of Martin V., Feb. 20, 1431)—"had irritated the laity beyond measure against the ecclesiastical order,"[2] so that it was to be feared lest, imitating the example of the Hussites, the popular indignation should rise up and sweep away the entire hierarchy.

Nor was this all. The Bohemians would be so encouraged by the corrupt state of things in Germany, as to be inspired to greater audacity in their invectives and complaints. To shut their mouths, and to take away every excuse for their course, it was absolutely essential that the council should proceed with the task of reform. If a general council was not held, a provincial council was absolutely essential. The danger was imminent. The entire hierarchy was threatened with destruction.

Such were the views of the legate, boldly expressed. They were shared fully by most of those acquainted with the facts of the case. Sigismund himself felt that hostile measures for the invasion of Bohemia were no longer wise or practicable. With his ready dissimulation he assumed a supplicating attitude, and hypocritically assured the Bohemians in writing of

[1] Richerius, iii. 323.   [2] Ib., 322.

his good-will and of his present inclination to come
to terms; to which they made reply—indicative of
their distrust—that his real intention was to draw
them away from the truth. In these circumstances
his only hope was in the conciliatory policy of the
council.

This policy was strongly urged by the cardinal
legate. He had seen enough to satisfy him that the
hope of subjecting Bohemia by crusading zeal was
vain and illusive. He had no wish to try again his
previous experiment. Yet he was deeply in earnest
to bring back the Bohemians to the unity of the
church. By means of the council which was now to
be convoked, he hoped that the object might be
accomplished.

The spiritual and temporal lords generally took
the same view of the case. They were strongly
inclined to make concessions. But this did not suit
the plans of the new pontiff. He was opposed to all
negotiation or compromise. He was urgent for a
renewal of the crusade, and scorned the humiliation
of treating with heretics who assumed a defiant attitude. Perhaps his fear of the council, which he
dreaded scarcely less than the Bohemian infection,
had not a little to do with it.

He beheld with apprehension the convocation of
a council in a city not only beyond his own jurisdiction, but where it would be subject to imperial
influence. He dreaded the freedom of its utterance.
He had reason to fear the bearing of its decisions
upon himself. The precedent of the council of Constance filled him with alarm. The result was, that

in spite of the emperor, the council of Basle was pronounced to be dissolved, and was convoked anew to meet at Bologna, (Nov. 11, 1431.) The reasons adduced by the pope for this procedure, were,[1] that Basle was not a place sufficiently secure, in part, on account of the Hussites, and in part, on account of the internal conflicts of the German princes; and that it was too distant for the deputation from the Greek church, in case they wished to prosecute the business of their union with the church of Rome. For this purpose an Italian city would be far preferable.[2]

This measure of the pope took the assembled bishops and theologians by surprise. Even the Cardinal Julian was dissatisfied with it, as at least impolitic. He replied to each of the reasons which the pope had adduced for the transfer of the council. The Greeks, he said, had been talking for three hundred years about union, but nothing had come of it; and as to the Hussites, or the civil discords and conflicts in Germany, no danger was to be apprehended. An uncertainty should not be surrendered for a certainty. The emperor and the princes regarded the council as the last resource for restoring peace to Bohemia; and, beside all, it was to be feared that if there were no speedy reform in the morals of the German clergy, the laity, who already had them in derision, would treat them no better than they had been treated by the Hussites.

---

[1] Schmidt's Geschichte der Deutschen, iv. 159.

[2] In addition to these reasons for the transfer of the council, the pope stated that many of the citizens of Basle adhered to the doctrines of the heretical and excommunicated Huss, and that the presence of the council there would breed daily scandals and quarrels.—*Bower,* iii. 219.

In spite of the papal mandate, the council resolved unanimously to remain at Basle, and proceed to business. The condition of Bohemia first invited their attention; but the papal urgency for the crusade was rendered futile by the open controversy between Eugenius and the council. At Basle it was no longer the question whether Bohemia should be subdued by force of arms. The Archduke of Austria and the Duke of Burgundy, who would have been selected as leaders in case of a crusade, were at open vari. ance. It would be no longer possible to combine in a single enterprise the forces of the empire. The invitation, moreover, given by the council to the Bohemians to be present at Basle, with the assurance that they should be indulgently heard, was a step which the pope represented as prejudicial to the authority of previous councils which had condemned them as heretical. He therefore renewed his decree removing the council to Bologna.

The old difficulty of the council of Constance was thus renewed. The pope and the council were at variance. It was in vain that Cardinal Julian attempted to dissuade Eugenius from the inflexibility of his purpose. "What," he asks,[1] "will the heretics say who have been already invited to Basle? Will they not be more strenuous, and must not the church confess itself overcome, if it refuses to await the arrival of those whom it has invited? Will they not think they see the finger of God in it, that after so many armies have been routed, the church itself flees before them, making it plain that the heretics can

---

[1] Richerius, iii. 326.

be overcome neither by arms, nor by learning and
conviction? What will the world say of the clergy?
Will they not hold that its corruption must be perpetual, and that if so many councils have been held
in vain, its reformation is hopeless? The whole
world is waiting in expectation of some result. If
this is again to be defeated, men will say that we
are making a mock of God and man; and as the hope
of reform vanishes, the laity will persecute us as the
Hussites have done." In a similar strain the emperor
himself addressed the pope. But all was in vain.
Either the court of Rome had gone too far in its
course of opposition to retreat with honor, or it was
inspired by a deeper policy than that which it
avowed. The council of Basle was an object of profound distrust. There was no relying upon it unless
it was removed to some Italian city. The cry of reformation had become exceedingly obnoxious, and
the pope could not be dissuaded from his purpose to
suppress it.

But on its side, the council was equally firm. It
felt that the eyes of the world were directed toward
the measures which it should adopt for restoring
Bohemia to the unity of the church. It was said
openly at Basle, that the Roman court was opposed
to all reform, and resolved to sacrifice the welfare of
all Christendom to its own interest. The decrees of
the fourth and fifth sessions of the council of Constance were confirmed, establishing the superiority of
general councils to the authority of the pope. The
decisions of Eugenius against the rights of the assembly were declared null, and it was decided that in case

the Holy See should become vacant, the election
should take place at Basle and no where else.   The
nomination of cardinals, pending the sessions of
the council, was forbidden, and the pope himself was
summoned to appear at Basle within the space of
three months.

These decisions were regarded at Rome as a formal declaration of war against the papal authority·
Nor were the measures of Eugenius more favorably
interpreted at Basle. Each party prepared itself for
the conflict, determined to maintain its superiority.
The ground was disputed, step by step. Eugenius
imagined that he had one decisive advantage. Sigismund had never yet received the imperial crown at
the hands of the pope.   He was now anxious for his
coronation.[1]   Eugenius determined to make his own
terms, and these were, the submission or transfer of
the council. Sigismund was in no condition to enforce his demand.   For a year he lingered in Italy,
and vainly summoned the German princes to his aid.
None came.   But even thus Sigismund held out.
He would not betray the cause of the council.   Eugenius at last receded so far as to consent that a
general council summoned by him should be held at
Basle. But this would not satisfy the council already
assembled.   What would be the fate of the sessions
already held ? They persevered in their cause in
spite alike of the threats and intrigues of the pope.

[1] The pope deferred the ceremony
as long as possible. He at length
yielded to Sigismund's demands, but
in doing so, gave full vent to his displeasure. He caused " the crown
to be placed awry on Sigismund's
head by another ecclesiastic, and
then pushed it straight with his foot
as the emperor knelt before him.—
Menzel's Germany, ii. 178.

At length, in the eleventh session, they cited him again to appear at Basle, threatening him with suspension if he failed to comply, and in case of continued persistence in his refusal, with deposition. Again the pope yielded, but the capitulation was partial. He recalled his decree dissolving or transferring the council. The return of the emperor from Italy suspended further hostile proceedings, and the year (1432) closed with an apparent reconciliation of the two parties, whose mutual irritation and violent designs were cloaked by hypocritical professions.[1]

The Bohemians at length were led to confide in the sincerity of the invitations that had been extended to them from Basle. Conscious of their own strength, they saw that the Roman church was no longer in a condition to prosecute hostile measures against them, and the obvious weakness produced by its threatened schism secured a confidence in its assurances which promises and safe-conducts alone never could have afforded. It was in the beginning of the next year (Jan. 4, 1433) that the Bohemian deputation, numbering three hundred, was chosen, from among the most noble in the land, and with Procopius the Great, the colleague of Zisca, the hero of many battles, the leader of many invasions, at its head. A curious spectacle was this—the reception with public honors, by a council representing the orthodoxy of Catholic Christendom, of a body of men who had stood forth for years, with arms in hand, as the champions of the martyred Huss—the heretic of Constance. They came in the conscious-

---

[1] Richerius, iii. 412, 414.

ness of strength, with the hard-won reputation of *invincible*, and in their bold, fearless, and haughty bearing, presented a striking contrast to the entrance of Huss or Jerome upon the scenes of their trial and martyrdom. They came with no tokens of inferiority or marks of submission, but to treat on equal terms with a body which represented the power and authority of the whole Catholic church.

The greatest curiosity prevailed to see these men who had rendered their names terrible throughout the world, and against whose impetuous heroism successive imperial armies had been dashed and shattered. Strange stories of their valor had gone abroad. The very means employed by calumny to make them odious and even horrible, had lifted them to fame. Procopius, with his hawk nose and his dark and ominous-looking countenance, led the band. He was attended by the shrewd and crafty Rokyzan, the head of the Bohemian clergy, Nicolas Biscupek, "The Little Bishop," the leading preacher among the Taborites, Ulric, the principal speaker among the Orphans, and Peter Payne, the Englishman.

As the Bohemians approached the city, they were met by an immense crowd, embracing a large number of the members of the council itself, who had dispersed themselves without the walls in anticipation of their arrival. "The public places and streets, along their passage, were thronged with spectators. Women, children, and even young girls filled the windows and occupied the roofs of the houses. The lookers-on pointed out to each other these foreign costumes, which had never before been seen there.

They gazed with surprise at the visages marked with scars, and those terrible eyes ; and in beholding men of stern appearance, they were the less astonished at the things which fame related of them."[1]   But it was to Procopius himself that particular attention was drawn.   He, the hero of so many sieges and battles, the destroyer of so many towns, who had subdued mighty armies, and was scarcely less terrible to his own countrymen by his massacres and plunderings than to the enemy by his victories, was the object of universal curiosity.

It had been only by pressing invitations, and strenuous efforts to overcome their distrust, that the Bohemians had been drawn to Basle.   The first letters sent them had remained unanswered.   No notice even was given the council that they had been received.   They had been first sent to Egra, and thence transmitted to Prague.   The deputies of the council, anxious for the success of their mission, sent through the senate of Nuremberg to inquire of the citizens of Egra how the invitation had been received at Prague. On learning that the Calixtine party, which preponderated there, had been inclined to regard it with favor, they renewed their application in hope of finally succeeding in their object.   A reply was returned, proposing a conference at Egra between the deputies of the council and the neighboring princes on one side, and the Hussites on the other, for the purpose of securing safe-conducts.   The twenty-seventh day of April (1432) was appointed for the conference.   But the Bohemians, on the ground that

---

[1] Æneas Sylvius.   Cochleius, 247.

no assurance had been given for their safety, even at
the conference, failed to appear.   This difficulty was
at last overcome ; but the Bohemians, complaining of
the injuries and wrongs they had suffered, and not
unmindful of the violation of the safe-conduct of
John Huss, demanded hostages for the fulfilment of
the promises made by the deputies of the council.
Nor would they accept any but those of princely or
noble birth.   At length the princes pledged themselves to see that the safe-conducts were faithfully
observed.   Even thus, however, the distrust of the
Bohemians could not be overcome until they had
sent two of their countrymen to Basle to be more
fully certified of the honest intentions of the council.
Upon their favorable report that the invitation was
sincerely and truly given, the deputation of the Bohemian nation was elected.

The next day after their arrival at Basle,[1] the
Bohemian deputation appeared before the council.
They were graciously received, and addressed by
Cardinal Julian, who presided at its sessions.   In behalf of the Bohemians, Rokyzan replied.   His address, composed for the most part of select passages
of scripture skilfully adapted to express the feelings
and views of the Bohemians, and expressing a measured confidence in the council, closed with demanding that a day should be appointed on which they
might be heard.   The sixteenth day of January was
appointed for opening the discussion, which was continued with few intervals for more than two months.

The Bohemians presented and defended their four

---

[1] Some say January 9 .

Calixtine articles. "These articles," say they, "we present to you, that, apprehending the unusual desire felt for peace and security, you may consent to approve them in the form subscribed, so that they may be freely held, taught, and irrevocably observed in the kingdom of Bohemia and the march of Moravia, and such places as adhere to the views they hold."[1]

In evidence of the sincerity of their desire for peace, the Bohemians say, "We are ready to be united, and to become one in the way in which all Christian believers are bound to be united, according to the law of God, and to adhere to and obey all legitimate ecclesiastical rulers in whatever they command accordant to the divine law. So that if council, pope, or prelate shall determine or command that to be done which is forbidden of God, or shall pass over, or command to pass over, what is written in the canon of the Bible—since the canons pronounce such things execrable and anathema—we shall be under no obligation to respect them or render them obedience. These conditions we offer, to be accepted and concluded mutually between you and us."

The Bohemians also insisted, that in case of the acceptance of their articles, the council should unitedly use its influence to produce concord in Bohemia and Moravia, silencing or restraining by its authority such as might be disposed to make disturbance, so that a safe and permanent peace might be the result.

The discussion of the articles was commenced by Rokyzan, who spoke for three days in defence of the

---

[1] Richerius, iv. 400.

first, on the communion of the cup. The second was argued by Nicholas de Peletz, who occupied two days; the third by Ulric, who occupied two more, and the fourth by Peter Payne, who spoke for three successive days. A perfect freedom of speech was allowed, and the council was compelled patiently to hear Wickliffe and Huss, who had been condemned as heretics at Constance, spoken of as evangelical doctors. In conclusion, the Bohemians thanked the council for the gracious hearing which had been allowed them. [1]

John of Ragusa, a theological professor, afterward a cardinal, then demanded to be heard in reply on the subject of the first article. For eight successive days he disputed the positions taken by Rokyzan. Before he commenced, however, John, a Cistercian abbot, exhorted the Bohemians to submit to the decisions of the church as represented by the council. But a blind submission was not to their taste, and they indignantly rejected the offensive proposal. They preferred a full and free discussion. John of Ragusa then proceeded with his remarks, but the terms " heretic " and " heresies " were so frequent upon his lips, that the patience of Procopius was exhausted. He rose up and indignantly complained to the council against such injustice. " This our countryman," said he, " does us great wrong, so often calling us heretics." " As I am your countryman both by tongue and nation," replied the speaker, " I do the more desire to bring you back to the church." Some of the Bohemians were, however, so offended, that

[1] Cochleius, 250.

they left the council, and would not hear the remainder of his disputation. Ten days more were occupied by others in reply to the three remaining articles, till the Bohemians grew weary of the tedious and protracted discussion. Still they maintained their ground.[1] Rokyzan defended his first positions for six successive days.

At last it was evident that the parties were brought no nearer together by prolonged disputations, and at the instance of the Duke of Bavaria, protector of the council, another plan was devised to reconcile matters. This was, that a certain number of the Bohemians and a certain number from the council should meet together, and in friendly conference decide upon terms of agreement. But here again they were met by an insuperable difficulty. Those of the council demanded that the Bohemians should first unite with the council, and then be bound by its decisions. But to this it was replied that there must first be a decision in regard to the four articles. All present union would be frivolous which resulted in a final disagreement. It was in vain that Cardinal Julian urged the Bohemians to acquiesce in the decisions of the council. They only replied, that they came to Basle to propound their four articles, and that not in their own name, but in the name of the whole kingdom of Bohemia. At length, as the Bohemians were preparing for their return home, it

---

[1] During the discussion, Procopius was reproached with having said that the monks were an invention of the devil. He did not palliate his guilt or deny the charge. "Whose else can they be?" he boldly replied; "for they were instituted neither by Moses, by the prophets, nor by Christ. —*Menzel*, ii. 170.

was resolved to send a deputation of the council with them, to see what could be effected at Prague.

The citizens of Prague, however, were no more inclined to sacrifice the integrity of their four articles than their ambassadors to the council had been. The eloquence of the deputation was wasted upon ears that had listened to the powerful arguments and representations of Rokyzan. The resolution of the Bohemians was inflexible, and the deputation could only carry back to Basle the four articles as the *ultimatum*. The council was reluctantly compelled so far to acquiesce as to send back word that if the Bohemians would accept, with the three articles, the union of the church, they should not be molested in regard to the fourth on the communion of the cup. To this, their reply—indicative of their wise and just caution—was, that they could give no decisive answer until they had a clearer understanding of what was to be done on the subject of the communion of the cup.

The formulary of the council's reply was drawn up with great art. It granted for a time permission to the Bohemian clergy to administer the communion in both kinds, enjoining however upon the communicants to believe that the body of Jesus Christ was not merely in the bread, and that his blood was not merely in the wine, but that his body entire was to be found in the sacrament under both kinds.

With these concessions many of the Calixtines were fain to acquiesce. The ambition of Rokyzan was flattered with the hope of obtaining the archbishopric of Prague, and multitudes, weary of civil

war and intestine conflict, were ready to accept almost
any conditions on which peace could be restored.
In the city of Prague the party composed of these
had the preponderance, and through their influence
deputies were sent to the council. In the following
year the definitive conditions of union, known in
history as the *Compactata*, were signed by both parties.

But if these measures were intended to secure the
peace of the kingdom, they failed in their design.
The Taborites could scarcely have been satisfied, even
with the full and entire concession of the four Calixtine articles. They had other demands and grievances which these did not meet. The proposed agreement became therefore the occasion of new disquiet.
Civil war broke out in the kingdom more furiously
than ever. The Catholics and the Calixtines, with a
large portion of the nobility anxious for peace, formed
one party, however incongruous in its elements, while
the Taborites, Orphans, and Horebites, united under
the two Procopii, formed the other. By the last,
the concessions of the council were regarded as perfectly illusory, and for the most part no union was
desired with the Catholic church. But their former
violence and the memory of their terrible ravages
stood in the way of their success. The nobility were
anxious that their vassals and serfs should return
to the cultivation of their neglected domains, and
that a stop should be put to the desolations of ma-
rauding bands.

The first open conflict occurred at Prague. The
Calixtines of the Old town rose against the Taborites

and Orphans who predominated in the New. A bloody battle was fought, and the Calixtines were victorious. Twenty thousand men were left on the field; and the lesser Procopius with the survivors joined his namesake, who was engaged in the siege of Pilsen.

Upon intelligence of the calamitous battle of Prague, the siege was raised, and the two Procopii, with all their forces, marched, in imitation of Zisca's former policy, upon the capital. They were met four miles and a half from Prague by the opposing army under Rosemberg, Newhauss, and Koska. Procopius resolved not to engage unless at a manifest advantage. But the indiscretion of a part of his troops precipitated the conflict. Confusion ensued on the part of the Taborites, and the orders of Procopius were imperfectly understood. His chariots were captured, and the general of his cavalry fled from the field. Gathering his bravest men around him, Procopius threw himself into the thickest of the fight, and made a manful stand against the hostile squadrons. But he was at last overcome by numbers, and, amid the unceasing shower of darts by which he was overwhelmed, he fell pierced by an unknown hand, "tired of conquering, rather than vanquished." Procopius the Less also fell in this terrible battle, and the prophecy of Sigismund[1] was fulfilled, that "the Bohemians will only be conquered by themselves."

The Taborites never recovered from this defeat. Internal peace was to a certain extent restored, but

[1] Menzel, ii. 177.

Bohemia was terrible no longer. The heroism of the nation was quenched in Taborite blood. While it lived, it resisted and defied pope, council, and emperor combined. It had met the successive hosts of crusading armies, and hurled them back routed from the Bohemian frontier. But the treacherous concessions of the council had shorn it of its unity, and Calixtine and Catholic banded together to crush what they regarded as a common foe. The last of the more prominent Taborites, Pardo Von Czorka, was hunted down like a wild beast, found under a rock, and hanged.

No obstacle stood any longer in the way of Sigismund's recovery of his hereditary kingdom, except such feeble demands as the emasculated energy of the Calixtine party might choose to present. But even these demands, which Sigismund did not dare to refuse, show how strongly the doctrines of Huss and Jacobel had rooted themselves in the Bohemian mind. The *Compactata* between the council and the states of Bohemia were approved by the emperor, July 12, 1436, but still further concessions were demanded and secured in treating with him. The citizens of Tabor were allowed for five years full and entire liberty of conscience. The emperor promised not to recall the banished monks, to leave the present possessors of ecclesiastical property unmolested, and to confirm Rokyzan in the archbishopric of Prague. But these promises were extorted by fear, and were soon violated. The necessity of the occasion forced his assent to what his inclinations disavowed. He put his own—a papal—interpretation upon the *Com-*

pactata; restored the Roman worship in the kingdom;
reopened the monasteries; recalled the monks; and,
with a retribution just in providence, but iniquitous
on his part, defeated the grasping ambition of Rokyzan by withholding from him the promised archbishopric unless he consented to abjure.

But the spirit of Huss was not yet extinct in Bohemia, and the rashness of Sigismund almost lost him
his hard-won crown. The states of Bohemia presented their complaints and demands at the council
of Basle, in 1438, and by their tenor was manifested
the tenacity with which the nation still clung to the
four articles. Among other things, they ask that the
permission of the use of the cup shall not be temporary only, and that the " gospels, epistles, and creed
may be sung and read in our vulgar tongue before
the people, to move them to devotion." But the danger to Sigismund was not merely in the yet unsub-
dued spirit of the nation, which might be provoked
too far, but it found a place within his own household.
He had designed his rich inheritance for Albert, Archduke of Austria, his son-in-law; but his second wife, by
culpable intrigues, countermined and frustrated his
projects. She represented to the Bohemians the danger which threatened them in case the sceptre should
fall into the hands of an ardent Catholic like Albert
of Austria, and she hoped to inflame the ambition
of the king of Poland by the offer of her hand and
the rich inheritance of the empire, upon the death
of Sigismund, prospectively near.

The intelligence of the conspiracy reached Sigismund at Prague. There, dangerously ill, almost

alone, and surrounded by a populace in which he
could not confide, he saw and felt the impending
danger. Calling around him his Hungarian nobility,
objects like himself of popular odium, he spoke to
them of his approaching death, and warned them
for their own safety to flee with him from a city in
which their lives would be no longer safe, the
moment he expired. He procured the circulation
of a report that he was going forth to meet his
daughter whom he wished to embrace before he
died, and then, " resuming all his dignity, he wreathed
his brow with laurel leaves, as on solemn feast-days,
invested himself with his imperial robes and insignia,
and decorated still more with his long white hair
which flowed freely over his shoulders, with his long
majestic beard, and the nobility stamped on his pale
visage, he had himself borne through the city, in an
open litter, in the sight of all, followed by his faithful Hungarians. It is said that he shed tears in regarding this city where his ancestors had so gloriously
reigned, and which he was beholding for the last
time. The people, affected at this unexpected and
imposing spectacle, forgot their vengeance, and saluted, with their adieus, their aged emperor." [1] The
illness and fatigue of the emperor allowed him to
proceed no further than Znoima in Moravia. Here
he had the empress arrested and imprisoned, and held
a long and secret conference with his son-in-law,
Albert of Austria. As his death drew near, he
charged the Hungarian, Moravian, and Bohemian
noblemen around him to remain united and loyal to

[1] Cochleius, 312.

the archduke, whom he designated as worthiest to succeed him, even if he was not his relative. Obtaining their assent, he named deputies who should secure the recognition of Albert as his successor to the throne. Among these was his able chancellor, Caspar Schlick, who had so resented the sentence of the council of Constance against Jerome. Almost immediately Sigismund expired (1437.)

The death of Sigismund left Bohemia again a prey to faction and popular turbulence. The accession of Albert of Austria to the Bohemian crown provoked opposition at Prague, where Cassamir, a younger brother of the king of Poland, was set up against him by those who still cherished the memory of Huss. Scarcely had he grasped the sceptre, when death snatched it from his hands, (1439,) and under the minority of his infant son, the control of the kingdom was a prize for the ambition of the nobility. In spiritual matters Rokyzan regained his former supremacy, and in temporal affairs Ptaczeck and George de Podiebrad were the real masters. The last was elected king on the death of Ladislaus, (1457,) although for many years the supreme power had been vested in his hands.

For fourteen years more George de Podiebrad governed Bohemia. His abilities and energy secured respect, and restored peace to the kingdom. A Calixtine in sentiment, policy forced him sometimes to violate his more humane convictions, and he yielded to the pressure which impelled him to treat the remnants of the Taborite party at times with great severity. He hoped to appease the pope and the

Calixtine party by making them a sacrifice to religious bigotry. In this course he was abetted by the time-serving Rokyzan. But it was not long before he discovered his error. The pope's favor was not to be secured even at such a price. In maintaining what he conceived the course of justice—the concordat of Iglau—George drew down upon himself the anger of the pontiff, Pius II., which manifested itself in the form of interdict. The articles of Prague—the *Compactata*—were revoked, under the pretext that no pope had signed them. The Catholics were incited to rise against the Calixtines, and when Paul II. succeeded to the tiara, the zeal of the Roman court against the Bohemian heretics became still more violent.

Meanwhile the warlike Taborites had disappeared from the scene. They no longer formed a national party. But the feeble remnants of that multitude that had once followed the standards of Zisca and Procopius still clung to their cherished faith, and, with the word of God as their only supreme authority, the United Brethren appear as their lineal representatives. How from such an origin should have sprung a people whose peaceful virtues and missionary zeal have been acknowledged by the world, is a problem only to be solved by admitting, that in the faith of the old Taborites, however they may have been guilty of fanatical excesses, there was to be found that fundamental principle of reverence for the authority of scripture alone, which they bequeathed as a cherished legacy to those who could apply and act upon it in more favorable circumstances and in more peaceful times.

CHAPTER XIX.

THE TABORITES AND MORAVIANS.[1]

1460 — 1517.

THE early history of the Moravian church abounds in scenes of deep and thrilling interest. For nearly three hundred years before John Wesley was the admiring witness of their calm faith amid ocean perils, they had exhibited to the world the most sublime illustrations of heroic constancy, under the severest hardships and persecutions. There might seem but little congeniality between the warlike Taborites

[1] The materials of this chapter have been derived from the various histories of the Moravians, and from a valuable work entitled " Reformation and Anti-Reformation in Bohemia," by Dr. Pescheck of Zittau, translated and published in London in two 8vo volumes, in 1845. "The History of the Brethren, or *Unitas Fratrum*," by David Crantz, translated into English by Benjamin La Trobe, was published in London in two 8vo volumes in 1780. Bost's History of the Moravians is a smaller and more popular work. Pescheck's volumes are largely compiled from extended documents, and are arranged with little regard to system, although for the most part of unquestionable authority and gathered with great diligence.

who followed the invincible Zisca to the field, and
the humble, peaceful, and peace-loving brethren,
whose gentle manners, honest industry, and simple-
minded devotion made Hernhut the radiating centre
of missionary influences, that have extended from
Greenland to the islands of tropic seas, from the
Eastern to the Western continent; but in the faith
of the former, who bowed with implicit submission
to the sole authority of the word of God, we recognize that living germ of the church of the United
Brethren, which more than two centuries of protracted persecution was unable to suppress. Through
a tedious but far from fruitless discipline, they were
brought to the exercise of those rare graces of the
spiritual life which have commended them to the
sympathy and respect of the Christian world. Like
the Israelites of old, they had their Red Sea and
desert to pass through; but the first was red with
the blood of martyrs, and the last was bitter with
the pains of plundered want and weary exile.

The attempts made through successive years, after
the close of the council of Constance, to crush out
the Bohemian heresy and subdue the followers of
Huss, had proved futile. Milder measures, as we
have already seen, were at last found necessary, and
the council of Basle (1431) listened patiently, for
fifty days, to discussions conducted by the Bohemians
on one side, and the representatives of the Romish
church on the other. Through the influence of the
able but intriguing Rokyzan, a compromise was at
last effected. The Bohemians were to retain the use
of the cup, but in other respects were to conform to

the rites and doctrines of the church, promising obedience to the Papal See. These articles—soon confirmed by the Emperor Sigismund at Iglau, and afterward known as the *Compactata* of Iglau—failed to
satisfy the demands of the more zealous portion of
the Hussites: but they were now in the minority;
and when their opposition had been effectually
crushed in a new appeal to arms, (1434,) they found
themselves constrained either to acquiesce in the
prevalent policy of the Utraquists, or enjoy their
proscribed worship in solitudes or secret retreats.

But the compromise measures were scarcely more
acceptable to the papal party than they had been to
the Taborites. They had been carried by the influence of Rokyzan, who aspired to become Archbishop
of Prague. The object of his ambition seemed just
within his grasp. At the diet of 1435, he was elected
to the post, and his election was confirmed by the
emperor. But the papal party refused to acknowledge him, and he was denied investiture unless he
would abandon the doctrine of the cup. Indignant
at being thus foiled in his purpose, and having the
object, whose pursuit must have cost him many a
reproof of conscience, snatched from his grasp, Rokyzan threatened to break entirely with the Roman
Catholic church. His hearers urged him on. In the
diet of 1450 he succeeded in procuring the appointment of an embassy to Constantinople, to seek a
union with the Greek church. The Patriarch Nico-
medis promised to ordain the Bohemian bishops, but
the Turkish conquest (1453) defeated the execution
of the design. Rokyzan became now more timid.

Hitherto he had not hesitated to denounce the *Compactata* which he had been so largely instrumental in procuring. He publicly taught that the forms of religion should be established according to the law of Christ alone. He introduced hymns, in the vulgar tongue, into the churches and schools of Bohemia.

But at length he began to draw back. He was too hesitating to take a decided step, or countenance the measures of the Taborites. The Regent, George Podiebrad, (1450,) was moreover inclined to adopt a temporizing policy, and Rokyzan henceforth stood more aloof from the "Brethren." His convictions were in their favor, but his ambition would not allow him to act upon them. When their assemblies were broken up, he replied to their complaints by advising them to maintain communion among themselves, and seek their mutual edification by the reading of the Bible and of good books. They had hoped for his sanction, but could not obtain it. Severe cruelties were inflicted upon them, through the influence of papal emissaries; and even Gregory—although a nephew of Rokyzan—was, as one of their number, cast into prison.

In 1451, Peter Maldoniewitz, the faithful notary of John de Chlum, and the friend of Huss at Constance, who had for many years been a Hussite preacher, engaged with others in zealous efforts to disseminate the knowledge of the gospel throughout Bohemia. But their efforts were met by violent opposition. Persecution was more bitterly revived. Three deacons of the Hussites were compelled to sacrifice their lives for their creed. One of them,

John, was burnt at Sobieslau; Wenzel was beheaded at Horzowitz, and the third, Vitus, not improbably the friend of Jerome at Constance, curate of Holonuz, was killed with several of his hearers in the church itself, for having administered the communion under both forms.[1]

But the zeal of their enemies went yet further. People of all ages and both sexes were made the victims of cruel intolerance. The pope sent to Bohemia bands of crusaders, warriors with the sign of the cross, who volunteered to attack the heretics, and who performed their task in the spirit of brigands. Many of them were students from Erfurth and Leipsig, in whom the ancient spirit of animosity against Prague had been revived. For years they ravaged Bohemia, encouraged by allies in the country itself. Many towns were plundered and burnt. The pursuits of agriculture were suspended, and hundreds perished of famine. To murder children was a mere amusement to the brutal invaders. But the popular vengeance, thus bitterly provoked, overtook them at last. Near Klattau 3,000 were left dead on the field of battle.

It was at this period that the first band of exiles left Bohemia, (1453.) Composed in part of Taborites, with Calixtine priests and even nobles among them, they retired in a numerous body to the neighborhood of Lititz not far from the Silesian mountains. Their avowed object was the enjoyment of the freedom of a purer worship. The *Compactata* of Iglau were pronounced by them unsatisfactory. The su-

[1] Pescheck, i. 30.

perfluous ceremonies which had been retained hitherto by the Calixtines, were rejected by the exiles.
None were admitted to their communion except upon
an examination as to their personal piety.   Gregory
—already mentioned as the nephew of Rokyzan—
a man of knightly rank, once a monk of Prague,
joined them, and became afterward consenior of the
church of the Brethren.   In 1457, a band under
Michael Bradazius, drew off to Kunewald, founding
their church on what they considered gospel principles, and calling themselves " Brethren of the Rule
of Christ."   As others joined them, they took the
name which they ever after retained, of the " United
Brethren."   Multitudes throughout Bohemia, who
were not yet prepared to become exiles from their
native land, found in them the organization toward
which their own sympathies were peculiarly drawn.

Already the time had arrived that would put their
principles to the test.   Taught by the errors and
experience of the Taborites, as well as by the lessons
of the word of God, that carnal weapons belong not
to the armor of the Christian soldier, they foreswore
all appeal save to prayer, reason, and the word of
God.   Yet if anything might have provoked them
to a departure from their principles, it was the treatment to which they were subjected, by Calixtines as
well as Romanists.   By both alike they were charged
with being heretics and anarchists.   They were summoned before the consistory of Prague, and were
accused of schism, even by Rokyzan, though they
claimed to have acted by his advice.

The regent, (George Podiebrad,) although inclined

to lenient measures, dared not venture so far to disregard his oath " to root out heretics," as to interpose
in their behalf.   Outrage of almost every kind was
heaped upon them.   They were known by the hated
name of Picards.   Notwithstanding their " apologies,"
stringent laws were enacted against them.   They
were denied civil rights.   In the cold of winter
they were driven from city and village, and their
goods were plundered.   Their character was assailed
with malicious slanders.   They were accused of blasphemy, murder, and witchcraft.[1]   Some were apprehended, and thrown into prison.   The sick were
forced to leave their homes, and perished in the fields.
To perform worship without Catholic ceremonies was
forbidden absolutely, under pain of death.   The
members of the church of the Brethren, in Bohemia
and Moravia, were forbidden to assemble together.
Some of their persecutors proposed imprisonment,
and some recommended the punishment of death.
The Bishop of Breslau opposed the last on the
ground that martyrdom multiplied the numbers of
the Brethren.   He advised their expulsion, with the
hope that, sooner than leave their native land, they
would rejoin the Romish church.

Upon this many took refuge in the forests.   They
lived in pits and caves, and thus obtained the nick-
name of Pit-dwellers (*Grubenheimer*).   In the day-
time they dared not kindle a fire, lest the smoke
should betray them.   At night they studied the
scriptures by the light of their blazing fagots.   Lest
the traces of their footsteps should be detected in

[1] Pescheck, i. 89.

the snow, they trod all in the same line, the last of
the party obliterating their tracks with the branch
of a tree, to give their path the appearance of having been made by a peasant dragging his brushwood
after him.[1] Sometimes, notwithstanding their precautions, they were arrested, and forced by cold,
hunger, chains, and torture, to confess their revolutionary projects, or betray the names of their associates. If nothing could be extorted from them,
they were cruelly maimed. Sometimes their hands
and feet were cut off. Sometimes they were hung,
or quartered, or buried alive. Many perished, and
multitudes were reduced to the extreme of wretchedness.

The Brethren at Lititz did not fail to send encouraging counsels to those whom they had left behind.
They were admonished that "such as would live
godly in Christ Jesus, must suffer persecution." Gregory, the nephew of Rokyzan, who bore the message, was reported to be in a dying state in the
prison where he had been cast. He was visited by
his uncle, who was constrained, by the anguish of a
guilty conscience, to exclaim as he saw him, "Nephew,
I would that I were where you are now!" His language excited hope in the Brethren, that all good
had not died out of the primate's heart. They were
encouraged to apply to him as the ecclesiastical
head (*summus theologus*) of the kingdom, to urge
forward the cause of evangelical reform, and relieve
them from the accusation of schism. He answered
them kindly, confessed his high estimate of their

---

[1] Pescheck, i. 39.

religious character, but told them that in attempting
to aid them he could accomplish nothing of any
account, and should only injure himself.[1]

The Brethren were disappointed. Rokyzan was
a trimmer and time-server. In taking leave of him
they could not suppress the expression of their mingled grief and disgust. "Thou art of the world
and wilt perish with the world," said they. The
language, however honest, truthful, or well meant,
was at least impolitic. Rokyzan was provoked to
renew the persecution against them. At his instance
the diet of 1468 issued what have justly been called
"the bloody decrees."

The hope of church reform by means of the ecclesiastical authorities was thus extinguished. The
Brethren found that they must provide for their
own government. Their numbers, increased by
accessions from the ranks of the more conscientious
Calixtines, had made this a necessity. To the New
Testament they looked for their model of church
order and discipline. If here they were in some
respects at fault, it was from no intentional departure from their acknowledged standard, but because
their peculiar circumstances modified the application
of their principles. A high testimony to their conscientious fidelity in framing their form of church
government is found in the language of Luther, who
declared its greater accordance with scriptural simplicity than his own. First of all, they elected elders
of their own number, by a majority of voices, and
to the discretion of those who were thus elected, the

rule of the churches was committed. At their summons the most eminent of the Bohemian and Moravian Brethren were convoked, to form such regulations as the interest of the churches required. General rules for the conducting of their worship, the observance of fast days, the doctrines and government of the church, were subjects of discussion, and these were definitely settled.

Their system of church order occasioned them some anxiety. A growing repugnance to the Romanizing tendencies of the Calixtines, from whom, moreover, they were repelled by persecution, forbade them to seek ordination at their hands. Even had they sought it, their application would doubtless have been rejected. The subject therefore was carefully considered in a synod held at Lhota in 1467.[1] They resolved to choose their own teachers, from among themselves. It shows their discreet caution that first of all they elected twenty persons as candidates. These twenty were to elect nine of their number, to whom the definitive choice of three was to be committed.

At another synod the question arose whether presbyters might be ordained without a bishop. It was answered in the affirmative. Both orders, it was said, were originally equal. Still, to avoid all occasion for scandal, it was deemed best to secure episcopal ordination. The three who had been elected as preachers were therefore sent for this purpose to the Waldensian church—the only one which they could recognize as pure and scriptural.

[1] Pescheck, i. 39.

These, after their ordination, returned to the Brethren and ordained others, as the necessities of the church required.

The circumstances of the Brethren—persecuted by the Romanists, and disowned by the Calixtines, who were apprehensive of the result if they should become in the least identified with them—led them to look abroad for sympathy. Might there not be—they asked—in other lands, those whose views and doctrines accorded with their own? Only among the Waldenses could such be found. But even of them, it was said that they did not confess the whole truth. Persecution had made them shrink from a bold and fearless avowal of all their convictions. Notwithstanding this, it was resolved that communion with them should be proposed, while they should be admonished of what the Brethren regarded as errors. The admonition was kindly received. The proposal of communion was accepted. The common faith which they held was endeared to them the more by the common hardships which a persecuting spirit inflicted on both. The result was most disastrous to the Waldenses. The fact of their communion with the Brethren (Picards) was betrayed. Their leader, Bishop Stephen, along with several others, was burned. Some were scattered abroad in other lands. Some fled to the march of Brandenburg, and others joined the Brethren. This year (1480) was marked by quite an accession to the church of the exiles, from this as well as other sources.

Meanwhile the Utraquists were not left unmolested. George Podiebrad, who from Regent had become king, was unwilling to favor the Brethren, or restrain their persecutors, lest the infamy of the hated "Picards" should attach to himself. Calixtine in sentiment, he held by the *Compactata* of Iglau. But this came far short of the standard of papal orthodoxy. Pius II., who had long pretended friendship for the king, at last won over to himself Matthias of Hungary, and in separating him from George, threw off the mask. The articles of Prague—allowing toleration to the Calixtines—were revoked, and George was put under interdict.

Paul II. (1465) was even more violent than his predecessor. In his zeal against the Bohemian heretics, he dispatched a legate, Rudolf, Bishop of Lavant, to Silesia, Saxony, and Bohemia, to preach up a crusade. The ambassadors of the king were driven out of Rome with rods. A murderous war sprang up on the frontiers of Bohemia between Catholics and Calixtines, each party branding its prisoners with the cup or the cross.[1] The invading hosts were manfully resisted; but at this juncture (1471) the king died. Ladislaus of Poland, whom the excommunicated monarch recommended on his death-bed as his successor, adopted another policy. He persecuted the Calixtines in order to conciliate the pope. A revolt took place. The exasperated citizens threw the Burgomaster out of the window of the council-house, and beheaded some of the town councillors. Their most furious attacks, however, were directed against the priests and monks. Tranquillity was at last restored by the sons of the late king, and Ladis-

[1] Menzel, ii. 192.

laus consenting to treat the Utraquists with less rigor.

The pope moreover found violent measures impolitic. He determined to try what kindness could effect. He withdrew therefore the excommunication and crusade, and, agreeably to the *Compactata,* declared the Bohemians, the Utraquists included, good sons of the church.

All this however was but a temporary expedient, demanded by the emergency. The oppressive measures were only deferred to a time more favorable to their execution. A short interval only elapsed before the administrators of the Utraquistic consistory, and several other ministers, were arrested and imprisoned. Some were put to the rack, or treated with such severity that they did not long survive.

On the 21st of August, 1480, Michael Pollack, curate of St. Giles in Old Prague, a man of irreproachable character and distinguished for his eloquence, and three other curates, were seized, because they had called the pope Antichrist, and conveyed to the royal castle (Karlstein), where Pollack perished of hunger and hardship, and the others were scarcely released at the intercession of the states. Other persons were banished, or, apprehensive of danger, fled the city. Among the latter were Lucas of Prague—subsequently a bishop of the Brethren—and his friend John Nix, a man of learning. The king moreover prohibited the singing of certain Hussite hymns, and when the prohibition was disregarded, the transgressors were committed to prison, and some were put to death by torture.

The monks, who had become more bold and even extravagant in their rage, " condemned the Hussites to hell." It was in vain that the people murmured. The magistrates of Prague conspired with the nobility opposed to reform, to exterminate the Calixtines. Various royal edicts of a persecuting nature were issued, and the night of the 24th of September, 1483, was long remembered as one that threatened to become almost as memorable for wholesale massacre as the French St. Bartholomew's of the succeeding century.[1]

The plot, however, was discovered. A great uproar took place among the people. Three public halls, and all the monasteries were plundered, and several monks and senators were killed. Ladislaus, at first indignant, refused to interfere when he learned how great had been the provocation offered to the Utraquists.[2]

In the public diet of 1485, the king, who seems to have become disgusted with the harsh measures of the persecutors, ordered a treaty to be confirmed between the opposing parties. They were required to promise mutual toleration and friendship. But in spite of this, mutual hatred still continued. The Calixtines as well as the Brethren were for many years subjected to vexatious and harrassing modes of persecution. Some of the more yielding among them joined the Catholic church. Others steadfastly adhered to their peculiar views, and refused to accept the ordination of the Romish bishops. Some of their

---

[1] Other authorities give the date of the contemplated massacre as Dec. 24th, 1485. It is possible that the failure of the first attempt may have led to a second.

[2] Pescheck, i. 43.

preachers were sent to Armenia, with commendatory
letters from the University of Prague (1499). As
reports of the Bohemian heresy had already reached
that country, they were closely examined. But their
general agreement of doctrine with the Armenian
church, especially in the use of the vulgar tongue
in church service, secured their approval, and they
were consequently ordained. Among them were
Martin of Tabor and his deacon, who were afterwards burned by their persecutors at Raudnitz.[1] At
length, after the appearance of Luther, the Utraquists
—many of them—preferred the ordination of the
reformers of Wittemberg to that of the Catholics.

The Brethren, meanwhile, notwithstanding the
harshness of their treatment, were increasing in numbers. To the false accusations brought against them
before the king, they replied by presenting him a
confession of their faith, (1493,) and a refutation of
the crimes laid to their charge.[2] No one can read
their "Agreement," drawn up by the Brethren in the
mountains of Richenau, and "given forth by the
seniors," as their bishops were called, without an admiration of its kindly, Christian, and Evangelical
spirit.[3] "Before all other things," it proceeds to say,
"we have agreed among ourselves, that we will
preserve to ourselves the faith of the Lord Jesus
Christ in purity, and confirm it in righteousness which
is of God, abiding together in love, and putting our
trust in the living God. This we are faithfully to
manifest, in word and deed. One is to assist another
faithfully in love, to lead a blameless life, and be ex-

---

[1] Pescheck, i. 40.   [2] Ib., 35.   [3] Ib., 45.

ercised in humility, submission, meekness, continence, and patience, in order to prove thereby that we have a true faith, real love, and sure hope, which is laid up for us. We have also agreed together that we will unanimously observe a willing and perfect obedience, even as the scriptures, given of God, enjoin upon us. One is to receive of another, instruction, warning, exhortation, and correction in the way of brotherly kindness, thereby to keep the covenant which we have made with God through our Lord Jesus Christ, in spirit. We have also unanimously agreed to strengthen one another in the truth which we confess, by the grace of the Lord, according to the measure which is given to each of us, and willing to do and undertake everything which shall be 'judged conducive to edification and improvement;' but especially to observe Christian obedience, to acknowledge one another in want and poverty, to be humble and in subjection, to have the fear of God always before our eyes, to improve after exhortation or correction, and acknowledge our guilt before God and man. But if one be found not to abide in all these, and refuse to keep the covenant made with God, and likewise with faithful Christian brethren,— we declare with sorrow that we cannot ensure such a one of his salvation; but the result may be, that we shall withdraw from him, and be under the necessity of excluding him from our communion in divine service. And if one be overtaken in a grievous sin, or in a decided heresy, for which he ought to be put away, we cannot readmit him, until he has entirely purged himself from it, and evidently amended his life.   It has been moreover determined, that every one is to abide faithfully in his calling, and in all things to keep a good conscience, according to the apostolic injunction.   The priests and teachers in particular are to set a good example, and in word and deed so to behave toward others that punishment and reproof may be avoided."

Faithful to the principles and rules thus clearly announced, the lives of the Brethren extorted praise even from their persecutors.   The constancy of their faith and the purity of their morals were exemplary.   One wretch, who had been a main instrument of their persecution by the slanders to which he testified, refused longer to perjure himself, and confessed that he knew no ill of the Brethren.[1]   His testimony had been accounted so important, that he had been taken by the persecuting party from village to village, and city to city, that he might retail his calumnies in the audience of the people.   Copies of his confession were sent where he could not be taken in person.   In this manner it was sought to overwhelm the Brethren with odium.[2]   But the conscience of the wretch smote him for his perjury, and he was terrified by the apprehension of the mischiefs which he was bringing down, in the basest manner, upon the heads of the innocent.

This event tended much to the furtherance of their cause.   Many were led, from curiosity or other motives, to frequent the meetings of the Brethren.   Some began to do it privately and in disguise; but what they saw won their approval, and at last led them openly

---

[1] Pescheck, i. 40.   [2] Bost. 54.

to join the calumniated and persecuted disciples.
Among the accessions to their ranks were several of
the nobility of Bohemia and Moravia, who, in various
districts, erected for them churches and houses of
prayer.   The king, moreover, was favorably impress-
ed by a perusal of their confession and apologies,
and mitigated the severity of his persecuting edicts.
He even received with favor to his Bohemian kingdom a portion of the church of the Brethren who had
been driven from Hungary, and for several years
had dwelt in Moldavia.

A favorable influence upon the condition of the
Brethren was also exerted by the political events of
the time. Ladislaus, upon his accession to the throne
of Bohemia, (1471,) had succeeded to the position
and duties of George de Podiebrad, as the enemy of
Matthias of Hungary. Eleven years later (1482)
the common interests of Ladislaus and the emperor
in opposing him, cemented between them an alliance
which resulted in the defeat of Matthias near Bruck
on the Leytra. But the latter, regaining strength,
laid siege to Vienna, whose inhabitants vainly em-
plored help of the emperor. The city fell into the
hands of Matthias, (1485,) but by the generous aid
of Albert of Saxony, he was soon after defeated.
In 1493, Maximilian succeeded his father Frederic
on the imperial throne. A milder policy for a time
prevailed. The daughter of Ladislaus was married
to the Archduke Ferdinand, son of Maximilian, and
Bohemia was thus again brought under the control
of the house of Hapsburg. During most of this
period the external dangers of Bohemia and the em-

pire, whose interests were one, withdrew attention
from the Taborites and Calixtines. These might be
regarded as well-nigh subjected, while the Turk,
thundering at the gates of Christendom, excited papal anxiety and more general apprehension.

Strange as it may seem, the Calixtines were now
more disposed to persecute the Brethren, than were
the party avowedly papal. Their aim was to retain
the cup, and yet be allowed the name of Catholic.
They wished to have their bishops consecrated at
Rome. To recommend themselves, it seemed politic
to appear as distinct as possible from the maligned
and hated " Picards." Hence they were jealous of
their reputation, and willingly adopted even persecuting measures to vindicate it from the reproach of
common sympathy with the Brethren. One result
of this course however, was, to drive the more honest
and conscientious of the Calixtines over to the persecuted body. The closing period of the fifteenth
century witnessed the slow but sure increase of the
churches of the Brethren. Although far from being
unmolested, they yet enjoyed comparative rest. At
the commencement of the sixteenth century, their
churches numbered two hundred in Bohemia and
Moravia. Almost all their communities possessed
each their own house of prayer. The scriptural simplicity of their rites and the purity of their doctrines
were confirmed by their familiarity with the sacred
writings. They procured the printing of two edi-
tions of the Bohemian Bible, the first at Venice, and
the second at Nuremberg. But these were insufficient to supply the demand, and three presses were

procured, and employed in Bohemia for the printing
of Bibles alone.   The version used was a translation
of the Vulgate, and answered its purpose for a hundred years.

The short peace of the Brethren was soon disturbed by fresh troubles.   Some of them had gone
so far in the zealous defence of their non-resistance
tenets, as to declare that a Christian could not with
a good conscience hold civil office, or bear arms.
These propositions were represented to the king as
of dangerous tendency; and in the diet of 1503, he
was urged to extirpate them from the kingdom.
Several of the states protested against these insinu-
ations, asserted the innocence of the Brethren, and
opposed the cruel measures which were contemplated.
But when the friends of the Brethren had withdrawn
from the assembly, their enemies prevailed upon the
king to sign a persecuting decree.

Against this the Brethren entered their remonstrance.   The king changed his mind, and sought to
bring about a union between them and the Calixtines.
With this view he directed that some of their principal preachers should visit Prague, and confer with
the professors of the university and the Calixtine consistory.   Though apprehensive of a plot against them,
the Brethren complied with the command, (Dec.,
1503.)   But on the very day on which the conference
was to have been opened, their most bitter enemy,
the rector of the university, died.   None of the rest
dared to meet them in a public discussion.   They
were afraid of being confounded in argument in the
presence of the citizens.   The conference was deferred

from day to day, till under various pretexts it was altogether abandoned.

From time to time, however, the work of persecution was revived. The views of the Brethren, as maintained in their apologies, were studiously misrepresented. Their non-resistance principles especially were so perverted by their enemies as to make them objects of odium and contempt. In 1508 this malice threatened to break out in a more violent manner. The Roman Catholic bishops succeeded by flattery in obtaining from Ladislaus several severe decrees against the Brethren. These were met by a presentation to the king of their confession. This, with their apologies, was all the resistance they could offer to the measures of their persecutors. Yet if any thing could have justified a departure from their principles by the use of physical force, it was the decree of August 10th, 1508. In this it was commanded that "all Picardines, without distinction of sex or age, should be punished with death."[1] An anecdote in this connection illustrates the fearless spirit of the Brethren, notwithstanding their view of non-resistance. The chancellor, Albert, on his return from the diet where the decree had been ratified, paid a visit to the Baron of Coldicium, and reported to him what all had agreed upon. The baron turned to his servant Simon, one of the Brethren, and asked him how he liked it. "All have not agreed to it," was his reply. "Who are they," asked the chancellor, "who dare oppose all the states of the kingdom?" "There is in heaven," replied the servant,

[1] Pescheck, i. 41.

lifting up his hand, " One, who if he were not present at your counsels, you have taken counsel in vain."

The murderous character of the edict disgusted
some of the principal nobility. Through their opposition its execution was deferred. But in 1510 it
received the second assent of the states, and to some
extent was enforced. Many of the Brethren became
its victims. Numerous were the cases of imprisonment. Some were mutilated, some burned, and some
put to death by drowning. All varieties of torture
were employed to subdue the constancy of the martyrs. So far did the power of persecution prevail,
that divine service could only be performed in secret,
save in the district of Baron Schwamberg.

Already, as we have seen, the Brethren had
sought to discover in other lands Christian organiza-
tions to which they could extend their sympathy
and communion. These they had found among
the Waldenses alone. Their effort was now (1486)
renewed. Previous to this they had made the matter a subject of deliberation. But in the synod of that
year they gave evidence of their large views and
liberal spirit. They declared that the Catholic
church of God was not limited to any visible society
of believers, but was to be found in any part of
Christendom, wherever the holy Catholic faith,
agreeable to the truth of God, prevailed. Again
they sent forth brethren to Rome, Italy, France, and
the Waldenses, to search out those whom they
might recognize as their spiritual kindred. They
longed to enjoy the assurance that somewhere in the
world there were those whose doctrines and worship

were mainly identical with their own; that in their isolation, they were not altogether separate from spiritual kindred who in other scenes and other lands were bearing testimony to a pure gospel.

Some whom they sent out on this novel errand of searching for Christian brethren, went to Greece, to Russia, to Scythia, to Egypt, to Constantinople, and to Thrace. Others visited France, Rome, and various parts of Italy. Their report is indeed striking and significant. They found, they said, sighing souls, but no organized church with which they could unite. Hence, at a synod at which the report was made, (1489,) it was resolved: "If God anywhere in the world should stir up righteous teachers and reformers of the church, they would make common cause with them." Such was the truly catholic spirit by which they were animated.

The fame of Erasmus had already reached Bohemia. The Brethren looked to him—a Biblical scholar—with some degree of hope. In 1511 they presented to him their confession of faith—the same which had been exhibited to Ladislaus in 1480. They asked him to point out its errors, or show them in what respects it could be improved. True to his nature, the timid scholar gave it his secret approval, but advised them to keep quiet. He excused himself from coming out openly in their favor, as it would only injure himself and do them no good. In some of his writings, however, he expressed himself favorably in regard to them.[1]

---

[1] The language of Erasmus, in reply to one of the calumniators of the Brethren, was, " If the Brethren elect pastors from among themselves, it is nothing more than what the primitive Christians did; if they make choice

The interval between this and the appearance of
Luther as a reformer, was one of sore trial to the
Brethren. They were rarely left unmolested in the
enjoyment of religious worship. They grew weary
of their state of isolation, separated from the rest of
the religious world. Their condition was, with many
at least, that of seeming, if not actual, schism from
the Christian body. Some proposed that they should
reunite with the Calixtines, in the hope of peace
and larger usefulness. The subject was brought
before one of their synods. Here it was decided,
that if in another church than their own a priest of
pure doctrine and holy life was to be found, it was a
subject for gratitude to God; but this was no sufficient reason for reunion or communion with a church
which had been left because of its errors. The successor of the priest might be a man of a totally different character. Even though one might not enjoy
the membership of a properly organized church, all
might keep the unity of the spirit and of the body
of Christ. Nor was it without danger for believers
to forsake privileges accompanied by divine grace
among themselves, to seek them among strangers.
In case there should be found many priests of another
church united together in the work of a faithful min-
istration of the word of God, and properly consti-

of unlettered and uneducated men,
they may well be excused, since the
want of learning is sufficiently com-
pensated by the holiness of their
lives ; if they call one another *brother*
and *sister*, I see no harm in it; would
to God that this appellation, dictated by brotherly love, existed universally among Christians ; if they place
less confidence in their preachers
than in the Holy Scriptures, that is,
if they put more confidence in God
than in man, they are right. As to
holy days, I find their sentiments
little different from those which prevailed in the times of Saint Jerome ;
but festivals have now increased to
an enormous number."

tuted, they were not to be despised; but the elders
of the churches of the Brethren were to see whether,
in some way, a union might not be effected with
them. In case they were found to hold the fundamental articles of the Christian faith, they were to
be obeyed and listened to as teachers. If in this
respect they did not agree with the Brethren, they
were not to be contemned, but treated with kindness, both that the purity of faith might be preserved, and themselves brought to the enjoyment of clearer
light. "Finally," say they, "we recognize no multitude or assembly, however numerous, as the church
catholic,—that is, as containing the entire number
of believers, so that outside of it are none of God's
elect; but wherever the sole catholic Christian faith
is kept in truth, according to God's word, in whatever part of Christendom, there is the holy catholic
church, out of whose communion there is no hope of
salvation."

CHAPTER XX.

REFORMATION IN GERMANY. THE BRETHREN.

German Demand for Reform. — Ecclesiastical Impositions. — Extortion. — Indulgences. — Relics. — Appearance of Luther. — His Views Advocated at Prague. — Thomas Munzer. — Correspondence with Luther. — He Prints the Brethren's Confession. — His Letter to Melanchthon. — Deputation to Wittemberg. — Papal Policy in Bohemia. — Measures of the Legate. — Zahera. — The Reformation in Austria. — Lenient Policy of Ferdinand. — Capito and Bucer. — Bohemian Sympathy with the Reformers. — Harsh Measures against the brethren. — The Exiles. — George Israel. — The Baron of Shanow. — Decree. — Victims of Persecntion. — Introduction of the Jesuits. — Maximilian I. — Persecuting Measures Defeated. — John Crato. — Lenient Policy of Maximilian. — The Brethren's Bible. — Efforts for Union. — Prosperity. — The Brethren in Other Lands. — Rudolph II. — Toleration.

1517—1602.

For a whole century the Taborites and the United Brethren—as the followers of Huss—had borne their testimony against the apostasy and errors of the Roman Catholic church. Their enemies had persecuted them with calumny and violence. Pen and sword had been employed against them without scruple. The harshest measures had been adopted to shake their constancy. Beyond their own neighborhoods they were known by the odious name of Picards. In all Germany there was scarcely to be found an individual who had any proper acquaintance with their character or doctrines.

But their revolt against the dominant hierarchy

was now to be justified in a most striking manner. They were to find whole nations unconsciously array- ing themselves upon their side. Germany, from the days of the council of Constance, had been indig- nantly demanding reform; but her cry had been smothered. Instead of meeting the demand, the hierarchy only became more hopelessly corrupt, until the evil was no longer to be borne. An earlier reformation might have been less radical, but eccle- siastical authority and interested opposition had resisted and turned back the current of popular feeling, until now, become resistless, it broke over all restraint. Luther came forward, the exponent of long suppressed convictions, the champion of a purer Christianity, the leader in the cause of reform; and the Brethren, who had long waited and watched for the appearance of one to whom they could extend the hand of fellowship, greeted him, ere yet his prejudices against them had given way, as a fellow- laborer in their own great work.

Tardily, but surely, the career of Huss and the bold views he had put forth were vindicated from that very direction from which the bitterest hostility against him had proceeded. Germany had been taxed and plundered and abused, till her patience was exhausted. As the noble gave up his broad forests to the tramp of beasts, that he might himself enjoy the pleasures of the chase, so papal avarice seemed to hold Germany in reserve as the hunting- ground of ecclesiastical extortion.

The Germans had been a patient people. They had borne the yoke of Rome long and well. They had complained and submitted, till it seemed their habit. The grossest impositions, the most absurd dogmas, and the coolest impudence of ecclesiastical assumption, had failed to produce revolt. Rome felt that she might venture further. There was yet " in the lowest deep " of her avarice, " a lower deep " of unscrupulous and unblushing audacity. Alexander VI., whose unnatural vices and monstrous crimes had so eclipsed those of John XXIII. that the latter appeared almost as a saint by his side, had done all it was possible to do to make the Papal See odious to Christendom. His successor, Leo X., while patronizing ancient and modern art, surrounded himself with the splendors of the old Roman mythology, with heathen deities, and all the forms of polished licentiousness. The immense expense occasioned by the erection of St. Peter's at Rome, drained Germany and even Europe of its wealth, and an avaricious ingenuity was set at work to invent new methods of extortion, or wring new tribute from exhausted provinces. Novel taxes were imposed. Forms of penance were multiplied. The periodical recurrence of the jubilee at Rome was reduced successively from one hundred, to fifty, thirty-three, and finally twenty-five years. Millions of money were poured into the papal treasury; but the cry was still heard, " Give, give."

The system of indulgences was subjected to a new process of development. It was elaborately drawn out, and shaped by chancery rules. Absolution was made a matter of traffic. Bills of exchange on the court of heaven might be had on demand, for the premium in money. Scarce a sin could be imagined—scarce a crime ever known in the realm of the actual or ideal—but had its price. In political intrigue and treachery, papal artifice won the palm over every competitor. The difference between the papal and secular courts seemed to be merely that the latter could not dissolve the obligation of their own oaths.

The depravity of the church was such that good men shuddered to think of it. Everywhere it was to be met. The heart was diseased, and the whole body suffered. When the pope was a devil incarnate, it is not strange that prelates and priests copied from the model. Hypocrites and idlers abounded. Nobles were elevated to bishopricks, and used the vast revenues of the church to revel in wanton luxury. The priests were proverbially ignorant, brutal, and drunken. But one in ten—by a concession of the popes [1]—was required to study. The obligations of celibacy were unscrupulously eluded. The wealthy priests had poor vicars in their pay, who for the merest pittance discharged the drudgery of visitation, preaching, and clerical duty. The disorders of the monasteries and convents equalled those which had provoked in Bohemia the vengeance of Zisca. The wealthy abbots vied with the powerful secular lords.

As to the monks, John of Goch said at Mechlin, that " they did what the devil was ashamed to think." The abuses of the church in respect to relics were in some instances so ridiculous as to disarm indignation.

---

[1] Menzel's Germany, ii. 220.

Many a saint had several genuine bodies and innumerable limbs. A collection of the curiosities of ecclesiastical resources for revenue would have formed a rare museum for inspection. It would have had the chemise of the virgin, six feet long—the drum on which the march of the Jews was beaten as they crossed the Red Sea dry-shod—a piece of the head of Tobias' fish—at least five hoofs of the ass on which Christ rode into Jerusalem—and numerous other treasures, well known alike in Germany and in England, and long before made familiar by Erasmus' wit and by Chaucer's rhymes.

To all these things are to be added the burlesque sermons, the Ass' and Fools' festivals,[1] the buffooneries in the churches, and the sacrilegious traffic in indulgences, which finally exhausted even German patience, and placed the northern portion of the empire in an attitude of revolt against Rome.

In a way not unlike that by which Huss was led to take the position he did, Luther was trained for his work. The cause to which he devoted himself was the same—the vindication of a pure Christianity from corrupting innovations of past centuries. His fundamental position moreover, was like that of Huss —the supreme authority of the word of God. As the tones of his clarion voice rang out over Germany, hosts of friends rallied to his side. In the printing-press he found an ally which Huss never had. His sermons and invectives were printed and circulated —hawked abroad by colporteurs through the cities and villages of the land. The pulpit of Wittemberg

[1] Michelet's France.

had a thousand sounding-boards—awoke a thousand echoes. Rome was boldly impeached, before the tribunal of the public opinion of Christendom, of high crimes and misdemeanors. Consternation was excited among the advocates of the old abuses. There was alarm at the court of Rome. The eyes of Europe were directed toward the fearless monk who had dared to burn the papal bulls, and fling forth his challenge against the world.

We cannot be surprised, therefore, that, among a people holding such views as those of the Brethren, the appearance of Luther, as the German reformer, was heartily welcomed. Nowhere did his labors excite more hope and attention than in Bohemia. Many of the Utraquists or Calixtines, as well as of the Brethren, preferred the ordination of the reformers of Wittemberg to that of the Roman Catholic church. Two years after the publication of Luther's celebrated theses, (1519,) his principles had found their way to Prague. Matthias the hermit, arriving there as a pilgrim, publicly preached the doctrines of the Reformation, in connection however with peculiar opinions of his own. Many were won over to his views, but were subjected in consequence to repeated imprisonments.

The celebrated Thomas Munzer followed Matthias (1521). The sympathies of the Brethren were already strongly enlisted on the side of Luther. In 1523 they sent two of their number to congratulate him, and render an account of their doctrine and discipline. So satisfactory did these appear, and so gratified was he upon a perusal of their writings, that he publicly declared that the prejudice which he had hitherto entertained against them was unfounded. Some questions of church order for a time interrupted the friendliness of their intercourse; but in 1532 Luther printed their confession at his own press, and testified to the futility of his own suspicions in regard to the Brethren, declaring that, notwithstanding diversities of discipline and ceremony, they must be acknowledged, with all true believers, to belong to the one fold of Christ. "Although I cannot accept," he says, "the Brethren's forms of expression, I will neither urge nor force them to adopt mine, so long as in fact there subsists a real unity between us."[1]   In 1535 he wrote to Melanchthon

---

[1] Luther, on receiving in 1532 the confession of faith which the Brethren had presented to George of Brandenburg, caused it to be printed at Wittemburg with the following preface :

"While I was a papist, my zeal for religion made me cordially hate the Brethren, and consequently likewise the writings of Huss. I had indeed early discovered that he taught the doctrines of holy writ, purely and forcibly, so much so, that I was astonished that the pope and the council of Constance should have condemned so worthy a man to the flames. Still, such was my blind zeal for the pope and the council, that without hesitation I abandoned the reading of his books, wholly distrusting my own judgment. But since God hath discovered to me "the Son of Perdition," I think otherwise, and am constrained to honor those as saints and martyrs whom the pope condemned and murdered as heretics, for they died for the truth of their testimony. In this number I reckon the Brethren, commonly called *Picards;* for among them I have found what I deem a great wonder, and what is not to be met with in the whole extent of popedom; namely, that, setting aside all human traditions, they exercise themselves day and night in the law of the Lord; and though they are not so great proficients in Hebrew and Greek as some others, yet they are well skilled in the Holy Scriptures, have made experience of its doctrines, and teach them with clearness and accuracy. I therefore hope all true Christians will love and esteem them. Yea, we are bound to give hearty thanks to the God and Father of our Lord Jesus Christ, that according to the riches of his grace he hath commanded the light of his word to shine out of darkness, and raised us from death to life. We sincerely rejoice, both for their sakes and ours, that the suspicion which heretofore alienated us has been removed, and that we are now gathered into one fold, under the only Shepherd and Bishop of our souls, to whom be glory to all eternity. Amen."

on the subject: " While we are agreed in the main articles of Christian doctrine, let us accept one another in love, nor let the dissimilarity of usages and ceremonies separate our hearts." Another deputation, in the following year, (1536,) again urged a stricter church order; but Luther excused himself from compliance, on the ground that things were not ripe for it, nor had he leisure to attend to it amid the many tasks imposed upon him by his opponents in controversy.

In 1540 still another deputation was sent to Wittemberg, with the same request. It was headed by John Augusta, senior or bishop of the Brethren, who in 1524 had studied at Wittemberg, and whom Luther highly esteemed. After his return to Bohemia—under a compulsory decree of the emperor, who wished to prevent the further spread of the Reformation in his dominions, and to this end commanded all his subjects under pain of severe penalties to leave Wittemberg—he still kept up a correspondence with the German reformer. Luther received his former pupil with the utmost kindness, and promised that so soon as sufficient quiet was restored he would act upon the subject. As Augusta took leave, he extended to him, in the presence of the other professors, the right hand of fellowship, exclaiming, " Be ye the apostles of the Bohemians; I and mine will be the apostles of the Germans." " I admonish you in the Lord," so he wrote Augusta afterward, " that ye persevere with us to the end in the communion of the spirit and of doctrine."

At Prague, meanwhile, the different parties became

more divergent and alienated from one another.   In
1523, under the impulse and encouragement of the
Lutheran reformation, the influence of which had
powerfully extended to Bohemia, it was proposed in
a meeting of the states to adopt articles looking to
the promotion of the cause of reform.   These articles
were of a moderately protestant character; but they
were strenuously opposed by Gallus Zahera, curate of
Tein church in Old Prague.   Zahera had resided at
Wittemberg, and had been reputed a friend of Luther.   But his time-serving policy led him to abandon
his former principles, and he became an intolerant
Calixtine.

It was at this juncture that the pope, apprehensive
of the spread of the reformation in Bohemia, sent
his legate to Prague.   The latter, upon his arrival,
wrote to several persons of influence, among others
to Zahera, insinuating with much flattery the idea
of a union of the churches.   The party of John Pas-
sack of Wrat, elected chief magistrate of the city,
was now in the ascendant, and to this Zahera joined
himself.[1]

This new party, in the name of the consistory, extended a favorable reply to the legate.   Articles
were drawn up which looked toward a union of the
Calixtines with the papal party, and the influence
of the king and pope, of Passek and Zahera, was
employed to enforce them.   They were imposed upon
the laity as well as the clergy, and whoever refused
to subscribe them was banished from the city.   Six
preachers, including Martin of the Bethlehem church,

<hr />

[1] Pescheck, i. 59.

were driven from their posts. Sixty-five of the principal citizens shared the same fate. The Evangelicals were charged with conspiring to destroy their enemies. Three citizens were put to the rack to extort a confession. Others were scourged, others branded, and still others cast into prison. The progress of the cause of reform was checked by these measures of cruelty and violence.

For several years this harsh policy prevailed. Scenes of horrid barbarity were not infrequent. The hermit, Matthias, the earliest preacher of Lutheran doctrines in Bohemia, whose unassuming manners and irreproachable life had secured him universal respect, was no longer suffered to speak, as he had been wont, in the streets and in the market-places. He had admonished Zahera for his apostasy and evil-doings, and had thus invited the vengeance of the persecutor. Invited to a conference, he was seized and cast into prison, and subsequently banished. The fate of Nicolas Wrzetenarz was still more cruel. He, with his aged housekeeper, who shared his faith, was condemned to the flames. Both met with a cheerful and heroic spirit their terrible fate. From time to time the funeral pile was lighted, but brighter than its flames glowed the faith of its victims.

Meanwhile the influence of the reformation had extended into the Austrian dominions. The doctrines of Luther were preached at Vienna by Paul von Spretten (Speratus), and were widely disseminated in the whole country around.[1] In spite of violence, the new opinions made progress. Speratus was ban-

---

[1] Menzel, ii. 244.

ished, and his successor, Tauler, was condemned to the
stake.   Hubmaier of Waldshut was also burnt.   But
fresh preachers, patronized by the nobility, arose to
disseminate their views, and the emperor, engaged
in a contest with the Turk, was constrained to leave
them for the most part unmolested.   In 1528 he
found that almost the entire Austrian nobility had
embraced Lutheranism.   In 1532 the estates demanded religious liberty; and in 1541 they repeated
their demand with new emphasis.   For ten years,
previous to 1538, not a single student in the University of Vienna had turned monk.

During this period Bohemia had fallen, by the
death of Louis, to the Archduke Ferdinand, who, to
distance his rivals and win the Calixtines, initiated a
milder policy.   There was good reason for it.   Persecution might well by this time have grown weary
in its task.   The people became disgusted with such
scenes of intolerance.   Several who had been foremost in the cruel work, were overtaken by sudden
and startling calamity, which was regarded in the
light of divine vengeance for their crimes.   One
hung himself in his own house, and was secretly
buried.   Zahera was banished, and ended his life
miserably in Franconia.   The king, Ferdinand, on
his accession to the throne, changed the city council,
and the year 1530 was a season of jubilee to the
exiles, who were allowed to return.

Better prospects now opened before the Brethren.
As the reformation spread, they found new sympa-
thizers, and a deeper interest was taken in their condition and doctrines.   Their fame went abroad.   At

Strasbourg, Capito and Bucer heard of them. They wrote to inquire more carefully in regard to their views and usages. They even sent one of their number, Matthias Erythreus, to obtain fuller information. So satisfactory was the report, and so grateful to the feelings of Bucer, that at the assembly of the Strasbourg theologians he could not restrain himself from tears. "I believe," so he wrote to the Brethren, "that at this present time ye are the only ones among whom not only a pure doctrine, but a becoming, gentle, and useful church order prevails."

Calvin was present at the time at Strasbourg. He was deeply interested in the accounts which he received of the Brethren, and, in the church constitution which he afterward framed at Geneva, adopted several of their peculiar principles. Thus the influence of the Brethren reached both the leading reformers of the sixteenth century. Without becoming involved in any of their peculiar controversies, they had the sympathy, friendship, and respect of both, extending to each the hand of Christian fellowship.

From this period, their cause is identified with that of the Reformation generally. In the hopes and fears of the German protestants, they likewise shared. The merciless resolve of Charles V. to crush out the reformers from every part of his dominions, excited in their behalf the ardent sympathy, not only of the Brethren, but to a great extent of the Bohemian Calixtines.

At the time of the celebrated league of Smalcald, the authority of Ferdinand over his subjects was insufficient to enable him to procure levies from Bohemia to aid the imperial arms. The object of the war was to crush what the Brethren regarded as their own cause. Here they were sustained by a large portion even of the Calixtines. So strong were the feelings of repugnance and disgust at the demand of Ferdinand for auxiliary troops, that the states and free towns, one and all, excused themselves from compliance. On the ground of their common faith, as well as that of their ancient confederacy with the house of Saxony, they declined acceding to the demand.

This provocation was not forgotten by Ferdinand. When the triumph of the emperor's arms had laid Germany at his feet, the crime of the Bohemains was recalled, and they were charged with rebellion. Ferdinand entered Bohemia with his victorious army, and seized the city of Prague (1547.) The " bloody diet " was convened. Many of the nobles, barons, and citizens were thrown into prison. Some were scourged, others beheaded. Some were almost beggared by the heavy fines imposed ; others were utterly despoiled of their estates. Prague was deprived of its arsenal and all its privileges. Many of the inhabitants were banished, and more went into voluntary exile.

But while the rage of the king was directed against the Calixtines generally, the Brethren were especially pointed at as the authors of rebellion. Every effort was made to draw down upon them the hatred of the king. The calumnies against them were poured into willing ears, and the churches of the Brethren were first ordered to be closed. All who professed their doctrines were then commanded to leave the country, unless they would connect themselves with the Roman Catholics or the Utraquists. Six weeks only were allowed them to make their choice. The test was a severe one, but the Brethren met it in the spirit of martyrdom. Dear as their native land was to them, those who were able to remove preferred exile to a violation of their conscientious convictions.

Some, however, were not allowed to escape unmolested. The senior of the Brethren, John Augusta, was thrice tortured to extort from him a confession of his guilt, and when these measures failed, was cast into prison, where he remained for sixteen years. Many other teachers were arrested, and subjected to similar treatment. There was no safety but in flight.

The exiles emigrated for the most part in three divisions. The first, gathered from parts about Leitomischel, Bidschow, and Chlumer, amounting to five hundred souls, passed with above sixty wagons through the country of Glatz and upper Silesia. The second band, consisting of three hundred, proceeded by the way of lower Silesia. The third, like the second, from Brandeis and Turnau, took the same route. Some of their deliverances upon their journey were remarkable. Several bands of robbers attempted to plunder them of their scant treasures. Their course led them through Poland, at that time entirely papal; yet a kind Providence carried them safe to their common destination at Posen, not without a large experience of sympathy and kindness from those who were of the same faith with their royal persecutor.

At Posen they were courteously and hospitably entertained, but even here they were not allowed to rest. An order was received from the king[1] for their expulsion. They were thus forced to proceed, and directed their steps to the confines of Prussia. To Duke Albert of Brandenburg they sent a deputation, asking leave to settle in his dominions. At Königsberg they were examined by the Lutheran theologians, and by them were acknowledged as brethren. Seven towns, among them Soldau and Guidzin, were assigned them for their residence. The bishop, Paul Sprettin (Speratus), a former pupil of Luther, who was well acquainted with their ritual and doctrine, showed them many tokens of Christian kindness.

One by one, as they were able to make good their escape, their teachers followed them. George Israel, pastor of the church of Turnau, who afterward became the apostle of the Poles, refused to allow his friends to pay the penalty of his non-appearance before the magistrate. Thanking them for their kindness, he appeared at the castle of Prague and surrendered himself. "It is enough," said he, "to have been once redeemed fully by the blood of Christ, and there is no need of being bought again by the gold of man." He was thrown into prison, but in the course of a few weeks made good his escape and followed his fellow-exiles to Prussia.[2]

[1] Some authorities speak of the Bishop of Posen as the instigator to harsh measures.

[2] He ventured to walk out of the place of his confinement in the castle of Prague in broad day, through the

Such of the Brethren as remained in Bohemia were subjected to the most cruel hardships. The Baron of Schanow was put to the rack to extort a confession of his having opposed the king. In the midst of his tortures, with heroic indignation, he bit off his tongue. When asked the reason of his conduct, he wrote, "If I tell the truth according to my conscience, you will not believe me; and that I might not be induced by pain to declare what is false against myself and others, I have disabled myself from speaking at all."

The baron died of the tortures that had been inflicted. He was a distinguished victim, and counted worthy of a distinguished fate. The humbler classes of the Brethren were subjected to vexations scarcely less cruel. It was decreed at Prague, that no one of suspected faith should be admitted to the workshops of the mechanics, or should be allowed the rights of citizenship. The act was confirmed by the king, and almost every kind of outrage against the hated "Picards" was perpetrated with impunity. If any one was unwilling to pay his creditor, he only needed to accuse him of "Picardism," and all was settled by the banishment of the creditor. One man, for having in his possession a book of one of the reformers on the sacraments, was scourged in the market-place, and then banished. Another was branded on the forehead. Another was thrown into a dungeon and there murdered.

midst of the guards, in the habit of a clerk, with a pen behind his ear, carrying an ink-horn and some paper, and made good his escape to his brethren who had preceded him to Prussia. In the space of six years, twenty congregations of the Brethren were established by him in the country.—*Bost.* 79.   *Lochner's Life of George Israel,* 59, 60.

A chapter of thrilling interest would be afforded
by the history of the martyrdoms of this period.
Never was the heroism of Christian faith more nobly
illustrated.   The victims met their fate with a constancy and a cheerfulness that showed the strength
of their convictions and the fervor of their devotion.
"Thither, where our God is, must I look," said one,
lifting her eyes to heaven, as the image of the cross
was presented to her at the stake.   They counted it
" a grace given them to suffer for the law of God."
" On my wedding day," said one, " I did not feel so
happy as I do now." [1]

The churches of the Brethren were now closed,
and their ministers were persecuted wherever they
could be met.   Some found temporary rest and security in Moravia; others hid themselves in the day-
time, but crept forth from their holes and hiding-
places by night to comfort and instruct their suffering brethren.

The Calixtines, moreover, were not left unmolested.
In 1538 the communion of the cup was prohibited
by Ferdinand, in an order issued by him at Vienna.
He did indeed at one time solicit the pope for a
grant of the cup, but his object was merely to procure peace and prevent any further defection from
the papacy.

In the years 1554–5, emissaries of the newly-
founded order of the Jesuits had found their way to
Prague.   They had been sent for the purpose of
" manufacturing genuine Catholic priests."   It was a
timely movement on the part of Rome.   " There were

Pescheck, i. 57,

so few orthodox priests in Bohemia," says Pessina, " that had it not been for the Jesuits, the Catholic religion would have been suppressed." At first they spoke in the mildest tone. They assumed the most bland and winning manners. All that cunning, zeal, perseverance, and genius could accomplish, they effected. They laid hold of the court. They condescended to the masses. At the confessional, in the pulpit, in the lecturer's chair, their power was felt. Among them " were saints, equalling in faith the martyrs of old; poets, overflowing with philanthropy; bold and unflinching despots; smooth-tongued divines, versed in the art of lying." While the popes negotiated, they acted. They discerned the problem to be solved, and set themselves to the task with fearless energy and unscrupulous policy. Nothing seemed to them too desperate that might enlarge the authority of the Papal See.

With the arts of the Jesuits, the feebleness of the king, as he advanced in years, contributed to produce a relaxation of the severity employed against the Protestants. The council of Trent disappointed the hopes and refused the demands of Ferdinand, and his previous zeal for orthodoxy was sensibly diminished. The closing years of the sixteenth century were years of comparative security and repose to the Brethren. Some of them screened themselves under the name of the Utraquists, to whom an almost complete toleration was allowed.

In 1562 Maximilian II. succeeded to the throne, and soon after was elected emperor. His policy was more· lenient. The Brethren were allowed, for the most part, freedom from molestation. A dangerous attempt against their privileges met with a signal failure. In 1563 the Archchancellor of Bohemia repaired to Vienna, and by continued importunity prevailed on the emperor to sign a persecuting decree against them. But on his return, exultant in his success, he was arrested in the execution of his designs. He had scarcely left the gates of Vienna and reached the bridge over the Danube, when the part upon which he stood sunk under him, and he himself, with his suit and baggage, was plunged into the stream. Some fishermen hasted to the rescue of the chancellor, who had been seized by his gold chain, and supported in the water by one of his young attendants; but he was too far gone to be restored. The casket which held the persecuting edict was swept down with the current, and never recovered.

In the following year brighter prospects opened before them. They obtained the liberty of opening their places of worship, and engaging in public religious services. These privileges were granted by the emperor himself. When measures for enforcing conformity were about to be put in execution, the Brethren applied to him asking his protection. Their application was favorably received, especially when the emperor had perused their confession of faith, and they were left for a period unmolested. The principle of religious toleration was becoming popular at court. Maximilian had been educated by one who was himself a pupil of Melanchthon. His physician was John Crato, one of the Brethren whom Maximilian made his confidant. Once as they were riding together, the emperor lamented the religious dissensions of the empire, and asked Crato which, of all the various sects, approached the nearest to apostolic simplicity. "The Brethren, known as Picards," replied Crato, "may bear away the palm." "I think so too," was the significant testimony of the emperor. His mind was evidently strongly inclined to the reformed opinions, although he wished to preserve the Roman hierarchy. His disposition accorded well with that of his contemporary, Henry IV. of France. His education and his tastes confirmed him in his convictions of the impolicy of attempting to restrict human belief. To force conscience he conceived to be to assail heaven, as he once told the Bishop of Olmütz. On one occasion he wrote to Paul Eber, at Wittemberg, "that he wished the pure gospel everywhere preached, though the Roman hierarchy should be retained." Catholic writers censure him for a neglect of duty in restraining the spread of heresy. It was even rumored abroad that he was a follower of the Lutheran doctrine.

This charge was not altogether without reason. In 1565, Maximilian urged Pius IV. to abrogate the rule requiring the celibacy of the clergy. He granted the free exercise of their religion to the Austrian nobility, and to the cities of Lintz, Steyer, Enns, Wels, Freistadt, Gmunden, and Vœcklabruck. He tolerated the introduction of the Protestant worship into Austria (1568) by Chytræus von Rostock. He allowed the Bible to be translated for the use of the Sclavonians in Carniola, Corinthia, and Styria; and protected, even in Vienna, the Protestants as well as the Jesuits. He even boxed the ear of his son—afterward Rudolph II.—for having attacked a Protestant church at the instigation of the Jesuits.

In 1566 the Bohemian Brethren dedicated their hymn-book to him. In the preface they ventured to say, "that the right form of the primitive church had been altered, the true worship abandoned, the light of truth made dim, the word of God adulterated, and the sacraments rent asunder; that error, superstition, and abuse had been introduced, and that the true doctrine must be again established." The confession of the Brethren, moreover, was kindly received. It was eminently evangelical, and met the warm approval of the theologians of Wittemberg (1575.) To the petition of toleration presented by the Brethren, Maximilian replied, with the assurance that neither during his reign, nor that of his son, should they be molested.

It was during the period of comparative quiet that followed, that the Brethren pursued the task of a new translation of the scriptures, from the original Hebrew and Greek, into the Bohemian language. It was published with annotations, under the title of the "*Brethren's Bible.*" An excellent copy of this now rare work is still preserved in the museum of Prague.

During this favorable period, the Bohemian Brethren found themselves in a somewhat peculiar position. They were not the only Protestants of the kingdom, and each party of the Lutherans and Reformed strove to draw them over to their side. Repeated efforts were made to secure a more formal union.

In 1557 a synod was held at Sleza in Moravia, which was attended by more than two hundred ministers, as well as a large number of Polish noblemen. A principal object of the convocation was to consider the proposed union of the Brethren with the Reformed of Poland and Switzerland. But there were great difficulties in the way, and nothing could be effected. In 1560 the attempt was renewed, at a synod held at Buntzlau, in Bohemia, the place of their principal settlement. A correspondence was opened with the Reformed, and the most kindly feelings were mutually expressed. At the synod of Xyans, in the same year, the matter was brought to an issue. The Brethren dropped the title of bishop for that of elder; both parties retained their confessions; and the strict discipline of the Brethren was adopted, with slight modifications.

With the Lutherans, the Brethren encountered greater difficulties. In Poland the matter was prosecuted with most success, although even in other lands the seed of truth, scattered by the Bohemian exiles, had taken root and had begun to bear fruit. In this kingdom, soon after the period of the most extensive emigration, already referred to, (1551,) forty churches of the Brethren had sprung up. Although strongly reluctant to yield one iota of their church order and discipline—now endeared to them by the experience of a century and a half—the sympathies of the Brethren were warmly extended to all that embraced evangelical views. The subject of a union was discussed at the synod of Posen, in 1567. No compromise could be effected, and the subject was remitted in the following year to the judgment of the Wittemberg theologians. Their advice was of a liberal and tolerant character. The result was, that at a second synod at Posen, in 1570, both parties acknowledged the harmony between the Brethren's confession and that of Augsburg. Soon after, at the synod of Sendomir, the union of all the Protestants in Poland was accomplished (1578). The *Consensus* of Sendomir was the basis of compromise received and adopted, and for more than a century adhered to in Poland.

Each church retained its peculiar rites and usages, but obtained the benefits of a practical union and mutual aid. The scene that was witnessed on the publication of this agreement was deeply affecting. Many wept for joy, while the members of the synod, as they sang the *Te Deum*, gave each other the right hand of fellowship. Successive attempts were made to disturb this union of the different churches, but they all proved futile. In 1627, at the synod of Ostrog, a more entire union was effected between the Reformed and the Brethren, so that they were no longer distinctly known.

In Bohemia this period of calm was one of great external prosperity. Enlarged efforts were made to evangelize the land, and numerous synods were held. At one of these there were present, beside ministers, not less than seventeen of the most distinguished barons of Bohemia, and one hundred and forty-six nobles of inferior rank.

Meanwhile the Jesuits, although largely favored by the emperor, failed to stem the tide of religious and ecclesiastical reform. The number of the Calixtines as well as Brethren vastly increased. It contributed not a little to this result, that the priests of the papal party were not only few in number, but at once ignorant and infamous. Repeated complaints were made of their gluttony and drunkenness; in some cases, of their profanity and licentiousness. It were better, said some, to be altogether without curates than to have such. In evident contrast stood the scriptural simplicity of worship and doctrine, and the exemplary life, of the Brethren. A marked progress was manifest in the cause of evangelical reform.

With brief exceptions, the reign of Rudolph II. was characterized by a tolerant spirit, (1576–1612.) In 1602, at the instigation of the Jesuits, the old edicts against the Picards were revived. The increasing number and prosperity of the Protestants began to excite apprehension lest Bohemia should soon be lost to the Papal See. "The principal Bohemian and Moravian nobility, says Pelzel, joined the Calvinists or Lutherans." At the urgent remonstrance of their enemies, the old severe measures were again resorted to. Their meetings were forbidden, their churches closed, and the Calvinists and Picards (Brethren) were ordered to leave the country.[1] They were declared incapable of holding public office, or, if discharging such duty, they were deposed. Some of their schools and churches were either demolished or shut up. But the mind of the emperor was not without misgivings. When the news of the capture of Stuhlweissenberg, in Hungary, by the Turks, reached him, he is reported to have said, "Something

---

[1] Ranke. Hist. of the Popes, 278.

of the kind struck my mind to-day, when I began
to usurp the province of God,—which is the province
of conscience."[1] The old decrees were again revoked.
The Brethren for several years were left unmolested.
The Bethlehem church, in which John Huss preached, was allowed to them as true followers of that
faithful martyr, by the University of Prague. But
they could not obtain possession of it. Three members out of twelve, however, were allowed them in
the consistory of the university, and they were permitted to build themselves churches, and have advocates to maintain their rights. There were some,
indeed, beside the papal party, who would have excluded them from toleration on the ground of their
separation from the Calixtines, which might now be
called—embracing as it did nearly two-thirds of the
population—the national church; but the diet would
not allow of their exclusion from the common privilege.

In their prosperity, however, they were subjected
to a new danger. "With the freedom of religion,"
says Comenius, their historian and bishop, "there
sprang up freedom of the flesh." They were more
disposed to a laxity of principle and to worldly conformity. But this danger was to be but of brief
duration.

[1] Pescheck, i. 126.

CHAPTER XXI.

PROTESTANTISM IN BOHEMIA, DOWN TO THE CLOSE OF THE THIRTY YEARS' WAR.

1602 — 1650.

THE closing years of the sixteenth century were, to the Protestants of Bohemia, years at once of security and of danger. The lenient policy of their rulers had disarmed their fears, while the seed sown by Jesuit policy was springing up to its harvest.

Ferdinand had need of the aid of his Protestant subjects to meet the expenses of the Turkish war. Maximilian II. leaned from conviction toward the doctrines of the Brethren, and Rudolph II., though educated by the Jesuits, was not a promising pupil. A pedant rather than a king, he indulged his learned indolence in the arts of the laboratory rather than in the arts of statesmanship, and buried himself from the sight of his subjects in his museum of curiosities and antiques.

But while the Protestants were almost unmolested, and were rapidly increasing in numbers, their Jesuit antagonists were not idle. If the first had acquired the ascendency in Austria, and to a large extent in Bohemia, the latter had seized upon the seats of learning, and presided over the education of those who were destined to wield the sceptre. Maximilian had tolerated both. The rival elements of future strife had been developed side by side. The papacy, moreover, was regaining its lost vigor. The tiara no longer rested on the brow of John XXIII., or on that of an Alexander VI. Paul IV. commenced the restoration. Pius IV., through the decisions of the council of Trent, reorganized if he did not regenerate the hierarchy. Pius V. exchanged the milder policy that had prevailed, for the sword and fagot, sanctioning, by precept and example, the cruelties of Alva in the Spanish Netherlands. Gregory XIII. conciliated favor as the representative of Jesuit learning, and Sixtus V. displayed the pomp of the old and undivided church. Protestant strength encouraged Protestant division. Henry IV., to secure him-

self against Spain, had sought the alliance of the
Protestants of the German empire; but this hasty
union was dissolved by his death, (1610,) while it
had given occasion for the formation of a counter
alliance, the "Catholic League," (July 11, 1609.)

The meaning of this league was well understood
at Prague, for at this juncture the Protestants had
just succeeded in extorting from Rudolph important
religious immunities. The persecution of 1602 was
scarcely passed, when, at the instigation of the Jesuits,
and through pontifical suggestion, it was proposed to
renew it. The success of the Protestants, and the
spread of their doctrines, had been such as to excite
apprehension lest the Roman Catholic church should
be utterly exterminated from the land.

In 1605 the alarm was sounded at Prague by the
archbishop, at the instigation of the pope. The
principal nobles of Bohemia had joined the Lutherans, the Calvinists, or the Brethren, and the clergy
became apprehensive lest their flocks should dwindle
quite away.[1] The archbishop, the Jesuits, the Capu-
chins, and the Roman Catholic nobility clamorously
demanded of Rudolph severe and persecuting measures. They would have only "Catholics" and Utraquists tolerated in the kingdom.

Their demand was granted. Rudolph forbade the
meetings of the Protestants, and decreed the banishment of the Brethren and the Reformed. None but
"Catholics" might hold office. Schools were demolished, and churches closed. The archbishop had
been enjoined by the pope "to destroy and root out

[1] Pescheck, i. 130—quotes from Pelzel.

heretical errors," and the work was now begun. Deeds of harshness and violence followed.[1] Protestant preachers were expelled, or silenced. The observance of the commemoration days of Huss and Jerome was prohibited. Special tortures were devised against offenders. Some were thrown to the hounds to be worried. Others were deprived of their ears or tongues. Others were tortured in subterranean vaults by incessant showers of water. Property was confiscated. The wafer was thrust down the throats of the victims by force. Printers were forbidden to print Protestant books; and burial in the graveyards was denied to those of the evangelical faith.[2]

But this state of things could not long continue. Policy was forced to revoke what justice should have forbidden. The Bohemians refused to aid Rudolph in the Turkish war, and he was forced to conclude a disadvantageous peace. At this very juncture, Hungary, where the Protestants were decidedly in the ascendant, demanded and obtained freedom of religious worship.

The grant had been made by the Archduke Matthias, brother of Rudolph, who witnessed with indignation the inefficiency of the emperor, and the impolicy of his administration. At a conference with the princes of the empire he was charged to interfere, and remedy the evils that had followed perverse counsels. Austria and Moravia were ripe for revolt, and were won to his banners by the promise of religious freedom. At the head of an army he pro-

---

[1] Pescheck, i. 134.   [2] Ib.

ceeded to Prague, and, sword in hand, dictated terms
to his brother.

In this measure he was encouraged by the state of
things at Prague. The patience of the Protestants
was exhausted, and the principal nobles were prepared to welcome one who came as their deliverer.
Already the evangelical states had ventured to present to the emperor their demands. At the instance
of Wenzel Budowa—a man of devoted piety, who
uniformly opened the meetings for deliberation with
singing, prayer, and a religious address—fifteen
articles were drawn up, setting forth the claims of
the Protestants. They were intended to secure the
freedom of Protestant worship, and check the intriguing designs of the Jesuits.

These articles were approved and adopted by two
hundred lords and three hundred knights, as well as
by deputies from the royal cities. The imperial counsellor, Martinitz, objected to them, but he was threatened with being cast from the windows if he persisted. Rudolph was forced to grant and ratify the
demands of the Protestants, in regard to most of the
articles (1608). Some however were rejected.

In the diet of the following year, the Protestants
again presented their demands, and their warlike
preparations showed that they were in earnest. Rudolph's advisers favored compliance. Even the archbishop took this ground. Although with great reluctance, Rudolph accepted the advice. " He indignantly cursed his fate, which so meanly and disgrace-
fully exposed him to the arrogance of the faithless,
and deprived him of the only right of heirship."

But the imminency of the danger forbade hesitation. The aid of Matthias might be invoked, and Rudolph himself lose the kingdom.   The articles of the Protestants were embodied in a "charter," by which their rights were secured, and the charter was signed by Rudolph, July 9, 1609.

As intelligence of the concession went abroad, it was received with transports of joy.   Budowa announced the signature of the charter, adding that now the Protestants, equally with the Jews of Prague, might enjoy full liberty of worship.   The fifteenth day of July was celebrated as a day of thanksgiving, and a sermon was preached upon the occasion in one of the old Hussite churches of Prague that had long remained unopened.   Throughout Bohemia there was great rejoicing over the restoration of religious privileges.   Churches that had long been closed were opened, and new ones were erected.   At Prague the German Lutherans erected themselves houses of worship.   Evangelical schools were established; and within twelve years after the granting of the charter, the Protestant churches of the kingdom were estimated at about five hundred.

But the success of the Protestants was a new occasion of danger.   The Jesuits regarded them with a jealous eye.   There was a stealthy encroachment upon their privileges, and step by step the University of Prague was wrested from the control of the Calixtines.   Nor was this all.   Assured of the support, if not directly invited by Rudolph, the Archduke Leopold of Austria, who was also Bishop of Passau, entered the kingdom with an army of plunderers,

and directed his efforts to the suppression of Protestant worship and the restoration of "Catholic"
ascendency.   But though ferociously orthodox himself, his troops were more brigands than soldiers.
His violence and injustice united the Bohemians to
repel his assaults, and recover the stolen booty.
The troops of Hungary, by direction of Matthias,
hastened to Prague, and the invaders were forced to
retreat.

Rudolph did not long retain the sceptre.   Dejected
and humiliated, he died Jan. 20, 1612.   He was
succeeded by Matthias, who had already wrested
from him the government of Bohemia, Silesia, and
Lusatia.   The Bohemians rejoiced in his accession to
the throne, confident from his past course that he
would concede to them their religious freedom.   But,
secure in his possessions, he no longer found it necessary to court the friendship of the Protestants.   His
confessor, moreover, was a Jesuit, Melchior Clesel,
not an unfair specimen of his order.   He was cool,
crafty, sagacious.   Mildness of manner concealed
firmness of purpose, and, by stealthy measures, he
prepared the way for the suppression of Protestant
privileges.   By wrong and outrage the Protestants
were provoked to insurrection and rebellion, that a
a pretext might be found for a repeal of their charters.   They appealed to Matthias.   They remonstrated against the wrongs done them.   But access
to their monarch was denied.   The Jesuit kept his
ear if not his conscience, and the petitioners only
made themselves obnoxious by their troublesome
complaints.

Wearied out and exasperated by persistent injustice, they urged their "defenders" to active measures in vindication of their rights. It was in vain that the latter counselled patience. They were themselves suspected of weakness and cowardice. Continued provocation forced the oppressed to violent reprisals, and the long sought pretext for retaliation was given.

It increased the strength of Protestant indignation, that Matthias, old and childless, wished to adopt as his successor his cousin Ferdinand, of Styria, a grandson like himself of Ferdinand I. He attempted to dictate to the states, in violation of their privilege of electing their own monarch. All the resources of hope and fear, flattery and threats, were employed to overcome opposition. Several of the nobility, who could not be overawed, withdrew dissatisfied. Count Thurn, Fels, and others openly opposed the project. They understood too well the character of Ferdinand. Many of his measures for the suppression of Protestant worship in his hereditary states were well known. He had proved himself an inexorable zealot for the popish faith. He tolerated the Jews, yet prohibited Lutheran worship by three successive edicts. Ruled by his Jesuit confessor, Bishop Stobeus, of Laybach, he had banished Protestant ministers, burned Protestant books, and endeavored to subdue his people to a perfect conformity to the Roman church.

In spite of opposition, Ferdinand was elected, (1617,) although the Protestants secured his approval of their charters. But the value of such security

was trifling. The guarantee of their religious freedom was not worth the parchment upon which it
was recorded. Ferdinand was a pupil of the Jesuits,
and their ready tool. At the age of twelve years
he had been placed under the care of the bigoted
Duke of Bavaria, and his education was conducted
by the Jesuit professors of Ingolstadt. From the
first he was instructed to abhor the heresy of the
Protestants. His bigotry was of the true Spanish type. At the age of seventeen he returned to
his hereditary states to put his principles in practice.
For some years policy restrained him from open
violence; but after he had sought in person at Loretto, with edifying devotion, the favor of the Virgin, and had received at Rome the apostolic benediction at the feet of Clement VIII., he was ready
for his task.

Craftily and vigorously he proceeded to execute
his projects. Dealing with his Protestant cities in
detail, he succeeded, to the astonishment of Germany, in the suppression of Protestant worship
throughout his dominions. He had found it in the
ascendant. In a few years almost every trace of it
was obliterated. Banishment, stealthy encroachment, annoyance, and persecution had done their
work.

This success was due to the aid and counsel afforded
by the Jesuits. All his steps were guided by the
members of that order. "He yielded himself," says
a Roman Catholic author, "to the guidance of the
clergy, but chiefly of the Jesuits and other monks,
even in political affairs. Hence originated his great

intolerance and hatred against all who would not be
Roman Catholics." His gloomy reserve secured him
the reputation of exemplary devotion.

His character excited the distrust of the Bohemians; and with good reason. On the death of Matthias, (1618,) his policy began to be developed.
Now were seen the fruits of his Jesuit training.
When Clesel, Matthias' confessor, mildly expressed
the hope that Bohemia would be leniently treated,
Ferdinand was offended, and exclaimed, "Better a
desert than a country full of heretics." His people,
he resolved, should be of the same faith with himself. He is said to have declared that "he would
rather, with his wife and children, beg his bread,
staff in hand, from door to door, than have a heretic
in his service, or tolerate one in his dominions.[1] His
own Jesuit confessor, more intolerant than Clesel,
advised the extermination of the Lutherans; and no
advice could have been more grateful. There was
but one person in the world whom Ferdinand could
have envied, and that was his bigoted model, Philip
II. of Spain.

Ferdinand was crowned in the Cathedral of Prague,
by the Archbishop Lohelius. Almost immediately
he withdrew from Bohemia, leaving the government
in the hands of his creature, Slawata, a renegade
Protestant, and Martinitz, a supple tool of the Jesuits.
A harsh policy of encroachment on Protestant privileges was adopted. In spite of the charter, a strict
censorship was established. Jesuit works alone were
unmutilated. The new churches which the Protes-

[1] Pescheck, i. 258.

tants were erecting at Braunau and Klostergrab were ordered to be demolished, and the remonstrances of the aggrieved parties were treated with contempt.

The Jesuits felt that their hour of triumph had come.[1] They were open and loud in their exultation. When Ferdinand, soon after his " reception," departed to be proclaimed in Moravia, they erected in Olmutz a triumphal arch, and among other decorations, they placed upon it the Austrian coat of arms. On one side of this was the Bohemian lion, and on the other, the Moravian eagle, both chained to it. Underneath was a sleeping hare, with open eyes, and the superscription, "This is natural to me." Such was the ridicule hurled at the Protestant states, who had allowed themselves, with their eyes open, to be chained and bound; and their feebleness was thus portrayed. From the pulpits they were openly derided and menaced. Count Thurn was deposed from his office as governor of the castle and keeper of the regalia, and his place was supplied by the Jesuit tool, Martinitz. An attempt was made to wrest the university from the control of the Protestants. The patience of the latter was exhausted, and a call for a meeting of the states at Prague was issued simultaneously from the Protestant pulpits. But the imperial councillors resolved to prevent the meeting. Martinitz and Slawata, already extremely odious to the evangelicals, were commissioned by the sovereign to prevent their assembling in the Caroline chamber; to summon the ringleaders; and to threaten them with punishment, unless

[1] Pescheck, i. 273.

they would remain quiet.[1] The states, moreover, were required to repair to the palace to hear the mandate of the emperor, now absent from Prague, read to them. They appeared, listened to the reading of the document, received copies at their own request, and promised to return the next morning with their reply.

They did so. On the eventful May 23, 1618, they met together, and proceeded to the palace where the four councillors (governors) awaited their appearance. Among their number were some of the most prominent of the Bohemian nobility,—Thurn, Fels, Schlick, Raupowa, Lobkowitz, Kapliztz, and others. They were not without arms. They had pistols in their girdles, while the people who followed them were provided with muskets and sabres. All the avenues to the castle were occupied; and the leaders passed to the green chamber, where they consulted on the answer which they should return to the royal commands.

Count Thurn was the leading speaker.[2] Though not a Bohemian by birth, he had estates in the kingdom, and had risen to posts of honor from which he had recently been removed. A thirst for vengeance, a restless and aspiring ambition, a burning indignation against the insults and wrongs of the Protestants, not without the impulse of his own impetuous zeal, combined to make him a reckless and headstrong counsellor in this emergency. But he had the confidence of the Utraquists, and his burning words and unscrupulous daring bore down all the opposition

---

[1] Pescheck, i. 289.   [2] Thirty Years' War, 52.

which might have been offered by more cool or prudent counsels. He depicted in eloquent invective the wrongs of the Protestants, and designated the obnoxious advisers, from whom they had proceeded and by whom they were sanctioned. While these stood in the way, religious liberty would never be established in Bohemia.

He declared Martinitz and Slawata to be the principal offenders. They were said to have driven their evangelical subjects to mass with dogs and scourges;[1] to have wrenched their mouths open that the wafer might be thrust down their throats; to have denied them the rites of marriage, baptism, and burial. These men, said Thurn, must be put out of the way. They must be made a sacrifice. Some opposed the rash and hasty decision, but others approved it, and a rush was made for the hall in which the councillors were seated. Paul of Rziczan was the spokesman in the name of the Utraquistic states. He charged Slawata and Martinitz with being disturbers of the peace, and with having sought to deprive the Utraquists of their charter.

Each of them was now asked whether he had had a hand in the imperial mandate. Some who were with them remonstrated against this tumultuous and disorderly proceeding. Fels replied that they had nothing to say against Sternberg or Lobkowitz, but that Slawata and Martinitz, who were now put upon their defence, had on every occasion opposed the Utraquists.

At this critical moment, when indecision threatened

---

[1] Pescheck, i. 292.

to be fatal, and the Protestants had gone too far to retreat, one of their number, Wenzel Raupowa, called out—"The best way is, *straight out the window*, after the old Bohemian fashion." These were fatal words. Some stepped forward to lay hold of one of their victims, when Lobkowitz interfered to lead them out of the room. But Martinitz and Slawata asserted their innocence, and prayed that if they were guilty they might be judged according to the laws. The matter, however, had gone too far: reconciliation or procrastination was now out of the question. Martinitz was seized by several at once, who bore him to the window and threw him out. He fell sixty feet, into the moat; but the force of his fall was broken by a heap of dung, which saved his life. Slawata was next seized and treated in the same manner, and the tragedy was completed by throwing down the secretary, Philip Fabricius Platter, who was also implicated, after the other two.[1]

Singularly enough, not one of the three was killed; not even a limb was broken. Platter was the first that was able to rise. He went back to his house in the Old town, and hastily proceeded to Vienna to acquaint the emperor with what had happened. The servants of Martinitz and Slawata, although fired upon in the attempt, ran to their aid, and succeeded by means of a ladder in bringing them over into the adjoining house of the Chancellor Lobkowitz. The means to restore them were diligently and successfully employed. Thurn came and demanded them, but the prudent and bold Polyrena softened down

[1] Pescheck, i. 294.

his fury by assuring them that they were both in a pitiable state.

Martinitz soon after made good his escape. Cutting off his beard, blackening his face with gunpowder, and disguising himself so as to defy recognition, he got safe to the White Hill, and subsequently to Munich. Slawata was unable to follow him, and he was allowed a physician, though kept under close guard. The three men, grateful for their wonderful escape, united in the present of a golden diadem, set with precious stones, to the Lady of Loretto.

There was danger lest the violence at the castle should be imitated in the city. The multitude in their exasperation commenced an attack upon the Catholics, but Thurn, mounting his horse, hastened to the place of danger, and deprecated all violent proceedings. The Braunau prisoners, however, were set at liberty.

The states immediately wrote to the emperor, acquainting him with what they had done. In two successive letters, termed their apologies, they detailed the grievous persecutions they had suffered, and vindicated the course they had pursued. They united together in a league of mutual defence, and took measures for their own security.[1] The governor of the castle and the three councillors were compelled to swear allegiance to the officers whom the Union saw fit to appoint. One of the bishops, and the abbots of Strahow and Braunau, were banished. A severe decree was issued against the Jesuits; they

---

[1] Pescheck, i. 327.

were forced to evacuate their colleges at Prague,
Kruman, Neuhaus, and Glätz, and within fourteen
days to leave the country. None was to grant them
shelter, or intercede for them. Thus, says Pelzel,
did the Protestants make enemies of those "who
had in their hands the hearts of the Romanist mon-
archs."

Unwisely enough, the Protestants had now furnished their foes with the long-sought pretext for
violent retaliation. But aware of their danger, they
determined to anticipate it by timely measures.
They knew what they would have to expect from
Ferdinand if he should be suffered unmolested to
take possession of the kingdom, and they therefore
solemnly deposed him, and elected Frederic V. Elector Palatine, a Calvinist in his religious sentiments,
as king of Bohemia. Undoubtedly they had felt
that in the troubles which surrounded Ferdinand,
and with the support which they expected from
England or its continental allies in behalf of the
son-in-law of the English monarch, they could safely
maintain their cause.

But they had committed a great error. The very
weakness of Ferdinand proved his security. The
Catholic league, while he was pressed by Protestant
invasion even at the gates of his palace in Vienna,
came forward to his help. His own casting vote as
king of Bohemia, and consequently imperial elector,
secured for him, on the death of Matthias, (1620,)
in spite of the protest of the Bohemians, the imperial
crown. Frederic of the Palatinate, moreover, proved
himself utterly unfitted for the post which he was

called to fill. His Calvinistic sympathies, and imprudent measures in stripping the churches of their
ornaments, alienated his Lutheran subjects, and when
the league began to act in earnest in support of
Ferdinand, Bohemia was the first to feel the weight
of its vengeance. Its king was merely an incum-
brance. Without energy himself, he only inspired
his subjects with disgust, and alienated the sympathy of the German Lutherans, while he was coldly
abandoned by his own father-in-law, the king of England.

And now commenced that terrible episode of
crime, violence, plunder, and invasion, known in the
history of Europe as " The thirty years' war." The
real date of its commencement is from May 23, 1618,
when the imperial councillors were thrown from the
windows of the royal palace at Prague. But it was
some months before the cloud of vengeance burst
upon the devoted country. At length it came. The
emperor, recovering from his depression and humiliation at Vienna, was now prepared to subdue Bohemia. His army marched direct to Prague. Unpre-
pared for the attack, the army that defended the
city, and which consisted of Hungarians, Moravians,
and Bohemians, was defeated in the battle of the
White Hill, Oct. 29, 1620. The weak monarch,
though a manful resistance might have yet been offered, abandoned his capital, and earned by his brief
residence the reproachful title of " the summer king."
Prague lay at the mercy of the victor; and what that
mercy would be, his own character only too clearly
foreshadowed.

The days of Protestant ascendancy and even toleration, in Bohemia, were now numbered.　The concentrated vengeance of the papacy, the emperor, and
the Jesuits was poured out on the devoted land.　It
would be entering upon another and an arduous task
to trace the fortunes of the Protestant states of Europe during the thirty years' war, and, happily, there
is no need of it, for it has been already done by an
able hand.[1]　The horrors of war, carnage, devastation, and violence, fiendish cruelties and reckless
deeds, marked with aggravated enormities the progress of the fearful drama.　Generals like Wallen-
stein, Tilly, Pappenheim, and the wonderful Gustavus
Adolphus, appeared upon the scene, and excited al-
ternate hope and fear as they led their victorious
hosts from city to city.　Europe at last sank exhausted under its own efforts; and after a whole
generation had been made to feel that war is the
natural condition of humanity on the globe, the exhausted combatants, worn out by their own efforts
rather than by defeats sustained from their foes, laid
down their arms.　German Protestantism was secured
from its imminent peril, but Bohemia and Hungary,
in the general pacification, were abandoned to their
fate.　This result was the more readily acquiesced in,
that already Protestantism was well-nigh crushed
out from these devoted lands.　They scarcely dared
to lift a voice of protest, or to make their claims
heard in the ear of Europe, and the sympathies of
Lutheran Germany abandoned Bohemia to its fate.

Under Rudolph and Matthias the condition of the

[1] Schiller.

country was enviable, compared with what it now
became under the rule of the bigoted Ferdinand.
From time to time gleams of light stole in upon her
through the broken clouds, as the beleaguering hosts
were forced to tremble before a foreign foe.   But for
the most part her feeble opposition was crushed.   It
could only break out in ill-timed and ill-managed
insurrections.   Bohemia had her full share of the
ravages and cruelties of this dark period.   The imperial will found nothing to stay its vengeance.   The
palace of the mysterious, Mephistophelian Wallen-
stein, who could convoke armies at a word, and
whose nature was constituted without the element of
mercy, rose proudly, with menacing aspect, by the
Hradschin of Prague.   A savage soldiery dragooned
the trembling fugitives, till they abandoned in exile
their native land.   Every attempt at national resistance was trampled down.   The choicest spirits of
Bohemia sighed in prisons, or wandered in foreign
lands.   Twenty-seven of her ablest defenders, in the
opening scene of the fearful drama of retribution,
perished on the scaffold.

Nor was this the worst.   The banished Jesuits,
expelled by the states for their incendiary principles
and obnoxious measures, *were readmitted at the point
of the sword.*   Volumes could not fitly display the
results of the fact stated in that single sentence.
With them came back all that Bohemia had most to
dread.   Ferdinand was only their bigoted tool.   What
with them was policy, with him was principle.   It
may easily be imagined what was the nature of the
measures to be taken, when at that very time the

English Jesuit Campian—a fair representative of the
order, for the order was as near as possible a unit in
spirit and sentiment—was saying, "The Lutherans
and Calvinists ought to be killed with the sword;
they ought to be banished and oppressed; they
ought to be burned with fire, sulphur, and pitch;
drowned in water; impoverished, hunted down, deprived of their estates, annihilated; in a word, they
ought to be rooted out, and persecuted to death by
every imaginable kind of excessive torture and pain."
No wonder the Protestants should say, that they
would rather have the devil for their master than
Ferdinand with his Jesuitical principles. In his bitter
intolerance, the most remorseless cruelties were covered with the sanction of churchly zeal.

The battle of the White Hill was followed by a
train of most odious crime and gratuitous outrage
on the part of the emperor. Neither rank nor age
was regarded. Of the twenty-seven distinguished
citizens of Bohemia who perished on the scaffold,
twenty-four belonged to the nobility. Some of them
had grown grey in the imperial service. Men they
were, of lofty patriotism, of heroic spirit, and of
Christian principle. The history of the martyrs
scarce furnishes a more sublime illustration of a triumphant faith than that afforded by the scenes of
their imprisonment and execution. They might have
said, each, with the Duke of Argyle, "I *could* die as
a Roman, but I choose rather to die as a Christian."

Some of the sufferers were members of the Brethren church. One of them was Wenzel Budowecz of
Budowa. For talents, learning, sagacity, integrity,

and Christian zeal he stood foremost among them
all. He has been called the last Bohemian, as Brutus
was called the last of the Romans. When urged in
prison to seek the clemency of the emperor, his reply
was, " I will rather die than see the ruin of my country." " See my Paradise," said he, pointing to the
Bible in his hand. " It has never offered me such
sweet heavenly food as now." When Count Schlick
was offered a cup of wine, he declined it. " I will
only look forward to a cup of heavenly joy," was his
reply. " May God forgive my enemies," prayed the
dying Harant, and then commended his spirit to
Christ. " The flesh is ready to fail," said the venerable Rosacius, " but I am no longer afraid." " Tell
your emperor," was the language of the fearless Procopius Dworshezky, " that I stand now before his
unrighteous judgment, and remind him of God's
righteous tribunal." " Thanks be to God," exclaimed
another, as the summons to leave his prison for the
scaffold was announced, " worldly distress has ceased;
I hasten to Christ." In such a spirit these noble men
met their fate.

But this was by no means the last act of this terrible drama of vindictive tyranny. Seven hundred
and twenty-eight of the nobility, who were induced
by a promise of pardon to confess their participation
in the rebellion, were deprived of their estates.
Forty million dollars were collected by confiscation
alone. Five hundred noble and thirty-six thousand
citizen families emigrated. Bohemia lost the whole
of her ancient privileges. The charter granted by
Rudolph, in favor of toleration, was torn by the

emperor's own hands. All heretical works, especially those of the ancient Hussites, were sought for
and devoted to the flames. Nor did the dead escape.
Zisca's monument was destroyed. Rokyzan's remains
were disinterred and burnt. Every visible memorial
of the heroism of Bohemia was obliterated. No
trace of religious liberty was left, to remind the citizen of privileges that his ancestors had once enjoyed.
The emperor declared himself in conscience bound
to exterminate all heretics.

It was a serious question what measures should be
adopted for the purpose. The matter was agitated
even in the conclave of Rome. Bloody executions
would only sow the seed of new martyrs, and were
deemed impolitic. Prompt banishment was proposed. " No, not yet," was the reply of crafty malice ; " at present they have too much to take with
them. They would bear off too much money. The
exile would too easily be borne. They must first be
fleeced."

This was the plan adopted. A brief space intervened before the terrible work began. There was
an oppressive sullenness as it were, like the lull that
ushers in the tempest. Men lived in fearful expectation. At length the storm came in its fury, and
swept all before it. Even the peasantry were imprisoned by the hundred, and forced by starvation
to recant. The Protestants were deprived of their
churches. Some of them were shut up ; some burned
and destroyed. Pulpits and statues were torn down.
The tombs were broken open. The altars or furniture were lashed and whipped, in the imbecile

rage that attacked even inanimate objects. When the Jesuits recovered their church at Prague, they strewed the floor with gunpowder, and set fire to it to destroy the poison of heresy with smoke and flame. Hussite pastors, who failed to make good their escape, fell a prey to the savage soldiery. They were tortured to extort confessions of guilt, or the place where their money was stored. In one case they filled their victim's mouth with gunpowder and set fire to it, when his throat was burst asunder Some were beaten, some left for dead, some plundered. These indeed were the acts of a licentious soldiery, but they were countenanced by imperial authority. Iniquity and violence were framed and legalized by statute. Imperial clemency was a commentary on what scripture declares of the tender mercies of the wicked. A fugitive nobleman was offered pardon if he would return to his country. His answer was significant. "What sort of pardon ? A Bohemian one ? Heads off ! A Moravian one ? Imprisonment for life ! An Austrian one ? Confiscation !" Ferdinand's confessor, Lamormain, superintended these horrors enacted at his master's command. What a terrible light is thrown upon his conduct by the title which he assumed in reference to the immense confiscations that took place—"God's clerk of the exchequer !"

All through the space of the thirty years' war persecution raged, till the materials on which to wreak its vengeance seemed to be exhausted. But the work of plunder and proscription still went on. Even the books of the Protestants were sought as

eagerly as their persons. The friends of the Bible
were forced to conceal it, sometimes in the space
beneath the dog-kennels. *A Bohemian book* became
synonymous with a rare work. Nothing was allowed
to be printed unless by the approving signature of
the officials of the Inquisition. Whatever Protestant works could be gathered were piled up under
the gallows, and then destroyed by fire. The work
of forced conversions was carried on with a high
hand. The Jesuits threw off the mask of mildness,
and called in to their aid Lichtenstein's dragoons.
The peasants were driven to church at the point of
the sword ; and a licentious soldiery won the title
of "Conversionists." Count Dohna boasted of his
having been able to do more than Peter, who converted three thousand on the day of Pentecost. He
had accomplished more without preaching a single
sermon. One Jesuit father wrote " with a trembling
hand, a little before his death, a summary of his conversions." " He had restored 33,140 to Christ and
the church, with enviable success." Priests of the
vilest character and most scandalous life were put
in the place of the exiled pastors. The people were
forced, by terrors of torture and death, to swear " that,
without compulsion, they renounced the evangelical
doctrine."

But even these measures were only partially effectual. The praying people could not be exterminated.
They met in the hours of night, in the mountains and
the forests, to enjoy their worship. Denied all civil
rights, prohibited from marrying, from solemnizing
the burial of the dead or the rite of baptism, many

still clung to their cherished faith. Even when
arrested and thrown into prison, the steadfastness of
their purpose could not be shaken. Among the
humbler victims was a clerk, whose dungeon was in
so horrible a state that both his legs rotted off. Yet,
supported by his faith, he still sung cheerful songs.
Such cruelties often rose beyond the point of endurance. Several times the peasants rose in insurrection, but they were crushed by the imperial power.
The sighings of the suffering martyrs beneath the
shadow of the Alps, found echo among the forests
and mountains of Bohemia. Thousands indeed
escaped, to swell the numbers of the Brethren's
churches beyond the borders. For a whole generation—from 1622 to 1652, during the whole period of
the thirty years' war—the work of expatriation continued, with only such abatement as the dearth of victims rendered necessary. Precious indeed amid their
hardships were the promises so beautifully expressed
in the Brethren's hymn-book—songs composed in
the midst of trial, and calculated to cheer the hearts
of the poor exiles amid their depression.

To the prosperity of Bohemia these inroads of
persecution were fatally disastrous. "As high," says
the Romanist author, Pelzel, "as the Bohemians had
risen in the arts and sciences, under Maximilian and
Rudolph, just so low were they now sinking. I do
not know a single example of a learned man, who
distinguished himself in Bohemia by any marks of
erudition, after the expulsion of the Protestants."
Pessina, in his work on Prague cathedral, confesses
that nothing worse or more melancholy could have

happened to Bohemia.   The last traces of her ancient
liberty disappeared.   The heel of the tyrant was on
the nation's heart, and crushed its throbbing energies
to the dust.   Protestantism in Bohemia was murdered by inches.

A large part of the exiles joined their brethren
in foreign lands.   " They sought," says an old author,
" a place where the doctrines of the gospel and the
scriptural use of the holy sacraments, are purely,
clearly, distinctly taught and propagated, and they
do not care so much for their personal and temporal
interests as for their spiritual and everlasting welfare."   As persecution relaxed from time to time,
some of them returned to their native land.   But
they were rarely left unmolested.   Many a time the
gloom of despair shrouded the prospects of the
Brethren's churches, but with unswerving fidelity
they clung to the faith of their fathers, until in
more peaceful times they were allowed to extend
their labors and influence to a wider sphere, and to
become the first missionary church of modern times.

We have traced from its origin to its close by a
violent suppression, and a catastrophe of carnage
and crime, one of the most remarkable religious
movements of modern times.   In connection with
the revival of learning and the evils of the schism,
as well as a growing religious consciousness which
brought to light the corruptions of the church, an
encouragement was given to the long suppressed
demand for the revival of a purer type of Christianity, and at the opportune moment the men were

raised up, in the providence of God, who were to give
utterance to that demand.   Conrad Waldhauser,
John Milicz, and Matthias of Janow were the precur-
sors of John Huss.   They prepared the way for his
labors, and more or less clearly apprehended the
radical conflict which existed between the interests of
a corrupt hierarchy and the claims of Christian truth.

Huss inherited their views, but he brought to
their elucidation and application a bold and fearless
spirit, a stern consciousness, a discriminating mind,
and a rare self-command.   With a purpose that
never wavered, and an energy that never wearied—
sometimes in the face of royal authority, and in spite
of unjust excommunication—he pursued the line of
duty marked out by his conscientious convictions,
reprobating the iniquity of the times and the abuses
of the hierarchy, and holding up before the world
his ideal of the church of Christ.   All human authority was made by him subordinate to the authority of
the Great Master himself.   Hence, constantly appealing to the scriptures in support of his views and in
defence of his course, he led men to look beyond the
decisions of councils or the bulls of popes, and to
study for themselves the word of God.   The impulse
was thus given to a reform more radical than he had
himself contemplated.   Before he was aware, he had
come into conflict with the whole hierarchical system,
and stood forth single-handed, and almost alone, as
the champion of truth against the errors by which
it was overlaid and well-nigh suppressed.

In this conflict he fell—a victim overpowered by
numerous and bitter foes.   Men that stood by him

at first, forsook him at the critical moment, and joined the ranks of his assailants. The force of his convictions had brought him to recognize in Wickliffe a fellow-laborer in the same great cause, and the odium that rested on the name of the English reformer was inherited by himself. The council of Constance gladly surrendered him as a sacrifice to the prejudices by which it was itself environed and controlled.

His associate, Jerome of Prague, met the same fate. His chivalrous nature scorned to retract his conscientious convictions as to the character, the truth and integrity, of one whom he had known and loved. And now was illustrated the trite adage that " the blood of the martyrs is the seed of the church." Hundreds and thousands in their native land stood ready to receive the bequest of their falling mantle. A nation imbued with their spirit set the council at defiance, and boldly remonstrated against the iniquity of the deed which had canonized for ever the memory of the martyrs.

Meanwhile an enlarged acquaintance with scripture had led to the restoration, in Bohemia, of the use of the cup in the eucharist. Considered as a mere rite, this innovation was a matter of small account. But it symbolized an element of independent thought, which appealed from popes and councils to scripture alone. It was of the nature of a practical and popular protest against errors which had crept into the church, under the sanction of ecclesiastical authority and antiquated usage. Its acceptance was an endorsement of the right of private judgment, and an impeachment of synodical and pontifical infallibility. It was a rent in the external unity of the church—an ominous crack, like that of the dome of St. Peter—which inspired terror by its portentous augury of what was yet to come.

All the resources of papal authority and of ecclesiastical interest were consequently marshalled to suppress the rite. But it was found that many of its adherents had already made it the first step to more radical innovations. Diverse tendencies had already begun to develop themselves among the followers of Huss, and the Taborites and Calixtines, as two radically diverse parties, appear upon the stage. In connection with the first, we find a puritanic severity of morals, a demand for evangelical simplicity of worship and purity of doctrine, a valor nurtured by religious principle, and sometimes allied with a wild fanaticism. In connection with the other, we note the timidity and the prudence of a cautious conservatism, a lingering respect for ancient usage, a jealousy of further innovations, and a disposition to watch and restrain what they regarded as the dangerous tendencies of their rivals.

But a common interest temporarily cements the alliance of these two opposite parties, and renders them, while they retain this attitude, invincible to all foreign invasion. Classed together, as alike heretical, they are threatened with the same fate, and papal fulminations and crusading armies are met by both with a bold defiance and stern resistance. One invasion after another is hurled back from the Bohemian frontier, like the waves dashed to foam upon the rocks.

But the very humiliation of the foe opened the way for the development of the conflicting tendencies which had been temporarily restrained. Internal division was the result of foreign triumph. Calixtine and Taborite were now ranged in open and avowed hostility. It was scarcely a question which must triumph in the conflict. The Taborite was indisputably superior in all the elements of uncompromising zeal, of fierce resolve, and of desperate if not fanatical courage, to his Calixtine rival. He thought more earnestly if not profoundly. He felt more deeply. His wrongs had been greater, and his vengeance was more terrible. The strife that now arose was scarcely less bitter than that of the united Hussites against the imperialists. It ranged neighbor against neighbor, and brother against brother; but, steeled against compassion and sympathy, the Taborites swept down before them all resistance, and encamped before Prague, ready to visit upon it such retribution as it had challenged. To save it from its threatened fate, its defenders submitted to negotiate, and the result was, the concession, in the main, of the demands of the Taborites and the establishment of their supremacy.

But the anarchy of the kingdom required that authority should be deputed to able hands, and that the monarch to be selected should be one whom all should be constrained to acknowledge. Sigismund, as the rightful heir, was preferred by many who differed from him in their religious views. The *Compactata* devised by the synod of Basle, opened the way for his recognition, but reproduced the old divisions between Calixtine and Taborite. The latter were defeated in the open rupture which followed, and Sigismund at last secured his hard-won crown.

From the Taborites, who now abandoned all further appeals to physical force in their own defence, sprang the church of the United Brethren. Through a century of persecution they still maintained their fidelity to an evangelical creed and the memory of Huss. The Calixtines, sometimes leaning toward Rome, and sometimes repelled by her bigotry, wavered in uncertainty as to their position, although still holding fast their four articles. At length the advent of Luther extended to both parties a new strength, and the current of the Bohemian reformation was swollen by the powerful tributary of German reform.

With intervals of persecution, Protestantism made steady progress in Bohemia for another century, till it had almost secured the complete ascendancy. But its bold and violent measures provoked the vengeance of the " Catholic " league, and the bigoted Ferdinand, with unfaltering purpose, resolved to suppress it. The tide of the thirty years' war swept over northern and central Europe, covering its track with desolation and crime. Of all the states that suffered, Bohemia was the most signal victim. In the general pacification, she was abandoned by her German allies, and left to the tender mercies of her unscrupulous and bigoted monarch. His vengeance was terrible. He deliberately preferred a desert to a kingdom of " heretics," and his preference was well-nigh realized. Bohemian art, literature, and enterprise received a blow from which they have never recovered. Protestantism was almost utterly suppressed. Its ablest champions pined in exile, or in prison, or atoned for their patriotism and Protestantism on the scaffold. The nation that five centuries ago was among the foremost of Europe, dwindled into insignificance; and for more than two centuries Bohemia has ranked as little more than a province of the Austrian empire. Her old renown has been commemorated by the noble achievements of Moravian missionaries, who trace their spiritual lineage to her great reformer; but her condition to-day is such as to render her a signal monument of the impolicy of persecution, and the incalculable mischiefs that have flowed from the violent suppression of religious freedom.

The day may not be far distant when upon her own soil the memories of her own glorious past shall be revived. Her hills and valleys have witnessed the heroism of men who stood forward as champions of scriptural authority, and the rights and privileges of religious freedom. Her plains have been moistened and fertilized with the blood of martyrs. Many a locality has been immortalized by the valor of her sons, and the names of Huss and Jerome, of Jacobel, Zisca, and Procopius, will never die out of her annals, whoever may guide the pen. A national partiality even now triumphs over ecclesiastical prejudice, and men who would contemn Huss as a heretic, honor him as a patriot.

INDEX.